D1233774

THE HISTORY OF

ROCK & ROLL

volume one

ALSO BY ED WARD

Rock of Ages
(coauthored with Geoffrey Stokes and Ken Tucker)
Michael Bloomfield: The Rise and Fall of an American Guitar Hero
The Bar at the End of the Regime
(Kindle e-book)
Two Blues Stories: Fiction by Ed Ward
(Kindle e-book)

THE HISTORY OF
ROCK & ROLL

volume one
1920–1963

ED WARD

FLATIRON
BOOKS
NEW YORK

www.flatironbooks.com

Designed by Steven Seighman

The Library of Congress Cataloging-in-Publication Data is available upon request.

ISBN 978-1-250-07116-3 (hardcover)
ISBN 978-1-250-07117-0 (e-book)

Our books may be purchased in bulk for promotional, educational, or business use. Please contact your local bookseller or the Macmillan Corporate and Premium Sales Department at (800) 221-7945, extension 5442, or by e-mail at MacmillanSpecialMarkets@macmillan.com.

First Edition: November 2016

10 9 8 7 6 5 4 3 2 1

*To the Obamas, a First Family so rock & roll
they named their dog after Bo Diddley.*

CONTENTS

HOW TO USE THIS BOOK

This book is written to be read from the first page to the last, telling a story in sequential form, just like any other narrative history. It's possible to do this at much greater length and much greater detail—witness Taylor Branch's magisterial three-part history of America's struggle for civil rights led by Martin Luther King Jr. or Claude Manceron's almost novelistic five-parter on the French Revolution—but I wanted to make this story thorough yet accessible to the kind of people who don't enjoy gigantic reads as much as I do. I also wanted to try to impart the excitement I experienced once I grabbed a ride on what turned out to be a lot more than popular music, a corner that was turned after this book's narrative ends, but one we can see approaching in its last pages.

I deliberately steered away from the Great Performer approach to this story, because although you can't ignore the Elvis Presleys and Ray Charleses here, the less well-known figures gave context to what they achieved and played their parts in shaping the eras in which they were active—often, in this part of the story, only in one part of the country and to a non-mainstream audience. They were, many of them, rediscovered after their years in the spotlight and influenced a lot of music several decades later, which also gave many of them second careers. Also, the people who took it upon themselves to supply the music these people made to the marketplace of jukebox operators, radio stations, and record stores—record biz people like Sam Phillips, Syd Nathan, Art Rupe, Mimi Trepel, Vivian Carter, Berry Gordy, Phil Spector, and Florence Greenberg—need their roles documented, and I've threaded them in among the performers, as well as songwriters and instrumentalists in this era before the writer/performer became the default model.

To this end, I've tried to make the experience of reading this book as smooth as possible, but there are a couple of places where the reader is presented with some long lists of names or songs and/or performers—as, for instance, the fat list of records released in 1957 that are considered essential classics today but never even hit the regional, let alone national charts (see page 154). These should be welcomed as opportunities to explore: if you already know the material, you'll get the point, but if you don't, the ease of finding this music presented by online sources these days sets you up for hours of exploration and, I hope, enjoyment. Some of the sounds take a bit of getting used to, but I envy the person hearing this music for the first time, as I'm sure a lot of you would be doing. Make playlists, check out videos, or—as old-fashioned as it may seem—go deeper by buying actual CDs, which often have liner notes illuminating the music far deeper than I can and, at their best, can provide an in-depth look at a performer or genre.

And you may notice that with a cast of characters as large as this, many of them drop out of sight after their first appearance or after their careers take off. If reading what I have to say about them here and your subsequent enjoyment of their music whets your interest, by all means pick up books dedicated entirely to them. Such authors as Peter Guralnick (his two-volume biography of Elvis and books dedicated to Sam Cooke and Sam Phillips are unparalleled), Robert Gordon (on Muddy Waters and Stax Records), R. J. Smith (Central Avenue and James Brown), and many others listed in the bibliography are the places to start. Only Pete Frame's astonishing *Restless Generation*, about British rock & roll up to 1960, wasn't published in the United States, but again, it's well worth finding.

From the records and books, you can progress to the films, of which there are an increasing number, many of them well-researched documentaries. But don't stop at the documentaries; some of the contemporary films are worth watching, too. I'd list *The Girl Can't Help It*, *Jailhouse Rock*, *Rebel Without a Cause*, and *Blackboard Jungle* as essential, and even the various films that exist mostly to highlight live performances and exploit what was perceived as a short-lived fad have fine performances wedged in with the less memorable ones. Later fiction films like *Ray* (about Ray Charles), *La Bamba* (Ritchie Valens), and *American Hot Wax* (Alan Freed) are very true to their subjects, while others push agendas (*The Buddy Holly Story* famously omits Norman Petty entirely and callously misrepresents the Holley family) or, like *Cadillac Records*, ostensibly about Chess Records, warp history to make it more like what Hollywood thinks it should be. Armed with the facts, though, there are moments in all of them that are both relatively accurate and highly entertaining.

In the end, though, this book is about the music and how it came to be made, and at the risk of repeating myself, I want you to use it as a springboard to new discoveries, new genres, and new performers. Pretty soon, you'll be wondering why I haven't mentioned H-Bomb Ferguson, or Ronnie Dawkins, or the Slades. That's when you'll know I've done my job here: rock & roll is a big world and contains many fascinating histories. Welcome to it. Tell us what you find.

Ed Ward
Austin, Texas
November 2016

THE HISTORY OF

ROCK & ROLL

volume one

chapter zero

IN THE BEGINNING

The Bogtrotters, with Uncle Eck Dunford *(far left)*.
*(Library of Congress, Prints & Photographs Division, Lomax Collection,
LC-DIG-ppmsc-00401)*

I n mid-nineteenth-century rural Southern America, which is as good a place as any to start this story, music wasn't something you did. Or, rather, it could have been just one of the things you did, if you did it, like smoking hams, mending the roof and the fences, and hoeing the vegetable patch. Black or white, Northern or Southern, rural life consisted of one job after another, just to stay alive. Sometimes, particularly among African Americans, music accompanied work, as it also did among sailors or excavating crews. "Field hollers" may have been African survivals, and recordings of prisoners in the fields doing agricultural work, giving off with whoops and pieces of melody, sound eerie to our ears. Along with chain gang songs and songs laborers sang while laying or mending railroad tracks, this music gave solidarity to groups of people engaged in common work. White rural people, who often lived close to blacks, especially in farming communities, had their own uses for music: women in particular memorized long ancient stories in the forms of ballads handed down through the generations and often sang them doing "women's work" like spinning, weaving, or sewing, or else used them as lullabies. Both groups sang communally in church, and both used instruments for socializing and to play music for dancing: fiddle, which the whites had brought with them (along with a lot of its repertoire) from the old country and which blacks had picked up during slavery from the masters; banjo, which was based on a West African instrument called the *banjar* (among many other names) and, being easily made from things one had around (wood, hide, gut strings), caught on right away; and guitar, which, being store-bought, was precious and at least at first not in common use.

What's shocking to us these days is the extent to which black string-band music from this era, some of which, performed by old men, was recorded in the 1930s by the black folklorist John Work, sounds like white string-band music. Poor rural people didn't worry as much about race as they did about survival, and more than one of the early string bands to record in the 1920s was biracial. A good tune was a good tune, and if one group learned it from the other, that was how the process worked; any variation or change was more likely up to the individual than to a folk tradition. But the important thing was, none of it was professional. It was a part of everyday life that existed around events like the annual hog butchering or the happy event of a friend's visit or a wedding, or simply to blow off steam after a week's work. It was, in the purest sense of the term, folk music.

Which isn't to say that America didn't have professional showbiz back then; it was just limited to the cities. Rural people had neither money nor transportation—nor, in most cases, the inclination—to engage with the wandering troupes of minstrels, light opera singers, and, after 1871, ensembles singing Negro spirituals, who descended from the Fisk Jubilee Singers. This branch of entertainment was for the middle class and up. It was performed by professionals, people who worked at making their art and were paid for it. And except for providing venues, a template for touring, and a few songs leaking into the folk pool, it doesn't have too much to do with our story, at least not until the very last days of the 1800s, when the phonograph was born.

The earliest phonographs, once the world adopted Emile Berliner's disc format over Edison's cylinder, and Berliner's standard of playing from the outside in rather than Pathé's inside out, were sturdy furniture. They had to be: the acoustic signal coming off the disc through a steel or cactus-thorn needle needed room for amplification in a large chamber, although the fascinated owners still had to sit close to the machine. You couldn't play a record in the next room and expect to hear it.

What were people listening to? The kind of music people of their economic class—upper middle and above—might be expected to listen to included classics, light classics, operatic arias, songs from the musical theater that was thriving in New York, patriotic music (John Philip Sousa's band was popular, and not just for his famous marches, since he composed other things for them), comic sketches from the vaudeville stage (often in Jewish, Negro, or Irish dialect), and the occasional novelty, like a Negro jubilee ensemble singing spirituals or, even more novel, the Dinwiddie Colored Quartet's mashup of "Dem Bones" with what sounds like a blackface minstrel comedy interlude.

Off the record, independent of this mainstream, some major changes were happening. For one thing, medicine shows, a sort of low-rent spinoff of the touring minstrel show, began to appear in rural Southern America, bringing black and white performers—sometimes together—to communities that had never before seen professional entertainers. They'd play and sing and prepare the locals for a pitch for some miracle drug (mostly alcohol, with additives that could be anything from opium to gasoline) that would do incredible things and was available just until the caravan pulled out of town for a low, low price. The people who performed at these shows were considered lowlifes by polite society, but out in the boondocks, they were visitors from another world. If the medicine show was from far away, they might well be exposing the locals to instrumental styles and even forms of music they'd never heard before. In addition, the better-funded medicine shows handed out "singers," cheap booklets with some of the songs performed in the show, thereby spreading everything from Stephen Foster songs to hymns and drinking songs to places where they'd been previously unknown. (One "singer" was found to have had half its contents recorded by one act or another during the 1920s and '30s.) The medicine shows lasted almost a century and became laboratories for young musicians honing their performing skills and welcome employment for entertainers who were too rural for the vaudeville stage.

Starting in the very last years of the nineteenth century, a new musical form emerged out of nowhere in the Deep South. Nobody can pinpoint the place or time when blues was invented, nor does it have a legendary inventor, but it did have a chronicler in the person of W. C. Handy, a trumpet player and bandleader from Memphis, who was famously waiting for a train in the early days of the twentieth century in rural Tutwiler, Mississippi, when a ragged black man with a guitar sat down next to him and, running a knife blade over the strings, began to sing "the weirdest music I ever heard," improvising lyrics about the train they were waiting for. Handy went on to make much out of his "discovery," even advertising himself as the "father of the blues," but blues was an evolution from other black traditions, including the "songster" genre, which survived in the work of "Ragtime Texas" Henry Thomas, Mississippi John Hurt, and Mance Lipscomb, among others, and is responsible for such black ballads as "Frankie and Johnny," "Stackolee," and "The Titanic." Blues was actually something new and easy enough to write: in its classic form, the first two lines repeat, and then a third line closes the thought: "Woke up this morning, blues all around my bed / Woke up this morning, blues all around my bed / I tell you people, they're the worst blues I've ever had." Some blues told stories, advancing the story (usually of heartbreak) verse by verse. Other blues were made up of what are called "floating verses" like the one just quoted, or the blues would start with a story and go on to floating verses that fit the mood. Either way, the form had the advantage of having spaces between lines where an instrumentalist could play some licks, and the space between verses for more extended solo work.

Blues probably started out being accompanied by guitars, which became more available as mail-order sources like Sears, Roebuck & Company and Montgomery Ward found their way into rural areas, but the form lent itself to the piano, too, which meant that it soon spread to the cities, where blues singers, almost invariably female, wound up on the black vaudeville stages. Gertrude "Ma" Rainey, one of the first to find fame, was a centerpiece of the Rabbit Foot Minstrels, one of the top black touring outfits, and her influence on younger singers was immense.

The rise of urban blues was parallel to and to some extent integrated with the rise of the music that came to be called jazz. Although it was undeniably a popular music—far more popular than some of the other music of its time—jazz only concerns us here as an ingredient of other forms. It's worth noting that many jazz scholars consider the blues-singing women of the 1920s as jazz musicians while ignoring or discounting rural blues performers. The harmonic structure of blues, however, was with jazz from its very earliest days, and the power of the word is evident in the way songs that aren't blues at all—W. C. Handy's "St. Louis Blues," to give a prominent example—use the word, if not the form.

If blues was a central ingredient to black music in the Deep South, there was another form that arrived about the same time that was just as important on the eastern seaboard: ragtime. This was a piano-based, composed and notated, syncopated musical form that came into being simultaneously with the earliest jazz—and in many of the same venues. Ragtime might be what the "piano professor" was playing in whorehouses with enough class to have a parlor with a piano, but it quickly escaped its seedy origins to become a fad in vaudeville and the politer parlors of the middle class. Most notably, it was promoted by the sheet music publishers who had Scott Joplin, a black pianist with some training, under contract. Joplin was hardly the only ragtime composer to make money for an ambitious publisher, but his prodigious output included music for small instrumental ensembles and an opera, among other works.

And while ragtime wasn't particularly transposable to the guitar, its ideas were, and so guitarists who heard pianists playing a form of ragtime called barrelhouse in turpentine camps in Georgia tried out the harmonies and came up with intricate fingerpicking techniques to form melodies on them and invented a guitar style that mimicked the multiple lines and tricky rhythms of the piano music. This became the basis of the black rural popular music of Georgia and the Carolinas.

Another place where ragtime's ideas showed up was in the medicine shows, where comic songs were common. Again, the chord progressions made a great base for a type of music that became known as hokum, which spread to both the black and white traditions. White medicine show performers like Uncle Dave Macon and Harmonica

Frank Floyd salted their repertoires with hokum, and black perform-ers in Memphis made it a signature of the city's music, as it was largely what the jug bands there played (Gus Cannon of Cannon's Jug Stom-pers had a long career with the shows), as well as the successful Memphis Sheiks. Not surprisingly, all these groups were in high de-mand among the city's moneyed whites for party entertainment.

These developments happened slowly, and they didn't all happen in the same places at the same time, since there was no mass media even remotely interested in this minority-interest stuff—and in some places, they didn't happen at all. But soon after the end of World War I, enough of these new sounds were in evidence for the immense changes that would come in the 1920s and kick off the arrival of a distinctly American wave of music.

chapter one

THE RECORD INDUSTRY:
RACE AND COUNTRY

Paramount Records ad from the Chicago *Defender*, a black
newspaper often circulated by Pullman porters.
(GAB Archive/Contributor)

On February 14 (or maybe August 10: it wasn't considered important enough to keep notes), 1920, a black vaudeville singer took advantage of another singer's canceled session to cut a record. Mamie Smith was backed by a band assembled by Perry Bradford, a young black veteran of minstrel shows, songwriter, and what would today be called record producer who'd convinced the fledgling Okeh Records label that black people owned phonographs in sufficient quantity to buy records. He'd worked with Smith before, when she'd recorded two of his tunes, "That Thing Called Love" and "You Can't Keep a Good Man Down," and the record had sold between fifty thousand and one hundred thousand copies—a very respectable number. When the opportunity to record her again came along, he grabbed two more of his songs and gave them to her. "Crazy Blues" wasn't even a blues song, but it was the first song with *blues* in the title to be recorded. It sold seventy-five thousand copies in a month and over a million copies in its first year, making Smith a star, giving Bradford the chance to work with other up-and-coming stars like Louis Armstrong, putting Okeh Records on the map, and igniting a craze for blues. Female blues singers suddenly appeared on records, singing blues songs that actually were blues songs, and—curiously enough—many of them were named Smith: Bessie, Alberta, Clara, and Trixie, among others. Most of them adopted the elaborate gowns, big hats, and flashy jewelry that Mamie had introduced as blues singer attire, and sang songs in the classic AAB form. They didn't just come out of the blue; a woman named Gertrude "Ma" Rainey had been singing blues for years, in an act with her husband, as Assassinators of the Blues. At first, the Raineys toured with the famous Rabbit Foot Minstrels, a show in which, much later, young Rufus Thomas began a career that would make him a Memphis icon well into the second half of the century, and then they graduated to a series of tent shows. Ma Rainey didn't leap on Mamie Smith's bandwagon, but when she did start recording in 1923, she made over one hundred sides.

The label she recorded for is worth noting: Paramount Records was a spinoff of the Wisconsin Chair Company in Port Washington, Wisconsin, which had started making Victrolas as they became popular. In 1917, they decided to form a record company to make something to play on them. The first Paramount releases were the usual mixed bag of stuff: Hawaiian tunes, Irish novelties, comic routines, and, for some reason, a lot of marimba orchestra records. Then Mamie Smith woke them up, and they announced that they were entering what was beginning to be called the "race market." Their first star was Alberta Hunter, a genteel vocalist who could do pop as well as blues, and her success alerted a former NFL player and graduate of Brown University, J. Mayo "Ink" Williams, to a possibility. Williams had been hanging around Chicago, doing small-time hustles, and one day he headed to Port Washington to talk to Paramount. He later remembered the walk from the train station, with little kids staring at him and, the more adventurous ones, touching him. They'd never seen a black person before. Williams told Paramount that he knew the black music world well—didn't he live in Chicago, a mecca of African American music-making?—and when he discovered they needed someone to run their new recording studio in Chicago, a deal was made. Williams went right to work: before long, he'd recorded Papa Charlie Jackson, a popular banjo-playing street performer from Chicago, blues singers Ma Rainey, Ethel Waters, Ida Cox, and further sessions for Alberta Hunter, and jazz musicians, largely but not entirely from New Orleans, who had found a ready audience in Chicago like Fletcher Henderson, Freddie Keppard, King Oliver (with and without Louis Armstrong), and Ferdinand LaMenthe, who called himself Jelly Roll Morton.

Williams didn't even like blues—he was more partial to classical music—but considered it part of his people's heritage. This resulted in his being open to blues besides the kind played on the vaudeville stages: a Paramount dealer in Dallas alerted Williams to a street performer who was drawing good crowds, and Williams sent for him. It was a wise investment; Blind Lemon Jefferson was phenomenally popular and recorded close to one hundred sides for Paramount before his mysterious death in Chicago in 1929. Some of his songs became classics, and "Matchbox Blues" was recorded by Carl Perkins and by the Beatles. As if that weren't enough of a claim on immortality, Jefferson's "lead boys," youngsters he'd hire to guide him along the streets, included Aaron "T-Bone" Walker and Joshua White. Jefferson's success opened the door for other guitar-playing blues performers of a rural bent. Blind Arthur Blake, a guitar virtuoso about whom absolutely nothing is known for certain, recorded close to eighty sides for Paramount before vanishing as mysteriously as he came, preserving a guitar style that has great hunks of jazz and ragtime in it.

Williams really lucked out by forming a relationship with H. C. Speir, a white store owner in Jackson, Mississippi's black neighborhood who took notice of the fact that there was a lot of black musical talent in the surrounding area. They'd come in and buy gramophones from him, and records, too. Speir's innovation was to buy a recording machine so that he could cut demos of people who wanted to record and send them on to record companies, who'd pay him a finder's fee if the artist was of interest. Speir was by no means exclusively dealing with Paramount—he also sent performers to Victor and Decca and, most famously, later got Robert Johnson hooked up with the American Recording Company, which was eventually absorbed by Columbia— but he hit gold with Williams, up until his mysterious departure from Paramount in 1927. The label began sending tickets to many of Speir's finds to come up to Wisconsin to record, and Speir sent some of the less commercial artists up there, including Charley Patton, who was a bridge between the songster and blues traditions and a great mentor to everyone from Johnson to Roebuck Staples (who later founded the gospel sensations the Staple Singers) and Chester Burnett (later known as Howlin' Wolf), and Nehemiah "Skip" James, whose career suffered from Paramount's not promoting his 1931 records and by James getting religion later that year. Speir also sent Williams Patton's friend and rival Son House, the mysterious King Solomon Hill, Ishman Bracey, Tommy Johnson, and Geechie Wiley and Elvie Thomas, whose identities weren't confirmed until the twenty-first century, to Paramount's studios to make records that would be rediscovered thirty years later by a totally different audience from the one they were made for. Country blues like this didn't sell spectacularly, although some artists like Tommy Johnson and the piano-guitar duo of Scrapper Blackwell and Leroy Carr certainly justified their record companies' investment in them, and other artists like Patton sold well enough in small regions where they were popular through live performances to be asked back to do further sessions. Hokum and jug band records also did well, with the Mississippi Sheiks, the Memphis Jug Band, and Cannon's Jug Stompers selling respectably, in part because they were popular with white people in Memphis, where they lived. Essentially, record companies were initiating a tradition: record it and see if it sells.

Paramount was far from the only company getting into the race music market. Most companies that dared going after such an uncertain audience just dipped a toe in, and the usual thing was to treat race music as just one of a number of small markets that might produce a return with a left-field smash like "Crazy Blues." Okeh, Mamie Smith's label, was run by a German immigrant named Otto K. Heineman, and was a bit more dedicated to minority music, including Yiddish music, but most race labels concentrated on jazz, because it had a crossover white audience from the start and was beginning a golden era with artists like Louis Armstrong and Duke Ellington. It was also produced in urban centers like New York and Chicago, close to where the record companies were.

It's really little wonder, then, that it took as long as it did for the nascent industry to investigate rural white music. Actually, they didn't go to it—it came to them. In 1922, directly after winning a fiddle festival, A. C. "Eck" Robertson, of Amarillo, Texas, and Henry Gilli-land, from Virginia, took a train to New York and, dressed in a cowboy outfit (Robertson) and a Confederate uniform (Gilliland), walked into the Victor Recording Company and asked to be recorded. Possibly just to get rid of them, Victor did so, cutting "Arkansas Traveler" and "Sallie Gooden." It was an odd record, just two fiddles—and two fiddlers from different traditions, at that—but somebody decided to put it out, and, to Victor's amazement, it sold. Word got out about Victor's interest, and in 1924, Marion Try Slaughter, a vocalist who had recorded light opera and popular songs, revived his career by taking the name of two Texas towns, Vernon and Dalhart, and recorded "The Prisoner's Song" for them. It became a huge hit, in part because Slaughter sang with a Southern accent, and made Vernon Dalhart a star. Other, more traditional musicians saw their chance, and Fiddlin' John Carson, Henry Whittier, Ernest "Pop" Stoneman, and Uncle Dave Macon began their recording careers with repertoires that were at least somewhat traditional.

At this point, Victor saw a chance. Ralph Peer was a Southerner who'd begun his career at Okeh, okaying the recording of "Crazy Blues" and a couple of years later discovering Fiddlin' John Carson, one of the first commercially successful traditional country artists. Aware of his ear for unusual music, Victor hired him to do a talent search. He picked the city of Bristol, straddling the Virginia and Tennessee borders (the state line actually runs down the center of State Street), mostly because other artists he'd already recorded for Victor, Pop Stoneman and Henry Whittier, lived in the vicinity and could help publicize his call for talent to audition for Victor Records. He announced it for July 25 to August 5, 1927, and when responses were slow, he arranged for the Stoneman Family to do a session and invited a newspaper reporter to watch. The subsequent article emphasized how much money the Stonemans made from records and touring, and Peer was suddenly in business: by automobile, horse, and even on foot, prospective stars came to Bristol to try their luck. On August 1, a trio from Maces Springs, Virginia, sat before the microphone, the Carter Family, A. C. and his wife, Sara, and Sara's sister, Maybelle. They wound up recording six sides that day and the next. On August

4, a singer Peer had met in Mississippi—who'd been rejected by H. C. Speir—recorded. He'd come to town with his group, the Tenneva Ramblers, but something happened—nobody really knows what—and so Jimmie Rodgers recorded without them, and they recorded later that day with another musician.

The Carter Family and Jimmie Rodgers weren't the only discoveries the 1927 Bristol sessions produced—Eck Dunford and Blind Alfred Reed were among the others—but they were by far the most significant. The Carters were almost an overnight success, and Rodgers was asked by Victor to do another session for them that produced the first of his "Blue Yodels," launching him into stardom. The fact that these two artists were making so much money for Victor made the label decide to open a regional office in Nashville, Tennessee, which had been the home of a successful local radio show, the *Grand Ole Opry*, since 1925. Although the establishment in Nashville, a city previously best known for insurance and Bible printing, hated the idea at least through the 1980s, country music and the country music end of the record business was largely centered there from then on.

Victor tried Bristol again in 1928, and similar cattle calls were held by other labels—most notably Columbia Records in Johnson City, Tennessee, in 1928 and '29—but calling the 1927 sessions, as a collection of the complete Bristol recordings did, the "Big Bang" of country music is entirely accurate. The Carter Family mingled songs written by A. C. Carter with folk material prettied up for commercial reasons by rewriting lyrics and adding verses. They also, later in their career, had a black chauffeur to get them from place to place on tour, and he was known to go song hunting for them. As for Rodgers, he was very much in the pop tradition, but influenced by black music he heard as a sickly youth hanging around the railroad yards where his father worked, which produced both his "blue yodel" and his use of a Hawaiian steel guitar on his records. Both acts were self-consciously pop artists, composing and copyrighting their material, a rarity in the "hillbilly" record field. Of course, since they were inventing an entire field of music that hadn't previously existed, they were free to experiment as they wished, a freedom Rodgers, in particular, took advantage of, recording with the more conservative Carters, and, on a couple of sides, with Victor's other major success story, Louis Armstrong.

It's worth noting that the first radio station to play records—and that only on a small segment of its broadcast day—began the practice in 1926, just as all this ferment was happening. The vast majority of music on the radio was live, be it dance orchestras broadcasting from ritzy hotels in New York over network radio or hillbilly bands and gospel quartets getting up early in the morning to draw listeners to the farm report and, via their sponsors, to sell flour or patent medicine on small local stations. Radio was becoming an increasingly important factor in American life, but as a medium for news, drama, comedy, and light entertainment. Country music was beamed by WSM's *Grand Ole Opry* and the WLS *Barn Dance* in Chicago, but those shows were anomalies, albeit ones with enormous listenerships, including black people. There was no blues on the radio, even the most sophisticated stuff like Bessie Smith and Alberta Hunter were recording. After all, who would listen to it?

With radio not yet important for record sales, and with no real feedback on releases other than sales, record companies tried everything. Ethnic communities had thriving entertainment scenes going on in cities like New York and Chicago, so Ukrainian and Yiddish music was easy enough to find and record, and record company catalogs, which were provided to every retail outlet, had those records' serial numbers in case the retailers wanted to order some. Mexican music was popular in the Southwest and Greek music in New England. And blues, both urban and rural, was in the catalogs' race section.

Another genre that emerged during this time was Western music. As movies got sound, the singing cowboy entered American popular culture. For the most part, they sang songs written for them by Hollywood songwriters, most of which weren't particularly memorable, rehashing clichés about the open range and herding cattle. Gene Autry, for instance, started his career by singing songs that sounded a whole lot like Jimmie Rodgers, although some of them were more risqué than anything Rodgers would have recorded, and soon graduated

to Hollywood cowboy stuff. But while most singing cowboys were actors first and singers second, one important musician took the opposite
route. Bob Wills was born in Limestone County, Texas, and learned
to fiddle from his father and grandfather as they farmed cotton on land
they'd bought in Turkey, a dot on the map of west Texas. Wills was
soon a local celebrity for his fiddling—and as Turkey's barber—but in
1929, he'd had enough of Turkey and lit out for the big city, Fort
Worth. There, he played medicine shows with his friend Herman
Arnspiger, and soon ran into the Brown brothers, Milton and his teenage brother, Derwood. This quartet was soon hired by an ambitious
hustler (and future Texas governor) W. Lee "Pappy" O'Daniel for a
radio program sponsored by Light Crust Flour. He renamed the band
the Light Crust Doughboys, but O'Daniel was no fun to work for
(besides his authoritarian personality, he was a staunch Prohibitionist),
and soon the Browns jumped ship to concentrate on one part of the
Doughboys' repertoire, a strange hybrid that was influenced by hokum, jazz, and the urban blues of singers like Bessie Smith. They called
it Western swing and established a base from which to perform it at
Crystal Springs, a resort and recreation area outside of town where the
Doughboys had performed despite O'Daniel's disapproval. Milton
Brown's Musical Brownies recorded a number of sides for Decca between 1932 and 1936, the year Milton died in an auto accident. In
1933, Wills, too, quit the Doughboys and started his own band with a
couple of others who'd left, and, just to make his point, got sponsor-
ship from Play Boy Flour. He moved to Tulsa, Oklahoma, got a daily
broadcast on KVOO, based himself in a large dance hall called Cain's
Dancing Academy, and called his band the Texas Playboys. In September 1935, they did the first of many recording sessions for Vocalion/
Okeh, which included "Osage Stomp," based on the Memphis Jug
Band's "Rukus Juice and Chittlin'," the Mississippi Sheiks' "Sittin' On
Top of the World," and Big Bill Broonzy's "I Can't Be Satisfied." This
was not the Carter Family's country music. It was also wildly popular
and spawned many another hot ensemble: Bill Boyd and His Cowboy
Ramblers, Jimmie Revard and His Oklahoma Playboys, Cliff Bruner's
Texas Wanderers, and Ted Daffan's Texans, among many others.

     Western swing was also a good thing to have in your band's book even if you didn't specialize in it: Adolph Hofner's orchestra traveled more widely than most Texas polka bands because they could play a non-Czech-Tex crowd with an entire program of swing, and the Sons of the Pioneers, a vocal group led by Roy Rogers and Bob Nolan and best known for pure Western songs like "Tumbling Tumbleweeds," added Texans Hugh and Karl Farr early on in the group's existence, not only for Karl's bass singing but for his hot fiddling and duets with his guitarist brother. The Sons, of course, appeared in many of Roy Rogers's films, and eventually Bob Wills, too, made movies, especially after moving to a large restaurant / dance hall / dude ranch complex he built near Sacramento, California, called Wills Point. Western swing itself, although never a huge genre outside its birthplace (Texas and Oklahoma, and, after the Dust Bowl migrations of the 1930s, California), continued through at least the late 1950s, although it only occasionally hit the country charts.

The record business was hit hard by the Depression. Although this period gave birth to the economic rule that entertainment does better during hard economic times, the entertainment it refers to is the kind with high production values (e.g., Busby Berkeley film musicals or movies like *The Wizard of Oz* or *Gone with the Wind*) or live music. Spending a dollar on an item that at most gave six minutes of music was an insane extravagance next to spending ten or twenty-five cents to go to a dance by a good band. (Even the three-for-a-dollar bargain labels only gave you six songs for your buck, and the records wore out more quickly.) And the sort of people who bought blues and country music had less discretionary spending money than ever, which indirectly killed the recording career of Robert Johnson, now the most famous Delta bluesman of all. Johnson recorded late—his two sessions were in 1936 and '37—and only his first release, "Terraplane Blues," sold at all. The rest, although undeniably virtuosic and brilliantly written, mostly languished unsold in the warehouses, causing a legend to build up that he'd sold his soul to the devil in order to play like that. Whether he did or not, he certainly died in 1938, probably poisoned by a jealous husband.

Paramount went under in 1932, announcing to its workers that it was closing during their Christmas party. Some of them celebrated by going to the factory's rooftop and using the metal record stampers as discuses, sailing them into the river.

Victor created Bluebird, a budget line to compete with ARC and Decca, who were selling three records for a dollar, putting out records by Western swingster Bill Boyd, the Blue Sky Boys, Earl and Bill Bolick, whose "brother harmonies" started a new genre of country music, and Bill and Charlie Monroe, who began recording in 1936. Charlie was tired of working with his cantankerous brother by 1939, and Bill formed an acoustic band emphasizing instrumental virtuosity and tight harmonies, the Blue Grass Boys. Like Western swing, bluegrass was never a lucrative field, but it was popular in the area where it was born; Monroe had almost immediate competition from Ralph and Carter Stanley. Bluegrass would prove very successful in hillbilly ghettoes in the Midwest after the war, as well as in rural areas east of the Mississippi.

Bluebird also had a blues operation going in Chicago, overseen by Lester Melrose, who had the brilliant idea of having the blues artists under contract to Bluebird play in supporting roles on each other's records. Musicians like Tampa Red and Roosevelt Sykes, Arthur Crudup, Sonny Boy Williamson (the original, not the postwar musician), and Big Bill Broonzy made innumerable records to supplement their income from appearances in Chicago nightclubs, and Bluebird recorded some of the first electric blues. They also had a very important hit with Lil Green's "Romance in the Dark," one of the first records that highlighted a growing trend that mixed small-combo jazz with blues. The master of this was Louis Jordan, a diminutive, hyperactive alto saxophonist whose novelty songs lit up jukeboxes practically from the moment he was forced to start his own band after the death of his former employer, drummer / big band leader Chick Webb. Probably because an unknown was better off carrying as few musicians as possible, Jordan and his band, the Tympany Five (who almost always numbered more than five and never featured tympani), downplayed solos (except for the leader) and emphasized slice-of-life comedy and wordplay. The latter was one of his most outstanding features: years later, Chuck Berry would say that when he began writing songs, he was trying to imitate Louis Jordan.

World War II halted all this activity that hadn't already been halted by declining record sales. Records were pressed on shellac, and the world's supply was located in the South Pacific, which was under Japanese control. Rubber for tires and gasoline for tour buses were rationed, making it harder for big bands to tour. The American Federation of Musicians, the national musicians' union, in the person of its leader, James Caesar Petrillo, claiming worry because working musicians were supposedly having their livelihoods taken away by recordings played on the radio, enacted a pair of recording bans in 1942, and in 1947–1948, resulting in some crucial American musical history being lost, most notably the beginnings of bebop. This affected all recording artists, be they orchestras or hillbilly fiddlers: in order to record, you had to belong to the American Federation of Musicians, and Petrillo was very powerful. On a positive note, demographics changed, as skilled workers went to where the jobs were, changing the racial and social makeup of the country's larger cities. When peace returned, things sounded different indeed.

chapter two

INDEPENDENCE

Rhythm and Blues show ad, early 1950s.
(The Michael Barson Collection)

usicians called it the Stroll. Every decent-sized town with a black presence had one: the strip where the nightclubs were, where the barbershops were, where the barbecue and chicken-and-waffle joints were. The "colored" movie theater was on the Stroll, along with doctors, dentists, insurance companies, and morticians who catered to the black community. Off to the side stood the churches. Occasionally, fraternal organizations like the black Elks would have a hall there that they rented out. The Stroll was the main street of the black community, and its heartbeat. Some were bigger than others, and some, like 125th Street in New York, Beale Street in Memphis, and Central Avenue in Los Angeles, were legendary and spoken of in terms white people reserved for Fifth Avenue and the Champs-Elysées. And while World War II had made things difficult for the black entertainment business, it certainly didn't shut it down. The biggest stars paid the bills by touring as much as they could (and in weird places, too; there's a famous recording of the Duke Ellington orchestra playing in Fargo, North Dakota, in 1941 to what must have been an all-white crowd), but many smaller bands, often with a male and a female vocalist and a couple of instrumental soloists, stayed within a given geographic area, their touring limited by rationing. Their repertoire was broad: pop tunes mixed with blues and Louis Jordan–style novelties.

The blues these groups played tended to be very smooth and so-phisticated, quite unlike the stuff being played by Chicago's Bluebird crowd of transplanted rural Southerners. One model for this new music was provided by the Nat King Cole Trio, piano, guitar, and bass. Cole began by recording straightforward jazz, and although he didn't like the way his voice sounded, he was outvoted by his band (and, later, audiences) and started recording vocals. This unit proved very popular and would have risen faster if the war and the recording ban hadn't interfered, but their sound made a nice contrast from brassy, horn-led combos. Cole's turf was Hollywood, but his peers played the Stroll, Central Avenue.

Central Avenue had been legendary almost from the start, when black railroad workers from Texas settled there in the early twentieth century, and by 1920, Central Avenue pretty much was black Los Angeles. Traversing its length, however, could hardly be called a stroll: just along Central, it was a thirty-block stretch, and of course the residential part went onto the side streets. But there were some legendary structures on Central: the Dunbar Hotel, a luxurious black-owned place much frequented by well-heeled black people and with a famous nightclub, the Apex, next door. The club later changed its name to the Club Alabam, and it became Los Angeles's answer to New York's Cotton Club, only without the slumming white folks. At Twelfth and Central stood Spikes Brothers Music, a venerable store selling instruments and sheet music—and later, records—to the community, and just down a couple of blocks was the black musicians union. At the corner of Vernon and Central was Ivie Anderson's Chicken Shack, run by the woman who had been Duke Ellington's greatest vocalist, and a little farther down was Bronze Recording Studios, with another Ellington connection: one of its investors was Herb Jeffries, once an Ellington vocalist and now a star in black cinema, Westerns a specialty, earning him the nickname "the Bronze Buckaroo."

Much farther down Central, though, things changed. This is where the later arrivals settled, in the area called Watts. The entertainment they sought wasn't the slick Nat Cole variety; it was blues. When Franklin D. Roosevelt integrated the war industries, black people with shipbuilding, welding, and other useful skills left Louisiana,

Oklahoma, and Texas and headed straight to California, and a whole lot of them settled around Central or in Watts. The former Japanese neighborhood downtown, too, had been emptied, its residents sent to internment camps and their property seized, and the neighborhood was transformed as black people moved in. The new arrivals did what they could to integrate with their sophisticated neighbors, but a certain amount of friction remained. It was evident in the clubs. Bebop and what was to be known as rhythm and blues hit Central more or less simultaneously: Charlie Parker and Dizzy Gillespie's ill-fated 1945 booking at Billy Berg's in Hollywood may have been a total bust financially, but one reason the club didn't make money was that young local guys like Dexter Gordon, Wardell Gray, Charles Mingus, and others sat at the bar, nursing Coca-Colas and hearing the music of the future. Meanwhile, three Oklahomans, Jimmy and Joe Liggins and Roy Milton, had come to town and assembled three small bands playing less harmonically sophisticated music largely based on blues forms and singing catchy tunes for dancing. Pee Wee Crayton, a guitarist from Texas, settled in, assembling a band that included another Texan, alto saxophonist Ornette Coleman. A former sewing-machine salesman, Big Jay McNeely, was purveying a honking, primitive style with his tenor sax and getting a following. And black Los Angeles, flush with wartime wages, made it all thrive.

Chicago, too, was a magnet for black war workers, and they mostly came from Mississippi and Tennessee, thanks to the Illinois Central Railroad, which would take them from Memphis straight to Chicago. Many of these workers were less skilled than the ones in Los Angeles, increasingly displaced from tenant farming jobs by a new cotton-picking machine that made hand labor all but obsolete. But you didn't need much skill to work in a steel plant or a slaughterhouse, and rural Southern black people had been migrating north for some time, so having relatives in town was a distinct possibility. That's what happened to McKinley Morganfield, who'd grown up on Stovall's Plantation, the same plantation that Charley Patton and Son House had lived on, where he'd worked his way up from agricultural laborer to truck and tractor driver, as well as one of the plantation's entertainers.

One day in 1941, two men documenting black folk music for the Library of Congress—Alan Lomax, from Washington, D.C., and black folklorist John Work from Memphis—came by with a huge recording device and recorded three songs with Morganfield. When Lomax got back to Washington, he compiled the best of the recordings from the trip into a five-disc "album." The only performer to get a whole disc to himself was Morganfield, and Lomax sent him a copy. Morganfield, upon receiving it, heard himself for the first time. He promptly put on his best suit, grabbed the record, and went to the nearest photo studio to have his picture taken holding it. Lomax and Work came back the next summer and recorded more. By the summer after that, Morganfield had joined the exodus north. His mother had a relative he could stay with until he found his own place.

As the war wound down, shellac supplies were still depleted, although replacement plastics had been developed for wartime use. Nobody was buying records because there were no records to buy. And then . . . then there was one. The story that was circulated at the time was that at a war bonds rally in 1944, a little black soldier visiting from Nashville had asked to play a tune, and he was so well received that someone made a record of it with him. "I Wonder" was a perfect song for wartime: the singer wonders if his lover, so far away, has been faithful, a situation loads of GIs faced. But the truth is more prosaic: Private Cecil Gant had wandered into Bronze Recording Studios and asked to make a record. The man in charge, Leroy Hurte, didn't tell him that there wasn't any shellac to press one on, but he listened to the songs Gant was playing and liked one of them. "I figured that one would sell," Hurte said later. He had some copies pressed up—heaven knows where he got the shellac—and distributed them locally. The song took off. But one night Hurte heard a radio DJ announce the record as "a Gilt-Edge recording." Gilt-Edge was another tiny label, but owned by a white guy with good connections. Gant had walked into his company and asked if he could re-record his song for them, and of course, with the record already selling, the guy, Richard Nelson, said yes. In the ensuing mess, each label disputed the other's copyright, and a judge found for Nelson.

Hurte actually bought a record press and pressed more Bronze copies of the song and distributed it to Pullman porters to sell on the trains they worked on (a time-honored distribution system not only for records but for the Negro press) and by hand to retailers on the Stroll, and Nelson activated a network of distributors nationwide and got radio airplay across the country. As for Gant, he made a few more records for Gilt-Edge, which sold respectably, and then vanished for three years. He shows up again on the Nashville label Bullet in 1948 and died in 1951 of pneumonia.

Hurte wasn't finished, though. Word on Central was that there was a combo that had a song that they played for what seemed like hours and that just kept people dancing and dancing. This was worth looking into, and Hurte eventually got Joe Liggins, whose band it was, to come down to the Bronze studio and record it. "The Honeydripper" was recorded in two parts, and slapped on either side of a record, but for some reason, Hurte didn't put it out right away. Disgusted, Liggins dragged Leon René, another black entrepreneur, down to the club and had the band do one of their deluxe versions of the tune. René witnessed the frenzy and rushed the band after the set and told them he'd record them for his label, Exclusive. This came out in the summer of 1945 and took straight off. Although Hurte eventually raised the money to put out his recording of it, the Exclusive version is better recorded and better played. The blunder almost cost Hurte his business, and to make up for it, he offered the service of his record press to three Jewish guys who'd appeared on Central. Jules, Joe, and Saul Bihari were Hungarians from Tulsa, Oklahoma, who got into the record business slowly. Jules started working for a record distributor and jukebox firm in Little Tokyo in 1942, which meant instant familiarity with what was going on on Central. His biggest problem was a lack of material to stock the jukeboxes with: record companies weren't putting out enough blues and jazz to keep them fresh. His brother Joe suggested that they start making them themselves. There was money in it, as "I Wonder" was proving every day.

Jules agreed enthusiastically. During his rounds, he'd heard a young woman playing some light classics in a music store. Hadda Hopgood was well educated, middle class, light skinned, and tremendously talented. Jules fell in love on the spot and asked her if she could play a boogie. Intrigued, Hadda improvised one, and Jules asked her if she'd ever thought of making a record. Would she like to? Well, why not? She was intrigued by this ambitious young man, and thus started a love affair and an important record label. Re-christened Hadda Brooks, she rehearsed a couple of tunes that she called "Swingin' the Boogie" and "Bluesin' the Boogie" and Jules submitted the tapes to Hurte to master and press demo copies. When they had the performance and the sound right, the brothers incorporated as Modern Music Co. at 111 South San Pedro and pressed up Modern Music 101. They had to go elsewhere to get the record pressed, though; Hurte was still hand-pressing copies of "I Wonder" on his single press. From this single record, a mighty independent label was to grow.

Meanwhile, in Chicago, another couple of ambitious Jewish brothers were also looking at the black music being made in their neighborhood. Lejzor and Fiszel Czyz were the sons of a Polish immigrant who'd opened a successful liquor store in Chicago. As soon as the boys could, they started running jazz clubs and changed their names to Leonard and Philip Chess. By the mid-1940s, they'd opened a highly successful club, the Macomba Lounge, and observed that the audiences loved some of the talent they were presenting, but the performers were stuck because they had no way to publicize themselves. In 1947, Leonard invested in a tiny record label called Aristocrat Records, and soon he and Phil had taken it over. Their first records (after the 1947 recording ban was lifted) were by unknowns: the Five Blazers were on Aristocrat 201, and Clarence Samuels, Jump Jackson, Andrew Tibbs, and Tom Archia (a regular performer at the Macomba) also made records. But, although they didn't know it, the Chess brothers were waiting for McKinley Morganfield.

He'd been lucky: a friend from Stovall's, Dan Jones Sr., who used his truck to clear apartments for landlords, hired the young man to help him. Not only did they get the pick of appliances and other stuff people had left behind, they also got early word of vacancies, and before long, Morganfield had a nice large apartment for twelve dollars a month. A place to live was one thing, but work in his chosen field was another. By this time, he was calling himself Muddy Waters, a name that evoked the Deep South as much as his slide guitar playing did. He was also playing an electric guitar, a nice Gretsch (an earlier guitar, which gave him problems all the time, had been stolen at a club), and holding down a regular gig with some friends. Finally, he had a chance to record, with none other than J. Mayo "Ink" Williams running the session. "Mean Red Spider" was the B side of "Let Me Be Your Coal Man" by James "Sweet Lucy" Carter and His Orchestra, and Muddy is buried underneath clarinets and saxophones: this was very much the old-time Chicago sound. But on that session, he met someone who introduced him to Leroy "Baby Face" Foster, who played guitar and drums. Muddy was already working with Jimmy Rogers, a hot young guitarist who doubled on harmonica, and once this group had solidified, they started packing the clubs. On September 27, 1946, they went into the studio with Lester Melrose, the man who'd forged the Bluebird sound, and recorded eight sides for Columbia, three featuring Muddy, the rest in combination with a couple of other vocalists. The tracks by pianist Jimmy Clark came out, but Muddy's remained unreleased for years.

The third time was the charm. By this time, the Muddy Waters–Jimmy Rogers–Baby Face Foster band had added another artist: Marion Walter Jacobs, whom Rogers knew from Mississippi as "a little squirrel-faced kid" who played harmonica. After being blasted out of bed one morning by the sound of a harmonica player performing at the Maxwell Street Market near his house, Rogers headed down there to find the kid, now an adult, playing like crazy, and took him over to meet Muddy. In no time, the band found a home at the Club Zanzibar, at Ashland and Thirteenth, just around the corner from Muddy's home, where they started playing blues with a power and authority that was brand new. Some of it was the volume from those electric instruments (and Little Walter's using a microphone to amplify his harmonica), and some of it was the down-home sound, including that of the slide guitar that Muddy transformed with electricity, that reminded homesick immigrants of life in the South—but with the electric sound of the city. Nobody else in Chicago was doing this, and other musicians would come to gape. By this time, the Chess brothers had hired a talent scout for Aristocrat, a black man incongruously named Sammy Goldberg, and he heard word of Muddy's talent. He ran into him at the musicians' union hall one day, asked to hear him play, and he liked what he heard. Shortly thereafter, the Chess brothers were doing a session, and pianist Sunnyland Slim talked himself into playing on it. During a break, he told the brothers they should hear Muddy Waters, and Goldberg enthusiastically agreed. Leonard Chess ordered Sunnyland to go get him—now. They tracked him down at work (he was by now driving a truck for the Westerngrade Venetian Blinds company) and told him his mother was sick and he should come home. Muddy's mother was worse than sick—she'd been dead for several years—so Muddy figured something important was happening and arrived at his house to find Sunnyland, who explained there was a session in progress waiting for him to show up. Muddy lost no time grabbing his guitar and driving down to Aristocrat. It took until February 1948 for the sides under Muddy's name to be released, and they didn't sell very well, but a synergy had been established that neither the Chess brothers nor Muddy Waters could have envisioned, where one would make the other famous, and vice versa.

The Aristocrat / Muddy Waters story was the story of black urban popular music in the late 1940s in miniature. The question was how to make money with it, and one way to do that was to make records, which sold musicians' reputations to an audience while the musicians were busy elsewhere performing live. The initial investment, as Leroy Hurte had discovered, was fairly small. If all you wanted to do was reach locals, knowing your Stroll as intimately as Jules Bihari or Leonard Chess did was essential; there were few record stores, but plenty of jukeboxes, as well as beauty shops, newsstands, tobacconists, and radio repair shops willing to feature a rack of 78s. And lord knows there was talent begging to be recorded.

One ambitious musician stopped by a construction site on Union Avenue in Memphis, where a redheaded guy just out of the Army Signal Corps and currently employed by a local radio station as an engineer was working hard on something. The musician, one-man band Joe Hill Louis, asked the young man what he was doing. "I'm going to build a recording studio here once I get the building into shape," he replied. "Man," said Joe Hill, "that's just what we need here in Memphis." And it was; Joe Hill had a contract with Columbia, and a hometown place to record for them would fit into his— and other artists'—plans nicely. Much recording was still done at radio stations at night, when they were off the air, but a dedicated recording studio would result in much higher quality sound. Some black Memphis talent went all the way to Nashville, where Jim Bulleit's Bullet Records put out blues records, but, like Chicago, Memphis had developed a stripped-down electric sound that younger fans liked and Bulleit didn't understand. As soon as Sam Phillips opened the doors to the Memphis Recording Service in 1950, though, people started appearing to show what they had. He immediately hired a woman he knew from his radio station, Marion Keisker, to help him out. Phillips well knew that he stood in a perfect place to attract musicians: black musicians came north from the Mississippi Delta and stayed, as they had for decades, and there was a whole coterie of country musicians who deeply resented Nashville's grip on the music they wanted to make. Now he was finding out just how lucky he'd been.

Farther north, in Cincinnati, a similarly fortuitous geographic conjunction brought together black and white musicians of all kinds, and King Records had been there since 1943, mostly to record the odd kinds of hillbilly music the area abounded in. King was anchored by a nearly blind, irascible Jewish man named Syd Nathan, whose doctor had told him to get into a less stressful business than the one he was in, resulting in him setting up a record store selling used jukebox records. This led to his setting up King Records to release some of the music he heard on live broadcasts on WLW, including bluegrass (which always sold well in Ohio) and some non-Nashville country artists, but his distributors told him there was a huge demand for "race" records, so he formed the Queen label, which soon merged into King. By all accounts, unlike Phillips, Nathan initially had no idea what he was doing and was very, very lucky.

If there was a single thing that characterized postwar black popular music, it was the size of the group making it. The big band era had died with wartime gasoline and rubber rationing, but a decent arranger could make a big sound out of a saxophone or two, a trumpet, an electric guitar played softly, and a piano, bass, and drums. If one of the instrumentalists also sang, that was a bonus. Jump blues they called some of the more sophisticated music that was drawing people to the clubs and record stores. It was pretty diverse stuff. Johnny Moore was a guitarist who worked with bass and drums and usually had a blues-singing pianist with him: at first Ivory Joe Hunter, but most famously a thin six-footer from Texas City, Texas, named Charles Brown, whose smooth voice fit in well with Johnny Moore's Three Blazers. Their 1946 hit "Driftin' Blues" was a languid, silken lament, and "Merry Christmas, Baby" the next year was an even bigger smash. (It was re-recorded several times, but the original was on Exclusive.) It's said that throughout the 1950s, if a black household had two singles, that was one of them, and it is further claimed that it was the bestselling record by a black artist until Michael Jackson's heyday. By the time it came out, Johnny Moore had been joined by his guitarist brother, Oscar, who'd been with the Nat King Cole Trio. On the other end of jump blues' spectrum was Wynonie Harris. Subtlety was quite beyond him, both musically and lyrically, and once he'd moved to King Records in 1948, various songwriters fed him risqué lyrics aplenty: he was the blues shouter par excellence. And in the middle were countless others: Jimmy Witherspoon and Big Joe Turner (who'd arguably started this whole genre in the '30s), Roy Brown, New Orleans based and Wynonie Harris's closest competitor; Ivory Joe Hunter, who had a touch of country music in his compositions; Roy Milton, one of the rulers of Central Avenue, his band made even more powerful by the piano and vocals of Camille Howard; Jimmy Liggins, and his brother, Joe, two other bandleaders vying for supremacy on LA's Stroll; and Bull Moose Jackson, Floyd Dixon, Wynona Carr, Amos Milburn, and Eddie "Cleanhead" Vinson.

Country music, too, came out of the war with something new: Hank Williams. Williams's influence on every country performer who came after him (and not a few who were starting their careers when he was) is so pervasive that today it's hard to hear him as the revolutionary he was, and although his sound wasn't groundbreaking, his songwriting was. His legend has him learning guitar and blues from a local black street performer, Tee Tot, in Montgomery, Alabama, where he grew up, and the result was that Williams wrote songs differently from earlier country songwriters. From the time of the Carter Family, who'd set the initial template for commercial country music, country songs had been about longing for an idealized past, a lost home, a parent who'd passed on to heaven, a lover lost to circumstance or death—all things beyond the singer's ability to change them. Country was about fatalism and nostalgia for a better past, ideal for homesick people who had moved from the rural South to the industrial north. Hank Williams had internalized the blues and changed the rules. His songs said, "This happened to me, or this is happening to me, and here's the way I feel about it." He fell in love and was happy. His lover had left him and he was angry or vindictive. He was looking forward to a good time with or without somebody. The titles illustrate this: "You're Gonna Change (or I'm Gonna Leave)," "I Just Don't Like This Kind of Livin'" "I Can't Help It (If I'm Still in Love with You)," "I'm So Lonesome I Could Cry," "Honky Tonkin'." These songs hit country audiences hard, and they made Williams a star, which was a mixed blessing for him: already a serious alcoholic, he became more unstable and unreliable, and he died from an overdose of prescription drugs in the backseat of a limo taking him to a New Year's Eve show in West Virginia in 1953, age twenty-nine. In his short time, he had not only changed country music but had been recognized by the pop mainstream as a serious songwriter whose songs were recorded by everyone from Margaret Whiting to Fats Domino.

Another game changer in the country field happened accidentally in 1945, when at the end of a recording session for someone called Cecil Campbell and the Briarhoppers, the session guitarist, Arthur Smith, played a boogie-woogie on his guitar and it was recorded. Boogie-woogie had been an immense craze in the 1930s, and many a black piano player had established a career with a strong left hand to put down the walking bass while the right hand played a melody.

Indeed, Hadda Brooks recorded a lot of boogieing-the-classics numbers early in her career, but by then, the craze had already mostly
died down with black audiences. Smith's record of "Guitar Boogie,"
though, caught the public fancy, and soon, country acts were recording boogies. Not all of them, of course; the majority were chasing
Hank Williams's lead, but on the West Coast, in particular, hillbilly
boogie gave guitarists an outlet. True, some of it came from Texas as
part of the Western swing tradition, and one of the most notable acts
purveying it, the Delmore Brothers, whose "Freight Train Boogie" was
a big hit in 1946, were from Alabama, but based in Cincinnati, where
they could be near WLW, whose program *Boone County Jamboree* was
a talent incubator for their label, King Records. Although the Del-
mores were proficient instrumentalists, they got a lot of help from the
Jamboree's star guitarist, Merle Travis, on their records and had a gospel
group with him and Grandpa Jones, a banjo-playing novelty act, called
the Brown's Ferry Four. Travis was from nearby western Kentucky,
where he'd come under the influence of a black guitarist named Arnold Shultz, as well as a very influential local country guitarist, Ike
Everly, who had a radio show with his wife and two sons. Travis's picking style enabled a bass line played with the thumb and a melody on
the upper strings simultaneously, so the challenge of boogie-woogie on
the guitar was perfect for him, and in 1946, he was signed by Capitol
Records in Los Angeles as a performer. He also functioned as a studio
musician for Capitol and other West Coast country labels and was
an important part of the sound of Capitol's top hillbilly boogie artist,
Tennessee Ernie Ford. Not all the hillbilly boogie crowd played guitar: one notable star whom even Jerry Lee Lewis acknowledged as an
influence was Aubrey "Moon" Mullican, from Beaumont, Texas,
whose records on King and, later, Starday, were rambunctious enough
to qualify as early rock & roll, although he was in his forties by the
time his career really took off.

But Capitol was emblematic of the change in the record industry
after the war. There were the big labels, based in New York: RCA
Victor (a merger of the veteran label with a radio network), Columbia,
Decca. Each had a Nashville office, and each ignored the West Coast.

They recorded mainstream pop music in New York and mainstream country in Nashville. MGM, for whom Hank Williams recorded, was based in New York, but barely took itself seriously as a record label, being a division of a major film studio in Hollywood. Capitol had been started in 1942 by a successful songwriter, Johnny Mercer, with help from Buddy DeSylva, another songwriter with film connections, and the owner of Hollywood's biggest record store, Wallichs Music City. Mercer's goal was simple: he knew there was a lot of pop talent in Los Angeles that nobody in New York was touching, and a lot of songs being written for the movies that could be recorded with studio orchestras. After all, he was writing some himself. He also had a soft spot for country music and knew that, if not in Hollywood, certainly in the San Fernando Valley and Bakersfield nearby, there was an audience for it and that clubs were attracting performers from all over the country, many of whom settled in California. "We're going into the open market for the best songs and the best performances we can give the public," Glen Wallichs announced. "We plan a complete catalogue that will offer sweet music, swing music, Hawaiian, hill billy [sic] and race music." Mercer had plenty of financing and plenty of connections in the record biz thanks to Wallichs, and so he didn't have to rely on any established network of distribution or talent pool; in many ways he had California all to himself. Capitol was an independent label.

Of course, so were Exclusive and Bronze and Modern, but they took the path of narrowly focusing on the emerging black popular music in the city. They weren't the only ones. Art Rupe, a fan of black music from suburban Pittsburgh, had founded Juke Box Records with some partners, but soon bought them out and renamed the label Specialty. Rupe had fallen in love with blues and gospel as a teenager and was attracted to Central Avenue the minute he saw it. Specialty immediately signed deals with some of the Stroll's top young blues talent—Joe and Jimmy Liggins, Roy Milton, Percy Mayfield—and went after some of the top names in gospel music, which was undergoing a modernization of its own. The Soul Stirrers, Professor Alex Bradford, and the Pilgrim Travelers were among his early signings; few of the top gospel acts would pass up the opportunity to perform at one of LA's Shrine Auditorium's spectacular gospel programs, after all. He also got some sales and jukebox action out of Wynona Carr's gospel novelties like "The Ball Game" and "Dragnet for Jesus."

Leo and Eddie Mesner's Aladdin Records started in 1945 as Philo Records, a jazz label, but soon turned its interest toward blues, after having a smash with Amos Milburn's "Chicken Shack Boogie" in 1948. Then there was Lew Chudd, whose Imperial label was set up to exploit what Chudd felt was an untapped market for music made by Los Angeles's Mexican community and managed to score some hits with both Edmundo Martinez Tostado, a.k.a. Don Tosti, whose "Pachuco Boogie" on Taxco was a rallying cry for East Los Angeles's teenagers and the first of his many hits, and Lalo Guerrero, whose "Muy Sabroso Blues" and "Marihuana Boogie" were also huge hits for Imperial. But after he'd leased a couple of small hits with music recorded in New Orleans, Chudd went down there scouting talent, and bandleader Dave Bartholomew took him to the Hideaway Club where they found a twenty-year-old pianist, Antoine "Fats" Domino, who was the current heir to the "piano professor" tradition that stretched all the way back to Jelly Roll Morton and before. Chudd intuited there was much more money to be made in New Orleans than in East LA.

There was Swingtime, founded on South San Pedro by Jack Lauderdale, a short, chubby black guy with questionable connections, who had a genius for buying masters other people had recorded, and was notable for releasing Lowell Fulson's "Every Day I Have the Blues" and buying "Lonely Boy" by a black guy in Seattle who was playing with a country band up there, Ray Charles. John Dolphin was a record store owner whose shop, opened in 1948, was one of the biggest ones on Central, with a DJ playing records in the window, and in 1950, Dolphin started his label, Recorded in Hollywood (which was miles away, but close enough), to feature blues artists he discovered. And Modern, thanks to the money from Hadda Brooks's success, was buying up talent, too, from tiny labels like Four Star in

Houston (Lightnin' Hopkins) and Down Town, an Oakland label that got them master recordings by Lowell Fulson and Jimmy Mc-Cracklin.

Los Angeles led the nation in independent labels, but there were others. Besides Chess in Chicago, there was Mercury, which was analogous to Capitol in that it was founded by music-biz veterans and recorded pop music and blues instead of country, but far more sophisticated blues than Chess was recording: Chess had Muddy Waters, and Mercury had Dinah Washington, who could be said to combine the traditions of Bessie Smith and Billie Holiday as she straddled blues and jazz in her repertoire. New York, where one would expect a lot of this sort of action, was very slow in catching the postwar trend, and initially, only Atlantic Records, formed in 1947 by pre-war record vet Herb Abramson and Ahmet Ertegun, son of the former Turkish ambassador to the United States, was looking for the same sort of artists as the West Coast labels were. Ertegun, along with his brother, Nesuhi, was a huge jazz fan and had been famous for his huge record collection and occasional jazz concerts at the embassy. Now he intended to seek out New York's jazz artists and record them, with an eye toward turning Atlantic into America's top jazz label. Based in New York, though, he wouldn't have heard any local blues, so blues was absent from Atlantic's roster. Uptown from Atlantic, Apollo Records was the fiefdom of Bess Berman, who ran a Harlem record store with her husband, Ike. Apollo released all kinds of music, recording some early bebop, some early sides by Wynonie Harris, and Dean Martin's first efforts, but really took off when they found a young woman from New Orleans named Mahalia Jackson, who took the gospel world by storm, almost making the pop charts in 1947 with "Move Up a Little Higher," and even found fans in the jazz world.

This was the scene in the record business at the end of the 1940s, but there were already some hints of what was to come. Country music, particularly on the West Coast, was featuring the electric guitar more (its use in country had been pioneered by Bob Wills's band and by Ernest Tubb, a Texan who defended his use of the instrument as the only way to be heard in the west Texas oil patch bars his band, the Texas Troubadours, played) and was exploring the new kind of lyrics Hank Williams had introduced. Black music was radically shaken by the jump blues phenomenon, and, in Chicago, the loud, aggressive electric sound coming out of its clubs. Then, out of the Midwest, came a clarion call: "Have you heard the news?" Wynonie Harris asked. "There's good rockin' tonight."

chapter three

BLUES, BIRDS,
AND A MOONDOG

Left to right: Joe Bihari, B.B. King, Los Angeles DJ Hunter Hancock,
and *Cash Box* editor Joel Friedman presenting an award from the magazine.
(Michael Ochs Archives/Stringer)

B y 1950, the shellac crisis was over, and a few record labels were switching to vinyl polychloride, which was cheaper and unbreakable—at least compared to shellac. James Petrillo, the head of the American Federation of Musicians, had conceded that the future was upon him, and the union took a more conciliatory attitude toward recording and stopped striking. There were lots of records flooding into the market, even in minority-interest genres like blues and country. But who was buying them?

The answer was jukebox operators, at least for the independent record labels: the men who added and subtracted records from the machines. Jukeboxes were everywhere: bars, diners, roadhouses, even barbershops and places you'd never expect; some churches had recreational areas outside the sanctuary where a jukebox filled with gospel records gave ambience to church dinners and other social events, for instance. Jukeboxes also had heavy tonearms and ground down the records they played, particularly if they were made of shellac, which meant replacing a big hit every couple of weeks. If an individual consumer was actually interested enough in a record, there were used record stores stocking records they'd bought from jukebox operators. Relatively few country or blues records were bought new by individual consumers.

Mainstream pop was played on the radio during the disc jockeys' time slots, but the evening, when the largest listening audience was tuned in, was still the province of live orchestras playing "sweet" dance music (or "Mickey Mouse music," as all too many of the musicians who played it called it). There was virtually no blues and no country on the radio with a couple of notable exceptions. Country had weekly live broadcasts, from WSM's *Grand Ole Opry* in Nashville, to the WLS *Barn Dance* in Chicago, and the *Louisiana Hayride* (started in 1948 in Shreveport, Louisiana, on KWKH), and of course short local shows, usually early in the morning, with live performers. These were notable because the *Opry, Barn Dance,* and *Hayride* went out on so-called clear channel stations that were allowed to operate on a stronger signal at night when most other stations were silent and, therefore, could be heard by listeners far away from the original signal, thanks to the "ozone skip" where the atmosphere bounced the signal back down to earth.

Another Nashville station, WLAC, also had a clear channel signal, and it was there that something remarkable happened. Most radio stations offered airtime to whoever could buy it, so that often someone would show up with a suggestion for a show sponsored by someone (or someones) who'd buy the airtime in exchange for commercials. WLAC, by 1950, had three disc jockeys at night, after its network programming shut off, who changed the face of American music: Bill "Hoss" Allen, Gene Nobles, and John "John R." Richbourg.

Nobles had started in 1947, and his sponsor was Randy's Record Shop in suburban Gallatin, Tennessee, owned by Randy Woods. Nobles, a white man, was a swing fan, so he naturally gravitated toward jump blues and boogie music on his program, from 10:00 to 10:45 at night, on which he noted that his sponsor could get any record you liked. Within a few weeks, Woods called him and asked what all these odd titles people had ordered were. Were they race records? They were indeed, and so Woods contacted a wholesaler and started buying them. Then he got the smart idea of offering packages: five records for $2.98 plus COD and handling. Most of these were hits, some were not. It was a great way of getting rid of overstock and duds. Then Ernest Young, who owned a store in Nashville, decided this was a good way to make money, so he bought forty-five minutes and Nobles's services from 9:00 to 9:45. Ernie's Record Mart, too, started shipping rhythm and blues packages via mail order. Finally, Buckley's Record Store, also in Nashville, bought an hour from midnight to 1:00 A.M., and Nobles did that, too. In the summer of 1947, he decided he needed a vacation, so the station told their newscaster, John Richbourg, to take over. They also found a young man just out of college, Bill Allen, to take some of the slots. Randy's and Ernie's were friendly competitors, and confused listeners often ordered the latest package from the wrong store, and they'd simply hand the order over. The on-air personalities of Gene Nobles, Hoss Allen, and John R., though, seeped through the night to any ears that would receive them, and as odd as it may have seemed to some, not a few of those ears were attached to high school- and college-age white kids, who loved the extroverted DJs and the music they played. WLAC's signal reached over twenty states: Bob Dylan, as a youngster, would lie awake listening to it in Minnesota. But of course, WLAC didn't invest in market research, which barely existed at the time. Randy's and Ernie's had no idea who they were selling to and might not have snapped if they'd investigated: it was a common ploy to have the record packages sent to a relative or friend to avoid parental scrutiny, and especially down south, listeners to this forbidden music formed a sort of secret society.

Up in New York, Atlantic noticed a surge in sales among their southern distributors every time one of their records made it into one of the packages, and it wasn't long until the sponsors realized that they were missing out on some money and started their own labels. Randy Woods started Dot in 1950, and Ernie Young had Excello (for blues) and Nashboro (gospel) up and running by 1952.

Meanwhile, there was Wynonie Harris's important question. Harris was a six-footer from Omaha with lady-killing good looks and a vocal style indebted to, but not a copy of, Big Joe Turner's. He hooked up with Lucky Millinder's popular large band in 1944 and was the vocalist on Millinder's hit song "Who Threw the Whiskey in the Well?" This boosted his profile enough for him to go solo, and he made a great many undistinguished records for Bess Berman at

Apollo. What he clearly needed was someone who could write good lyrics, because his singing chops were never in doubt. In 1947, things came together; he signed with King Records, where he worked with the A&R team of Henry Glover (another Lucky Millinder alumnus) and Ralph Bass. A&R, at least back then, was what it said: artists and repertoire, with the A&R department of a record company responsible for hooking performing talent up with song material they could do a good job with. Harris continued to tour but hadn't had any hits on King by the day he played New Orleans and refused to see a guy named Roy Brown, who idolized him. Brown was a short, rotund ex-boxer who'd been working the clubs in New Orleans and had written a song he wanted to get to Harris. Dejected at having been turned away, he contacted another singer playing the clubs there, Cecil Gant, and played the song for him. Gant was still well connected and immediately called the president of New Jersey–based De Luxe Records, Jules Braun (at, legend has it, 4:00 A.M.). Braun sent Brown a contract first thing, and he went into the studio and cut the song, "Good Rockin' Tonight." One of the King A&R team heard the song and sent Harris into the studio to record it, and, with King's higher profile, the song took off faster and topped the black charts just as the summer of 1948 came on. Brown's version didn't do too badly, either, although it peaked at #13.

Two careers were made by one song, and something of a line was drawn. Bestselling blues songs were rarely very explicit about sex, but although the "rockin'" in the lyrics might have been about dancing and playing music, there was the couplet "Gonna hold my baby tight as I can / Tonight she'll know I'm a mighty, mighty man." That was pushing it, but nobody made much of a squawk; it was "just colored folks," and it wasn't like white bands were playing this material or impressionable white children were listening to it. Except, maybe, for the ones who were buying those records from WLAC. After all, the record shops there offered all-King packages and always salted them with at least one smash hit. And that may not be where a teenager, recently relocated from Tupelo, Mississippi, to Memphis, got a copy of it, but young Elvis Presley did indeed have a copy of it and played it over and over. He was a nice kid, fond of his mother, and always went to church with her on Sundays—sometimes twice, if he could convince her to head down the road to the black church after the services at their church was over. He often could. He could be remarkably persuasive, even if he was a little shy, and his mother, Gladys, found it hard to deny him anything.

Elvis may not have been aware of it, but music in black churches was changing, as was the music on the little-noticed gospel touring circuit. There wasn't much money to be made by record companies in gospel music—after all, most record sales were to jukebox operators, and the last thing you'd want on a bar's juke was an admonition to repent—but some were recording it, anyway. Art Rupe of Specialty Records liked gospel music as a fan and adjured his representatives in the field to push "our spiritual line" when selling to retail accounts. He'd started recording gospel in 1947, when James Petrillo called the last of his musicians' union strikes, forbidding instrumentalists from recording. No problem: some of the most popular gospel groups were vocal ensembles, and singing without instruments was how they honed their arrangements, only adding a piano or guitar or organ at the last minute. The Pilgrim Travelers were Rupe's first group, and they were a perfect bridge between what had been and what was coming. The group had been in existence since 1930, shifting membership around a central core, as with all long-lived gospel groups, the core being in this case Joe Johnson and two brothers named Davis. By the time they signed with Rupe, Johnson and the Davises were long gone, and the group was under the capable leadership of J. W. Alexander, who helped them move away from the archaic style of a lead vocalist with the group making rhythmic syllables in the background to the more modern style of everyone singing the same words in harmony, led by a solo vocalist. This wasn't exactly a new style, because black pop groups like the Mills Brothers had pioneered it in the '30s, but it was new to gospel. (It's also important to note that gospel wasn't performed at weekly church services, which emphasized congregational singing led by a pastor or music director and perhaps the church's own choir, but, rather, at special shows called programs featuring traveling acts, big and small, in a more showbizzy context.)

Alexander's Pilgrim Travelers were (as were most savvy gospel groups) chasing the Soul Stirrers, a Chicago-based group that had been around since the mid-1920s. By 1950, they were under the leadership of R. H. Harris, who was acutely aware of showmanship, since gospel programs were fiercely competitive, and who was also recording in this new style for Specialty. (Harris also led the group to record songs with social content, like "Why Do You Like Roosevelt (Poor Man's Friend)" and "Jesus Hits Like the Atom Bomb.") In 1951, Harris, who was continually trying to have the best singers in his group, hired a young, handsome kid named Sam Cooke for the group and noted with approval the number of teenage girls who turned out for the programs as a result. Actually, he must have known what would happen: Sam had been lead vocalist in a group called the Highway QCs, who had a habit of turning up when a program was in town and blowing all competition away, even though they were still teenagers. (He was replaced there by another Chicago teenager named Lou Rawls.) There was no doubt the new sound of gospel was popular; a group called the Trumpeteers managed to hit the #1 slot on the Race chart in 1949 with "Milky White Way."

But of course, not every group of black teenage boys wanted to sing gospel, as you'd expect; group singing was fun, Jesus often wasn't, and you didn't have to be R. H. Harris to note that the women at a gospel program were mostly older. But one thing the gospel groups had gotten right was the economic model: all you needed were your singers and maybe a piano or guitar. So the late 1940s saw a rush of secular vocal groups, starting with the Ravens. Except for youth, there wasn't much difference between the Ravens and the Mills Brothers, but an accident at New York's famous Apollo Theater amateur show set them apart: bass singer Jimmy "Ricky" Ricks started singing before the rest of the group because he was so nervous, and the others had the smarts to back him up as the lead singer. Snapped up by National Records, a tiny New York indie label, run by Herb Abramson and engineer (and former Manhattan Project prodigy: he'd done top-secret work on the atomic bomb while studying nuclear physics at Columbia University) Tom Dowd, they managed eight records in 1948, most of which hit the R&B top ten, culminating in December with a two-sided Christmas hit of "Silent Night" and "White Christmas," the latter of which had a swinging arrangement that was later copied by both Billy Ward and His Dominoes and the Drifters. The Ravens were followed by the Orioles, whose lead singer, Sonny Til, had a voice as airy and light as Ricky Ricks's was plummy and deep. The Orioles' harmonies were complex, and their debut single, "It's Too Soon to Know," blew the roof off the Apollo after their manager (and author of the song) got them onto the show after they'd lost on *Arthur Godfrey's Talent Scouts* TV show. Deborah Chessler—a teenage department store clerk in Baltimore who first encouraged, then wrote songs for, and finally managed the Orioles—was a dynamo, and the group wound up on the amusingly named It's A Natural label, largely as a result of her work and that appearance at the Apollo.

It was obvious that things were changing in the black music world, and to reflect this, in mid-1949, a young journalist named Gerald Wexler, who was pretty aware of the scene, convinced his employer, *Billboard,* one of the two top trade magazines for the record business (the other being *Cash Box*) to change the name of its Race Records chart to Rhythm and Blues, the term record dealers and people in the street used for the emerging music. The term embraced all manner of black music; #1 records on *Billboard*'s chart between 1948 and 1950 included pure blues (Memphis Slim, Arbee Stidham, Pee Wee Crayton, John Lee Hooker, and Lonnie Johnson), jump blues (Bull Moose Jackson, Wynonie Harris, Amos Milburn, Roy Brown, Charles Brown, and multiple entries by Louis Jordan), instrumentals (Sonny Thompson, Hal Singer, and Big Jay McNeely), and black pop (Nat King Cole, Dinah Washington, Percy Mayfield, and the Orioles). Very few of these crossed over to the white charts.

Somehow, the Ertegun brothers, Ahmet and Nesuhi, thought they could break into this in a big way and enlisted Herb Abramson and Tom Dowd (who were still working for National) and Abramson's formidable wife, Miriam, to join Atlantic Records. National was falling apart anyway, so the Abramsons and Dowd found themselves working for the most ridiculously underprepared record label in New York. Capitalized largely by the sale of the brothers' immense record collection, they'd set up offices in the Ritz Hotel just in time for the 1947 Petrillo strike. Soon, they moved to far more modest quarters in the Hotel Jefferson. They released a bunch of random stuff—some jazz, some spoken word (at one point Ahmet Ertegun told *Billboard* they were going to release the complete works of Shakespeare on 78), even some country—and then had a stroke of luck. A distributor complained that there was a hit record, a blues record called "Drinkin' Wine Spo-Dee-O-Dee," by Stick McGhee that he couldn't get enough copies of, and he wondered if Ertegun could help. The only blues artist Ertegun knew in New York was Brownie McGhee, so he found him and asked him about it. It turned out that Stick McGhee was Brownie's brother and just happened to be visiting Brownie at his place in Harlem. A session was quickly organized, and Atlantic had its first hit.

Its second one came from the center of the Stroll in Detroit. The Flame Show Bar was hands down the most prestigious black nightclub in the city, so much so that Duke Ellington played there within months of its opening. He was quite impressed with a young vocalist, Ruth Brown, that he heard there. She'd been working with Lucky Millinder's band, and Ellington mentioned her to Willis Conover, the jazz disc jockey with the Voice of America, and Conover mentioned her to Herb Abramson, who found her on tour near Washington, D.C., and summoned her to New York to record. She was on her way with her manager, Blanche Calloway (bandleader Cab Calloway's wife), when they had an automobile accident just outside Philadelphia. As soon as she was able, Brown went to New York, surprising the crew at Atlantic, who were busy recording Eddie Condon, a retro-jazz guitarist who led a band with some remarkable talents in it. Brown limped in, and Condon's band were impressed with the song she'd chosen to record, "So Long," so they spent extra time on the arrangement, and the song was a top-ten hit in the last months of 1949. Miriam Abramson signed on as her manager, and Brown began a career that would provide Atlantic with a couple of dozen hits over the next decade. She was versatile enough that her style partook of blues, jazz, and pop, which, given the taste among Atlantic's management, made her the ideal artist for them.

Another denizen of the Stroll in Detroit was an illiterate auto worker from northern Mississippi, John Lee Hooker, whose music couldn't have been further from Ruth Brown's. His sparse, primitive blues (a lot of his songs only had one chord), accompanied only by his guitar, appealed to people like him: poor black folk who'd left the South for work in the North, and the only concession he'd made to his urban setting was to get an electric guitar so he could be louder than the crowds he played for. In 1949, somebody he'd hired as his manager sent a demo of two of his tunes to Modern Records in Los Angeles, and they released it as is, with the label correctly identifying the contents: "Boogie Chillen," by John Lee Hooker & His Guitar. The record flew in the face of postwar sophistication: one man and one guitar playing one chord, essentially, and not making much of an effort vocally, either. It was a smash.

The Biharis wondered if this were a trend, and picked up a master by a Houston bluesman who'd recorded some fairly primitive stuff for Gold Star Records there, Sam "Lightnin'" Hopkins (so named because a few of his early recordings were with a pianist, "Thunder" Smith, and someone suggested that Thunder and Lightnin' would make a good name for an act). Hopkins had had a couple of local hits ("Katie Mae," "Short Haired Woman") on Gold Star Records, but the record Modern put out was "Tim Moore's Farm," a song current with several Texas bluesmen at the time about a real farmer in Grimes County notorious for his mistreatment of black workers. The man's real name was Tom, but nobody in that part of Texas needed to be told who it was about, and the story was universal enough to sell it to jukebox patrons all over the country. Hooker and Hopkins had little in common other than being solo acts and their practice of recording under a bewildering number of names for anyone who'd pay them.

Electric guitar players were hardly novelties in black popular music at this point—T-Bone Walker had had hits in the '30s—but this kind of stripped-down country blues was certainly an odd trend. Jules and Saul Bihari decided to accept a long-standing invitation to look for talent in Memphis in mid-1950, and while visiting WDIA (the "mother station of the Negroes," with all-white management but a pioneering all-black air staff), they heard a demo by a guitarist who also had a popular program on the station, Riley King. B. B. King, as he was known professionally (the initials stood for Blues Boy), had made quite an impression on Memphis music fans since he came to town from his native Itta Bena, Mississippi, with his guitar protected from the elements by a gunnysack. He'd already recorded for Bullet Records in Nashville to no great effect, but the Biharis heard a great singer who played blues guitar with a pure tone and an endlessly inventive flow of ideas and decided to get him into the studio right away. Fortunately, unlike a lot of Southern metropolises, Memphis had a brand-new, technically up-to-date, great-sounding studio. All that was needed was to assemble a band and get King over to Union Avenue to cut some tunes. Sam Phillips was ready for them. He'd tried a bunch of stuff to get the Memphis Recording Service off the ground, and now here was the nation's top rhythm and blues label asking him to record one of the city's top names—and offering first refusal on anything else he had to offer, which included his early encourager Joe Hill Louis, harmonica player Big Walter Horton, and others, who wound up on Modern. B. B., though, wasn't coming up with anything.

Phillips, meanwhile, was enjoying the scouting services of a teenage pianist from Clarksdale, Mississippi, Ike Turner. Turner's mother had run a hotel-cum–rooming house for musicians, one of those refuges where touring black performers could stay in the segregated South, and he'd learned a lot about what was good and what people wanted. He also had his own band, the Kings of Rhythm, and although he was more than willing to use them to back up others on sessions, he really wanted his own career. At B. B. King's urging, he brought them up to Memphis in 1951, and in no time he found himself on a session with Sam Phillips. One of the tunes they recorded featured his saxophonist, Jackie Brenston, doing a tune he'd do during their live show, "Rocket 88."

Leonard Chess happened to be in town on a scouting expedition similar to the one the Biharis had done the year before and heard it. Knowing that it was a hit, he bought it on the spot from Phillips and asked if he had other masters for sale. As a matter of fact, he did. One was by a very unusual performer Turner had found, a huge forty-one-year-old ex-farmer from West Helena, Arkansas, who'd played the blues all his life and had, as a youth, traveled with Charley Patton.

Chester Burnett played guitar and harmonica, but his real attraction was his voice; Sam Phillips has memorably described it as "where the soul of man never dies," and it lent credibility to Burnett's stage name, Howlin' Wolf. He was unabashedly old-fashioned, but maintained a band of young players, so his music spoke across generations. Chess picked up the recordings Phillips had and took them back to Chicago with him. The ones Chess rejected Sam sent to Modern.

Then, something unfortunate—for some—happened: "Rocket 88" took off like its namesake. The Biharis were not happy; one of the biggest hits of 1951 (as it turned out to be) had been sold outright to their biggest competitor instead of being offered to them first. Ike Turner wasn't happy; the record came out under the name Jackie Brenston and His Delta Cats, not Ike Turner and His Kings of Rhythm, featuring Jackie Brenston. The result was that the Biharis refused to deal with Phillips or his studio anymore, and Turner refused to deal with him *or* Chess. Chess won all around; they kept up their relationship with Sam, and although they didn't realize it yet, in Howlin' Wolf they'd acquired another important talent who would sustain their label for years to come. The Biharis, meanwhile, were eager to record B. B. King again, and Sam's studio was the only game in town. Well, not when you're in touch with Ike Turner, it's not; he swung by the colored YMCA and told the Biharis he'd found a place to record. Joe Bihari came to town lugging a couple of tape recorders, Ike found a bunch of blankets to hang on the walls of the gymnasium, and they got to work. B. B. recorded an old Lowell Fulson tune, "Three O'Clock Blues," and a few other tracks, Ike played piano, and Bihari also got in sessions with some other locals Ike had recommended to him, including Johnny Ace and Bobby Bland, before the YMCA demanded their room back. Joe packed up the tape recorders and headed back to Los Angeles, and released "Three O'Clock Blues" toward the end of the year. B. B. promptly forgot about it until Bihari sent him a telegram telling him they'd sold one hundred thousand copies of the song and it was still gathering momentum.

Leonard Chess, for his part, not only had the Jackie Brenston record, but Muddy Waters was turning out to be a major signing. True, his sales were modest and mostly confined to the South and

Chicago, but starting in January, he'd put "Louisiana Blues" and three other records on the national charts. Then, at the end of the year, Chess's first release of Howlin' Wolf turned out to be a double-sided hit: the furious "How Many More Years" and "Moanin' at Midnight," a spectral performance that begins with a wordless moan and continues on to highlight Wolf's famous howl (which, he noted later, he intended to sound like Jimmie Rodgers's yodeling). On "Louisiana Blues," Waters spoke of going to New Orleans to buy a mojo hand. Was Southern mumbo-jumbo taking over the turf formerly occupied by more sophisticated urban performers?

Well, no; among others, Charles Brown had had a top hit with "Black Night," which was harmonically sophisticated if depressing, and Earl Bostic had scored with "Flamingo," a lovely instrumental. And then there were those vocal groups that kept popping up. It was hard keeping track of them, since at first they all seemed to be named after birds: the Ravens and the Orioles were followed by the Robins, the Cardinals, the Swallows, the Larks, and the Crows, although the Clovers, the Moonglows, the Dominoes, and the Five Satins also appeared in 1951. The Dominoes even managed to cross over to the pop charts with their classic, bass-led "Sixty Minute Man," whose lyrics were suggestive, but not outright bawdy, although lots of radio stations wouldn't play it. None of these groups had yet hit on a style—they all tended to be slightly modernized versions of the old vocal groups—but that would change.

Probably the strangest thing that happened in 1951 was that Alan Freed, a hard-drinking, trombone-playing Wagner fan (he'd named his daughter Sieglinde) in Cleveland who had had a bit of a problem holding down a job on the various Ohio radio stations he'd worked for and had finally been relegated to the late-night ghetto at WJW, had a conversation with a guy named Eliot Mintz, who owned the Record Rendezvous, one of the city's largest record stores. Mintz said that he had a constant stream of white teenagers coming into the store and requesting obscure black records. Here, Mintz told Freed, was an audience for a radio show that played nothing but black records on a white station. Freed thought this was a risky proposition—and how would he square it with the brass, especially with his reputation as a troublemaker?—but Mintz promised not only to advertise heavily but to get other businesses to advertise, too. So in June, Freed debuted "The Moondog Show," playing records Mintz said were popular and blasting them out on WJW's fifty-thousand-watt clear-channel signal to Ohio, Pennsylvania, and, if atmospheric conditions were right, other parts of the country, too. It didn't take long before distributors noted this surge in sales in Cleveland, of all places, and WJW, noticing the rise in late-night listenership, left Freed alone, even though he was howling, shouting, "Go! Go!" over sax solos, and pounding on a Cleveland phone book he kept close to the mike and otherwise acting like a lunatic.

Freed wasn't the first white DJ to play black records, of course; as we've seen, the guys at WLAC had been doing it for a while, and another maniac, Dewey Phillips (no relation to Sam, although they did co-own a record label for a while), was enchanting Memphis teenagers with a canny mixture of blues, rhythm and blues, and some of the hotter hillbilly boogie records, and in Los Angeles, Hunter Hancock, a lanky Texan, was a big enough star on KGFJ that his *Huntin' with Hunter* show was being syndicated via sixteen-inch discs to radio stations nationwide. But Freed was in Cleveland, which, compared to Chicago or Detroit, had a very small black music scene. It was teenagers who were driving this phenomenon—white teenagers, mostly. And somewhere along the way, Freed started calling the music he played by one of the terms its audience was already using for certain kinds of records: rock & roll. He was far from the first to use the term to designate rhythmic black music (although he later tried to copyright it), and instances of its use go back to at least the 1930s, but it gave the kids a banner around which to gather, a code name squares couldn't penetrate.

chapter four

BLACK VOICES IN THE HEARTLAND

Atlantic Records event with: *(front row, left to right)* Jerry Wexler, Alan Freed, and Ahmet Ertegun; *(back row, beginning third from left)* Ruth Brown, Big Joe Turner, and Mrs. Turner.
(Charlie Gillett Collection/Contributor)

L ew Chudd was concerned. The Mesner brothers, who ran the Aladdin label, had managed to score a coup by going to New Orleans to record Amos Milburn, and were getting hit out of hit from him. Chudd was on a talent-scouting tour in Houston at Don Robey's Peacock Club and saw a set by a New Orleans trumpet player named Dave Bartholomew, who was a huge draw down there with his band, which included Red Tyler and Lee Allen on saxophones and a wiry drummer named Earl Palmer. Chudd immediately offered Bartholomew a contract, and asked him to look out for talent back home in New Orleans for him, with a nice signing bonus for acts he found. A few weeks later, Bartholomew sent him the results of the first session he'd done back home at Cosimo Matassa's recording studio (the only one in town), Jewel King's "$3 \times 7 = 21$," which became a top-ten hit right off. Next came a piano player, a twenty-two-year-old named Antoine Domino, whom everyone called "Fats." Fats's theme song was a thinly disguised rewrite of another New Orleans pianist's signature tune, "Champion" Jack Dupree's "Junker Blues," whose lyrics dealt with heroin use and were not destined to adorn the rhythm and blues hit parade. "The Fat Man," though, propelled by Fats's signature right-hand triplets and his ingratiating voice, didn't sound like anything else out there and just missed the top of the R&B charts in 1950, the first of what would be nearly sixty chart successes for him on Imperial over the next twelve years. Then Chudd and Bartholomew had an argument—over what, nobody remembers now—and Bartholomew got his revenge. In early 1952, Specialty's Art Rupe was sniffing around town, giving mostly unsuccessful auditions, and he was about to give up when the next singer up broke down crying in the middle of his song. Rupe was impressed and set up a session. Who better to use as backup than Dave Bartholomew—and Fats Domino on piano? The only reason Lloyd Price's "Lawdy Miss Clawdy" wasn't a Fats Domino record was that Price sang it. It was the top-selling R&B record of 1952 and sold lots of copies to white teenagers, too—not enough to chart, but enough for Alan Freed and Hunter Hancock to notice, and enough to cause Lew Chudd to beg Bartholomew to come back to work for him. Just to show there were no hard feelings, Bartholomew was allowed to work for other labels, and agreed to record Lloyd Price for Aladdin, a plan that was interrupted by the Mesners hearing a demo some teenagers had made at Cosimo's. They spent several days looking for the kids, who eluded them, thinking that the only reason white guys would be looking for them was that they were in trouble, but once the Mesners found them, they dismissed most of the group and formed a duo of Shirley Goodman and Leonard Lee, whose on-record romance as Shirley & Lee enthralled teenagers for years later. (Price continued to record for Specialty until he was drafted in 1954.)

Shenanigans like this were what drove Sam Phillips up in Memphis to a desperate act in January 1952. He'd delivered Jackie Brenston to the Chess brothers, incurring the wrath of the Biharis at Modern in LA, and then he'd sent Howlin' Wolf's recordings to both of them, and, to top it off, he was watching the beginning of B. B. King's rise to the top on the Biharis' RPM label, which they'd set up, apparently, just for him. Sam had also made recordings by other artists for other labels that hadn't done much—but what if one had? He was, as an old saying went, tired of fattening frogs for snakes. "I truly did not want to open a record label," he said years later. "It honestly was the last thing. But I was forced into it by those labels either coming into Memphis to record, or taking my artists elsewhere." He asked Jim Bulleit over in Nashville for some capital and came up with a name for the label, Sun, and a label design in yellow and brown, courtesy of an artist he'd known in school, featuring a rooster, a half-circle sun emitting rays, musical notes (which don't form a tune), and a notation at the bottom of the circle saying *Memphis, Tennessee.* In February, he sent a dub of "Selling My Whiskey," by Jackie Boy & Little Walter, to a couple of DJs in Memphis. Jackie Boy was vocalist Jack Kelly, and Little Walter wasn't Muddy Waters's remarkable harmonica player, but Walter "Mumbles" Horton (known as Big Walter after Little Walter achieved fame). The DJs hated it, and it wasn't issued. Instead, he released an instrumental by Johnny London (identified on the label as an "Alto Wizard"), an alto saxophonist of undeniable talent whom Sam liked. Sun 174 was the number on the label, and it went precisely nowhere, but Sun Records was in business, sort of.

Sort of, because he discovered right off the bat that there were two other Sun Records companies in business, too. One was in New Mexico, making records to sell to Indians, and the other was a New York label recording Yiddish music. Somehow, Sam prevailed against them. But he couldn't prevail against the fact that he hadn't bothered to set up a distributor, relying on his brother, Jud, to drive around the South with boxes of records in his car. He knew the Biharis and the Chess brothers didn't do that. And, with Sun trying to get a foothold, Sam still had to send artists he recorded to Chess, most notably Harmonica Frank Floyd. Sam had often told his secretary / right hand / mistress, Marion Keisker, that "if I could find a white boy with the authentic colored sound and feel I could make a billion dollars," and Floyd fit those requirements except for the "boy" part; when Sam started recording him, he was forty-four years old, but his sound had been shaped by years of traveling the rural South with medicine shows. Chess put his records out, too, although it's anybody's guess who they thought they'd sell them to. Sam, meanwhile, was primed to record anyone he could, and that included country musicians. Nashville and Memphis have a history of country music rivalry, but Memphis has always lost, and part of it, Sam would discover, is because so many Memphis country performers were at least partially going for that authentic colored sound and feel.

Nashville, on the other hand, had taken Hank Williams's new realism to heart. Things had been changing since 1949, when Floyd Tillman's "Slipping Around" had been recorded by both the duo of Margaret Whiting and Jimmy Wakely and Ernest Tubb, both records topping the country charts. The breakthrough record was Hank Thompson's 1952 smash "The Wild Side of Life," lamenting that he'd lost his girlfriend to the bar scene, where she'd be "anybody's sweetheart" for the price of a drink. It was swiftly followed by an answer song by Kitty Wells, "It Wasn't God Who Made Honky Tonk Angels," which decried the mind-set that put "the blame . . . on the women" when it was male misbehavior that drove them to it. Then Webb Pierce arrived to talk about his "Back Street Affair," and, late in 1953, "There Stands the Glass," celebrating the liquor that would obliterate his heartbreak and misery, and admitting that "it's my first one today." Nashville was getting gritty, singing about cheating and drinking, which became country staples, although blues artists had been singing about them since the '20s. But you weren't going to sell records like those to teenagers.

Nor did they seem hot on instrumentals, although some classics were coming out, mostly by jazz artists slumming in rhythm and blues: Jimmy Forrest's "Night Train," Illinois Jacquet's "Port of Rico," Count Basie's "Paradise Squat," and Johnny Hodges's "A Pound of Blues." But one of the biggest records of 1952 on the R&B side was a harmonica instrumental by Little Walter that he often performed to start off a set by the Muddy Waters band. He called it "Your Cat Will Play," and it was tossed off during a recording session one day. Leonard Chess changed its title to "Juke" and decided to release it under Walter's name, and it took off. On tour in Louisiana, Walter discovered it was selling like crazy, quit Muddy in the middle of the tour, and headed back to Chicago to put a band of his own together. That wasn't difficult; he took over another young harmonica player's band, the Aces, and changed their name to the Jukes. The harmonica player he'd replaced, Junior Wells, then joined Muddy's band. That's the way it worked in Chicago. Muddy's band was informally known as the Headhunters because when they heard of a new talent in town, they'd go see what the noise was about and then do battle while

Muddy relaxed with a drink at the bar. If the new kid shut Muddy's guy down, he'd sometimes get an invitation to replace his rival. If, as was more often the case, Muddy's band member triumphed, it was a reminder of who was at the top of the heap, a place Muddy Waters occupied for the entire decade. But now Chess had two major national blues stars.

The period of 1952–1953, in retrospect, seems to have been a stylistic watershed for rhythm and blues. Old-style jump blues was still around—Big Joe Turner was making some classic stuff for Atlantic, and Roy Milton, Charles Brown, and Amos Milburn had hits—but other solo artists were exploring a new area somewhere between blues and pop. One of the brightest stars was Johnny Ace, yet another Memphis singer, who was one of an informal group of young guys, the Beale Streeters, who hung around together and were locally popular. Ace's "My Song" was a #1 record, and teenage girls went for him in a big way. (It was released on Duke, a brand-new label featuring Memphis talent, and Houston's Don Robey, who already had a label called Peacock after his Bronze Peacock club, went to Memphis and bought Duke—and Johnny Ace—outright.) Texan Floyd Dixon wrote and sang in a wide variety of styles, and his "Call Operator 210" rocked the jukeboxes all year long.

Specialty had found a couple of local artists who would accomplish great things. Percy Mayfield was a songwriter and singer who was touted as "The Poet of the Blues," although his work was far more in a pop vein. It wasn't just hype, either; his "Please Send Me Someone to Love" is both harmonically sophisticated and lyrically accomplished. He, too, was very handsome, and had a devoted following, but an automobile accident in 1952 disfigured his face in a way that made him afraid to go out in public, which killed his performing career, although he continued to record and write. Jesse Belvin might have become as famous as any of this crowd if he'd stuck to a solo career, but he also recorded as Jesse and Marvin with Marvin Phillips (who went on to other hits as Marvin and Jesse, with a number of other vocalists being "Jesse" over the years) and was a member of the Hollywood Flames, one of LA's pioneering vocal groups.

Another entertainment entrepreneur was Johnny Otis, who not

only played drums and vibes with his own band, which he featured at his nightclub, the Barrelhouse, in Watts, but also served as a talent scout for labels like Savoy and Modern. His first big find was Little Esther (Phillips), who was fifteen when he discovered her and propelled her, backed by the Robins (and, of course, the Johnny Otis Quintette, under whose name the record was released) to the top of the charts with "Double Crossing Blues" in 1950. Esther's foil on a lot of her records was Mel Walker, who also released records under his own name, backed by Otis's crew. Few who knew about Otis realized that he was white; he was born John Veliotes, son of a couple of Greeks who ran a grocery in Berkeley, California. His first autobiography, *Listen to the Lambs,* concludes with a weird description of how he "became" black. Certainly the oddest rhythm and blues star of 1952 was a gay white singer who wore hearing aids and broke down crying during his act. Johnnie Ray may have been an anomaly, but he had a solid pedigree, being a star attraction at Al Green's Flame Show Bar in Detroit, and his song "Cry" topped the pop and R&B charts. And on the East Coast, Atlantic was still having success with Ruth Brown, and, at the end of 1952, signed a guy who sounded a lot like Charles Brown and had had a couple of records out on Swingtime, Ray Charles.

But it was vocal groups who were really inventing a new style. The Dominoes, who'd scored with "Sixty Minute Man," had a lead singer, Clyde McPhatter, whose emotional style was rooted in his early gospel experiences, and their "Have Mercy Baby" was 1952's #3 R&B hit thanks to McPhatter's pleading vocal. Gospel was the starting point for a lot of these groups. At Apollo Records, Bess Berman inserted a clause into the contracts of all her gospel signings saying that if they didn't sell what the record company deemed a sufficient number of records, they should try secular music, a clause that made her top-selling gospel act, Mahalia Jackson, stomp off the label after it was suggested that if she sold *that* many gospel records, imagine how many R&B records she'd sell. (Jackson had, indeed, sung, but not recorded, blues in New Orleans before being saved.)

In 1951, Apollo had signed a gospel group from Winston-Salem, North Carolina, called the Royal Sons Quintet. They were showmen, ripping up gospel programs throughout the South with their vigorous choreography and bass singer Lowman Pauling's stinging guitar. After a few gospel 45s that didn't really do much, Bess invoked her secular music clause, but the group had no problem with it; they were young, and a lot of what they'd been doing could be rewritten as rhythm and blues. In October 1952, they stepped into the studio to try it out and recorded a handful of sides—"Baby Don't Do It," "Help Me Somebody," "Crazy, Crazy, Crazy," and "Laundromat Blues"—that would make them stars in 1953 under their new name, the "5" Royales. In fact, once they started selling records and touring, they found that another group, the Royals (who recorded for the King subsidiary Federal) was showing up and playing their gigs, as well as pretending to be the Royales. A lawsuit settled that, and the Royals became Hank Ballard and the Midnighters.

In Cleveland, Alan Freed had discovered a Chicago group, the Moonglows, whose leader, Harvey Fuqua, was a talented songwriter, singer, and vocal arranger, so Freed signed them to a management contract.

The first big hit of 1953 in the R&B world was a shot across the bow of the sophisticated crooners in the big cities. Willie Mae "Big Mama" Thornton came by her nickname honestly, and she growled, howled, and yipped her way through "Hound Dog," calling out a no-good man who was little better than a cur and taking time for someone in the backing band—listed on the label as "Kansas City Bill," but in reality Johnny Otis—to scream out a guitar solo. And those who might be inclined to dismiss it as just another piece of Negro depravity would be in for a surprise when they learned who had written it: a couple of former students of LA's Fairfax High, sons of well-educated Jewish intellectuals. Jerry Leiber and Mike Stoller had moved with their parents to Los Angeles in 1950, and Stoller had dropped out of high school to work as a musician with local dance bands. A drummer in one of them introduced him to Leiber, who was still in school, as a guy who wrote lyrics he thought might make good songs. Stoller was skeptical—"I thought he had in mind something that I would find saccharine and uninteresting"—but it turned out that Leiber was influenced by the records he sold at a record store after school, R&B records that were bought by black and white teenagers alike. "I wouldn't say we were the only Caucasians interested in the blues," Stoller remembered later, "but generally speaking it was unusual for teenage white kids to be involved, knowledgeable, and interested in black popular music." They began to write songs, made a connection with Modern Records in the person of Modern's sales manager, Lester Sill, who got one of their songs to Gene Norman, a local promoter of big blues shows, and through him they got to stand in the audience of a Gene Norman Blues Jamboree and the Shrine Auditorium in 1950 and hear Jimmy Witherspoon sing one of their songs. Not long afterward, Sill took them to New York to meet the A&R men who gave songs to performers to record, including Bobby Shad of Mercury and Ralph Bass of King. Bass moved to Los Angeles shortly thereafter to open a new King subsidiary, Federal, and gave the two regular work. Johnny Otis got the word that there were a couple of good songwriters in his backyard, so he'd have them over to his house to work with his latest discoveries, which was how they met Big Mama Thornton. "Hound Dog" was their first really large hit, on Don Robey's Peacock label, and, because they were only twenty when it took off, they had to get their mothers to sign as their legal guardians in order to deposit the check. It bounced.

Imitation may be a sincere form of flattery, but in the music business, it can get you sued. One fad that was gaining force was the answer record, where the "5" Royales' "Baby Don't Do It" got answered by Annisteen Allen's "Baby I'm Doin' It" and Ruth Brown's smash "(Mama) He Treats Your Daughter Mean" harvested a bunch of answers like "Daughter (That's Your Red Wagon)," by Swinging Sax Kari with Gloria Irving, "Papa (I Don't Treat That Little Girl Mean)" by Scatman Crothers, "Pappa!" by Bennie Brown, and Wynonie Harris claiming that "Mama, Your Daughter's Done Lied on Me." The majority of these records disappeared shortly after being released, but more than a few of them copied the melody, arrangement, and a good part of the lyrics of the original. Nobody cared because the record would be dead by the time they got a lawsuit together, and anyway, there was no real money involved. But not everyone was so lucky.

Sam Phillips had had a rotten 1952 and after a couple of releases suspended Sun Records and went away for a little nervous break-down, something he'd done before. In January 1953, though, he brought his brother, Jud, into the business as business manager and got him to stake him some more operating capital, since he'd run through Jim Bulleit's pretty quickly. There was a sense of urgency; that same month, Lester, the eldest of the Bihari brothers, came to Memphis to open yet another in the Modern family of labels, Meteor, and Don Robey had already grabbed up the Duke label on the strength of one artist's hit. This was formidable competition, but Sam had several years' experience on the ground in Memphis, which nei-ther of the other men had. (He might also have been relieved to know that Lester Bihari was sent to Memphis as much to get him out of the Modern offices, where he ran the stockroom and chatted end-lessly with customers instead of taking care of business, as to establish a beachhead in Memphis.) Sam immediately released three records he'd recorded in late 1952, including one by Joe Hill Lewis, and al-though they only sold locally, they sold: as part of his untangling his previous affairs he'd assigned distribution to Jim Bulleit, one less thing for him to worry about. Then, in March, he decided to get in on the answer record fad, and "Hound Dog" was a perfect target. As for the singer, he chose a prominent longtime local showman, Rufus Thomas Jr., who had a show on WDIA, and emceed the talent shows at the Palace Theater, where B. B. King had gotten his break along with a long list of others. "Bear Cat" was no masterpiece, but it was entertaining enough—and close enough to the original to get shot down right away, but it had gone into the R&B top ten before the cease-and-desist order was signed. June saw Rufus stick with the me-nagerie and record "Tiger Man," a superior record that didn't do as well, but wasn't going to get anyone sued since Joe Hill Lewis wrote it specifically for him.

Acts wanting to get signed had always come to Sam, but now he was someone to be reckoned with—he'd had a hit, even if it had got-ten him sued.

Joe Calloway, who worked in radio in Memphis, had gone out to the Tennessee State Penitentiary in Nashville to produce a news story on five guys who'd formed a singing group in prison, and thought that not only did they have talent, but they'd written a song, "Just Walkin' in the Rain," that could be a hit. Sam agreed, and arranged for the group to record it at Sun, surrounded by armed guards. He then named them the Prisonaires and had DJ copies of the record pressed on clear yellow plastic with black bars. It was a lovely light ballad in the mode of the Orioles, with Johnny Bragg's lead tenor sounding a lot like Sonny Til's. The record sold fifty thousand copies almost immediately, but a tour was out of the question, although the group did do occasional weekend shows, heavily escorted by lawmen, around the Nashville area.

An act that wasn't constrained that way, one of the city's top attractions, stopped in that June and recorded the first in a series of classic sides for Sun. Herman "Little Junior" Parker had been a member of the band Howlin' Wolf had left behind when he moved to Chicago, and he was one of the Beale Streeters along with Bobby Bland, Johnny Ace, and Rosco Gordon. Putting together his own band, the Blue Flames, he cut "Feelin' Good" for Sam and watched it go into the R&B top ten. In August he came back and recorded "Mystery Train," but it only sold locally. And if proof that Sam's fortunes had changed were needed, Ike Turner returned to him that summer with some talent: Johnny O'Neal, "Little" Milton Campbell, and the star of Ike's latest version of the Kings of Rhythm, his wife, Bonnie. The tapes piled up; none were issued, presumably because Sam knew not to expand too rapidly, and it was all he and Jud could do to keep filling the orders for the records they'd already issued.

Vocal groups really charged ahead in 1953, with the Orioles scoring a massive summertime hit with "Crying in the Chapel," a country tune that had been a hit for Darrell Glenn and cowboy movie star Rex Allen that spring, but which fit Sonny Til and his crew like a glove, so much so that it almost cracked the pop top ten. Billy Ward and His Dominoes were enjoying a wonderful year, thanks to Clyde McPhatter; they followed up a top-ten hit, "I'd Be Satisfied," with one of the most bizarre records yet, "The Bells." McPhatter becomes more and more unhinged as he listens to the church bells tolling for his girlfriend's funeral and ends the record screaming with grief. It's not an easy record to listen to, but it achieved a #3 position on the R&B charts and became a highlight of the Dominoes' show. The other side, "Pedal Pushin' Papa," was a hit, too, although it was David McNeil on lead vocals, and then Clyde came back with "These Foolish Things (Remind Me of You)."

Because vocal groups were big on the East Coast, the Dominoes played Harlem's Apollo Theater and Birdland frequently. Atlantic's Ahmet Ertegun was at Birdland one night that summer to see them and noticed that McPhatter was missing. Between sets, he went backstage and casually asked Ward why. Ward was known as a hard guy to work for, with numerous demands put on his employees and a hair-trigger temper. His answer to Ertegun was concise: "I fired his ass." Ertegun was soon on the pavement outside the club hailing a cab and talking the driver into taking him to McPhatter's Harlem apartment, and took the singer to dinner, where he convinced him that he should sign with Atlantic. McPhatter had some friends with a gospel group, the Thrasher Wonders, who wanted to go secular and sing with him, and after auditioning at Atlantic, they were signed, too, and took the name the Drifters. Their first song for the label, "Money Honey," became the top-selling R&B song of the year. (Billy Ward wasn't too upset—Atlantic had just inherited his problems, in his opinion—and he found another lead singer named Jackie Wilson, a former boxer who had been singing gospel and pop tunes in Detroit at the Flame Show Bar.)

Atlantic wasn't much on vocal groups, although the Clovers were on the label and selling respectably, but the Drifters weren't a street-corner-style group, and had a couple of guys who could take the lead; in this they bridged old and new vocal group styles. Producing "Money Honey" was in the hands of Ahmet Ertegun and Jerry Wexler, the young former *Billboard* journalist who'd coined the term "rhythm and blues" at the magazine, who'd been hired when Herb Abramson was drafted, and who was at last ready to get his hands dirty in the record business.

Atlantic was slowly gathering force, which Abramson's departure only interrupted a little bit. They had Ruth Brown, who was proving a most versatile artist (her 1953 hit "Wild Wild Young Men" is an early rock & roll classic, while her big hit that year, "(Mama) He Treats Your Daughter Mean," was black pop at its finest), Big Joe Turner (who was doing some of his best work ever for them), LaVern Baker, formerly known as "Miss Cornshucks," who was still a developing talent, the Clovers and the Cardinals and the Drifters, and Ray Charles, Ahmet's pet project, with whom he and Abramson had already cut a couple of singles that hadn't gone anywhere. Two of them, "Losing Hand" and "Mess Around," are the subjects of a remarkable tape recorded on May 10, 1953, with Ertegun teaching Charles the latter tune, which he'd written, practically bar by bar. A lot of label owners reflexively took all or part of the songwriting credit for their artists' tunes, aware that the publishing copyright was far more valuable than ownership of a recording, but it's obvious from this that Ahmet Ertegun (or A. Nugetre, as he signed himself) was a fan and a lover of the music and that he understood what made it tick, even if he couldn't sing and had to talk the lyrics in his crisp, accented voice. (Nugetre's songwriting was so varied and so successful that Syd Nathan ordered Carl Lebow, his A&R head, to find him and lure him away. Finding no Nugetres in the New York phone book, he called Atlantic asking how he could find him. The person on the other end of the phone suggested he spell the name backward and hung up.) One thing was certain, though: under Ertegun, Abramson, and Wexler's guidance, Charles was leaving his Charles Brown imitations behind and using more gospel techniques in his vocals.

One artist everyone wanted to land was Elmore James, a Mississippi-based guitarist whose style consisted of one guitar lick based on the one Robert Johnson had used in "I Believe I'll Dust My Broom," which James had re-recorded in 1952 as "Dust My Broom" for Trumpet, a Jackson, Mississippi, label owned by Lillian McMurry, whose husband owned a radio repair shop in which James worked. This version of the tune, which James re-recorded often, featured harmonica work by a guy who called himself Sonny Boy Williamson, whether in homage to the Bluebird blues star who'd been murdered in 1948 or just to confuse people who didn't know that the original was dead. At any rate, this Sonny Boy had been born in 1910 (four years before the other guy), had been one of the musicians who'd hit the road with Charley Patton in the '30s, and was probably named Aleck "Rice" Miller. The record was a top-ten hit, and both Modern and Chess went looking for him. Mrs. McMurry, who wanted to establish a music industry in Jackson for the Mississippi musicians who hadn't defected to Memphis or Chicago, held firm, but that didn't stop James from taking a bus to Memphis and presenting himself to Lester Bihari, who immediately recorded him and issued the first Meteor recording, "I Believe" (practically identical to "Dust My Broom") as fast as he could. It, too, went into the top ten. Presumably his brothers back in Los Angeles were finally proud of him. They didn't know (nor did Lester) that he was about to make a huge mistake.

chapter five

1953–1954: THE STARS ALIGN

Sam Phillips, Elvis, and Marion Keisker standing outside
Sun's office/studio at 706 Union, Memphis.
(Courtesy of Tom Salva)

Or maybe not. Here's what we know for certain. On June 3, 1953, Elvis Aron Presley graduated from Humes High School in Memphis. There was a musical program at the graduation ceremony, but he wasn't part of it. For some years since moving with his family from his birthplace in Tupelo to Memphis, he'd been taking guitar lessons from the son of a woman his mother knew from church, and although he wasn't too talented as a guitarist, he could come up with enough chords to accompany songs he liked, which were mostly pop songs he'd heard on the radio. Since moving to Memphis, his interest in music—as a consumer and as a performer— had grown to the point where he carried his guitar around with him, entered a couple of talent contests, and could be heard entertaining at informal get-togethers in the courtyard of the apartment complex where he lived, or, when the Presleys were evicted for making too much money to live in public housing, on the front porch of the house they rented subsequently. He was a weird kid: polite to his elders, an indifferent student, but dressing oddly in flamboyant clothes (black and pink was a favorite combination), wearing loud socks, and combing his hair in a complex, stacked-up way that echoed the complex dos of the black performers he may well have seen on the Sunday night shows at the Handy Theater, which were reserved for a whites-only audience. Like a lot of his friends, he listened to Dewey Phillips's program *Red Hot & Blue* on WHBQ, a Memphis station that let this hillbilly madman (no relation to Sam) sing along with and speed-rap over the R&B records he played, as well as read out dedications and do free-form commercials. Elvis also hung out at a record store called Charlie's, which had a jukebox featuring the records for sale in the store instead of listening booths (but it still cost a nickel to play) and attracted a lot of dedicated music fans. We know that the morning he graduated, Elvis went to the Tennessee Employment Security Office and got a job at the M. B. Parker Machinists' Shop. He'd start the next day. We also know that he was looking for something that would involve his singing. He wanted, maybe, to make a record.

Here's what we don't know. It's possible that he figured that Meteor would be a good bet. Sun was just getting on its feet, but it had had a hit, and with a black artist at that. He'd have wanted someone who was recording country performers, perhaps, and Meteor would fill that bill nicely, although they, too, had had only one hit, and that was with Elmore James. According to Jules Bihari, people were always dropping in at Meteor looking to audition, and most failed to impress Leonard. Elvis, he remembered, was one of them, and Leonard told him to go visit Sam Phillips; maybe he could do something for him. If this is what happened, Elvis may have considered it a failure on his part, and yet the Memphis Recording Service was, in fact, a better deal; they didn't have to like you. All you had to do was have the money to cut your song: $3.98 plus tax for a two-sided acetate disc, and for another dollar you could have a tape copy made, too. So in August he figured okay, he'd try that. And we know that he did.

Much has been written and conjectured about what happened and who was there since then, but at the moment it happened, it was of so little significance that we pretty much have to take the word of the only one of the two people who were there to have been interviewed—Sam Phillips's partner-cum-secretary, Marion Keisker. Interviewed by Elvis biographer Jerry Hopkins for his 1971 book, she remembered that it was a Saturday afternoon and that, for some reason, she was the only person there except for a bunch of people wanting to use the recording service. (Sam may have been elsewhere in the building or at the café next door, which was the informal Sun business office.) She told this kid with his beat-up guitar that he'd have to wait, and he agreed. While he was waiting she got into a conversation with him, and as she remembered, it went like this: Elvis mentioned that he was a singer, and she asked, "What kind of singer are you?"

"I sing all kinds."

"Who do you sound like?"

"I don't sound like nobody."

Her reaction, she said, was to think, *Oh yeah, one of those.* "Hillbilly?" she asked him.

"Yeah, I sing hillbilly."

"Who do you sound like in hillbilly?"

"I don't sound like nobody."

Eventually they made it into the studio, and Ms. Keisker set up the disc for the acetate recording. Elvis's first tune was the Ink Spots' "My Happiness," and halfway through, Ms. Keisker did something unusual: she threaded some tape into the tape recorder, despite the fact that he hadn't ordered a tape copy. "Now, this is something we never did," she told Hopkins, "but I wanted Sam to hear this." She recorded part of the first song and all of another Ink Spots' song, "That's When Your Heartaches Begin." She took down his name, address, phone number (which belonged to the folks upstairs, Rabbi Alfred Fruchter and his wife), and noted on the tape box "Good ballad singer. Hold." Which they did. For a long time. Elvis would drop in from time to time—his pretext was that he hoped Ms. Keisker would have heard of a band that needed a singer—but there was no news. In January 1954, he recorded another acetate, Joni James's "I'll Never Stand in Your Way," and "It Wouldn't Be the Same Without You," an obscure Jimmy Wakely tune. He kept talking about trying out for a gospel group at his church, but he didn't talk about the fact that when they finally auditioned him, they rejected him. He heard that an up-and-coming local country star, Eddie Bond, was looking for a singer, and he went out to the club where he was performing, did a couple of numbers, and never heard from Bond again. Then, on June 26, Sam—or Marion Keisker, to be exact—called. Elvis later joked that he was at 706 Union before she hung up the phone. Sam had found a song, given to him by Red Wortham, who'd discovered the Prisonaires, and he heard a hit in the demo. Who could do it? Ah, that kid, the kind of shy one. So Ms. Keisker phoned, Elvis arrived, and Sam played him the song, "Without You." They spent most of the afternoon going over and over and over the song, but nothing clicked. Sam had him sing songs he was already familiar with, listening intensely. He still didn't hear a record. So he sent the kid home but turned the events of that afternoon over in his head. There had to be something . . .

In New York, Atlantic was recording a lot with Ray Charles when he was in town. He was building up a reputation on the road, so he was touring, especially down South. One day in October 1953, he'd found himself in New Orleans, hired to do a session and provide an arrangement for the artist Guitar Slim. Johnny Vincent, an Italian American entrepreneur from Jackson, Mississippi, had been hired by Specialty's Art Rupe to scout talent, supervise recording sessions, and generally take care of business for the label, which hoped for another "Lawdy Miss Clawdy"–sized smash from down there. Guitar Slim (real name: Eddie Jones) had the makings of someone who could deliver one. A regular at New Orleans's notorious Dew Drop Inn, he was a flamboyant dresser, a virtuoso guitar player with a lot of the tricks T-Bone Walker had introduced like playing behind his back, picking with his teeth, and walking out of the club while playing, trailing a long cord plugged into his amplifier. He was also a bad drunk, so getting him through a session could be a problem, as Vincent knew, because he'd recorded him on one of the record labels he'd had before joining Specialty. Ray Charles threw the arrangement of the song, "The Things I Used to Do," together on the spot, ran the band through it, and finally got a take they could use, with Slim's stinging guitar punctuating the verses and, way back in the mix, you can hear Ray shout with delight just before the band plays the last two notes. It's a great performance, even if Art Rupe snarled at Johnny Vincent for sending him such a sloppy record and threatened to fire him if it didn't become a hit. Fortunately for Vincent, he watched it reach the top of the R&B charts at the start of 1954.

Maybe all the talent in New Orleans hadn't been signed up after all. As for Ray Charles, the record didn't do much for him—he wasn't credited on the label, after all—but Atlantic slipped out one of his new recordings in the spring and got some action. It was kind of a novelty item, but it did showcase Charles's new voice, one that owed an awful lot to gospel singers, on the chorus, as he wailed "It Should Have Been Me." Atlantic got it into the R&B top ten and started rooting around in its tapes for something to follow it with.

While that was happening, the Detroit vocal group that had just changed its name from the Royals to the Midnighters ignited a scandal that would have far-reaching repercussions. "Work with Me, Annie" was the record that white parents feared their teenagers were listening to—and they were. The lyrics were really something: the kind of work Annie was being asked to perform sounded a whole lot like . . . something else, and lead vocalist Hank Ballard's begging her to "give me all my meat" was certainly lurid enough. Worse, it was catchy as could be. And after it had become #1, they followed it up with "Sexy Ways," which was, well, something you just didn't sing about, and Ballard's vocal left little doubt about the effect those sexy ways were having on him. It got played on the radio, though, primarily on black stations, which tended to be low power and go off the air at sunset. By this time, the kids looking for dirty records knew what to ask for, so when "Annie Had a Baby" came out in the summer, airplay didn't really matter, although, again, there probably was some, late at night.

Radio, though, was in an uproar—not so much about the Midnighters' records, but about the fact that R&B was popular enough that stations wanting to attract teen listeners found themselves forced to devote airtime to it. *Billboard* ran a survey in 1953 that found that 25 percent of all radio stations had an R&B program on for an average of two and a half hours a week. The pre-recorded programs Hunter Hancock and Alan Freed were sending out were very popular, and some stations, like WNJR in Newark, New Jersey, had eighteen hours daily of jazz and R&B programming, including a taped Freed show, and that same issue of *Billboard* reported aggregate sales of R&B records had reached $15 million in 1953, the result, they felt, of teenage kids wanting dance music with a big beat, like the music that had given rise to the pre-war swing kids.

By the time the "Annie" records were in full swing, a correction was trying to establish itself. A club of self-policing R&B disc jockeys on the East Coast banded together to "combat smut and racial derogation," with *Billboard* reporting that "tunes that the club hopes to stop play on are those that deal with sex in a suggestive manner, those that deal with drinking, and those that hold the Negro up to ridicule. The club is not against blues records as such, but it is against a record in which 'rock,' 'roll,' or 'ride' doesn't deal with the rhythm and meter of the tune." It was the white DJs, obviously, who were most offended. "I don't like to feature blues," said Bill Laws of KLX in Oakland, "but the requests keep coming in." And, tellingly, in Lynn, Massachusetts, WLYN's Don Sherman told *Billboard* that "I've found it necessary to start including some of the less offensive R&B records on my pop show. The teenage crowd seems to know nothing else." In Memphis, the police cracked down, confiscating jukeboxes with offensive records on them.

One of those records was soon going to need a little explanation. Bull Moose Jackson's "Big Ten-Inch Record" is a masterpiece of double entendre and timing, and it sold well enough under the counter, but its subject was changing. Not sex: records. The ten-inch 78 was on its way out. Between 1948 and 1950, Columbia and RCA each introduced a new kind of record. Columbia's was the long-playing record, which ran at 33⅓ RPM and was issued in both ten-inch and twelve-inch sizes. (The 78s were also available as twelve-inchers, but for classical repertoire almost exclusively.) RCA, on the other hand, had a seven-inch record with a much larger hole in the center, and it played at 45 RPM. Each had its advantages, and both sounded better than 78s. This was becoming an issue to higher-end consumers (most of whom had never heard of Bull Moose Jackson), especially jazz fans, who for the first time could buy records with full-length, uninterrupted recordings of extended performances. Classical fans, too, welcomed a medium where you could get over twenty minutes of music before having to turn the disc over; it revolutionized listening to opera, for one thing. The long-playing record, or LP, was also a great medium for collecting singles by popular artists, as Capitol soon realized by putting out Frank Sinatra albums. In 1955, *Billboard* would inaugurate a chart for long-players.

The 45, however, was ideal for singles; using the latest mastering technology, they could sound vastly better on even a jukebox's primitive sound system, and if one took care, it was possible to put two songs on each side, thereby giving birth to the extended-play record, or EP. This format was endorsed immediately by the pop music industry, which loved the lighter weight, improved sound, and reduced manufacturing costs, and both 45 singles and EPs were soon available in addition to their larger, clunkier cousins. EPs were also ideal for artists who couldn't fill up an entire twelve-inch album; country and R&B artists were especially popular in the EP format, and jukebox operators who'd converted to 45 were happy to charge more for selected discs. One of the classic EPs from this era was the Midnighters' entire "Annie" trilogy—"Work with Me, Annie," "Sexy Ways," "Annie Had a Baby," and their first hit, "Moonrise"—all on one Federal EP. And another thing the 33 and 45 had in common was that they were made of polyvinyl chloride, which stood up to wear better and could be dropped without shattering. (The 78 hung on a good long while, though, especially outside the United States; Indian Odeon issued a 78 of the Beatles' "Paperback Writer" and "Rain" in 1966.)

Alan Freed was a major beneficiary of all this interest in R&B (it would be interesting to know if he played the "Annie" records), and had been putting on "Moondog Ball" shows in Cleveland to sold-out audiences. He expanded to other Ohio cities, offering two or three headliners and an orchestra backing them that would play pepped-up pop jazz. Then he started growing and moving out of town. In May 1954, he put on a show at the Newark Armory with a sky-high ticket price of two dollars, which drew around ten thousand paid admissions and a few thousand disappointed kids who were too late to get into the sold-out show. *Billboard* reported that the audience was largely between fifteen and twenty years old and 20 percent white.

His next show was at Ebbets Field in Brooklyn, with the Clovers, the Dominoes, the Orioles, Fats Domino, Muddy Waters, Little Walter, Count Basie's Orchestra, and Buddy Johnson's Orchestra. One reason Freed may have been spending so much time in New York was that he was deep in negotiations to move his show there, and in July, he announced that he'd signed a contract with WINS, 1010 AM, for an astronomical $75,000, which included his keeping his syndicated show. He returned to Ohio, put on one more "Moondog Ball" in Akron, broadcast it live over WJW, and went home to pack his bags. About the only major change he had to make was to drop the "Moondog" handle, because it already belonged to a blind, bearded giant whose real name was Louis Hardin, who hung around Sixth Avenue dressed in Viking regalia, performing his percussion compositions to anyone who'd pay him.

Vocal groups were popping up everywhere. Atlantic had the Clovers (whose "Your Cash Ain't Nothin' but Trash" was a hit this year), the Drifters (who made their contribution to the smut crisis with "Such a Night"), and, over on their newly formed Cat label, the Chords, with "Sh-Boom," a song loaded with nonsense syllables, expertly harmonized. In the Midwest, King's Federal label had not only the Midnighters but the Charms, a Cincinnati group fronted by the charismatic Otis Williams, who delivered "Hearts of Stone" to the charts, and they'd also signed a group from Los Angeles called the Platters who didn't seem to have much sense of what they were doing. In Chicago, a new label called Vee-Jay had made the wise decision not to compete with Chess for blues artists (they had offices right across the street for a while) and put their toe in the water with a local group called the Spaniels, whose "Goodnite, Sweetheart, Goodnite" was a perfect slow last-dance number that put the group and the label on the map. They also grabbed a local group, the Flamingos, from whom great things would be heard, but not in 1954. Realizing that Chicago was a center for gospel music, they also signed up a couple of acts, most notably the Staple Singers, a family act held together by Roebuck "Pops" Staples, who, in his pre-saved days, had been among the young blues musicians who had followed Charley Patton around, and whose electric guitar playing, the only backing the group had, featuring deeply reverbed and oddly voiced slow ostinati, gave an ominous backing to the family's songs of hope.

Chess was more interested in finding more blues artists than vocal groups, but you couldn't deny their popularity, and their picking up the Moonglows, the Chicago group that had moved to Cleveland to be near Alan Freed, was a very good move, as "Sincerely" became a hit late in 1954—and the group's connection to Freed couldn't hurt the label's relations with him.

Out west, the fledgling Dootone label (owned by Dootsie Williams, whose other income source was Redd Foxx's party comedy records) put out "Earth Angel" by the Penguins, as primitive a slab of harmonizing as had ever had success, but it was a national hit nonetheless. And a couple of out-of-nowhere classics, songs that would be used as audition pieces by innumerable vocal groups to come, also made their appearance in '54: "A Sunday Kind of Love" introduced the Harptones, at least locally in New York (the record never charted), slowing down a pop hit co-written by Louis Prima, the better to showcase their lead singer, Willie Winfield, while the Cadillacs, also from New York, took "Gloria," which had been recorded by both Charles Brown and the Mills Brothers, to vocal group heaven with lead singer Earl "Speedy" (or "Speedo," as we'll see) Carroll reaching into falsetto territory in praise of the girl of the title. It, too, joined the pantheon without charting. And the Drifters closed out 1954 with a version of "White Christmas" that owed more than a little to Clyde McPhatter's former employers the Dominoes' arrangement, except that Clyde took over from the bass lead to exercise his own kind of drama on the tune, leading to grumbles from Irving Berlin's lawyers. Berlin shouldn't have bothered; not only was the group on firm ground by rearranging the song, but it also managed to chart over the next two Christmases and earn him lots of money.

One of the biggest successes with the teenagers was forty-three-year-old Big Joe Turner, of all people. He'd finished out 1953 with "Honey Hush," a classic boogie-woogie tune, and started 1954 with "TV Mama," which featured Elmore James doing his thing on the slide guitar, something completely unlike the Kansas City–style jump blues Turner was known for. But those records were overshadowed by one that was on the charts for most of the year (thirty-two weeks!): "Shake, Rattle and Roll." It, too, was part of the smut crisis, as Joe admired his girlfriend's "dresses, the sun comes shining through" and compared himself to a one-eyed cat peeping in a seafood store. It also swung like crazy, making it one of the first rock & roll classics. Turner's version never made the pop charts, but you'd better believe white teenagers knew about it. So did a twenty-nine-year-old Western swing bandleader in Pennsylvania who'd been recording hot records with titles like "Rock This Joint" for regional labels, and had done a cover of "Rocket 88."

Bill Haley and the Saddlemen were pretty popular around the Philadelphia area, and Haley had no doubt been listening to some of the R&B records that were sent to him in his day job as a disc jockey at WPWA. In mid-1953, he recorded a hot tune called "Crazy Man, Crazy," that almost made the top ten, and made enough noise for Decca to sign him, changing the name of his band to the Comets. His version of "Shake, Rattle and Roll" did make the pop top ten, although of course he cleaned up the lyrics and his band wasn't close to the caliber of the jazzmen Atlantic had enlisted to back up Big Joe.

Still, Haley's success pointed out one solution to the smut crisis and the problem of white youth buying black records: cover versions. This was an industry term for a re-recording of another person's record, and it had a long and venerable history reaching back to the 1920s, before records were even how most people accessed a song. The Chords' "Sh-Boom" was a great, catchy, tricky tune, so Mercury had a white group, the Crew-Cuts (formerly the Canadaires) record a cover version that almost killed the Chords' version. Almost—both went into the top ten, but the Crew-Cuts made #1. Ruth Brown had a pretty little number called "Oh, What a Dream" riding the charts in the summertime. Patti Page grabbed it, but didn't have much luck with it. So far, cover versions weren't much of a threat. That would change soon. And, of course, there was another way to deal with some of the unruly performers; Clyde McPhatter was drafted in May. Fortunately, there was stuff in the can, and the Drifters were unaffected, because Atlantic had pulled Clyde from the group and started recording him as a solo artist, replacing him in the group with a near soundalike, Little David Baughan.

The real crisis was brewing in Memphis, however. A guitarist from a local country band called the Starlite Ramblers was hanging out at the Memphis Recording Service, and Sam Phillips took a shine to him. Scotty Moore had ambitions of playing jazz, although he was completely self-taught, and, like Sam, had an intuition that something new was on the horizon, which they'd discuss over coffee. Sam did a single on the Starlite Ramblers, and it didn't sell, like most Memphis country music, but Scotty kept hanging around. Eventually, someone mentioned the kid who'd been looking for a band, Elvis Presley, and Scotty offered to take a listen to him. The Ramblers' bass player, Bill Black, lived a couple of doors away from him, and Scotty invited him over to work with the kid. On July 4, Elvis showed up at the Moores' house and Bill came over and they stumbled through some tunes together. Between songs, Bill discovered that Elvis knew his brother Johnny, who had moved to Texas. They ambled through some more songs, and finally Elvis left. Scotty called Sam and said he wasn't much impressed, but the kid did have a good voice. Sam thought it would be a good idea to record him, because sometimes people sound different on tape. They made an appointment at the studio—Bill Black agreed to come, too— and so at 7:00 P.M. the next day, Scotty, Bill, Elvis, and Sam convened, and, after a little conversation, rolled the tape.

They went through several takes of an old Ernest Tubb hit, "I Love You Because," a ballad with a recitation in it, and although the voice was there, and Sam was convinced that Elvis was a ballad singer, it wasn't exactly what he was looking for. Hours passed, and then something happened. Elvis, out of sheer nervous energy, perhaps, started whanging away on a tune he'd been playing for some time, Arthur Crudup's "That's All Right (Mama)," which the bluesman had recorded for Bluebird in the 1940s. Scotty told Jerry Hopkins that Elvis was "jumping around the studio, just acting the fool. And Bill started beating on his bass and I joined in. Just making a bunch of racket, we thought. The door to the control room was open, and when we was halfway through the thing, Sam come running out and said, 'What the devil are you doing?' We said, 'We don't know.' He said, 'Well, find out real quick and don't lose it. Run through it again and let's put it on tape.' So to the best of our knowledge we repeated what we just done and went through the whole thing." Now, this was interesting. All they had to do was record another song and they'd have a record.

It took four more sessions. Elvis, Scotty, and Bill sitting around the studio, tossing around songs to do, doing them, and coming up with nothing. Finally, they were between songs, just like the last time, and somehow Bill Monroe's name came up. The bluegrass master was known for not having much of a sense of humor, and at the moment the country stations were playing "Blue Moon of Kentucky," his latest record, in an attempt to make it a hit. Elvis started mocking him, jumping up "Blue Moon of Kentucky," and, laughing, the other two joined in, making up the arrangement as they went along, trying not to crack up too much. When it was over, Sam walked into the studio and said, "Fine, man, fine. Hell, that's different. That's a pop song now, nearly 'bout. That's good." Not good enough to use, so they did one more take. Sam gave the two-sided curiosity the number Sun 209.

Then, after everyone had gone home and Sam sat alone in the studio, Dewey Phillips stopped by. Dewey and Sam had a history going back before Sun; they'd briefly had a record label, It's The Phillips!, that flopped, and of course Dewey was essential to exposing the blues records Sam was cutting. The two men sat up, drinking beer and listening to "That's All Right (Mama)," a song whose original Dewey had played many times on his show—perhaps that's where Elvis had heard it. Sam was just a bit tentative about playing it at first; Dewey was known to prefer non-local performers, rhythm and blues stars from faraway Strolls like Central Avenue or 125th Street. But he liked this record. In fact, he called Sam the next morning and told him that he wanted two copies for his show that evening, and Sam warmed up the acetate-cutting lathe. After taking the records to WHBQ, Sam told Elvis, Scotty, and Bill that Dewey would be playing it that night, and Elvis, nervous as he could be, turned the family radio on to WHBQ after dinner that evening and ran off to the movies. At about ten o'clock, Dewey announced that he had a record that

Sam would be putting out next week, and here it was, by a local boy, Elvis Presley. Back at the Presley house, his mother, Gladys, was so shocked by hearing his name on the radio that she couldn't pay attention to the record. No matter; Dewey played it again. And again. And again. Something like eleven times in a row. Then the phone rang at the Presleys'. It was Dewey, demanding that they find Elvis and bring him down to the station for an interview so that the phones would stop ringing at the station. They went down to the theater and pulled Elvis out of his seat and out onto the sidewalk and down to WHBQ, where Dewey greeted him warmly and told him to hang on because he was going to interview him. Elvis, scared to death, said he didn't know anything about being interviewed, and Dewey just told him not to say anything dirty. He kept talking, and "I asked him where he went to high school," Phillips told Stanley Booth, "and he said, 'Humes.' I wanted to get that out, because a lot of people listening thought he was colored." They continued to chat, and finally Dewey thanked him and Elvis asked when he was going to get interviewed. "'I already have,' I said. 'The mike's been open the whole time.'" Now Dewey had to deal with the phones; they'd been jammed since he played the record the first time and weren't letting up. Elvis, no doubt a bit preoccupied, slowly walked home. In teenage Memphis, though, the word was out. That weird-looking guy? The one who dressed funny and was obsessed with his hair? He'd made a record. And what a record!

Back then, *Billboard* ran regional charts for R&B and "hillbilly" records, which are fascinating because individual geographical areas have very specific tastes in both genres. Sun 209 showed up fairly quickly on the Memphis chart—it should have, because Sam had had to change his order with the pressing plant from whatever his usual testing-the-waters quantity was to five thousand copies to seven thousand copies right off the bat, so it was selling. Promoting the record was hard; if the singer was white, why was he singing Arthur Crudup, and if he was black, what in the world was he doing with Bill Monroe, of all people? The first place to get it was Texas; a promotion woman named Alta Hayes at Big State Distribution in Dallas managed to get it some airplay, and then it showed up on the Dallas charts. Emboldened, Sam called in a favor at the *Grand Ole Opry*, and in September, Elvis got to sing his record on the show. Contrary to legend, Opry manager Jim Denny did not tell Elvis not to quit his truck-driving job—in fact, he was slightly impressed, according to eyewitnesses—and Elvis's worst fear came and went when he bumped into Bill Monroe backstage and Monroe told him how much he'd liked "Blue Moon of Kentucky," which he was re-cutting the next week to turn it from a waltz to a 4/4 arrangement. Elvis got to introduce Scotty Moore to Chet Atkins (his idol), and later, at *The Midnight Jamboree* at the Ernest Tubb Record Shop, a popular post-*Opry* show, he had an encouraging conversation with Tubb. Sometime after the Opry appearance and his appearance on the *Louisiana Hayride* (the second-most important live country music radio show), he went back into the studio to record the next single, "Good Rockin' Tonight."

At some point after the release of the single, but before the Opry, Elvis played Bethel Spring, Tennessee, and three brothers who had a band went to see him. They'd heard of him, and at least one of the boys had heard him on the radio. His wife had made him listen: "It sounds like *you*!" she'd said. And, he thought, as "Blue Moon of Kentucky" played, it did. The Perkins Brothers had been playing music that way since 1946, when they talked their way into a gig at a place called the Cotton Boll. Carl Lee Perkins was three years older than Elvis Presley, was married, and had kids. But he and his brothers Clayton and Jay were working their way up out of the cotton fields by playing music in the honky-tonks at night. He'd begged his parents for a guitar when he was six and learned to play from "Uncle" John Westbrook, a black man who worked with the Perkinses in the cotton fields. In fact, the Perkins house was in an area that wasn't so much integrated as a place where poor people who sharecropped cotton lived in terrible conditions. Some of them happened to be black, some white. Carl was determined to play the Opry, which his father listened to religiously each week, but his attempt to replicate the music he heard didn't go so well. He liked Uncle John's approach too much, and it infected a lot of what he played. Of course, that had been the key to the Perkins Brothers' success; they were more rhythmic than a lot of other bands, and they got people dancing. Part of this happened when Carl convinced Clayton that he should switch to bass, and then demonstrated a playing technique in which the strings bounced off the neck, providing a rhythmic clicking as well as the bass note. Bit by bit, the Perkins Brothers got better, and eventually acquired a guy named "Fluke" Holland, who'd beat on the side of Clayton's bass with drumsticks, enhancing the rhythmic impact they made.

They all had day jobs, though, and Carl didn't like that. After the Bethel Spring show, Carl had approached Elvis in the parking lot to tell him how much he'd enjoyed the show. (Elvis needed some cheering up; after his last number, he'd tripped over a cable onstage and landed on his butt.) He asked if Sun Records was looking for artists, and Elvis said he didn't know. And that was that. Okay, only one way to find out. As Perkins told his biographer, David McGee, years later, "Presley nailed it. He jumped right in the middle of what I was doing, and the minute I heard it I knew it. I started knowing I had a shot then, because, you know, if you record 'Blue Moon of Kentucky' by Elvis, you might record it by me too, because I sang it. I was a big enough fool to think if I'd go down there and sing it, [Sam Phillips] might like me singin' it too." So in October 1954, the Perkins Brothers loaded their stuff into Fluke Holland's car and headed to Union Avenue. The minute Carl walked in to ask about recording, Marion Keisker blew him off. They had their hands full with Presley and didn't need any more acts. He protested that they sounded like Elvis, and she countered that that wasn't going to help them. Furthermore, Mr. Phillips wasn't there, so auditioning wouldn't do any good. Carl went back out to the car, and just as they were about to drive away, a large blue Buick drove up in front of the studio, and a guy they reckoned was Sam got out. Carl leaped to intercept him and begged him to listen to them. Impatient, Sam said he had a couple of minutes, but no more, and ushered them into the studio. (Years later he told Carl he thought the boy's world would end if he said no, and from what Carl has said, that wasn't too far off.) Jay, who did a mean

Ernest Tubb, stepped up and started one of his original tunes, but Sam cut him off. He then began singing a Tubb number, and Sam informed him that Ernest Tubb already existed. Carl immediately launched into a song he'd written years ago—the first one he'd ever written, in fact—called "Movie Magg" and Sam listened. He listened all the way to the end. And then he asked Carl if he could do it without jumping around, and he did, although by now he was nervous. Sam agreed the second time wasn't so hot, but he liked the song. "You come in with another thing like that and we'll talk about a record deal. But right now, man, this guy Elvis's got my hands tied." Well, okay, Carl figured. He could do that. Carl and Sam made an appointment for a couple of weeks later, and Carl and the band returned to Jackson to wait the time out. When they came back, Fluke Holland had a drum kit, which gave Sam a bit of a start, but it was his car they were driving in, so he let him set up. They recorded "Movie Magg" in an all-new version Carl had worked up, and then "Honky Tonk Gal," a newer song. Sam didn't like that for a B-side for "Movie Magg," so they did another, "Turn Around," that was more country. Carl had a bunch of them, though, and he was ready to record them all.

Up the Mississippi River from Memphis, in St. Louis, something of the opposite phenomenon was happening. Charles Edward "Chuck" Berry, a preacher's wayward son, had done time for armed robbery and car theft while fresh out of high school, and by 1952, he was playing in the Tommy Stevens Combo, a small band that fed versions of popular black hits to the crowds at Huff's Garden, a relatively sophisticated nightclub for black patrons. One night, possibly out of boredom, Berry struck up and performed a country tune for the crowd, which went wild. Stevens encouraged him; a little showmanship couldn't hurt, and soon the whole group was acting nutty, with Berry's country tunes and novelties a highlight of the show. Observing from the sidelines was Johnny Johnson, a boogie-woogie pianist two years older than Berry, who'd been working with an act called the Sir John's Trio in a considerably less sophisticated venue, the Cosmopolitan. At the end of December, Sir John's saxophonist got sick and wasn't going to be able to make the New Year's Eve show, and Johnson (who, after all, was the Sir John of the band's name) asked Berry if he'd like to do his country act as part of the evening's entertainment. By the end of the night, the club's owner insisted that Berry join the band and incorporate this part of the entertainment permanently. This arrangement lasted until Tommy Stevens called Berry one day in 1954 and told him that his band was going to become the house band at the Crank Club, working more and each getting over twice what Berry was making with Sir John. Berry was back with them in a heartbeat. Not long after, a local label owner called to ask if Chuck would play guitar on a record he was making with a guy he was writing songs for, Calypso Joe. The experience of recording energized Berry to the point where, when the Cosmopolitan's owner begged him to come back, he said he would on three conditions: he would be bandleader, he would have a contract, and the band would actively pursue a record deal. Done, done, and done, although who would record them, St. Louis not being awash in rhythm and blues labels, was a good question.

And while Sam Phillips was discovering that talent would come to him, Ahmet Ertegun and Jerry Wexler were having to travel to record their talent; determined to get another hit out of Ray Charles, they went to Cosimo Matassa's studio in August 1953 to record two numbers (one of them by Guitar Slim), radio station WDSU, also in New Orleans, that December, and, in November 1954, to WGST in Atlanta to record him. He was making money on the road, not via his records, so all but the first New Orleans date featured his road band, which shifted personnel but had picked up its first core member, a young saxophonist from Fort Worth, David "Fathead" Newman. The results were all fine tunes, but it was the last session that produced a two-sided hit that Atlantic released in December. "I've Got a Woman" was a quick rewrite of a gospel house-wrecker, "I've Got a Savior," and Ray put everything into it. The B side, "Come Back Baby," had a gospel piano underlying a breathtaking blues vocal punctuated by falsetto hoots. The A side went to #1 on the R&B charts in short order, and the B side got to #4. It looked like Ray Charles had finally found his audience. The hooting was probably influenced by Professor Alex Bradford, who'd had a gospel smash for Specialty in 1953 with "Too Close to Heaven," where he took flight with it a couple of times. That song was no doubt noticed by a young blues singer who'd been doing the Southern circuit and recording for RCA. Richard Penniman—or Little Richard, as he billed himself—was known for a high-energy stage show, but his records were undistinguished blues. After RCA dropped him, he recorded a session for Duke-Peacock in 1953, since Don Robey knew the kid had drawing power and got Johnny Otis's band to back him. Robey didn't even bother to release the records. But Penniman wasn't through yet.

Nor was Otis. On an engagement at San Francisco's Fillmore Auditorium, he was confronted by a brash, light-skinned fifteen-year-old named Jamesetta Hawkins who wanted to audition for him right there and then. He let her try out and then got her parents' permission to take her with him when the band returned to Los Angeles. They gave her the stage name of Etta James and cobbled together an answer record to Hank Ballard's "Annie" records called "Roll with Me, Henry" and presented it to Modern, who insisted on a title change to "The Wallflower." It shot up the R&B charts, and suddenly Etta James was a touring member of the Johnny Otis Revue.

chapter six

1955: ROCK & ROLL
IS BORN . . . MAYBE

The "5" Royales: *(left to right, clockwise from top)* Jimmy Moore, Johnny Tanner, Lowman "Pete" Pauling, Eugene Tanner, and Obediah Carter.
(Michael Ochs Archives/Stringer)

Don Robey did not have a merry Christmas in 1954. Up until Christmas Eve, the year had been very good to him. His Buffalo Booking Agency, administered by the formidable Evelyn Johnson, handled bookings in the area for just about every major black touring act, and acted as an exclusive booking agency for B. B. King, among others. His Bronze Peacock club was also the only conceivable stop for first-class touring acts coming through Houston, and it was one of the swankiest clubs on the circuit, which is why acts vied for week-long engagements there. Robey treated his people well most of the time. His record labels were doing just okay nationally, but locally Clarence "Gatemouth" Brown was racking up local hits, the Songbird label's gospel records were steady sellers, and Duke, the label he'd bought to acquire Johnny Ace, had proven a great investment; ever since Ace had been with Robey, every single one of his records had been an R&B top-ten seller. His next one, "Pledging My Love," looked like it was going to go through the roof, so Robey was holding back on releasing it until after Christmas was over. Ace was going to premiere it at the grand Christmas Eve show at Houston City Auditorium, where he'd headline over a bunch of Robey-managed acts, including Willie Mae "Big Mama" Thornton, who was sharing a dressing room with Ace and his band.

Accounts of what actually happened there differ, but not wildly.

Anyone would tell you that Johnny Ace loved guns and carried them with him all the time. In part, this was something a lot of performers— not just black ones—who worked the club circuit had to do. Often, threatening the club owner or concert promoter was the only way to get the money legitimately owed you out of them at evening's end. Robberies in dressing rooms were not unknown. Johnny, though, was a bit *too* gun-crazy, shooting road signs when on tour and displaying his weapon at inappropriate times. One version of Christmas Eve has him pulling his gun in front of a female admirer who objected, whereupon he told her he knew what he was doing, put the gun in his mouth, and pulled the trigger, having forgotten that there was a bullet in the chamber. Other versions having him playing Russian roulette, although just why he'd want to do this is never explained. The caliber of the gun is disputed: some say it was a .22, others a .32. Whatever happened, one thing was clear: in a second, Johnny Ace was dead. The incident would propel "Pledging My Love" to the top of the charts and instigate a weird death cult among black teenage girls, who erected shrines to him in their bedrooms in extreme cases. Nobody had ever seen anything like it. Don Robey, once he got over the shock, knew just what to do; he took all the stuff Ace had recorded and re- leased a ten-inch LP album, the *Johnny Ace Memorial Album,* one of R&B's first long players.

Sam Phillips was doing a bit better; "Good Rockin' Tonight" was selling well, and on January 1, 1955, Elvis had signed a management deal with Bob Neal, a local country music figure who had great con- nections in both the world of clubs and in Nashville. With Neal in the picture, Scotty Moore could stop booking the band and go back to doing what he did best: playing guitar. And Elvis's fame was spreading beyond Tennessee; that Texas connection had proven firm, and Elvis, Scotty, and Bill had played a big New Year's Eve show in Houston. A larger Texas tour was in the offing, and at some point early in the year, they went to Lubbock, way out in west Texas, but a town with a univer- sity and a legendary club, the Cotton Club, not named after the place in Harlem, but for one of the area's main crops. Managed by Western swing fiddler Tommy Hancock, it featured black and white enter- tainment (on separate evenings, of course), up to and including Duke

Ellington and Ernest Tubb. Naturally, Elvis drew a crowd of curious locals, including an up-and-coming country duo and their manager. Charles Hardin "Buddy" Holley and Bob Montgomery played "Western and Bop," according to their business card, which also gave their management contact as Hi Pockets Duncan, a DJ on local country station KDAV. Buddy and Bob played whatever gigs they could, and studied the competition thoroughly. They also recorded some at the radio station during its downtime. But, like most Lubbock teens, they didn't actually listen to the station; country music was just a bit square. It was something of a revelation to see this kid their own age tearing it up onstage at the Cotton Club. In between sets, Buddy and Bob went over to talk to the kid, who was sitting alone in a corner drinking a Coke. "You know," Buddy told Hi Pockets later, "he's a really nice, friendly fellow." The next day, there was a show at a Pontiac dealership's grand opening, and Elvis, Scotty, and Bill played that, as did Buddy and Bob, and they struck up something of a friendship with the guys from Tennessee. And in the next few weeks, Buddy and Bob were getting more and more requests for Elvis Presley tunes, so they learned them. The next time Elvis came, he'd moved up to a bus, which Buddy and Bob intercepted at the city limits. Elvis got out and into their car, and they took him on a tour of Lubbock's hot spots, such as they were, and then opened for him at the Cotton Club.

On the West Coast, the arrival of the new wave shook things up. Modern was the first victim: they all but shuttered the Modern label, and concentrated everything on their relatively new RPM label, which had the only consistently selling artist in their roster, B. B. King. They did use Modern to introduce Etta James, whose "The Wallflower" (also known as "Roll with Me, Henry") was a cleaned-up version of "Work with Me, Annie" where the work was clearly dancing. White singer Georgia Gibbs hopped right on it, and her version of the tune, "Dance with Me, Henry" (*also* known as "Wallflower"), was a #1 pop hit in March. (Gibbs had already started the year with a cover of LaVern Baker's "Tweedle Dee," which cut off Baker's rise on the pop charts right away. It was her first record, and she and the folks at Atlantic, which had issued the original, weren't pleased.) At least Hank Ballard had a sense of humor about James's (and Gibbs's) appropriation of his tune, and released "Henry's Got Flat Feet (Can't Dance No More)" later in the year. But James's stay with Modern wouldn't last long.

Over at Specialty, Art Rupe was having trouble with everything but gospel. His relationship with Johnny Vincent was going sour and resulted in Vincent's striking out on his own with Ace Records (named after a brand of comb) based in Jackson, Mississippi, but with Vincent's ears still cocked to New Orleans for talent. But Rupe desperately needed someone on the ground in New Orleans. In order to try to modernize his roster of R&B artists, he'd picked up an ambitious young black kid from Seattle (where he'd worked in a jazz band that had Ray Charles as pianist and a young trumpet player, Quincy Jones), Robert "Bumps" Blackwell. Blackwell had a good rapport with musicians, and, although not a top-notch instrumentalist, he had a way with arrangements, and Rupe figured he'd make a good producer. He set him to plowing through the demo tapes that were piling up at the office, and on his second week, he found a tape that had been mailed in a brown paper bag with grease stains on it. When he threaded it onto the machine, a voice said, "Mr. Art Rupe, you are now going to hear Little Richard and his Upsetters." He listened to a bit, then tossed the tape onto a pile of stuff to be mailed back to the senders. "The reason we listened to it a second time," Rupe remembered later, "was that Richard kept calling us and bothering us. He was calling us practically every other day." There was a reason for that; Richard was desperate. His records for Don Robey hadn't sold—the ones that had finally been issued, that is—and he was working the very lowest level of the chitlin' circuit when he wasn't washing dishes in the Macon bus station for a living. Rupe, his patience exhausted, went down to the audition studio and had Blackwell dig out the tape so they could both listen to it. "I made the decision that Richard did not sound like B. B. King, but he had the same feeling, and that, coupled with the gospel sound and a little more energy, was the basis for us being interested and deciding to sign him." In early March, he sent Richard's manager, Clint Brantley, a contract and set up a session in Atlanta. Unfortunately, it developed that Richard was still under contract to Robey, so the session was canceled until arrangements were made to buy him out of that contract. It took a while.

The vocal-group thing hadn't really taken off in California yet, with a couple of exceptions. Capitol had signed the Five Keys, who'd had an immense hit in 1951 with "The Glory of Love" on Aladdin and then disappeared. They started 1955 off with a novelty hit, "Ling Ting Tong," a racist bit about the title character, who lived in Chinatown and had a song he sung: "Eye a smokum boo-eye-ay, eye a smokum boo." It's unlikely many Chinese Americans bought the record, but plenty of other people did; it almost made the top ten on the pop charts. The vocal group record that did make the top-ten pop, though, was one nobody would have predicted: "Earth Angel" by the Penguins. Despite being primitive and seemingly uncopyable, the Crew-Cuts jumped in with their anodyne version, which chased the Penguins up and down the charts. The Penguins, however, did much better on the jukebox charts, which probably reflected better what teenagers really wanted. Realizing this, Mercury Records in Chicago went to the Penguins' manager, a guy named Buck Ram, who'd kicked around LA doing arrangements for bands, and begged him to let them sign the group. Ram agreed, as long as they'd also take another group he'd been managing, the Platters, who'd flopped on King. Mercury figured it'd be worth the risk; the Penguins clearly had what record buyers wanted, and the Platters didn't, but if that was what it took, they'd sign the deal. Of course, the Penguins never had anything close to a hit after that, but Ram had added a woman to the Platters, Zola Taylor, and somehow she was the missing element. They were allowed to cut a single in April, lead singer Tony Williams found a voice he'd never used in the studio before, the other Platters closed in around him with harmonies, and "Only You (And You Alone)" became the first of 45 crossover chart records for the group.

In Chicago, the Chess brothers were doing just fine. Muddy Waters, it seemed, could do no wrong, and Howlin' Wolf was right behind him. Little Walter still hadn't surpassed "Juke," but not for want of trying, and the group Allen Freed had brought them, the Moonglows, had hit big with "Sincerely," so big that their stay on the pop charts was only broken by the McGuire Sisters' cover, which went to the top. No matter—the group had more where that came from, and "We Belong Together" followed shortly, and didn't get covered—or pop airplay. The brothers' open-door policy paid off yet again in February, when Ellas McDaniel and Billy Boy Arnold showed up with a demo they'd cut, "I'm a Man" and "Uncle John." Asked to return the next day, McDaniel and Arnold found an audience waiting to hear the demo: Muddy Waters, Little Walter, and both Chess brothers. Everyone loved both tunes. "Uncle John" had a pounding, insistent beat over which McDaniel sang what were essentially nursery rhymes, and "I'm a Man" exuded menace over a slow, stop-time backing. A couple of changes had to be made, though; it was bad enough that McDaniel, in real life a retired boxer, looked like an accountant with his black-framed glasses, but the name had to go. Billy Boy remembered the Southern practice of nailing a wire to a barn and attaching the other end to a broom, then twanging it to make sounds: the diddley-bow. His friend became Bo Diddley, and the next day, March 2, they split a session, with a friend of theirs, Jerome Green, playing maracas. Billy Boy's songs didn't get issued. Bo Diddley's did, and "Bo Diddley" and "I'm a Man" was a two-sided hit right out of the box.

If we had to pick a moment when rock & roll was born as a major movement in American popular music (and we don't), May 1955 would be a good candidate. Bill Haley and the Comets had launched their sanitized version of Big Joe Turner's "Shake, Rattle and Roll" in August 1954, but his follow-ups like "Mambo Rock" and "Birth of the Boogie" didn't do nearly as well. Then, in May, something with a little more attitude and a lot better beat started showing life. "Rock Around the Clock" had been released in 1954 and had just lain there, but someone had made a film about juvenile delinquency in high school, *The Blackboard Jungle,* and as a way of starting it off with the right atmosphere, had run the song over the film's opening moments. That was all that was necessary; kids ran to the record stores for a copy of the song, and in May 1955, it topped the charts. Haley was a very unlikely teen idol—chubby, thirty years old, with a ridiculous spit curl on his forehead—and the rest of the Comets were around the same age, but there was something challenging, a line drawn in the sand, around this rather mild-sounding record. Something else happened, too: the film was released in England.

In mid-May, Muddy Waters told the Chess brothers about a guitar-and-piano duo he'd caught in a St. Louis club, the Cosmopolitan. Chuck Berry and Johnny Johnson had decided to see if they could get something going in Chicago and had contacted Muddy when they got into town. Berry said that Chess was his first choice and that he had just presented himself there, but other sources suggest that he'd been tossed out of Mercury first and had maybe gone to Vee-Jay. But the Chess brothers had heard Muddy's enthusiasm, and then Berry walked in with a demo tape he and Johnson had made. The song Berry was trying to sell was "Wee Wee Hours," which Johnson accurately referred to as "a regular old blues in G," but the song that lit up Phil Chess's ears was Berry's version of a country song, a fiddle tune with a long and venerable history, "Ida Red." It had been recorded by Bob Wills (in 1950, as "Ida Red Loves the Boogie"), by Jack Guthrie, and, probably the version Berry emulated because it was fairly current, Cowboy Copas. Berry, an admirer of Louis Jordan's tricky wordplay, had recast the lyrics, turning them into an exciting car chase as the singer pursues his girlfriend, running away with another guy. Said Phil Chess, it was "different . . . Like nothing we'd heard before. We figured if we could get that sound down on record we'd have a hit . . . The song had a new kind of feel about it." Of course, as "Ida Red," it couldn't be copyrighted, being traditional, so they suggested Berry work on another title. Since he'd also trained as a cosmetologist, he came up with "Maybellene," after the popular line of cosmetics, and then fiddled with the melody of the chorus a tiny bit. On May 21, they (Berry, Johnson, drummer Ebby Hardy, Chess house bassist Willie Dixon, and the omnipresent Jerome Green on maracas) went into the studio and cut it. It took them forever, since Phil and Leonard had no idea what they were looking for, and at one point, they stuck a microphone in the bathroom for Berry to sing into and get some echo. Berry claims it took thirty-five takes to get it right. But oh, did they get it right. So right that they didn't release it for two months; "Bo Diddley" was still selling well, and

Muddy's version of "I'm a Man," entitled "Manish [sic] Boy," was also a big hit. "Maybellene" (with "Wee Wee Hours" on the back) sat in the can for two months until Leonard went to New York for a business meeting with Alan Freed. He left an acetate of the record—no names, no song titles—with him and said, "Play this." Freed did. "By the time I got back to Chicago, Freed had called a dozen times, saying it was his biggest record ever." Chess was very conservative about new records, rarely pressing more than two thousand copies on a first run. "Maybellene" got them to press ten thousand just to satisfy the demand coming out of New York (on one show, Freed apparently played the record straight for two hours), and then things went insane. Cover versions (one by country singer Marty Robbins) appeared and were ignored. Answer records ("Come Back Maybellene") were recorded and ignored. Only the original would do. Teenagers purchasing copies and spinning it on jukeboxes certainly didn't notice that the first pressing listed Chuck Berry as sole author, and that pressings made after August added Alan Freed and one Russ Fratto, landlord of the building Chess was in. It's easy enough to see why Chess would cut Freed in for a piece of the pie, and one could speculate several good reasons for the landlord's presence in the credits, although Leonard Chess's son Marshall's speculation that Berry set the deal up with him as a cash advance against royalties seems unlikely; he hadn't become as sophisticated about the music business as he later became.

Another thing that happened in May was that Lew Chudd finally got the breakthrough he'd been hoping for from Fats Domino. Since "The Fat Man" in 1950, Fats had done well on the R&B charts, but although some pop radio played him, he hadn't charted. All that changed with "Ain't That a Shame," a mid-tempo song with a strolling piano line right up front and Fats's winsome vocal singing about heartbreak. It was irresistible, and not only topped the R&B charts, but also got to #10 on the pop charts and established him there. Chudd then grabbed another Dave Bartholomew–produced number he had by the guitarist Smiley Lewis, an old New Orleans tune called "I Hear You Knockin'," with yet another talented local pianist, Huey Smith, doing the honors, and got a hit out of that, too. Chudd seemed to have a lock on New Orleans, although the Chess brothers were trying to get a foothold there. In January, they'd gotten lucky with a vocal group called the Hawkettes, because they'd gotten their record "Mardi Gras Mambo" out in time for citywide saturation during that period, but the group was unstable and vanished, which was a shame; the young kid who'd sung the lead vocal, Aaron Neville, seemed to have something. (In October, via Johnny Vincent, they also put out a record by Bobby Charles, who'd sung "See You Later, Alligator" to one of the brothers over the phone. A couple of months later, they were shocked to discover that his real name was Robert Charles Guidry and that he was a white Cajun.)

As for Elvis, he'd been playing the *Louisiana Hayride* when he wasn't touring. A lot of the touring he was doing was on package shows, often headlined by Hank Snow, a diminutive Canadian who'd been cranking out hits since the '40s and who was managed by a large, rough—some would say crude—man called Colonel Tom Parker. Parker claimed to be an orphan who'd grown up in Florida, and had actually been a dogcatcher in Tampa for a while before getting a job with a traveling carnival. Carnivals were a prime outlet for up-and-coming country stars, and one, a tall, handsome lad with a fine voice, caught Parker's eye. Eddy Arnold was on his way to stardom, and Parker signed him to a management contract, which meant that when Arnold signed with RCA Records, Parker was exposed to a major record company and its workings. Everyone agreed that negotiating with Parker was essentially a lost cause; if you wanted Eddy Arnold, you dealt with the Colonel (an honorary title he'd gotten from the governor of Louisiana, former country star Jimmie Davis), and although he made the occasional small concession, he won all the big points. The carnival never left his blood; while Arnold was up onstage singing, the Colonel, a cigar jammed in his mouth, was hawking Eddy Arnold songbooks, souvenir programs, and glossy photographs (which the star would sign after the show). Attempts to change Arnold's fees were doomed; Parker would never budge. In fact, his unwillingness to budge cost him his star. Nobody's sure exactly what happened, but in 1953, Arnold fired him. Parker continued to book Arnold, but that was it. He had various other things going, especially with a few country artists, but by early 1954, he was working exclusively with Hank Snow, also an RCA artist, whose show also included his young son, Jimmie Rodgers Snow. With Elvis now in possession of a contract with the *Louisiana Hayride,* he was performing often on bills with both Eddy Arnold and Hank Snow, and Parker was becoming more and more interested in him.

On February 6, Elvis was booked on a show at Ellis Auditorium in Memphis, a good-sized venue where he performed fourth on the bill below Faron Young, Ferlin Husky, and gospel singer Martha Carson. His new manager, Bob Neal, had set up a meeting with Elvis and Scotty, Tom Parker, Sam Phillips, Oscar Davis (Parker's advance man), and Tom Diskin, who was a partner with the Colonel and Snow in Jamboree Attractions, the firm that handled the Hank Snow tours. Elvis was already booked on one, starting a few days hence, and Neal thought it would be a good idea to get all the people in Elvis's professional life together in one place, a restaurant around the corner from the Ellis. From all reports, it was pretty tense. Parker started off by insulting Sam, who had already developed a strong dislike for the old carny, by saying that Elvis wouldn't get far on Sun— certainly not as far as he would on RCA. Neal had to calm things down by introducing the subject of the coming tour, and noting that by working with Parker, he'd be able to get Elvis into territories he hadn't yet played, thus increase record sales. Neal and Parker were already working together on setting up tours and were looking forward to working together in the future. Elvis and Scotty just sat silently while this drama was going on and eventually left to play the show.

The tour went as planned; all through west Texas, one of Elvis's best markets, and, in May, down to Florida, where he met a woman named Mae Boren Axton, who was a promoter and had been balancing teaching school, journalism, and songwriting. She interviewed him and worked with Parker on promoting the shows, and noticed his increasing interest in Elvis; he had, she later said, "dollar marks in his eyes." An RCA promotion man who was down there to help out Jimmie Rodgers Snow was impressed by Elvis, and, seeing Parker's interest, went to a record store and bought Elvis's complete catalog—four

singles, at that point—and took them back to Nashville to give to Steve
Sholes, the head of RCA's country division. He, too, was impressed.
But there was no other movement; Elvis's agreement with Bob Neal
had been renegotiated and now ran through 1956. Country music,
though, was changing slightly. Twenty-three-year-old Faron Young
was aiming for younger fans when he recorded "Going Steady" in 1953,
his first hit, and he almost edged into juvenile delinquent territory with
his 1955 hit "Live Fast, Love Hard, Die Young (And Leave a Beautiful
Memory)," and the charts even welcomed two of Elvis's Sun records
that year: "Baby Let's Play House" (a cover of R&B artist Arthur
Gunter) and "I'm Left, You're Right, She's Gone," a song written by a
Memphis fan, and "I Forgot to Remember to Forget," written by a
young singer Sam was working with, Charlie Feathers, which had Junior Parker's "Mystery Train" on the other side. Neither of these dented
the pop charts; Elvis was still an eccentric country artist. Still, other
country hopefuls took notice. Roy Orbison, who had a band with its
own radio show elsewhere in west Texas, thought he was disgusting
and dressed badly; Bob Luman vowed to practice guitar more. Buddy
and Bob, in Lubbock, went to Nesman Recording Studios in Wichita
Falls, as well as a studio in Dallas—a long haul—and the KDAV studios where they now had a show, and recorded a bunch of originals as
demos to circulate to any record companies that might come knocking. They were pretty straight country tunes, and the boys had occasional help in the studio from fiddler Sonny Curtis and drummer Jerry
Allison.

As inevitably happens, summer passes and it's back to school
again. Alan Freed celebrated this by renting the Brooklyn Paramount
Theatre for the week of September 2 to hold his back-to-school show,
featuring Tony Bennett, the Harptones, Nappy Brown, the Moonglows, the Red Prysock Band (whose singles in 1955 included "Rock
and Roll" and "Zonked"), and, for the first time outside St. Louis
and Chicago's clubs, Chuck Berry, singing his hit "Maybellene," and,
at a climactic part of his short performance (the acts only got to do a
couple of songs in order to keep the show moving, and in any event,
that's as many as most of them had in their repertoire), sticking the
bottom of the guitar into his stomach, extending the neck straight

out, and, picking a repetitive pattern, executing an odd, bent-kneed walk across the stage, head bobbing in rhythm like a duck. The kids went wild. And there were lots of kids; Freed had no problem filling the theater show after show, grossing $154,000 for the week. Even after paying off production costs and cutting in his manager, Morris Levy, and WINS, his station, that was a pretty nice payday.

Freed might not have had a problem, but there was an increasing worry that American society had one. *The Blackboard Jungle* was an attempt to deal with it, as was, perhaps more sympathetically, *Rebel Without a Cause*. The former provoked riots in theaters—not all the time, but enough that some chains blocked it—and its story about kids out of control in the nation's public schools hit home. In its most symbolic scene, a teacher, played by Richard Riley, brings in his jazz records to try to reach the students in his inner-city classroom and they not only make fun of his taste but smash the records. There's no rock & roll (or, indeed, any music) in *Rebel,* based on a real-life case study from 1944 by Los Angeles psychologist Robert M. Lindner, but the three teenagers at its center were compelling. James Dean plays the seventeen-year-old Jim, a confused teenager who's new in town and has been picked up by the police for being drunk in public. Also at the police station are John, a smart but confused young man whose nickname is Plato, played by Sal Mineo, and Judy, played by Natalie Wood. As outsiders at their high school, they bond over their problems with their parents, and engage in some antisocial activity like drag racing, which winds up getting another delinquent youth killed. The subversive message of the film, although it has a fairly happy ending, is that sometimes bad behavior on the part of teen-agers is due to a bad upbringing at home, and that parents bear some responsibility for how their kids act out. This was a fairly radical no-tion for most of the country, and the fact that teenagers flocked to see the film again and again was upsetting. The fact that at least part of the reason they did so was to gaze on James Dean and Natalie Wood (and, perhaps some of them, the gay Sal Mineo) seemed not to matter. And of course there was the unspoken bit: although one rarely saw black people in anything but menial positions in films (al-though one of the juvenile delinquents in Glenn Ford's classroom is played by a young Sidney Poitier), rock & roll seemed to be either black people or white trash who were little better, socially speaking.

Ah, but worse was to come: with the recording sessions with Little Richard on hold until he could get his release from Don Robey, it was mid-September before Art Rupe and Richard's manager could get something together, and this time the most convenient place was New Orleans. Bumps Blackwell was still learning his job, and Rupe cast him into the fire: supervise a recording session with this guy and come back with a hit. On September 13, Bumps, Richard, and a handful of Dave Bartholomew's musicians convened at Cosimo Matassa's J&M Studio, site of all of New Orleans's hits (and still the only recording studio in town) and took stock of one another. Lee Allen and Red Tyler were on saxophones, Earl Palmer was on drums, and Huey Smith was on piano. Smith was later to say, "I played on the session before he became a piano player," and it's true that next to New Orleans pianists like Fats Domino or Roy "Professor Longhair" Byrd, Georgia-born Richard wasn't much of a virtuoso, and Richard felt the resentment in the studio: "They thought I was stupid and crazy and that I didn't know where I was going." They managed four songs that day, mostly slow blues, which is what Richard had been cutting for RCA and Peacock, and nobody was happy. These were tame numbers that he used to fill out his stage act. The next day they came back again and did four more tunes, and still nothing was happening. Bumps called a lunch break, and everyone headed down to the Dew Drop Inn, where Richard had played a number of times, as presumably the other musicians had, too. They ordered food and some drinks, and Richard spied the piano up on the bandstand. He jumped up and started playing a number he usually reserved for his shows at gay bars: "A-wop-bopa-lubop-a-good-god-damn! Tutti frutti, good booty!" and giving out with an Alex Bradford / Ray Charles gospel whoop. He was going nuts, beyond the pale of decent behavior with the lyrics, although not nearly as far beyond as some of the stuff that had been performed on the Dew Drop Inn's stage. He was also doing something that even inexperienced Bumps Blackwell could recognize as something different and new. But . . . those lyrics! Art Rupe had provided Blackwell with a huge list of resources in

New Orleans, and among them was a songwriter named Dorothy Labostrie. He ran to the bar's phone and called her to come to J&M and help rewrite the song. Richard was horrified; he couldn't even *recite* those lyrics to a lady! Bumps and Mrs. Labostrie reassured him that she was married and had had children and was there to help him out, so Richard took her into a corner and whispered the lyrics, line by line, as she scribbled into a notebook. Time was running out, the musicians were getting antsy, and the saxophonists were already breaking down their instruments and putting them into their cases. There was fifteen minutes left on the clock, not enough time for Huey Smith to learn the piano part, which meant Richard re-creating his performance from the Dew Drop Inn. "Wait a minute!" Bumps said to the horn players as Mrs. Labostrie finished up and showed him the lyrics. Richard took to the piano and laid out an arrangement with Bumps's help, and ten minutes later they had two takes. The musicians still thought it was stupid—"It sounded stupid to me when we did it," guitarist Justin Adams said later. "It wasn't sayin' nothin'. But I still get checks off of it!" The real key to the session, though, was drummer Earl Palmer, whose almost mechanical backbeat propelled the song without a hint of swing. "I just felt that's what it called for," he said with characteristic modesty. "I didn't think much of it at the time, that it was startin' anything." Oh, but it did; in the five minutes those two takes took, Earl Palmer had invented rock & roll drumming, setting a rhythmic template that would endure for decades and make him a wealthy, if unknown, musician. Little Richard, too, had invented something; reaching back through years of striving, of living in a shadow world of black Southern gay bars, of hollering his lungs out while washing dishes in bus stations and dives, he had finished inventing Little Richard. Blackwell took the tape back to Los Angeles, telling Mr. Rupe that it was the next "Maybellene," because, as Rupe explained, "It was up-tempo and had novelty lyrics. Actually, the reason I picked it wasn't solely for the tempo, it was because of the wild intro . . . What was interesting was how rapidly that thing caught on. I don't think we had had a record catch on that fast." By December, it was working its way up the pop charts— the *pop* charts!

America was about to enter a state of emergency. Already it was marshalling its defenses; in Nashville, Charles Eugene "Pat" Boone, a clean-cut, well-spoken young man who might have been some mad scientist's attempt at an anti-Elvis, was toiling away on Randy Woods's Dot label, releasing anodyne covers of black records: "Ain't That a Shame," "At My Front Door (Crazy Little Mama)," and, unbelievably enough, almost simultaneously with the original, "Tutti Frutti." (That didn't do too well, but there was more to come.) Studies were launched to see if this music caused juvenile delinquency. At least there was hope in the year's biggest fad: Walt Disney had a television program, *Disneyland*, which, like the amusement park, divided its weekly shows into Tomorrowland, Adventureland, Fantasyland, and Frontierland, and the Frontierland parts were serializing the life of Davy Crockett, the Tennessee outdoorsman who'd left the state for Texas (his famous quote, delivered to the Tennessee legislature, where he was serving: "I will go to Texas and you can go to hell") and died during the Texas revolution defending the Alamo. The episodes' theme song was a tremendous hit for no fewer than four performers (Bill Hayes, "Tennessee" Ernie Ford, Fess Parker, who played Crockett in Disney's series, and Walter Schumann) and set off a fad for coonskin caps and BB guns.

But, as 1955 ended and the Drifters' "White Christmas" started making its annual ascent of the charts, the change was only starting.

chapter seven

1956: INTO THE BIG TIME

The Teenagers: *(left to right)* Sherman Garnes, Frankie Lymon,
Jimmy Merchant, Herman Santiago, and Billy Lobrano.
(Pictorial Press Ltd./Alamy Stock Photo)

Colonel Tom Parker was unstoppable. He'd booked Elvis on package tours all over the South during the summer and early fall of 1955, and when the boy was on the road, he'd call the Presley household to assure them—well, mostly Elvis's mother, Gladys—that things were well. Gladys didn't much trust the Colonel. He was a smooth talker, and she saw through that. There was a while when he was pressuring the Presleys to sign a contract—Elvis was still twenty, too young—naming him as a "special advisor" to Bob Neal. Privately, he'd tell those close to him that he was just waiting for March 1956 when Elvis's deal with Neal expired, and that he'd just swoop on in and take over. Meanwhile, Neal and Sam Phillips were letting out the rumor that Elvis's Sun contract was for sale. Sam desperately needed money; the success of Elvis's records put him in a classic position. The label took on the risk of pressing the records on credit, then shipping them to the distributors, who had ninety days to pay up on the ones sold, returning unsold records for 100 percent credit. A sudden run on a given title, a hit, would mean that the label owed the pressing plants and hoped that the distributors would pay up on time. And Sun was no longer a one-artist label. It never had been, but Sam was developing Carl Perkins, and there was a new kid from Arkansas, Johnny Cash, for whom he saw great promise in the country market. And it wasn't just the pressing plants, either; Sam's brother, Jud, had invested in the label a year ago, buying out Jim Bulleit's share, and was hoping for some return. Given Decca's success with Bill Haley, maybe a major label taking on a rock & roll artist made sense. Mitch Miller at Columbia called Bill Neal and asked what the contract was going for, and Sam told Bill to ask $18,000, to which Miller said, "Oh, forget it, nobody's worth that much." Decca, Capitol, Mercury, Chess, Atlantic (who offered a colossal $25,000—which was "everything we had, including my desk," Ahmet Ertegun told Elvis biographer Jerry Hopkins), all of them made offers. None was sufficient.

Finally, in August, Parker got the Presleys and Neal to sign a document making him a "special advisor" to Elvis and Bob, and added a clause at the end that gave him the right to "negotiate all renewals on existing contracts." Elvis then went back out on the road with a better fee for performances (although the band was only getting a pittance, further reduced when they added D. J. Fontana on drums at Elvis's request), at one point touring with Bill Haley and playing as far away as Cleveland. Meanwhile, Parker and RCA were deep in negotiations, because that's where the Colonel wanted Elvis to wind up. At the end of October, Sam and the Colonel and Tom Diskin met in Memphis, and Parker told Sam that RCA was offering $25,000 for the contract and would go no higher. Sam, knowing that he had to pay Jud back and that he also owed Elvis $5,000 in unpaid back royalties, dug in his heels at $35,000. By the time of Nashville's annual DJ Week in November, Elvis was on everybody's mind. He'd been named most promising young country star by *Billboard* and *Cash Box*, and he was there with his parents, meeting and greeting industry people. Bob Neal was there, realizing he was about to be consigned to history, at least in terms of Elvis's story, and of course the Colonel was there; true to his roots, he'd tied a live elephant down at the Andrew Jackson Hotel, wearing a banner saying, "Like an elephant Hank Snow never forgets. Thanks Dee Jays." Elvis also ran into Mae Boren Axton, who insisted that a song she'd written would be his first million seller once he signed with RCA. Some friends had shown her a newspaper article about a teenager who'd committed suicide, leaving a note that read only "I walk a lonely street," and she'd populated that street with a hotel. Elvis really wasn't interested in being pitched songs, but Mrs. Axton had been so good to him in Florida that he took a couple of minutes out to listen to it and then had her play it over and over, probably memorizing it as she did.

On November 21, they had finally solidified all the deals around the new contract, including Bob Neal's payoff, and a gaggle of RCA folks, Sam, and Hank Snow (probably because he was the Colonel's partner in Jamboree Attractions) gathered at Sun and did the deed. RCA took over the matter of the unpaid royalties, $35,000 was the price, Elvis's royalty rate on records sold went from Sun's 3 percent to 5 percent, and there was a complex publishing deal with Hill and Range Music, one of the biggest music publishers in the country. In addition to Sun, Sam now owned radio station WHER, whose gimmick was all-female air personalities, one of whom was Marion Keisker, and so from the signing, Elvis and his parents and Hank Snow and the Colonel all jammed into the studio there while Ms. Keisker moderated a chat celebrating the signing. And so, two days after his twenty-first birthday, on January 10, 1956, Elvis walked into RCA Studios in New York to record "Heartbreak Hotel."

Nor was it just Elvis whose career was suddenly taking off. In early December 1955, Marty Robbins's manager, Eddie Crandall, had seen Buddy and Bob perform and had also probably been at an all-night jam session after the gig with Robbins's band and Holley and Montgomery's band at the Cotton Club. He wrote a note to Dave Stone, owner of WDAV, where the boys had their show that "I'm very confident that I can get Buddy Holley a recording contract. It may not be a major, but even a small one would be beneficial to someone who is trying to get a break." He then sent a telegram asking Stone to make a four-song demo on the boys, with the caveat "Don't change [Buddy's] style at all." Then he went to work; he finally got Jim Denny, who had a long association with the *Grand Ole Opry*, to make some inquiries on behalf of Buddy, and, after getting turned down by Columbia, he got Paul Cohen at Decca interested. Cohen asked for Buddy to call him, and in the lead-up to that conversation, he asked Denny if Bob Montgomery was supposed to go with him.

"He can't sing on the records," Denny said. "We want one singer, not two." And when he sat down with Bob to see how he felt about it, Buddy's mother remembered that he answered, "You've got your chance—now go ahead!" (Montgomery went on to become a very successful songwriter in Nashville and died in 2014.)

Buddy was good and ready to go, but first he needed a band, which, given his contacts around Lubbock, wouldn't be hard. But he also wanted a first-rate instrument for himself—an amplified acoustic guitar had been fine for the country numbers with Bob, and he had a cheap electric guitar, but he wanted something better—so he approached his older brother Larry for a loan of $1,000. Larry had his own business and was doing well, although he was a bit shocked at the fact that his brother was actually going to spend $600 on a Fender Stratocaster guitar. Still, he, like the rest of the family, was caught up in Buddy's absolute conviction that he was going to be a star, so he loaned him the money. Buddy got further into debt when the Holleys bought a new car and gave him the old one, provided he take over the payments. In late January, he loaded the band's equipment (with the bass fiddle in the traditional place, atop the car), and Sonny Curtis, who was now playing guitar, and Don Guess, his new bassist, into the car and took off on the long drive to Nashville and, they all hoped, stardom. They had to leave their drummer, Jerry Allison, behind because he had to go to high school.

The problems—or, if you were thinking positively, as Buddy was, adjustments—started as soon as they got into town. Decca told Buddy that they were okay with him using his band, but they didn't want him playing rhythm guitar because they were concerned about leakage into the vocal mike, so they called in Nashville session cat Grady Martin for that. They also didn't want rock & roll drumming—which they wouldn't get from Buddy's band because Allison was still in Lubbock—so they enlisted Doug Kirkham to play percussion. The Lubbock crew all had to join the musicians' union, too; the folks at Decca were shocked that they hadn't. Overseeing the sessions was the studio's owner, Owen Bradley, whose converted Quonset hut had legendary sonic properties and was known all over Nashville as Bradley's Barn. The session on January 26 resulted in four songs: "Blue

Days, Black Nights," "Don't Come Back Knockin'," "Love Me," and the only non-original, "Midnight Shift." (For those who think of Buddy as a kind of cute, innocent kid, the latter tune, a third cousin to the "Annie" songs that begins with the words "If you see ol' Annie, better give her a lift/Cause Annie's been working on the midnight shift," will give some insight into his dangerous side.) Having done their duty to Decca, they got back in the car and drove back to Lubbock. In April, a single came out: "Blue Days, Black Nights" b/w (backed with) "Love Me." Neither side was particularly representative of what Buddy wanted to do, and, as an extra problem, they'd misspelled his name as "Holly" on the label. And despite having Bill Haley on their label, Decca had no idea what to do with Buddy. (Haley had been signed through the New York office, which was more used to dealing with pop music than Nashville was.) In retrospect, Owen Bradley admitted to Holly biographer John Goldrosen that "it just wasn't the right combination; the chemistry wasn't right. It just wasn't meant to be. We didn't understand and he didn't know how to tell us." And the record's sales and radio play reflected just that. It was okay; there was still a contract, and there would be more sessions in Nashville later in the year.

Back at Sun, Carl Perkins had been awaiting his chance. He hung around as much as he could and became good friends with Elvis. Sam would rehearse him and hear the ideas he was working with, intrigued by his obvious talent with country tunes, but also his ability to rock. After all, he'd been doing it as long as Elvis had, and he wanted to get some recorded. One day, Sam suggested that because his music was so different, his stage clothes should reflect that, and mentioned Lansky's, where Elvis and a slew of Memphis R&B acts got their clothing. They did their shopping, and Elvis found a blue shirt for his friend and then said it'd look good with black slacks. Carl, who'd been intrigued by the silk stripe on tuxedo pants, took them home and had his wife sew a pink ribbon on the legs, which blew Elvis away the next time they met; Carl had just upstaged the Hillbilly Cat! Now he just had to get some music to match the clothes; Sam had a label called Flip that he used for non-union musicians, and Carl's first record had appeared there in February 1955. He switched him to Sun for a country release, "Gone, Gone, Gone" b/w "Let the Jukebox Keep On Playing," in September, but perhaps because of all the drama around Elvis at that point, nothing much came of it, although "Jukebox" was excellent for a Memphis country record, and "Gone" was inching toward rock & roll. The summer of 1955 saw Carl, Elvis, and Johnny Cash, Sam's latest signing, who had taken an instant shine to Carl, doing some small shows around Memphis, and one day in Parkin, Arkansas, they were hanging around in the dressing room when Cash asked Carl if he'd been writing anything recently. "Ain't nothin' worth writing home about," Carl told him.

"Tell you what," Cash replied, "I had an idea you ought to write you a song about blue suede shoes."

Carl shrugged. "I don't know nothin' about them shoes, John."

He had, however, noticed them showing up in places like Lansky's. But surely there were more important things to write about than footwear.

Then, in October, Union University in Jackson, Carl's hometown, asked the Perkins Brothers Band to play a show at a nightclub they'd rented, and they showed up and started rocking out, which the crowd appreciated. As performers will do, Carl fixed his gaze on a young couple who were dancing particularly well and watched them respond to what he was playing. At some point, between songs, he'd lost visual contact with them when he heard a threatening male voice say, "Uh-uh. Don't step on my suedes!" It was the boy he'd been watching, and the girl, sounding terrified, replied, "I'm sorry. I'm really sorry." Carl looked down, and the boy was wearing blue suede shoes, one of which now had a scuff mark on it. *Good gracious*, Carl thought as he packed up at the end of the evening. *A pretty little thing like that, and all he can think about is his blue suede shoes.* The trouble was, the memory of Cash's suggestion then entered his mind, and as he tried to get to sleep that evening, blue suede shoes was all *he* could think about. With his wife and kids sleeping peaceably, he went into the kitchen and grabbed his electric guitar, not plugging it in. A song was forming. There was a paper sack of potatoes on the counter, and he emptied it to give himself something to write on as the song came to him. Finally, the song completed, he went to bed. As soon as he woke up, though, he headed straight for his guitar to see if he still had it straight. He was playing through it and his wife, Valda, perked up. "Carl, I like that," she said. "I really *like* that!" Carl, who'd already mapped out an arrangement for the band, said, "Well, if you like it now, wait'll you hear it when Clayton, Jay, and W. S. join in." After breakfast, he got Jay from across the street, and they ran through the number. That Saturday, two things happened: Carl called Sam and told him he wanted to record this new song right away and even sang it over the phone to him. Sam was encouraging, but in no rush. That night, though, the Perkins Brothers played it at a dance in a honky-tonk and wound up playing it eight times—even better than rehearsing! But Sam was taking his time. The shows with Elvis and Cash continued to happen, and Carl's confidence was at an all-time high, so much so that he stole the show from Elvis twice in a row that fall, and mysteriously, Elvis never worked with him again. Then, on December 19, Sam called a session and said, "Do me that 'Shoes' song." Carl didn't have to be asked twice. They did three takes, and Carl was in orbit. He didn't even realize what he'd done and wanted to keep going, but Sam had already decided the second take was the one, and after a while, Carl realized he was right.

Now they needed another song for the other side of the record, and Carl whipped one out that the band didn't much like because it had an odd chord progression in its first few bars. Carl was feeling very certain of himself by now—"Blue Suede Shoes" had invigorated him, and after a bit of yelling at the band, they went through three takes of the song "Honey Don't." It, too, was a rocker, but not as crazed as "Blue Suede Shoes," and after three takes Sam figured they'd gotten it. Just to have some more Carl Perkins in the can, though, he got the band to record two more songs since they were all feeling pretty good by now. "Sure to Fall" was a duet with Jay, and a country ballad, expertly rendered, and next up was a very odd song Carl had written in tribute to his home state; "Tennessee" celebrated a number of things, with the chorus asking us to "give old Tennessee credit for music," but concluding with a verse celebrating the atomic bomb, of all things, the first of which, the song claimed, was made in Tennessee. (Oak

Ridge National Laboratory had, indeed, refined the uranium used in the first couple of bombs.) Then the band piled into their car and went back to Jackson, arriving in the early hours of the morning. Sam, for his part, had already gone to work, calling up Dewey Phillips and telling him that he had another smash hit. He mastered the tapes and sent out orders for stampers to be delivered to the pressing plant on two records, "Blue Suede Shoes" b/w "Honey Don't" and "Tennessee" b/w "Sure to Fall." He released the first one on New Year's Day 1956 and stuck two 78s in the mail to Carl. They arrived broken. Carl was so anxious to have a copy to play everyone that he went into town to the music store where he got strings and where the owner had sold him a Gibson Les Paul guitar on easy terms, and asked for a copy. He didn't recognize what he saw. "No, sir," he told the storekeeper, "that ain't my record. See, my record's a great big one with a little bitty hole in it." He'd never seen a 45 before, and he was devastated; everyone knew what a record looked like, and it didn't look like that. The man told him that that's what all the new records looked like, that juke-boxes were now stocked with them, but it didn't matter to Carl; he had nothing to play it on at home. After his wife calmed him down, he drove back to the music store and got a multispeed record player and a copy of the record to play.

He was lucky to get one; it had taken off beyond anyone's expecta-tions. Sam got a call from his distributor in Cleveland; Bill Randle, a veteran disc jockey who was one of the few who got rock & roll right from the start and judiciously added some to his programming, had jumped on the record, and the distributor wanted twenty-five thousand copies right away. Bob Neal was booking the Perkins Brothers, and sent them out on the road with Johnny Cash, and got Carl bookings on the *Big D Jamboree*, an *Opry*-like show in Dallas, where he went over just great, and soon the band was playing all over Texas and New Mexico. This was helped by Texas's long history of loving innovative and un-usual forms of country music—which is what rockabilly, the term Carl used for what he was doing, was thought of at that point—and everywhere they went, he and Cash used Sam's advice and promoted their records by showing up at radio stations to thank them for play-ing them. Cash's record, "So Doggone Lonesome" b/w "Folsom

Prison Blues," was also doing well, and Neal was able to ask more and more for gigs as January turned into February. And by the end of February, something major was happening: "Blue Suede Shoes" entered the pop charts—as did Elvis's first RCA single, Mae Boren Axton's "Heartbreak Hotel." Elvis was in a recording frenzy in the New York RCA studios, and was preparing to release an album as soon as he could. One of the songs he had in the can was "Blue Suede Shoes." Not that either he or RCA was going to release it as a single. It was just there. He played it on his second TV appearance, on *The Dorsey Brothers Stage Show,* but then, he'd played "Tutti Frutti," another song he had in the can, on his first appearance in February.

March was a blur of recording and performing for Carl, and in April he did the *Ozark Jamboree* television program, and Sam told him he'd gotten booked on a national show, Perry Como's show out of New York. What Sam didn't tell him was that he was going to surprise him by giving him the gold record for "Blue Suede Shoes" on the show: a million dollars' worth of records sold and certified by the Recording Industry Association of America.

On March 21, the band, which was by now traveling in a Chrysler limousine that Sam had rented so that they'd hit New York in style, stopped in Norfolk, Virginia, to play the Norfolk Auditorium. The promoter wanted Carl's opinion on a kid he'd just signed and was going to produce, Gene Craddock, who'd been mustered out of the Navy after a motorcycle accident had damaged his left leg. Carl watched the kid and his band and heard them do the song they were going to cut. Carl told the promoter that it was sort of like "Blue Suede Shoes," in that "there ain't a lot to it, but it's an effective ol' song." Then, after they'd sown pandemonium in a sold-out house once again, the boys got back into the limo and headed to New York. As the sun rose the next day, the limo's driver fell asleep at the wheel and rear-ended a truck. The limo then rolled four times, took out a guardrail, and went off the side of a bridge into a creek. Fluke Holland, the drummer, was the first to wake up and found Carl wedged under the backseat of the car, head in the stream. He grabbed him and pulled him to safety. Jay had a broken neck and internal injuries, and the rest of the band was battered but not gravely injured. The driver of the truck was dead. Carl had a broken collarbone and a concussion, among other injuries. Perry Como would have to wait. So would Carl Perkins.

Not Johnny Cash. In 1954, newly out of the Army, he'd been selling appliances in Memphis and relaxed by singing gospel tunes with two other guys in the shop, Marshall Grant and Luther Perkins (no relation to Carl). They thought they sounded pretty good, and so they auditioned for Sun. Sam was impressed, but he knew how many records gospel shifted, so he asked Cash to write some straight country material; at long last, maybe Memphis would prove a threat to the monolith of Nashville. Cash had the background for it; growing up dirt poor like Carl Perkins, only in Arkansas, with a penchant for getting into trouble, a couple of years in the Army and a turbulent marriage gave him material. But he wasn't exactly mainstream country, either; there were no fiddles, no steel guitar, no drums. Johnny Cash and the Tennessee Two were Cash, Grant on bass, and Perkins on guitar, and that was it. Still, beefed up a little with the famous Sun slapback echo sound, they had hits from the beginning, with "Folsom Prison Blues," in which Cash nonchalantly admits to killing a man in Reno just to watch him die, also not your standard country fare. It was a top-ten country record in 1955, anyway.

Television had been slow to warm to rock & roll, mostly because there was so little of it and most people felt it was just a fad; there were enough good musicians to have on your show without giving any more publicity to these animals. But as variety shows became more popular, more slots opened up for acts to play. A New York newspaper columnist, Ed Sullivan, had one of the most-watched variety shows, and he would seemingly book anything: acrobats, magicians, puppeteers, weird instrumentalists. In 1955, he'd asked Tommy "Dr. Jive" Smalls onto the show to give his audience a look at the R&B talent he played on his radio show, and Smalls delivered the goods: LaVern Baker, Bo Diddley, the Five Keys, and Willis "Gator Tail" Jackson's band to back them all. Unfortunately, one of Sullivan's producers decided to get creative; one of the big songs in the country that week was Merle Travis's tale of life in an Appalachian coal-mining town, "Sixteen Tons," and he decided that that guy with the guitar would play it on the show. No matter that Bo Diddley hadn't cut the tune or, for that matter, didn't know the words and the changes; they rehearsed him on it, wrote the lyrics on some cue cards, and he was going to do it. But, like most television in those days, Ed Sullivan went out live, and when Bo strolled onstage, he struck up *his* hit, ignoring the cue cards, and, when confronted by an irate production staff afterward, said, "Man, that might have been 'Sixteen Tons' on those cards, but all *I* saw was 'Bo Diddley.'" Must've been those glasses of his.

We don't hear as much about that show as we do about Elvis's appearances on *Sullivan*, but they were preceded by the Dorsey Brothers' shows, the first on January 28, 1956, where Elvis was introduced by Bill Randle and played a medley of Big Joe Turner songs and Ray Charles's current hit, "I Got a Woman," and then got off. The theater was only about half-full, and the audience reaction was confused, with laughter being heard during some of the performance and the engineer turning up the applause to make it sound like there were more people in the house than there were. There were two more to come, though, and on the second one there was a bigger audience, and Elvis did a couple of other people's hits. The third and final show saw him introducing "Heartbreak Hotel" and his version of "Blue Suede Shoes," and was pretty much of a flop, since the Dorsey Brothers' orchestra just couldn't figure out the "Heartbreak Hotel" arrangement, which screwed up Elvis's ability to work the stage. It was, however, the first time that the girls in the audience started to go wild. The Dorseys' producer sent the Colonel a contract for three more shows. After the last show, on March 28, the band drove back to Memphis, stopping off in Dover, Delaware, to see Carl Perkins in the hospital. Elvis stayed in New York to do press and to get ready to fly to Hollywood for a screen test and to do Milton Berle's TV show.

The world of American popular music had clearly gone insane; both "Blue Suede Shoes" and "Heartbreak Hotel" were chasing each other around the top tens of the pop, R&B, *and* country charts, the first time that had ever happened. The term *rock & roll* was making its way into public recognition, as proven by Kay Starr's hit record "Rock and Roll Waltz," a record that, its title aside, had not the slightest thing to do with rock & roll—it was a *waltz*, for heaven's sake! No, except for Bill Haley's reworking of Bobby Charles's hit, "See You Later, Alligator," the only sign of rock & roll in the pop top ten besides those two records in early 1956 was a telling one: "Why Do Fools Fall in Love," by Frankie Lymon and the Teenagers. Its appearance was due to a kind of mistake. The Teenagers were from a nice neighborhood in Harlem known as Sugar Hill, home to such black celebrities as Duke Ellington. The Teenagers had something of a gimmick: they were integrated. Herman Santiago and Joe Negroni were Puerto Rican, and the rest—Sherman Gaines, Jimmy Merchant, and Frankie Lymon—were black. They actually weren't even known as the Teenagers; they'd been calling themselves the Premieres, or the Ermines, or the Coupe deVilles. Santiago was the lead singer, and at some point Richard Barrett, who was scouting Latin bands for George Goldner, a guy downtown who owned a couple of labels recording New York's salsa bands, Tico and Rama, heard them and thought that not only were they good, but a lead singer with a Spanish accent was a great gimmick. Barrett got the kids to come downtown to audition for Goldner, who was confused because they didn't have any instruments like a real Latin band should, but Barrett convinced him to listen to a song called "Why Do Birds Sing So Gay," which they'd gotten from some friend of theirs whose girlfriend had written the lyrics. (It was not, as a story current at the time had it, written by Frankie out of unrequited love for one of his schoolteachers.) There are a lot of unclear details about what exactly happened, because for good reason Goldner was a fairly secretive guy, but somehow Frankie wound up singing lead, even though he was still a kid at thirteen. He was an instantly charismatic figure, and his voice was perfect, unlike a lot of children whose voices need a lot of work to keep them on pitch. Goldner was wowed, and, after changing the title of the song, cut it. He kept on with the Latin music and made a lot of important records in that field, but when he formed Gee Records to put out the Teenagers' stuff, he pioneered New York–based labels specializing in vocal groups.

Talent notwithstanding, it was smart of Goldner (or Barrett, it's not certain) to rename the group the Teenagers. For one thing, they *were* teenagers, unlike a lot of the new performers. For another, that's who was buying this music, so Frankie and his friends were just claiming the name. So were the Teen Queens, a one-hit group on RPM who scored early in the year with "Eddie My Love," and, in New York, the Six Teens, whose "A Casual Look" made full use of their boy-girl harmonies.

The guys who had driven from Georgia to Cincinnati on February 4 to do a session were more typical; all in their early twenties, the Flames had their genesis in a juvenile detention camp in Toccoa, Georgia, where their lead singer was doing time for stealing cars and joyriding, and Bobby Byrd, a Toccoa kid whose mother had a religious turn of mind that she'd passed on to her son, a gospel singer and piano player, who played the detention camp as part of his church outreach. Bobby kept running into this kid, who was called Music Box by the other inmates, singing gospel at the camp, and finally Mrs. Byrd agreed to sponsor Music Box in her home, with the hope of turning him toward the light. It was a textbook case; all the kid needed was people who loved and paid attention to him, and soon Bobby Byrd and Music Box, whose name was James Brown, were assembling a group to play local gigs. They were completely unlike anything anyone had seen, with the showmanship of gospel and the energy of young men having the time of their lives, and after three years of paying dues all over the South, they came to the attention of King Records' talent scout, Ralph Bass. Bass was particularly taken with a tape the group had cut at a local radio station, and was determined to make a professional dub of it. So when Bass showed up for work on February 4 and saw the car with Georgia plates, some guys asleep inside, and the bass tied to the top, he figured the Flames had made it. A few hours later, they went into the studio with musicians King often used on sessions and got to work. Syd Nathan walked into the control room and, after taking in what was happening, said, "What is this shit?" It wasn't just Syd, who was notoriously abrasive; the musicians hated it, too. Eventually, though, they finished the session—four songs, including the one everyone hated—and Bass went back on the road in search of more talent. One day, a King salesman told him to call the office. "You're fired," were Syd's first words to him. "He's just singing one word! You're fired." Ah,

Bass now knew what was happening; it was the Flames' record of "Please, Please, Please," a gospelly remake of Big Joe Williams' classic "Baby Please Don't Go." Bass pleaded for Syd to test-market it in the South, at least, give the record a chance. "Fuck it," said Syd. "I'm putting it out cross-country just to prove what a piece of shit it is." And on March 3, he did. It took a while to catch on, with John R. and Hoss Allen down in Gallatin the first to get on it, but soon it was selling like mad, and by the end of April it was a certified R&B hit. The only downside to the whole thing was that when the Flames got a copy of the record, they noticed that it was credited to "James Brown and the Famous Flames." How had that happened? What's ironic is that King had another group drenched in gospel, one that would have passed inspection with the studio musicians, under contract at the same time; the "5" Royales had jumped from Apollo, where they'd had several hits, to King in late 1954, and although they were putting out plenty of great records, they weren't selling. The Royales were touring and doing well—the Flames had seen them during this period and been wowed—but on the radio and on the charts, it was like they didn't exist. And the most gospel-flavored vocalist out there, Ray Charles, was enjoying success, but not with teenagers; his #1 R&B smash "Drown in My Own Tears" was a dramatic performance, but way down-tempo, and (although nobody bothered to monitor this kind of thing in those days) probably selling mostly to adults.

The kids preferred zippier fare, apparently; Little Richard was riding a two-sided smash in April, "Long Tall Sally" b/w "Slippin' and Slidin'," which was not only frantic but weird. The lyrics to the A side could very well have come out of Richard's gay-bar act, with Uncle John carrying on and hiding from Aunt Mary with a woman who was "built for speed." He followed that with two more blazers, "Rip It Up" b/w "Ready Teddy" (on which he declares that he's ready to rock and roll). Fats Domino had finally cracked the upper reaches of the top ten with "I'm in Love Again," which was about as up-tempo as the Fat Man got, but it was the record's other side that portended his future: the old standard "My Blue Heaven," which was also a substantial hit. Fats rode a succession of standards to year's end, first "When My Dreamboat Comes Home," and, in the fall,

"Blueberry Hill," which became so identified with him that few realize that the song dated to Glenn Miller's 1940 record of it. The Platters were another act who fell back on standards for material; their early 1956 hit "Great Pretender" had been written by their Svengali, Buck Ram, but their next hit, "My Prayer," was from decades earlier. But Chuck Berry knew what was really needed; at the beginning of the summer Chess released a record he'd recorded in April that was both sweet and defiant, and claimed a piece of turf for teenagers only. "Roll Over, Beethoven" described the rock & roller's world of 1956 perfectly: impatient to hear a song you loved on the radio, *very* impatient with all that old-people's crap that stood between you and it while wanting everyone to acknowledge your music. True, it was "rhythm and blues" he wanted everyone to dig, but kids knew what he meant. Although he wasn't one of them, he had a way of tapping into their world; his next record, "Too Much Monkey Business," expressed the frustrations of the kind of lowly jobs teenagers had. His next record, though, which had been recorded at the same session as it and "Roll Over, Beethoven," was quite different. "Brown Eyed Handsome Man" idealized the man of the title, an irresistible type for whom Venus de Milo had lost her arms trying to win in a wrestling match, women crawled across deserts to reach, and the judge's wife begs to be let off his vagrancy charge. It was lyrics as usual for Berry, comic, direct, and sharp: the man had been arrested "on charges of unemployment." And, although nobody came right out and said it, was it the man's brown *eyes* that made him irresistible?

More and more kids wanted to do this themselves, but some had advantages others didn't have. If you wanted to be a vocal group, that was fairly easy, assuming you and your friends had talent and someone was listening. But for young white kids, the desire was to be Elvis. That was much harder. Out in west Texas, Roy Orbison, son of an oil well worker, had been in a band for several years, the Wink Westerners, named after his hometown. As soon as they saw Elvis, they became the Teen Kings. In 1955, Roy was attending North Texas State College in Denton, north of Fort Worth, and one of his classmates, Pat Boone, started making records, but he'd married into country music royalty; his wife was the daughter of Randy Woods of

Dot Records, for whom Pat recorded. At a free concert at school, Roy heard two students, Wade Moore and Dick Penner, do a song, "The Ooby Dooby," and taught it to the Teen Kings. In early March 1956, they went to the nearest recording studio, which was Norman Petty's in Clovis, New Mexico, and cut it. The Teen Kings had a thirty-minute television show each week that was followed by a country show headed by Weldon Rogers, and one day someone suggested to Rogers that he should put out the tape the Teen Kings had made in Clovis. He formed a label, Je-Wel (for Jean Oliver and Weldon Rogers, Oliver being the daughter of the guy who cofinanced the record), and it became the rage of west Texas; one Lubbock store was selling 250 copies a week. The Teen Kings' show also hosted visiting teen-appeal artists, and Johnny Cash had appeared on it. After hearing Orbison and his band, he suggested Roy get in touch with Sam Phillips, who, in true Sam style, said, "Johnny Cash doesn't run my record company" and hung up. But when he heard the Je-Wel single, he recanted and invited Roy and his band to Memphis to record. He also got an injunction against Weldon Rogers to enforce Roy's contract with Sun, but the judgment didn't include not making more records, so Rogers had a chat with Norman Petty, and Petty financed a new pressing. Sam was re-cutting the record at his own studio, though, with something called "Go! Go! Go!" on the other side, and, in May, he released it. It took off immediately, and Sam, who had formed Stars Incorporated, a booking agency for his artists, with Bob Neal, told the Teen Kings to get ready to tour. Tour they did, with someone leading Roy up to the microphone (he was nearly blind, but wouldn't wear his thick glasses onstage). They finished the tour in Memphis on June 1 at the Overton Park band shell, and Elvis made a surprise appearance. The package they toured with included Johnny Cash, Carl Perkins (out of the hospital at last, finally appearing on the Perry Como TV show and with a new single, "Boppin' the Blues," making noise), and Warren Smith, a promising newcomer whose Sun record "Rock and Roll Ruby" was enjoying some action at the time.

"Ooby Dooby" would be Orbison's last hit for a while, and its lyrics were pretty silly, but silly lyrics have always been a part of

American popular music. Take, for instance, that kid Carl Perkins had been introduced to in Virginia the night before his accident, he of the "effective ol' song." Eugene Vincent Craddock was almost as unlikely a teen idol as Roy Orbison, with his crippled leg and gaunt face, and his first record, inspired by his love of Little Lulu comic books, was entitled "Be-Bop-A-Lula," which was right up there with "Tutti Frutti" for nonsense. But not quite nonsense: it was simultaneously rocking (although seriously down-tempo), and threatening (there was an ominous shudder in the vocal), and reeking of sexual longing (since Be-Bop-A-Lula was the girl who gave him "more, more, more"). Gene Vincent, as Craddock was re-christened for Capitol Records, was everything people thought Elvis was: a twenty-one-year-old hillbilly thug who was developing an alcohol and pill problem and whose escapades with women were both numerous and lurid. He was also the leader of a superb rock & roll band, the Blue Caps, guys like him who'd been working in the bars that catered to sailors in Norfolk, and featuring a truly great guitarist in Cliff Gallup. Between Vincent's instability and Capitol's getting caught flatfooted by his first record being a hit and then having absolutely no idea what to do with him, he gets overlooked a lot, and the Blue Caps even more.

It's all very well and good for guys to want to be Elvis, but what about girls? Someone eventually came up with Alis Lesley, "the female Elvis," who wore her hair in a kind of Elvis pompadour adapted for females, and more hair combed down to look like sideburns, but Capitol had nineteen-year-old Wanda Jackson, just the kind of double-barreled threat they had no idea what to do with. She'd been born in Oklahoma, and, guided by her very savvy father/manager, had been performing on the radio starting when she was thirteen. Her powerful, brassy voice could—and did—belt out country music, but she also could—and did—rock like crazy. She combined both in her stage act and in 1955–1956 she did a lot of shows with Elvis, with whom she shared Bob Neal's booking agency. But her forwardness and her good looks worked against her; her first appearance on the *Grand Ole Opry* in 1955 was marred by Ernest Tubb refusing to let her onstage wearing the sleeveless dress she'd bought for the occasion, sending her back to the dressing room for a jacket to cover her shoulders. That was also her last *Opry* appearance. Her first sides for Capitol were rockers—Elvis had given her a crash course by playing her his record collection—but songs like "Hot Dog! That Made Him Mad" and "I Gotta Know" got very little action. Later records like 1957's "Fujiyama Mama" (inexplicably a huge hit in Japan, but nowhere else) and "Let's Have a Party" (recorded by both Elvis and the Collins Kids in 1957, and an album track on her first album in 1958, which became a mild hit in 1960) had to wait until later to be discovered by rockabilly revivalists, who caught Wanda at the end of her successful country career and gave her a new audience.

The thing is, although it was where the money was, not all popular music was aimed at teenagers, and nowhere was this more evident than the black community. B. B. King was doing fine without a teenage audience; his big hit of 1956 was the lovely "Sweet Little Angel," a double entendre based around the angel spreading her wings. And the Chess brothers were making records teenagers wouldn't discover for nearly a decade. Howlin' Wolf had settled on a recording band that included Hubert Sumlin, a delicate-looking young man Wolf had hooked up with while still in Arkansas, and he proved to be the missing ingredient in Wolf's band—Wolf would never admit it, but he himself wasn't such a hot guitarist and didn't handle lead guitar at all well. Sumlin did, and he also could play rhythm alongside Wolf to make an almost orchestral sound. Wolf's big hit for 1956 was "Smokestack Lightnin'," as overwhelming yet enigmatic a record as anyone had ever made. What is it about? Hard to say, but in its odd phrasing and off-kilter meter, it lurches through its three minutes with Wolf bellowing its lyrics and howling when there were no words, and finally finishing off with some harmonica playing that sounds like the old Memphis instrumental favorite "Cats Squirrel." And just in case anyone thought you could mess with Wolf, his next hit of the year was "I Asked for Water (She Gave Me Gasoline)," which was every bit as evil as the title would suggest. Muddy Waters, too, continued his domination of Chicago's South Side, with three hits in 1956, and his former harmonica player, Little Walter, was still doing well not only with instrumentals, but also singing such classics as "Boom Boom (Out Go the Lights)." Sonny Boy Williamson, although he was close to sixty, was killing them in the clubs and making the occasional hit record for Chess, and Bo Diddley was playing both the teenage and the adult markets, with "You Pretty Thing" having teenage appeal and the dark, threatening "Who Do You Love" being something else entirely. Nor did Chess have a monopoly on hard-edged blues; Vee-Jay had found Jimmy Reed, a guitarist who played harmonica in a rack and had minimal backing, but who was incredibly popular in Chicago and, soon, elsewhere: his hits in 1956 included "Ain't That Lovin' You, Baby" and "Can't Stand to See You Go." The label also had a visit from Detroit bluesman John Lee Hooker, who signed no contracts, but laid down one of his classic tunes, "Dimples." And—not that anyone was—if anybody was worried that the blues would pass with this generation of South Side Chicago bluesmen, a rival scene of younger guys was rising on the West Side, and the biggest star there, the twenty-two-year-old lefty guitarist Otis Rush, chimed in with "I Can't Quit You Baby" on Cobra, a brand-new label (Rush's was its first single) run by a jukebox operator, Eli Toscano.

All of these artists were also of the age where they appealed to audiences in nightclubs serving hard liquor, where teenagers couldn't go. That audience had more disposable income, and was more likely to buy records, which meant that there was a generational spread in the R&B market. Performers like Ruth Brown were discovering that they could extend their careers by recording more sophisticated or adult material, while some newcomers started there and figured if they could pick up teens along the way, so much the better. Probably the most powerful example of this was Little Willie John, who had been performing since childhood and who once, as a young teenager visiting New York with a couple of guys who'd released a Christmas single of his, had escaped their clutches while they were watching television together and Count Basie came on. Willie vanished, ran to the TV studio, and talked his way into a guest appearance in front of the Basie band on live television as his handlers watched in utter disbelief. His first record was a rhythm-and-bluesy one, "All Around the World" (better known in a later version by Little Milton as "Grits Ain't Groceries"), but he settled into supper-club territory beautifully with his two 1956 hits, "I Need Your Love So Bad" and especially "Fever," which would reignite Peggy Lee's career two years later. He recorded for King, and it's a safe bet that Syd Nathan liked his music better than James Brown's, although the two performers later became fast friends.

Earlier that spring, the Colonel had gotten an offer from the New Frontier Hotel in Las Vegas for Elvis to play their Venus Room, and it turned out to be the first stumble of his career. The few people who came to see him couldn't make sense out of what they saw, and Elvis was as nervous as he'd ever been. By the end of the engagement two weeks later, Elvis had learned to relax, although his core audience of teenagers—and there were teenagers in Las Vegas—couldn't get in to see him. Probably the biggest thing that happened to Elvis was his opening act, Freddie Bell and the Bellboys, a hyperactive bunch who show up in some early rock & roll films. One of the songs they did was an arrangement of Willie Mae Thornton's "Hound Dog" that was pretty much unlike the original. Elvis knew the song, but this new approach was right up his alley. "We stole it straight from them," Scotty Moore admitted. *Newsweek* compared Elvis's appearance to "a jug of corn liquor at a champagne party," and *Variety* panned him. He'd be back.

Rock & roll, though, was definitely the flavor of the year, spearheaded by Elvis. His appearances on Milton Berle's show seemed to trigger something. The first, on April 3, went off just fine, but in June, the critics, who'd ignored him till then, went after him, with the New York *Journal-American*'s critic, Jack O'Brien, saying that "he can't sing a lick, makes up for vocal shortcomings with the weirdest and plainly planned suggestive animation short of an aborigine's mating dance." Ed Sullivan, reading the bad press, said that Elvis was too suggestive to appear on his show, which prompted his archrival, Steve Allen, to book him on *his* show, which aired at the same time on Sunday nights, for July 1. Allen didn't even like rock & roll: one of his routines was reading—declaiming, really—lyrics like "Tutti Frutti" and "Be-Bop-A-Lula" as poetry for the gag effect. And he didn't seem to much like Elvis, having him dress in a tuxedo and top hat and sing "Hound Dog" to a . . . hound dog. But for the first

time in the two men's rivalry, Allen wiped Sullivan out in the ratings. Sullivan swallowed his pride and offered the Colonel $50,000
for three appearances, starting in September. If you can't beat 'em . . .

Meanwhile, though, it was off to Hollywood to start filming on
Elvis's first movie, *Love Me Tender,* and to record the soundtrack
album. The Hollywood folks working on the film were impressed by
his dedication to the work he had to do, although he did complain
about having to spend all day one day on a scene that had him
plowing behind a couple of mules. In the evenings, he hung with
Nick Adams, a young actor who'd had a bit part in *Rebel Without a
Cause* and was busy talking his way into Elvis's film, Nick's room-
mate, Dennis Hopper, and their friend, also a *Rebel* veteran, Natalie
Wood. His cousin Gene was also around, and at one point Scotty
and the band came out to audition for the soundtrack album. Meanwhile, there was the Sullivan show to get ready for. Unfortunately, Ed
Sullivan himself couldn't prepare for it because he was laid up in the
aftermath of an automobile accident a few weeks earlier, so actor
Charles Laughton handled the hosting. It was on this show, on September 9, that he introduced the theme of his forthcoming movie,
Love Me Tender, and RCA, shortly thereafter, had orders for over a
million copies. He then flew to Memphis to play a predictably wild
homecoming show in the city of his birth, Tupelo, Mississippi.

By the time Elvis got back on the road—the film was now in
post-production, scheduled to open over the Thanksgiving weekend—
there was another film starting production that would put *Love Me
Tender* in the shadows. Elvis's movie was primarily a drama, without
a lot of music, and it was shot in black-and-white. Frank Tashlin, an
animator turned director, had taken on a quickie production for 20th
Century-Fox based on Garson Kanin's novel *Do Re Mi.* It was the
story of an alcoholic press agent hired by a gangster to turn his
girlfriend into a top singing sensation in six weeks—or else. This, of
course, means that he has to immerse himself in the current world of
pop music, with lots of opportunities for various currently popular
artists to appear. Tom Ewell played the press agent, Jayne Mansfield
the girlfriend, and Fats Domino, the Platters, Little Richard, Gene
Vincent and the Blue Caps, and a few others, now largely forgotten

(the Treniers, the Chuckles, Johnny Olenn), appeared as themselves, playing their latest records. One of Richard's songs gave the film its title, *The Girl Can't Help It*, and although on one level it's a disposable screwball comedy, on another it's a brilliant time capsule of rock & roll coming into its own. All the musical sequences are brilliantly shot (it also helps that the film's in color), with Gene Vincent and the Bluecaps and Little Richard in particular turning in sizzling performances. There's also a scene that shows the frenzy of the times in a particularly memorable way: Ewell's housekeeper is working in a room with the television on when Eddie Cochran comes on, doing "Twenty Flight Rock." This middle-aged black woman totally loses it, so excited by the music that she grabs Ewell to come look at the TV. There were no conventions, no market research, as to what rock & roll was or who its audience was. All anyone knew was that it was a fad, and they had to get this movie out before it peaked. Eddie Cochran hadn't even released "Twenty Flight Rock" then, but it hardly mattered. He'd been hanging around Hollywood since he was in his teens, and he'd been recording since he was fifteen, initially as the Cochran Brothers with Hank Cochran, no relation, who later became a very successful country songwriter. Besides being a charismatic performer, Cochran was a studio whiz, often recording and overdubbing to make a whole band out of himself. Like Nick Adams, who was now on tour with Elvis and opening his shows with impressions and comedy, he was a young man using rock & roll to stand out from the Hollywood crowd.

Rock & roll may have been a fad, but it was definitely taking over at the moment. One sign of this was the release, that summer, of "The Flying Saucer, Parts 1 and 2," by Buchanan and Goodman, a couple of colorful well-known New York music-biz guys. While waiting for work one day, they came upon the idea of putting out a record where snippets of other records were used in a pretend newscast, in this case about the landing of a flying saucer. Dickie Goodman played the role of John Cameron-Cameron (a reference to star newscaster John Cameron Swayze), reporting the alien craft's visit to Earth. Naturally, the space visitors' first words to Earth were "A-wop-bop-a-loo-bop-a-lop-bam-boom," and naturally, Buchanan and Goodman hadn't applied for the rights to use anything on the record. It was probably done as a gag for disc jockeys initially, but teenagers immediately wanted copies for themselves, and so the two men had set up a label, Luniverse, and pressed some up. With some of the most feared copyright lawyers in the business looking for them, they weren't making public appearances, but suddenly some odd things started happening. Dootsie Williams, for instance, noted that sales of "Earth Angel" by the Penguins, which had been cold for months, started picking up after it was quoted in the song. So did other not-current hits. Eventually, a judge ruled that the use was fair play under parody laws, and Buchanan and Goodman went on to make lots of other so-called break-in records, but for all its silliness (and it was 100 percent pure silliness), "Flying Saucer" proved an important point: nobody would have reacted to it if they hadn't been familiar with the records being used, and familiar enough that they thought that the juxtaposition was funny. It spoke directly to, and only to, the rock & roll crowd.

Of course, novelty records had always been around, and rock & roll was spawning them aplenty in 1956. Nervous Norvus was James Drake, a forty-two-year-old truck driver who, as a member of the Four Jokers, released a fairly dumb song called "Transfusion," which was picked up by Dot, home of Pat Boone, that summer and re-cut. The whole joke was that the guy was driving along and crashed his car, verse after verse, and ended up needing a blood transfusion, which he'd order with a quip like "Shoot some claret to me, Barrett." The production sounded like it had been recorded in a closet, the sound effects were crudely inserted, and it was banned on lots of radio stations, which didn't stop the record from reaching the top ten (or Norvus from following it up with "Ape Call," which stiffed). Then there was Jay Hawkins, a mediocre blues singer who'd been recording for Okeh to no great success. He was given a song, "I Put a Spell On You," to record, and, having troubles with the vocal, commenced drinking. Smashed out of his gourd, he managed to make his way through it, but interspersed the lyrics with weird whooping and gargling sounds. The label thought the rock & roll kids would like it, so they renamed him Screamin' Jay Hawkins and sat back as it became one of those under-the-counter hits. Hawkins, whose career started at this point and continued to his death in 2007, claimed he didn't even remember recording it. More professional (but not much more), and totally enigmatic, was "Rubber Biscuit," by the Chips, which was written when one of the Brooklyn group's members, Charles "Kenrod" Jackson, was in something called the Warwick School for Delinquent Teenagers—and sounds like it. Basically a polysyllabic one-chord chant from which English-sounding words occasionally emerge, it's interrupted at times by the bass singer, talking of biscuits, buns, and sandwiches, and the record concludes with him saying, "What do you want for nothing: a rrrrrrubber biscuit?" Neither the pop charts nor the R&B charts would pay host to this confusing slab of wax, but it endured in the hearts of record collectors. (One member of the Chips, Sammy Strain, would go on to become a member of Little Anthony and the Imperials, and, even later, the O'Jays.)

The Chips were, putting it mildly, an outlier in the rush of vocal groups entering the market in the second half of 1956. Chicago in particular was hot, probably because both Chess and Vee-Jay were aware of how cheaply you could record this stuff. The Flamingos had their first two hits (for Chess) this year, the Moonglows also kept up their winning streak, and Vee-Jay introduced the Dells, who'd been recording for small labels unsuccessfully since 1953, with "Oh What a Nite," starting a career that was to last until the '90s. Modern was doing vocal groups now, too, with the Cliques (Jesse Belvin multitracking his voice, actually) and the Cadets had a summerlong hit with the novelty "Stranded in the Jungle." Atlantic in New York, although its owners (particularly Jerry Wexler) didn't like vocal group music at all, managed to score some great landmarks in the style. They'd been enjoying hits for some time by the Clovers, who released one of the classics of the genre with "Devil or Angel," and the Drifters, who never seemed to be the same guys twice, were doing well, but the real kick for Atlantic came from Los Angeles, where Leiber and Stoller, looking for a group they could use for their most teenage material, took members of the Robins and the Cadets, moved them to New York, and invented the Coasters. Their first hit, "Down in Mexico," set the template for the comic songs with which they'd make their name. Elsewhere in New York, small labels issued records by hopefuls, including the Cadillacs, led by Earl "Speedy" Carroll, who was so nervous making this record that he mis-sung his own nick-name, and became known thereafter as "Speedo," which was fine with him after the record spent fifteen weeks on the charts. The Heartbeats, whose "A Thousand Miles Away" was another classic, were led by James "Shep" Shepherd, who had the unique experience of having another hit four years later as leader of Shep and the Limelites, which was an answer record: "Daddy's Home." This was also the year the first integrated vocal groups appeared, most notably the Dell Vikings, who met on an Air Force base in Pittsburgh and had a big hit with "Come Go with Me." And the Cleftones joined Frankie Lymon and the Teen-agers on George Goldner's Gee label with "Little Girl of Mine." But vocal groups were just getting started.

Elvis owned the radio for most of the second half of the year, with the first two-sided #1 smash, "Don't Be Cruel" b/w "Hound Dog" in August, which topped the charts until "Love Me Tender" came along in November to displace it. Two things are worth noting, especially in light of all the ridiculous charges aimed at Elvis over the years. First, his recording of "Hound Dog" sounds nothing at all like Willie Mae Thornton's; the melody and tempo are wildly different. Second, "Don't Be Cruel" features the vocal interjections and backup vocals of the Jordanaires, a white gospel quartet like the ones Elvis had admired in Memphis who would be featured on his records for some time.

Sam Phillips, flush with money from Elvis's contract sale, was put-ting out some classic stuff, too; Carl Perkins had "Boppin' the Blues" and "Dixie Fried," two classic slabs of rockabilly, Sonny Burgess gave us "We Wanna Boogie," and Warren Smith the borderline-racist "Ubangi Stomp," which at least gave credit to Africans for rock & roll. A young man from Louisiana, fresh from a Texas Bible college, had been hanging around Sun wanting to make records, and he was a good enough piano player that Sam used him on a few country ses-sions, finally giving in and letting Jerry Lee Lewis make his first rec-ord, "Crazy Arms" (an old Texas shuffle by Ray Price) b/w "End of the World" and releasing it to total indifference in December. On December 4, Elvis, on a much-needed break from filming, recording, and touring, was back in Memphis for the whole month, buying his parents a pair of Cadillacs and stopping by Sun to see what was shaking. He walked in on Carl Perkins and Jerry Lee Lewis singing hymns and joined right in; they weren't the Jordanaires, but they weren't bad! Sam saw what was happening, got on the phone, and called a photographer and Johnny Cash, and soon the Million Dollar Quartet, as they were dubbed years later, were singing, catching up with each other, and generally having a great old time, and most of it was captured on tape by Sam's new studio manager, Jack Clement. It was a fitting close to a great year for all concerned.

chapter eight

INTERLUDE IN
ANOTHER LAND

Teddy Boys, London.
(Photo by Popperfoto/Getty Images)

The old cliché has jazz coming up the Mississippi from New Orleans and settling in Chicago, which is hardly what happened, but it's an enduring myth. However, we can with some exactness pinpoint the moment when New Orleans jazz came to Britain, and even on which ship. Ken Colyer was a hard-drinking, reefer-smoking maniac with a Merchant Navy card and a blinding love of jazz that had caused him to buy the very best trumpet he could afford at the moment. Not that he could play it well, but he and his brother Bill hung around the pathetic postwar British jazz scene, watching its wannabe performers attempt to replicate what they'd been listening to on the records they'd been buying in specialty shops since the '30s. Ken went off to sea, trying to work up to a ship that would head to New Orleans with some cargo. He knew it would take ten days before they sailed back, and that shore leave was what he was living for. Finally, late in 1952, he succeeded. He rushed onto shore in Mobile and headed to the Greyhound station, where he caught a bus to his dream destination. There, he lost no time in finding some of the old guys who were still playing around, most notably clarinetist George Lewis, who, noticing the young Brit with the trumpet in his hands, silently fingering notes, asked him to sit in. Colyer did, and found that all the listening he'd done had paid off; he could just about keep up with the band, and, on subsequent nights, found himself catching up, often with handy hints from his new bandmates. Just in time to get busted: New Orleans had a law prohibiting black musicians and white musicians from playing on the same stage, and that's what alerted the cops, but they looked at his passport and realized he'd long overstayed his allowed time. He was thrown in jail to await deportation. During his thirty-eight days in the clink, Colyer sent letters detailing his adventures to his brother, who passed them on to the British jazz magazine *Melody Maker*, which printed them. Bail had been set at $500, which Colyer of course didn't have, but somebody did, because he was released in mid-February 1953, just in time for Mardi Gras. He partied for twenty-four hours. "I stayed on my feet til daybreak," he wrote to *Melody Maker*. George Lewis approached him about going on tour with the band, but Colyer was awaiting news from New York, which was where he was being deported from. Finally, word came down, and, in a nice twist of fate, he was assigned to the *United States*, the world's fastest luxury ocean liner, to get him back home. There, as he got off the train from Southampton in London's Waterloo Station, he was met by his brother and a young kid named Chris Barber, with whose band Bill Colyer had been playing.

There had been jazz fans in Britain going back to the 1930s, but the attempts they'd made to imitate what they heard were risible, which didn't stop them from getting gigs or occasionally recording. They also had very little choice in the records they bought, largely imports ordered by specialty stores that didn't really know who was on them. Thus, alongside the New Orleans and Chicago records of Louis Armstrong and Bunk Johnson (Colyer's idol) were blues records by Big Bill Broonzy, Josh White, the Mississippi Sheiks, and Lead Belly. There was nobody you could ask about this who had any knowledge at all; the British Musicians' Union, in its wisdom, denied visas to most foreign performers, and this most especially meant black Americans. Sidney Bechet had snuck into Britain in 1949 after a series of gigs in Paris and, at a late show, played with the Humphrey Lyttelton Band, which had a residency at the 100 Club at 100 Oxford Street in London, but was playing the Winter Garden Theatre on this particular night. That was an anomaly, though; the

British jazz scene was largely a case of the blind leading the blind. Chris Barber didn't care. Somewhere along the way, the teenager had picked up a trombone and learned to play it, and was bouncing from band to band getting experience, while amassing one of Britain's best jazz record collections.

Another young jazz fan, Tony Donegan, was obsessed with the blues records he heard. His favorites were by Lonnie Johnson, a virtuoso guitarist who straddled urban blues ("Racketeer Blues" on Okeh, risqué numbers with Victoria Spivey) and jazz ("The Mooche" by Duke Ellington). In 1948, after years in the shadows, Johnson emerged again with a smooth song, "Tomorrow Night," on King, that did okay on the race charts and re-established his career. That was what inspired Donegan to buy a guitar and learn to play it as well as he could. Drafted into the Army in 1950, he was sent off to Vienna, where he heard Armed Forces Radio for the first time, with its rich helping of country and western and rhythm and blues. Donegan was transfixed. Upon his discharge the next year he returned to London and started looking for an opportunity to play. A pub called the Fishmongers Arms hired him to fill the interval between sets for their regular jazz band, but Tony had bigger plans. He hung out at the 100 Club, checking the talent, and finally got a job playing banjo in Bill Brunskill's band, where he was good enough that soon the band was called Tony Donegan's band. The only problem was when he took the spotlight and began to sing; people (including his then girlfriend, many say) would head to the bar to get away from the noise. Still, he had great faith in himself, and took any opportunity he could to play in front of an audience, and by 1952, he was billing himself as Lonnie Donegan, no doubt in homage to his idol Lonnie Johnson. Under that name, he played an eighteen-act extravaganza at the Royal Albert Hall, just him and his guitar one evening in June. By his own admission he was awful, but he was doing something nobody else onstage had done, and the audience, if not the critics, went wild. And at the end of the month, he found himself onstage again, at Festival Hall on a bill organized by the National Federation of Jazz Organisations, featuring British, Dutch, and Swedish jazz musicians and two Americans, ragtime pianist Ralph Sutton and none other than Lonnie Johnson! Of course, he only got the gig after some of the bigger names on the bill withdrew in protest over the Musicians' Union's ban on foreign musicians, including the Americans, but Donegan wasn't in the union, so he went ahead. He was so nervous, though, that he didn't speak a word to his idol, who put on a show of supper-club music. Then, news came down that Chris Barber's band was falling apart. Donegan was onto him in a flash. As part of building a new band, they took on Bill Colyer as a manager, and, after meeting Ken Colyer at Waterloo Station, renamed the band Ken Colyer's Jazzmen. A Danish tour happened almost immediately.

And then, when they returned, they'd changed the name again: they were now Ken Colyer's Jazz and Skiffle Group. This was because the band had noticed that their between-sets music, with Barber on string bass, Donegan and Ken Colyer on guitar, and Bill Colyer playing washboard, performing acoustic blues tunes learned from American records, were just as popular as their New Orleans jazz. Bill reached into his record collection and found a group called Dan Burley and His Skiffle Boys on a couple of American Exclusive 78s. Burley played piano, Pops Foster bass, and Stick and Brownie McGhee played everything else. They used suitcases with wire brushes for percussion, played jugs and harmonicas, and generally just had a good time. Heaven knows where Burley et al. got the term, but Colyer snagged the word *skiffle* and applied it to what they were doing. In no time, half the Jazzmen's audience was people who came for the between-sets entertainment, and sang along with their favorite numbers, top among which was Lead Belly's "Midnight Special." But the Colyers were causing friction in the band—Ken's drinking, in particular, made him unmanageable—so in the middle of 1954, they left and the band became the Chris Barber Band again. Barber made sure everyone knew that it was the same band without the two brothers, and especially wanted the folks at Decca, for whom they'd already made a ten-inch album, to know that. Decca thought that a new album would be a good idea, so in July they cut *New Orleans Joys,* eight tracks, two of which were skiffle: "Rock Island Line" and "John Henry." Then Decca sat on the album for six months. When it finally came out in January 1955, it sold very well, considering that jazz was at best a minority interest in Britain. But wait: What were those two other tracks?

It hardly mattered; Decca was not interested in further product from the Barber band and let them go by the end of the year. They signed with another label, made another album, and there was no skiffle on it. That was because a Scottish fan with some technical expertise had made a whole album of the skiffle band, *Back Stairs Session,* and pressed up a bunch of copies. He had no distribution and no idea how to get the album into circulation, which is why it was such a shock for the band to learn in early January 1956 that something called the Lonnie Donegan Skiffle Group had a top-ten hit with "Rock Island Line." Someone at Decca had taken the two skiffle tracks off *New Orleans Joys* and released them as a single! The musicians who'd played on it—Donegan, Barber on bass, and Beryl Briden (a longtime friend of Barber's) on washboard—had gotten precisely three pounds, two shillings each as a recording fee. There would be no royalties of any sort. And just to make sure it hurt all the more, Decca put the record out in the United States, where it went into the pop top ten. Lonnie acquired an American manager, Manny Greenfield, who happened to be passing through London at the right moment, and then quit the Barber band and went on tour in the United States, appearing on the Perry Como show, as well as on package shows with Clyde McPhatter, Chuck Berry, the Cleftones, Frankie Lymon and the Teenagers, and Pat Boone. He got back to England in July, and the entire music industry had changed. Skiffle had become the new thing.

It had had a very modest beginning outside the Barber band; in September 1955, a club had started at the Roundhouse Pub in Soho at the corner of Brewer and Wardour Streets. (A "club," in the British sense, is just that: a group of enthusiasts who gather for a given purpose on a regular basis in a regular location. Thus, the Roundhouse could also in theory have hosted a jazz club, a poetry club, and a folk club on other days of the week.) The Roundhouse skiffle club was run by Bob Watson, who had his own skiffle band that played there and had been introduced to the music by the Colyer/Barber band; Watson had even taken guitar lessons from Lonnie Donegan, but soon Donegan had no time, so Watson sought out a guy who was reputed to know a lot about black American music, Alexis Korner. Korner had been hanging around Soho since he was a teenager blowing off school, teaching himself guitar and eventually sitting in with Barber on occasion, but he was also looking for other opportunities to play. He fell in with a band led by Dickie Bishop, which featured a guitarist named Cyril Davies and a bassist, Adrian Brand. When Bob Watson broached the idea of a skiffle club at the Roundhouse, Davies and Brand became the rest of the Bob Watson Skiffle Group, and officers in the club. The club was a hit from the first night, at the end of which the landlord gave them a lecture on maximum capacities and fire laws. The "group" was pretty flexible, and drop-ins by Donegan and Korner happened all the time. So did visits by an American who was living in London and called himself Ramblin' Jack Elliott. Nobody at the Roundhouse knew that he was the son of a Jewish dentist in Brooklyn and that his real name was Elliott Charles Adnopoz, nor would the fact that he'd lived with Woody Guthrie for a spell have impressed anyone because Britain had no idea who he was, but one undeniable fact was that Ramblin' Jack knew more songs than anyone. It didn't hurt that he'd also starred in a Christmas musical, *The Big Rock Candy Mountain*, written by a new Londoner, folklorist Alan Lomax, whose father, John, had discovered Lead Belly and been the first to record him doing "Midnight Special" and "Rock Island Line."

Soon there were two other skiffle clubs. The one at Richardson's Rehearsal Rooms on Gerrard Street in what was not yet London's Chinatown was called the 44 Skiffle Club, run by John Hasted, who taught atomic physics at University College, and who was also a communist. Again, the house band was kind of loose, and singers would include Shirley Collins and Margaret Barry. Then there was the one at the Princess Louise, a posh Victorian pub by Holborn Kingsway tube station, run by Russell Quaye and his girlfriend, Hylda Sims, an aspiring ballerina who'd taken up banjo and guitar. Quaye had a group called the City Ramblers who were the house band for his club, and they also had the usual numbers of droppers-in, including Cyril Davies and Jack Elliott and a dynamo of a young woman from Glasgow,

Nancy Whiskey, whose real name was Anne Wilson and who'd taken her stage moniker from a Scottish folk song. When Quaye, Sims, and Jack Elliott and his wife, June, all took off at the end of the summer to see what opportunities might await in Europe, one of the City Ramblers, Johnny Pilgrim, was left without anything to do. He took a day job, and soon thereafter a guy he'd met one night at the 100 Club, Wally Whyton, asked him if he'd be interested in joining his skiffle group, the Vipers. "We've got a residency at the 2 I's, a coffee bar in Old Compton Street, and the place is packed every night." Welcome to Ground Zero of British rock & roll.

The 2 I's wasn't the first espresso bar in London, but they were springing up with regularity. A lot of the new Bohemians in London didn't like the atmosphere in pubs, so they took to hanging out in places like the Gyre and Gimbel (known to its habitués as "the G") or the Nucleus ("the Nuke," of course), which were open late and had every manner of oddball hanging around. There was usually a guitar for people to use, and occasionally one guitarist teaching another so they could play together. The success of these two places ("success" being a relative term) led to more, but they tended to want a touch of respectability; one had a sign warning "Folk Songs, But No Skiffle." The manager at the 2 I's was happy to have it, though; the Vipers had accidentally walked in after playing on a flatbed truck during a street fair and continued playing, and as they were packing up to leave, the manager said, "Excuse me, lads, but I really enjoyed that." He invited them to return, and they said they'd be in some evening next week. And, like every residency of every skiffle band in every situation so far, they started attracting drop-ins. The most aggressive one was a kid who'd sworn he was going to make it in showbiz someday, and determined that the first step on that ladder would be to become the first Englishman to play rock & roll. His name was Tommy Hicks.

Rock & roll wasn't exactly a new thing in Britain. Decca, after all, was a British-owned record company, and so Bill Haley's records were made available, although the BBC didn't give them any needle time. They had something of an underground cachet until *The Blackboard Jungle* opened on October 17, 1955. That not only revived sales of "Rock Around the Clock" as it had done in America, it also gave teenagers an excuse to hang out. Ian Dury, a rowdy young Cockney who would find unexpected fame twenty years later, remembered, "It was the films that gave everybody a chance to congregate. Before there were many concerts, Sunday afternoon was when we used to sit round the big screen, telling jokes, singing songs, and spoiling the film." Rebels without a cause, they were the new audience. Now, if only there was some rock & roll for them. Tommy Hicks was ready; a school dropout who'd been to sea crewing on transatlantic liners, he'd heard rock & roll in America, and was hitting the skiffle scene, trying to get those musicians to back him on tunes like "Blue Suede Shoes" that nobody was familiar with. It hardly mattered; one night in the 2 I's, Hicks was playing a short set when a New Zealander named John Kennedy, a showbiz photographer who'd worked in Hollywood, where he'd shot Marilyn Monroe, among others, walked into the place and was transfixed. "I think I could make you a star very quickly," he told the lad, who replied, "What do you know about show business?" Kennedy had to admit that he didn't know much and asked Hicks what he knew about singing. "Nothing," he admitted. So they joined forces. First off was to change Tommy's name, since *Hicks* didn't sound like star quality. Steel, however, was his grandfather's name, and steel is hard and shiny, so they went with that. (Not long after, when Tommy made his first record, he was dismayed to see Decca had printed his name as Steele, no doubt adding the *e* that their American affiliate had dropped from Buddy Holley's name.) Next, Kennedy pulled the first of his publicity stunts; on Sunday, September 16, 1956, *The People*, a bestselling tabloid, had a picture of Tommy performing and driving a bunch of girls wild. ROCK AND ROLL HAS GOT THE DEBS, TOO! read the headline, although Kennedy later revealed that they were models he'd hired, and told them to give posh names when reporters asked, as "Patricia Scott-Brown" and "Valerie Thornton-Smith" did. The pictures were supposedly at the nation's "first society rock and roll party," with the evening's star declaring, "Gee, you cats have rocked me to a standstill," as he collapsed into a chair at party's end. In order to keep the hype rolling, Kennedy needed money, and he approached Larry Parnes, who'd been working in his family's fashion business but was trying to buy his way into show business, having invested in a flop play a year earlier. Parnes dropped in at the Stork Club, a semi-posh nightclub that had given Steele a three-week contract on the basis of the newspaper article, and when Kennedy introduced him to Parnes, Steele said, "Hello, guv. I understand you're to be my new manager." He already had three: two guys who'd introduced him to Kennedy and now Parnes. And a couple of weeks later, he was auditioning for Decca (in a bathroom; they'd mistakenly booked him into a studio that was being used) and getting ready to cut "Rock with the Caveman," written by Steele, a member of the Vipers named Mike Pratt, and a young student who hung around a sort of commune where the Vipers and others lived, Lionel Bart. On the other side was a song by Steele alone, "Rock Around the Town." It sounds sort of like a rock & roll record some-one who'd never heard rock & roll would write, which isn't far from the truth. The record was released on October 12, and although *Melody Maker* disdained to notice it—it wasn't jazz, after all—its feisty young competitor, *New Musical Express*, said, "Decca's British rock 'n' roll record by Tommy Steele lacks the essential authentic flavour. Best thing on the disc is Ronnie Scott's driving tenor sax playing." Nor did they like his first television appearance, asking, "Does Tommy Steele expect to gain more popularity by appearing with untidy hair?" Untidy hair! Would today's youth stop at nothing? But twenty-year-old Tommy was energetic, jumped around a lot while playing, and, best of all, looked perfectly harmless.

Steele's creative team could have been forgiven their rock & roll ignorance; in fact, until RCA started releasing Elvis's records on their British label late in 1956 and EMI, which had bought Capitol, inexplicably loosed "Be-Bop-A-Lula" on the unsuspecting country ("a straightforward idiot chant": *New Musical Express*) the only thing they'd had to go by was what Bill Haley was putting out, and after a couple of decent records, he was losing the thread, as witness "Mambo Rock." But the worst thing Haley did was sign up for a quickie film, *Rock Around the Clock*, thrown together with Alan Freed, the Platters, the Ernie Freeman Combo, Tony Martinez and His Band, and Freddie Bell and the Bellboys, Las Vegas's lounge rock attraction, who got to eat up far more celluloid than they deserved. This dire piece of cinema landed in Britain and teenagers got to see Haley, corpulent and with that ridiculous spit curl in the middle of his forehead, churn out a few numbers. In America, the film was the beginning of the end for Haley, whereas British youth were just confused. Fats Domino's "Blueberry Hill" got released ("It seems a great shame that a delightful song like 'Blueberry Hill' must be massacred by a weapon like the voice of Fats Domino": *NME* again), but the perfect indignity was "Why Do Fools Fall in Love," for which Frankie Lymon and the Teenagers took abuse in the British press for being young and black, and anyway, when a professional singing group (white and British) called the Stargazers performed it on a BBC television show, anyone could see that people who knew music could make something fairly respectable out of the song. As for Little Richard, who unaccountably had "Tutti Frutti" picked up by a British label, there was no chance that anyone would hear him. A newspaper compared him to "an animated golliwog."

Skiffle it was, then, as the Vipers were signed to Parlophone, where producer George Martin recorded their first single, "Aren't You Glad" b/w "Pick a Bale of Cotton." Novelty fare. Teenagers would eventually learn what quality was. Nobody in America had a thing to worry about; Britain was never going to compete in the rock & roll sweepstakes.

chapter nine

1957: ANNUS MIRABILIS 1

"It's got a beat and you can dance to it." Dick Clark *(center, with microphone)*
and a jukebox jury on *American Bandstand*.
(Pictorial Press Ltd./Alamy Stock Photo)

From time to time, forces converge in such a way that amazing cultural collisions occur in the space of a single year. There will be tremors before the fact, and aftershocks later on, but the year itself seems like a fast train ride through an incredible landscape; 1957 was one of those years for American culture. The most cursory glide through the year's high points will attest to this. In literature, John Cheever's *The Wapshot Chronicle*, Vladimir Nabokov's *Pnin*, and Jack Kerouac's *On the Road* appeared (as did Dr. Seuss's *The Cat in the Hat* and *How the Grinch Stole Christmas*), and copies of Allen Ginsberg's debut collection, *Howl and Other Poems*, were seized from City Lights Bookstore in San Francisco, the beginning of a landmark obscenity trial. On Broadway, Leonard Bernstein's *West Side Story* made its debut. One can pick up just about any jazz album from 1957 and hear genius; Miles Davis alone released *Bags' Groove*, *Birth of the Cool*, *Cookin'*, *Walkin'*, *Relaxin'*, *Miles Ahead*, and *'Round About Midnight*. Thelonious Monk released *Brilliant Corners* and *Thelonious Monk with John Coltrane*, John Coltrane had *Coltrane* and *Trane's Blues*, Charles Mingus released *The Clown*, and Sonny Rollins released *A Night at the Village Vanguard*, *Saxophone Colossus*, and *Way Out West*. Film and the fine arts also came up with masterpieces.

But popular music really blossomed. In just the first few months of the year, a slew of classic records appeared. The Johnny Burnette

Rock and Roll Trio's "Train Kept A-Rollin'," Chuck Berry's "You Can't Catch Me," Jerry Lee Lewis's "Crazy Arms," Warren Smith's "Rock 'n' Roll Ruby" and "Ubangi Stomp" (Lewis and Smith on Sun), Richard Berry and the Pharaohs' "Louie Louie" (*Billboard* gave it a 70), Charlie Feathers's "One Hand Loose," Sonny Burgess's "We Wanna Boogie" b/w "Red Headed Woman" (again, Burgess was on Sun), Buddy Holly's "Modern Don Juan," Johnny Horton's "I'm Comin' Home," Billy Lee Riley and the Little Green Men's "Flyin' Saucers Rock & Roll" (on Sun), Bobby Marchan's "Chickee Wah-Wah," Muddy Waters's "Got My Mojo Workin'," Bo Diddley's "Hey, Bo Diddley" b/w "Mona," and Carl Perkins's "Matchbox" (on—you guessed it—Sun) were among them, and it's worth noting that not a single one of those records made the pop charts and most didn't even make any country or R&B charts except the regional ones.

That list shows some interesting trends, though. Jerry Lee Lewis, Carl Perkins, Warren Smith, Sonny Burgess, and Billy Lee Riley proved that post-Presley, things were really heating up at 706 Union Avenue. Memphis was the rockabilly epicenter, as demonstrated by the Rock and Roll Trio, comprised of Johnny and Dorsey Burnette, two brothers whose dislike for each other was as legendary as their capacity for alcohol, and master guitarist Paul Burleson, who stayed out of their way and played some of the most stinging electric guitar ever. They'd been working the Memphis clubs since 1951, developing their style, and watched Elvis's progress with great interest.

Charlie Feathers, too, was from near Memphis in Mississippi, and, like Carl Perkins, had grown up with black people as friends and neighbors. Somehow he'd eluded Sam Phillips and wound up on King, which was absolutely unable to figure out what to do with him. Johnny Horton was more of a mainstream country artist, but young enough that he picked up on rockabilly, and "I'm Comin' Home" was his most rocking side to date. Over on the R&B side, Bobby Marchan contributed to the tradition of New Orleans nonsense songs, but missed the gold ring this time around, as he would as lead singer of Huey "Piano" Smith and the Clowns' 1957 "Just a Lonely Clown." Radio had to choose between Muddy's mojo and that of Ann Cole, which is probably why that classic slipped by. As for Richard Berry,

Billboard liked the other side of the record, yet another recording of "You Are My Sunshine," the country sing-along authored by the one-time governor of Louisiana, Jimmie Davis. Berry was just another Los Angeles R&B musician, singing with local vocal groups and picking up gigs where he could, including a stint with René Touzet's Cuban American cha-cha group. Their "El Loco Cha Cha" was a catchy thing, and Berry pinched some ideas from it, most notably the rhythm and the chord progression, and wrote lyrics about a Jamaican man pining for a woman vaguely based on the classic "One for My Baby (And One More for the Road)."

Berry's mistake was in recording a cha-cha, not a calypso. Calypso was the fad in early 1957, even if the only calypso artist to hit the charts was Harry Belafonte, Elvis's labelmate on RCA, who'd actually been born in Harlem, albeit to West Indian parents. He'd hit with "Jamaica Farewell" in late 1956, singing in light dialect, and 1957 would make him a star with "The Banana Boat Song (Day-O)," even though his record was competing with another version of the song by the Tarriers, an acoustic trio with banjoist Erik Darling and guitarist Alan Arkin, later best known as an actor. If someone were looking for a trend, they'd be better off looking at the Tarriers, but as of early 1957, people were so eager to see rock & roll off that they welcomed calypso as its successor. Unfortunately, Belafonte's stay on the charts was short (at least as a singles artist; he sold albums for years) and both the bandwagon-hoppers and authentic calypso records released in the United States at the time failed to make any noise.

Leave it to that other Berry, Chuck, to make it perfectly clear. On January 21, he, Johnny Johnson, Howlin' Wolf's guitarist Hubert Sumlin, and the rhythm section of Willie Dixon and Fred Below went into Chess Studios and cut an instrumental ("Deep Feeling"), a Spanish-language novelty ("La Juanda"), and the teenage national anthem "School Day (Ring Ring Goes the Bell)." For a thirty-year-old man, Berry certainly understood the teenage psyche, and this tale of waiting all day in school, hating every minute of it when suddenly *ring, ring* goes the bell and you were released to head down to the burger joint with its jukebox and, as Chuck sang, rrrrrroll the coin right into the slot to achieve liberation from all that the day had handed you so far. "Hail! Hail! Rock and roll," he sang. "Deliver me from the days of old." It was that simple, and any teen with a nickel (jukeboxes cost five cents a play, six for a quarter) could do it. There it was: an instruction manual for being a teenager, a map to the territory you could claim, an affirmation that your culture existed alongside another one and was different from and in many ways superior to it. Coming onto the charts in April, "School Day" stayed there for a whopping twenty-six weeks, reaching #3 on the pop chart and #1 on the R&B chart. This would be Chuck Berry's year, although Elvis and others would pass through it, too; the important point is that Berry's succeeding records were all more successful on the pop charts than on the R&B charts. And there was more where that came from, too.

Buddy Holly, though, was going through some tough times. Decca had utterly failed to figure him out, and the two singles they'd released on him sank without a trace. To compound his problems, his manager, Hi Pockets Duncan, had quit radio and moved to Amarillo, where he opened a nightclub, the Clover Club. He got a call from Buddy saying that the band sure could use some work, so he closed the bar for a night and promoted Buddy's appearance there as a teen dance, which did a lot better than expected, so it became a regular thing. Realizing that Decca wasn't going to stay in the picture much longer, Buddy changed course; first, he assembled a new band, consisting of Jerry Allison on drums and Niki Sullivan on second guitar. Next, he started visiting Clovis, New Mexico, right across the state line and not a terribly long drive from Lubbock. Clovis was the home of Norman Petty, leader of the Norman Petty Trio, an instrumental combo featuring Norman on organ, his wife, Vi, on piano, and Jack Vaughan, a drummer. They played what might be termed cocktail music, but in 1954 had had a hit with a rendition of "Mood Indigo" that had sold well and made enough money for Petty to open a studio in his hometown, equipped with the latest gear. Needless to say, it became a magnet for west Texas musicians, and a band called the Rhythm Orchids had cut a record there late in 1956, which resulted in two hits and launched two careers: Buddy Knox's "Party Doll" and Jimmy Bowen's "I'm Sticking with You," which they sold to Roulette. They were both on the same 45, and they both did very well, which seemed auspicious for Buddy's chances. Petty also had connections to Columbia Records' Mitch Miller, who was the head of the pop music department there, and had signed the Petty Trio. Buddy went over to Clovis in January with the band and recorded a couple of numbers, including a version of "Brown Eyed Handsome Man," and then returned at the end of February with two songs, one of which, "That'll Be the Day," he'd been working on for some time and had actually recorded in Nashville, and the other, "Looking for Someone to Love," knocked out just before the trip so there would be a B side for the demo they intended to send to Decca in New York to see if they understood him any better than the Nashville office had.

There was a bit of a problem: Buddy had been told Decca wasn't picking up his contract, but he also hadn't been released from it, and it specified that he couldn't re-record any of the material he'd done for them. Someone hit on the idea of crediting the demo to a group, so they began to search for a name. Over at Jerry Allison's house there was an encyclopedia, so they had it open to the article on insects, maybe thinking about the Spiders, a vocal group from New Orleans that had had a minor hit recently. First they were going to call themselves the Grasshoppers, but nobody thought much of that. They scrutinized the color plates of bugs for more inspiration. Aha! The Beetles! But Jerry said, "Aw, that's just a bug you want to step on," so that was out. He suggested the Crickets: didn't they make music by rubbing their legs together? By now everyone was tired of the game, so they all agreed on the Crickets, and played a few gigs under that name. Along the way they picked up a bassist, Joe B. Mauldin, who was still in high school but was a seasoned musician already. Now that the band was complete, they went back to Clovis on March 1 and recorded "Last Night," one of Joe's compositions, and a new song by Buddy, "Maybe Baby." They sent the demos off, not to Decca, but to Roulette, hoping for the success the Buddy Knox / Jimmy Bowen tunes had had. Then they headed to Amarillo to audition for *Arthur Godfrey's Talent Scouts* TV program. Godfrey turned them down. (He'd also turned down Elvis, who'd auditioned in 1955.) Then word came back from Roulette: not interested. Now

Petty took charge and contacted Murray Deutsch, of Peer-Southern Music, a big music publishing firm. Deutsch flipped when he heard the record, and he got turned down by Atlantic, Columbia, and RCA. Finally, he went to Bob Thiele, who'd been put in charge of Coral, a Decca sub-label that had Lawrence Welk, the McGuire Sisters, and Thiele's future wife, Teresa Brewer. Thiele didn't answer right away: he had to get anything he released past the brass at Decca, and they hated the record. Thiele and Deutsch loved it, but Thiele couldn't do anything. Finally, Deutsch prevailed on him to press up a thousand copies of "That'll Be the Day" so he could exercise his rights as publisher. Then things got really confusing. Although Buddy's first record had come out on Decca, the rest of the Nashville sessions were given to a subsidiary, Brunswick, which just sat on them. Now Buddy was on *another* Decca subsidiary, Coral, and in violation of his not-yet-expired contract with the main label. When the dust cleared, the new version of "That'll Be the Day" came out on Brunswick in May, Buddy had relinquished all rights to the earlier recording, and Norman Petty's Nor-Va-Jak Music had stepped in to make sure things ran smoothly from now on. Furthermore, there would be Buddy Holly records on Coral and Crickets records on Brunswick, all featuring the same musicians. But this wasn't the problem it seemed, because when "That'll Be the Day" came out that summer, it rocketed to the top of the charts and stayed there for twenty-two weeks.

Although Buddy Holly's guitar playing could get wild at times, there was still something gentler and more melodic about his records that pointed at another approach to rock & roll, one that found favor in Nashville, where Archie Bleyer thought he'd discovered another talent that would sell records. Heaven knows he needed it. He'd started Cadence Records in hopes that Arthur Godfrey, his old boss, would sign to it, and then found he wouldn't. He'd signed Steve Lawrence, a young crooner whose contract he'd bought from King, which had no idea what to do with him, and then the Chordettes, a female trio who'd appeared on Godfrey's television show and had had some hits including a cover of the Teen Queens' "Eddie My Love." (One of them was also Bleyer's wife.) But he wasn't really making waves until he approached two kids who'd grown up performing on their family's radio show in Shenandoah, Iowa. Don and Phil Everly grew up in a musical family. Their father, Ike, was from Kentucky and learned a lot of the local ballads and songs while developing into a monster guitar player, a skill he shared with several other guitarists who came to learn from him, most notably Merle Travis. But Ike never seriously considered a musical career and subsisted on a number of other occupations, including barber. His sons grew up on the family show, introduced as "Little Donny and Baby Boy Phil," and surviving recordings show that the close blend of their voices was with them from the start, no doubt influenced by the country brother-singing tradition started by the Blue Sky Boys, the Monroe Brothers, the Louvin Brothers, and the Delmore Brothers. Once the boys were out of high school, Ike moved the family closer to Nashville, and eventually Chet Atkins, who ran RCA's Nashville studio and was a friend of Ike's, invited them to try a record. He got them a deal with Columbia, for which they recorded one flop, and placed a song with Patsy Cline ("Thou Shalt Not Steal"), but they didn't really take off until Atkins introduced them to Wesley Rose at Acuff-Rose Music, a major force in Nashville music publishing. Rose signed them as writers and mentioned them to Archie Bleyer when he asked if Rose knew any talent he could record. Bleyer signed them in February 1957, and, perhaps wary of recording an original tune, put them onto Felice and Boudleaux Bryant, a married couple who'd become Nashville's first professional songwriters—they just wrote and never performed. Boudleaux was eager for the assignment—Ike Everly was his barber—and so he and Felice handed them "Bye Bye Love," an up-tempo number that showed off their voices (and had been rejected by thirty other acts) and suddenly Archie wasn't worried anymore; it just missed the #1 slot and stayed on the charts for twenty-seven weeks. It also had an Everlys original on the B side, "I Wonder If I Care as Much," that showed that any worries about their songwriting were unwarranted.

Patsy Cline, to whom the boys had sold that song, was another Nashville face going pop. Born Virginia Hensley, she'd been around a while, recording standard (and substandard) country fare for Four Star, a minor label affiliated with Decca, and making occasional appearances on the *Grand Ole Opry*, but it wasn't until she signed to Decca itself and recorded at Bradley's Barn that she began to see success. Owen Bradley saw that she had a strong, smoky voice without a hint of twang, as well as the ability to phrase like a jazz singer, so he just dispensed with the country trimmings entirely (much to the delight of some of his studio musicians, who frequently jammed with black musicians on the other side of town after hours) and went for a straightforward pop sound on "Walkin' After Midnight," her first record, and found that it sold well in both the pop and country markets. It would take a few more years for Cline's career to really take off, but the mere fact of her existence in the Nashville machine pointed to a new way of doing things in an increasingly sclerotic scene. Bradley didn't stop there, either: Decca had signed an eleven-year-old vocalist in 1956 named Brenda Lee who likewise didn't take off until Owen Bradley took over her production, which showed that even if he hadn't gotten Buddy Holly, he had ideas that would at the very least modernize country music and make those much-needed crossovers (a country "hit" generally only sold several thousand copies) more frequent. Brenda Lee was a belter, Patsy Cline more nuanced, the Everlys more country but teenage. Nashville was changing.

But the year's top country-to–rock & roll crossover was Jerry Lee Lewis. Sam Phillips knew he had something with this wild youngster with a seemingly unlimited number of songs in his repertoire, but he was damned if he could figure out just what it was. He'd used him on a bunch of sessions but wasn't quite sure what to do with him as a solo artist, and Jerry Lee wasn't helping. For one thing, he'd always been a musical sponge, even back in his childhood in Ferriday, Louisiana, when he and his cousins Mickey Gilley and Jimmy Swaggart would hang out behind a local club they were too young to get into and absorb the various blues singers who played there. Eventually, he convinced his parents to buy him a piano, and learned to play some of this, as well as the music he heard in church.

When it came time for him to make a follow-up to "Crazy Arms," Sam selected an amusing song Jack Clement had written, "It'll Be Me," about a guy so insecure that he's stalking his girlfriend in a bunch of unlikely places, which Lewis was trying to get right one day in

February on a session. At one point the band took a break and some-one mentioned a song Jerry Lee used to do when he backed up a guy named Johnny Littlejohn, an obscure Big Maybelle tune from 1953 that Roy Hall, Webb Pierce's piano player, had recorded. Jerry Lee thought for a moment, trying to remember how it went, got it, and then started attacking the piano like a madman, banging out a boogie and yelling out an invitation to a party in a barn where there was a whole lot of shakin' goin' on. It was a needed diversion to "It'll Be Me," and after it was over they got back to work. But Sam thought there was something to the song, even if he couldn't claim publishing on it, and a couple of days later, he assembled a slightly different band, including Jerry Lee's regular drummer, Jimmy van Eaton, and they tried "Whole Lotta Shakin' Goin' On" again. Two minutes and a few seconds later, they were done, and they put it out in March, whereupon it began its steady ascent to the upper reaches of the pop, R&B, and country charts. All of this proved something to Sam, too; he'd noticed the flood of wannabe Presleys and had been talking with Jack Clement, "saying that I wanted to get off this guitar scene and show that it could be done with other instruments," as he said later. Well, here he was, the guy who could do it. Of course, so could Little Richard, but not like this, not that he was worried about Jerry Lee Lewis. He was too busy blazing through up-tempo songs with girls' names: "Lucille," "Jenny, Jenny," and "Miss Ann," slowing down only for "Lucille"'s B side, "Send Me Some Lovin'," which showed that he could do a down-tempo gos-pel groove with the best of them.

With Richard screaming and whooping his way up and down the charts, you would have thought that Art Rupe would have welcomed a crooner with a proven ability to melt girls' hearts, not try to punish him. Sam Cooke had been singing with the veteran group the Soul Stirrers since late 1950, when he was only nineteen. Not only did he have a wonderful clear tenor, but in the Soul Stirrers, he frequently duetted with Paul Foster, who had a gritty shout that played well off Sam's smoother style. This gave a spurt to their record sales, and the Soul Stirrers' discs outsold all of Specialty's other gospel groups at the time. And as good as their records were, one can only get so much of an idea what they were like in person, when troops of teenage girls—a rarity in the gospel world, where the average female audience member was older—would show up to swoon. Fortunately, Specialty recorded a gospel program at the Shrine Auditorium in LA on July 22, 1955, and the CD reissue of it, pretty much the whole show in real time without overdubs, devotes nearly twenty minutes to the Soul Stirrers' three numbers, so that we can hear Cooke and Foster really getting into it, and driving the women nuts. But Cooke was thirsting for more, so with the encouragement of a growing number of people, including the Pilgrim Travelers' J. W. Alexander, he began to explore, timidly at first, the idea of crossing the line to pop. One of Cooke's showstoppers with the Soul Stirrers was a song called "Wonderful," and he talked to Bumps Blackwell about converting it into a secular song. Finally, in December, Bumps took Sam to New Orleans and booked a session with Cosimo Matassa for the twelfth. They cut four songs, but only released two of them: "Lovable" was a straightforward remake of "Wonderful" with different lyrics, and "Forever," on the B side, was a tune brought to the session by saxophonist Alvin "Red" Tyler. Hoping to head off any angry Soul Stirrers fans, the record came out as by "Dale Cooke" and promptly stiffed. Part of this was because the secret of "Dale"'s actual identity spread like crazy in the gospel world, and there was growing anger. Part of it was because Sam was getting lectured by other gospel performers about the uncertainty of the pop world and the sure thing he had going in gospel. Part of it was because "Dale" wasn't out there promoting the record. And part of it was because Art Rupe wasn't convinced it was a very good record and was becoming more and more sure that he didn't want Sam striking out on his own. He was also having his doubts about Bumps Blackwell, having discovered that the musical education he professed to have was something he'd invented to get a job. Paying for another pop session for Sam Cooke didn't sound like a very good idea.

But, having crossed the Rubicon into pop, Sam saw his options narrowing. He'd sent Bumps a tape of him playing several songs he wanted to record, accompanying himself on the guitar, and Bumps took it to Rupe, noting that if they didn't try another session on Sam they'd lose him to someone else. The Soul Stirrers, for their part, saw

Sam acting up; he was writing most of their songs at this point and chafing at the six-way split of the money coming in, although that was how most gospel groups did it, and the Soul Stirrers were no exception. Sam simply wanted more of the money, and the group was unmovable about that. They also sent Rupe a telegram asking him not to release any more Dale Cooke records, because they felt "Lovable" had cut into their sales. Torn, Sam had a conversation with the man he was beginning to see as a mentor, J. W. Alexander. J. W. had a clear, unsentimental vision that would stay with him for years to come, and he realized that the Soul Stirrers were fighting against cultural forces that were bigger than they were, that their and, indeed, the Pilgrim Travelers' days were numbered. Over dinner after a program both groups had appeared on, Sam dropped his star mask and asked J. W., somewhat timorously, if he thought he could make it as a secular singer. J. W. told him he'd have to forget the Dale Cooke persona and be himself, Sam, but yes, of course, he could make it. So on May 28, 1957, Sam got a ride from a friend to the Chicago airport and got on a plane to Los Angeles. He hadn't even bothered to tell the Soul Stirrers he was quitting, but he had.

In LA, Bumps had been busy. His days at Specialty were numbered, and Rupe had flat-out handed him all of Sam's unreleased material in preparation for figuring out a way to pay him off and cut him loose. Bumps put the word out that he was looking for another company who could use his talents, and found a startup that had promise. Keen Records was an investment for a Greek American manufacturer of airplane parts named John Siamas, who entrusted its running to a young clarinet player, Bob Keene. Keene heard that Bumps was looking, but, more importantly, he had Sam Cooke in tow, so he set up a meeting with Bumps and J. W. Alexander to start working out the details. Meanwhile, Sam was getting to know a Los Angeles that gospel singers knew little about, hanging out with a couple of young men who introduced him to a still-vital Central Avenue and hanging out at Dolphin's of Hollywood, the famous twenty-four-hour record store that had DJs spinning live on the radio in its window and was presided over by John Dolphin, the rotund, black, cigar-chomping owner. (It was the store where a lot of LA's white teenagers bought their R&B records, and Dolphin knew his store wasn't anywhere near Hollywood, but blacks weren't allowed in Hollywood, and he figured he'd make his own entertainment capital, and thus called his record label Recorded in Hollywood.) Sam cut a few more tunes for Bumps and then, on September 7, his first record on Keen, "Summertime" b/w "You Send Me," came out—masters that Rupe had given Bumps. It took off almost immediately once radio figured out that the supposed B side was the hit, and, because it was selling even better than his previous timid venture into secular music, it faced a wave of scorn from the gospel world. But it was a great start for Keen— and Keene—and Bumps began whispering in the ears of other gospel performers on Specialty that Rupe wasn't in such great shape and if they were thinking of crossing over, they might find a home at the new label.

Spiritual crisis was all around, it seemed. Jerry Lee Lewis's decision to head to Memphis to audition for Sun had been occasioned by his having been booted out of Bible college in east Texas after boogying up a hymn during worship services, and his decision to go secular was still not sitting well with him when the time came to record a follow-up to "Whole Lotta Shakin'." On October 8, he sat down with a couple of songs that had been sent to Sun for him by Otis Blackwell, a black songwriter and sometime performer who'd written "All Shook Up" and "Don't Be Cruel" for Elvis. "Great Balls of Fire" was the obvious choice, and Jerry Lee and the band were rehearsing it when suddenly the star balked. Fortunately, Jack Clement was prone to leaving the tape running during sessions, and he caught the discussion that followed. Alcohol was almost certainly involved, and all of a sudden the image of great balls of fire seized Jerry Lee's imagination and he refused to go any further. Sam came into the studio to try to talk sense to him, but the notion that he'd been recording "worldly music," as he put it, had paralyzed him and nothing Sam could say would budge him—not that Sam's argument was much more coherent than Jerry Lee's, although the tone of his voice shows a man trying to quell a panic-stricken young man. The tape ends with Jerry Lee saying, "Man, I got *the devil* in me! If I didn't have, I'd be a Christian!" It's not recorded how Sam turned things around, but fortunately for rock & roll, he did. How fortunate it was for Jerry Lee is hard to say; these demons were to follow him for quite some time.

And then there was Little Richard, who was under increasing pressure from former R&B saxophonist Joe Lutcher, who'd had a conversion experience and was now evangelizing pop musicians, to renounce his worldly ways. In October, when Russia launched the Sputnik satellite and made headlines, Richard and his band were on tour in Australia, and Richard believed he'd either seen the satellite from his plane, or, as he claimed, "it looked as though the big ball of fire came directly over the stadium about two or three hundred feet over our heads. It shook my mind." Shook it so badly, in fact, that he decided that night to quit show business. The next day at a press conference, he announced, "If you want to live for the Lord, you can't rock and roll, too. God doesn't like it." His saxophone player, Clifford Burks, joshed Richard about it as they took the ferry across Sydney Harbour, and Richard, to show his sincerity, took a ring valued at $8,000 and threw it into the water. They canceled the tour that day, stranding the other acts on the package, Gene Vincent and the Blue Caps and Alis Lesley (the "female Elvis"), and flew home to lawsuits and harsh words from Art Rupe, but Richard checked into a Bible college and refused to talk. Not everyone had the freedom Elvis had, to sing spirituals with the Jordanaires, a group not unlike the Stamps Quartet he idolized, and release them alongside his pop records. In fact, in April, he released two EPs, *Just for You*, with ballads, and *(There'll Be) Peace in the Valley (For Me)*, the title track of which had reached #25 on the pop charts.

Another group that had renounced gospel, the "5" Royales, were beginning to regret their decision to, if not go secular, at least sign with King Records. Since 1954, they'd been recording one great record after another, all with no result whatever. Whether a novelty like "Monkey Hips and Rice" or "Mohawk Squaw" or up-tempo rockers like "Women About to Make Me Go Crazy," "Right Around the Corner," or "Come On and Save Me" or soulful harmony numbers like "When You Walked Through the Door," or "Get Something Out of It"—all records that have the capacity to astonish even today—there was no response from radio, although certainly some of them appeared on jukeboxes throughout the South, where they were still touring relentlessly. It's a good thing King didn't drop them, and maybe someone decided that a change of studio might be indicated, because all of the above were recorded in New York with Mickey Baker, one of the great guitarists of the era, playing on them. But the Royales already had one of the great guitarists of the era in the group: their triple-threat guitarist / songwriter / bass singer Lowman "Pete" Pauling, so when they gave him a free hand on a session at King Studios in Cincinnati on February 28, great things happened—they recorded "Tears of Joy," a ballad, which was a top-ten R&B hit for them, and one of the most gospelly things they'd recorded yet, "Think." Featuring group hand-claps and the biting, incisive sound of Pauling's Gibson Les Paul guitar weaving in and out of the vocal arrangement, it was a workout that took a few seconds to sort out all the motion, after which the listener would presumably join in the fun. It was a top-ten R&B song and got as far as #66 on the pop charts and probably saved the "5" Royales' career. Now they were playing everywhere, including the Apollo Theater in New York, touring with the big package shows. Six months later, with "Think" still all over the place, they went back in and did it again, cutting four more songs, one of which would become a classic—but not, unfortunately, for them. "Messin' Up" was an up-tempo dance number of no great consequence, but its B side, "Say It," has Johnny Tanner's pleading, soulful lead vocal duetting with some of the most savage guitar playing Pauling ever recorded, on the edge of overdriving the amp. Nothing. But the next one, "Dedicated to the One I Love," would live on as a hit . . . by the Shirelles and, even later, the Mamas and the Papas. Its B side, "Don't Be Ashamed," was clearly a gospel remake, again with Lowman's guitar in full force. Incredible as it may seem, this record never saw the charts, although presumably it got some airplay. But in 1957, it was just another lost classic.

Part of the problem, of course, wasn't a problem at all; rock & roll, rhythm and blues, and country music were all minority-interest genres, although rock & roll's willingness to include the other two meant it was bigger than they were. Plus, trade magazines editorialized that any black record company that didn't give at least passing thought to the growing white teen market was shooting itself in the foot. That was only partially true. B. B. King was still having hits, Jimmy Reed was doing very well indeed, Chess was still releasing blues, Chuck Berry notwithstanding (and had a minor hit with Muddy Waters's guitarist Jimmy Rogers on "Walking By Myself"), and Don Robey was promoting a new generation of blues artists from Memphis on his Duke label. Johnny Ace belonged to the ages, but he'd lured Junior Parker away from Sam Phillips (whose interest in blues faded as soon as the rockabillies happened) and scored the first of many hits with "The Next Time You See Me," and had picked up another of Johnny Ace's circle, a young man named Bobby "Blue" Bland, who sang in a smooth voice that he occasionally interrupted with an odd growling sound, and whose "Farther Up the Road" introduced him to audiences outside his hometown for the first time.

The main obstacle—or non-obstacle—was that all media was regional. Network television and radio wasn't about to treat rock & roll as anything but a fad, occasional appearances by stars on shows like Ed Sullivan's or Steve Allen's notwithstanding. *Billboard* and the other trades still carried regional charts, knowing that something that was a hit in Detroit or Memphis or Chicago or Atlanta might go nationwide, but might also generate a lot of heat and then fade, never making that next step. Or perhaps it would spread to another couple of cities in the region—Chicago to Detroit and Cleveland, for instance—but never make the leap to the two cities that mattered to the mass media, New York and Los Angeles. But regionalism also meant that an explosion of talent could be tolerated by the pop ecosystem; the majority of the acts just couldn't get past a glass ceiling of popularity. This situation would soon change, but slowly. Two things helped it along: television and a new approach to radio.

Television, as noted, wasn't paying much attention to rock & roll. As sets got more affordable, more people bought them, and the viewing audience just exploded. Besides variety shows like Ed Sullivan's, there was a boom in half-hour situation comedies, family-oriented tales of mild misadventure, all heartwarmingly resolved at the end. One of the big ones was *The Adventures of Ozzie and Harriet*, featuring

Ozzie and Harriet Nelson and their two sons, David and Ricky. Ozzie Nelson had been a successful "sweet" bandleader, his wife, Harriet, had been his female vocalist, and they were very familiar with how Hollywood worked, so when Ozzie suggested a show based on his family to network radio, based on some sketches he'd done on Red Skelton's radio show, they went for it. The boys were played by actors for the first several years, but by 1952, when the show moved to ABC television, they played themselves. Ozzie wrote the scripts, the opening credits showed their actual house, not far from the western end of Hollywood Boulevard, and they had a hit on their hands. But when Ricky turned sixteen in 1956, he had a request: Ricky liked rock & roll, and badgered his father to let him make a rock & roll record. Ozzie, thinking it was a good idea if the kid would play it on the show, agreed, and pulled some strings in the music world to make it happen. A one-off deal with the jazz label Verve was set up, with a band assembled by (and featuring) Barney Kessel, the jazz guitarist who was doing A&R for Verve. They settled on a cover of Fats Domino's recent hit "I'm Walking" for the A side and something called "A Teenager's Romance" for the flip and put it out. Of course, Ozzie quickly worked up a scene where Ricky played his record on the show, and the record took off the next day, a double-sided hit that was #1 in a number of regional markets, and in the top ten nationally. Lew Chudd woke up to the fact that a song by one of his artists was making noise and asked Ozzie if Ricky would like to sign a deal with him, and soon enough, Ricky was signed to Imperial, their first teen star. For the show, Ricky used the same band he'd be using on the Imperial records, which included James Burton, a guitarist a year younger than Ricky who'd been playing with a guy named Dale Hawkins and who'd created an irresistible guitar riff for Hawkins's big hit "Susie Q," which hit the airwaves at about the same time as Ricky's second record, "Be Bop Baby." Teenagers now tuned in *The Adventures of Ozzie and Harriet* on the chance (increasingly likely) that Ricky would finish the show by playing a song with his band.

But that was just one performer, one show, once a week. ABC-TV's answer to the summer slump in ratings added more performers: an Alan Freed TV show, hosted by the charismatic radio star. This worked so well that in August, they added a daily show they'd picked up from their affiliate in Philadelphia, WFIL, to their national feed. Dubbed *American Bandstand*, it was hosted by a guy who looked like a teenager, but wasn't (he was twenty-seven at the time), Dick Clark. Clark had been in radio since he'd actually been a teenager, which was partially what made the show, which aired in the dead zone from 3:00 to 4:30 daily, a hit; the formula was to play records and have a carefully screened bunch of kids on to dance to them. Every day, a performer or two would come on to lip-synch to their latest hit, and there would be interaction with the dancers in the form of interviews (mentioning the high schools they went to, of course), and a jukebox jury of kids rating new releases and spawning the cliché "It's got a good beat and you can dance to it. I'll give it a 9." Clark also did a top-ten countdown each week, which, like the rest of the show, purported to be national, and, once ABC started to broadcast it from coast to coast, actually was.

The importance of *American Bandstand* to the summer of 1957 can't be overestimated. For the record industry, it was the first national exposure for their product; getting a record on *Bandstand* was tantamount to breaking it nationwide immediately instead of waiting for the regionals to report it. For the kids, though, it was a window to a teen paradise. Here were teenagers wearing teenage fashions, doing dances most teens had never seen (the first to break out was a sedate line dance, the stroll, which you could do to Chuck Willis's current hit, "C.C. Rider," for instance), being treated like their ideas were worth listening to when Clark interviewed them about their lives and schoolwork. Not only did the show make stars out of performers, it also made stars out of its regulars, who may not have been on every day (there were frequent casting calls at Philadelphia high schools) but were often enough to attract fan letters. True, it wasn't all as idyllic as it seemed (or was it? Firsthand reports from regulars detail make-out sessions and outright sex in the cloakroom and reefer smoking on the building's roof), and Dick Clark was busily making a little showbiz empire, with a few music-publishing companies, an investment in a record-pressing plant and a distributor, and very close relationships with some of Philadelphia's many record labels.

And *Bandstand* spawned imitators; rare was the urban center that didn't soon have a local jock doing the same thing, only with local teens and local talent, and in Newark, there was what amounted to a black *Bandstand* under the aegis of Doug "Jocko" Henderson. Jocko was on 4:00 P.M. to 6:00 P.M. on WDAS in Philadelphia, and then got on the train for New York, where he did it again from 10:00 P.M. to midnight on WOV. Henderson has never gotten the credit he deserves for turning teens on to current black hits and dances, not to mention the torrent of jive talk he spouted, which had white jocks trying to figure out enough of it so they could do it themselves. *Jocko's Rocket Ship Show* was, for teens in the New York area (those who could get it on their TV sets; the signal wasn't the greatest, even in Manhattan), a hipper alternative to Dick Clark and his crew.

Radio, however, remained the top means of getting news out about a record, although it was hopelessly regional. This was about to change; early in the year, Todd Stortz, a guy who owned a chain of radio stations in the Midwest, was sitting in a bar with his station manager, having what must have been more than a few drinks. Over the course of the session, they noticed that although there were a couple hundred selections on the jukebox, most customers played the same few over and over; Stortz estimated it was about forty records. But something else was going on, too; at the end of the night, the waitresses took some of their tip money and fed it to the jukebox to play as they cleaned and closed the place—and even though they'd heard the records all night long, they chose the same ones. Stortz got to work and introduced what he called the Top Forty formula on KOWH in Omaha. The equation for figuring out the mix was a trade secret, but must have included reports from jukebox operators and record stores, as well as the *Billboard* or *Cash Box* charts. Whatever it was, it worked, and pretty soon Stortz's other stations started leading the markets in their cities. In Fort Worth, Gordon McLendon, another businessman with multiple stations, came up with his own formula and tried it on his stations, and again, it worked. Oh, some DJs quit, of course, angry that they couldn't make their own programming decisions—and, no doubt, angry that the money some record companies were paying some of them to play records was now going elsewhere—but this was a lot more efficient for management than the anarchy that had prevailed up to then, and a godsend for record companies. If the Stortz or McLendon chains (or, ideally, both) went on one of your records, you were made; your record got added to dozens of stations at once, instead of piecemeal. Even better, you didn't have to worry whether the record was "good" or not; mathematics took care of that! The higher the ratings, the more money the chains made, and the more money they made, the more stations they could buy, soon either expanding out of the regional market they'd dominated or franchising the formula to other chains. Furthermore, with the decline of network radio as a source for broadcast drama and comedy shows, a role that was being completely taken over by television, this gave independent stations playing nothing but music and news (including local sports) a huge leg up in profitability. Radio was still big business, thanks to the Top Forty.

The summer of 1957 saw the first flowering of rock & roll as a national phenomenon, although it was still controversial. It was the summer of Elvis's "All Shook Up" and "(I Want to Be) Your Teddy Bear" and Little Richard's "Jenny, Jenny" and "Keep a-Knockin'," that old New Orleans whorehouse favorite, the Everly Brothers' "Bye Bye Love" and "Wake Up, Little Susie" (both written by the Bryants), of the Crickets' "That'll Be the Day," and Chuck Berry's "School Day." It was Fats Domino doing "I'm Walkin'" and "Blue Monday" (which he'd taken from Imperial's no-luck New Orleans guitarist Smiley Lewis), Clarence "Frogman" Henry's "I Ain't Got No Home" and Huey "Piano" Smith and the Clowns' "Rockin' Pneumonia and the Boogie-Woogie Flu," just in case anyone thought New Orleans didn't still have its mojo. Larry Williams celebrated "Bony Moronie" and "Short Fat Fannie," LaVern Baker raved about "Jim Dandy," and the Bobbettes harmonized about "Mr. Lee," a teacher they had a crush on. For those oh-so-crucial slow dances, the Platters offered "I'm Sorry" and "My Dream," Lee Andrews and the Hearts told of "Long Lonely Nights," the Tune Weavers wished a "Happy, Happy Birthday, Baby," and the Five Satins told of each step drawing closer "To the Aisle." When teens weren't slow dancing or doing the stroll, the Del-Vikings suggested the "Cool Shake" and Andre Williams the "Bacon Fat." Actually, that last one was probably a put-on, since Williams concedes that some do it like this and some do it like that, and, as his under-the-counter word-of-mouth hit "Jail Bait" proved, he wasn't too serious about anything.

It was a great year for Leiber and Stoller: Atlantic signed them to an A&R and production deal that enabled them to put together the Coasters and move to New York. Right out of the box, a group specializing in cleverly written comic songs about being a teenager was fated to succeed, and "Searchin'" and "Young Blood" started a run of hits that wouldn't abate for years, every one of them written by the dynamic duo. Not only that, but practically before they had time to unpack, Jerry and Mike were asked by Colonel Tom Parker to provide songs for Elvis's upcoming film (his third, after *Love Me Tender* and *Loving You*), *Jailhouse Rock*. Elvis was making films fast, but he loved the work, loved living in Hollywood with a circle of his friends who were laughingly referred to as the Memphis Mafia (and who would have acted like a real one had anyone tried to hurt him), and was even getting good reviews for *Loving You*. Certainly it was better than the quickie movies being made: *Rock Around the Clock*, which exposed way too much of Bill Haley and essentially sealed his doom as a teen favorite, *Don't Knock the Rock*, which had another memorable moment from Little Richard and too much of Bill Haley and the Treniers, *Mister Rock and Roll*, starring Alan Freed in the story of how he discovered rock & roll (really!), with contributions from Chuck Berry, Little Richard, Frankie Lymon, Clyde McPhatter, and Lionel Hampton, and the simultaneously fascinating and horrifying *Rock Baby-Rock It*. This last was the result of a Dallas wrestling promoter, J. G. Tiger, putting together a rock & roll package tour with some local talent, most notably Johnny Carroll, an Elvis wannabe signed to Decca. Apparently the tour ran out of money, and Tiger had the brilliant idea of taking the talent and doing a quickie movie around them while he still had them to hand. With luck, the film would make enough money to pay everyone off, so a script about a bunch of kids who held rock & roll parties at their clubhouse, which is suddenly menaced by bad guys who want to buy the property, was conjured up. The bad guys were played by Tiger's wrestlers, and the acting is only as good as you needed to be a semi-pro wrestler in Dallas in 1957. The good guys were the kids, many of whom were the musicians; besides Carroll, there were the Five Stars, a singing group, aging Sun blues pianist Rosco Gordon (whose gimmick was a dancing chicken atop his piano), Preacher Smith and the Deacons, who sounded a bit like Fats Domino, and the Belew Twins. None of these people made even a dent in the national charts (although Carroll would be one of the Texas rockabillies rediscovered by a later generation), so the film is a slice of life in a healthy local rock & roll scene in a city that is also the center of a regional country scene, and the home of a radio program, the *Big D Jamboree*, that mixed both of them in its weekly broadcast from Tiger's wrestling arena. More films were promised for the fall, led by *Jailhouse Rock*, which was actually pretty good and with a knockout score (the title tune immediately shot to #1, and the scene where Elvis sings the title tune is a proto–rock video), and *Jamboree*, a Warner Bros. production that was essentially a package tour on film, with Jerry Lee Lewis, Fats Domino, Buddy Knox, Jimmy Bowen, Charlie Gracie, the Four Coins, Carl Perkins, Frankie Avalon, Lewis Lymon and the Teenchords (yes, Frankie Lymon's younger brother), Slim Whitman, Connie Francis, and the Count Basie Orchestra featuring Joe Williams. The film was also arranged so that local DJs could cut scenes to be inserted, and Dick Clark, Jocko Henderson, and various other American, Canadian, British, and German jocks did them.

In Memphis, Sam Phillips, having abandoned blues and begun assembling a stable of rockabillies, started a new label, Phillips International (PI), to concentrate on pop music, stuff with less of a twang. Its logo had the words "New York—Memphis—Hollywood," which was maybe wishful thinking, and it launched in September with records by Buddy Blake, Hayden Thompson, Barbara Pittman, Johnny Carroll (whom he poached from Decca), and Bill Justis. The motive behind PI was just a little bit cynical; Sam knew the Dutch label Philips was going to enter the U.S. market eventually, and he planned to have a similarly named label up and running by that time so they'd have to buy him out. He told Johnny Carroll that he'd release all five singles at the same time, and whichever of the artists sold, he'd write them a longer-term contract. That was a bet he didn't exactly win: of the five records, Bill Justis's "Raunchy" took off, an instrumental that was instantly catchy and wound up as a #1 pop record—Sun's biggest triumph since Elvis. Justis was already employed by Sam as his studio bandleader, so in a way he already had a contract. But the real surprise came just after PI launched: Marion Keisker, who'd been at Sam's side since 1950 when they were both on the same radio station, suddenly quit to join the Air Force. She and Sam had had a big fight, and she'd just walked out. When Elvis came by at Christmas, he realized that things had changed at Sun, and one of those was that Ms. Keisker was no longer there. Another thing—although they wouldn't find this out for another couple of weeks—is that Carl Perkins, having not had a hit in ages, was about to sign with Columbia. That's okay, there was still Jerry Lee.

The year ended on a very high note; in May, Chuck Berry had gone into Chess Studios with pianist Lafayette Leake and a rhythm section of Willie Dixon and Fred Below and cut another session, which included a couple of obscure tunes ("Oh Baby Doll," "How You've Changed"), one of his trickier lyrics ("13 Question Method"), and the anthem teenage America had been waiting for. "Rock and Roll Music" was, even more than "School Day," a celebration of the music's central place in teen life, a declaration of independence, and a performance like Berry had never before given, with guitar pyrotechnics supporting a great lyric. He made it perfectly clear: he had nothing against other types of music, provided they were well played, but "It's gotta be rock and roll music / If you wanna dance with me." And what teenager in his or her right mind could disagree?

chapter ten

1958: HOODLUM
FRIENDS OUTSIDE

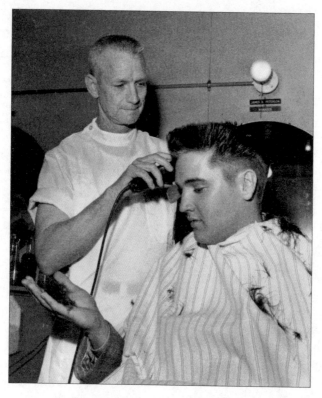

Elvis receives his regulation military haircut.
(Bettmann/Contributor)

On December 19, 1957, Elvis Presley got a phone call from the head of the local draft board. He'd been expecting to hear from them ever since, some months back, he'd been classified 1-A, and now he had. He'd waved off offers from some of the armed forces, offering to give him special treatment, like assignment to a special Elvis Presley unit filled with guys from Memphis, or else the kind of deal some other performers got, working with entertainers on the USO circuit while in uniform. Elvis was at the height of his career; he'd just bought Graceland, an eighteen-room mansion on Highway 51 south of town, that had belonged to a respected physician whose daughter was a classical musician. It cost $102,500 just for the house and acreage, but Elvis had hired the decorator who was doing Sam Phillips's new house and had ordered cast-iron gates with music notes on them, as well as a large swimming pool out back, all of which would cost him a half million dollars before it was finished. A chicken house for his mother's chickens was also constructed, and by the end of the year Graceland had become Elvis's clubhouse, with a fully functioning soda fountain for Elvis and his friends to use. The walls were painted new colors, selected by Elvis and his mother. He was touring constantly when he wasn't making movies—1957 had seen his first dates in Hawaii—and there were new films being lined up all the time, so it was good to finally have a place to relax during the downtime.

Elvis drove downtown to pick up his draft notice, stopped in at Sun to show it off, and then went back to Graceland, where his friend George Klein saw the notice and asked what he was going to do. "Man, I don't know," he told Klein. "The Colonel says we might could get a deferment to make *King Creole* [his next film], but he says I probably got to go." The Colonel was adamant that no boats should be rocked at any time in Elvis's career, for a good reason that didn't surface for many, many years: everyone knew he'd bought his "Colonel" title, but he wasn't Tom Parker at all. He was Andreas van Kuijk, a Dutch citizen who'd escaped the law (perhaps, as his sister later surmised, for indictment for murder) and stowed away on a ship to America in his late teens. He wasn't an American citizen, didn't have a passport because he was in the country illegally, and, thus, would never leave the United States and deflected all the government's gaze away from Elvis and, by association, himself. Throughout Elvis's career, he paid their taxes with the simplified Form 1040, although it meant giving up loads of deductions he could have claimed (and, at a 50 percent management fee, wildly disproportionate to the 15–20 percent other managers charged, taking money out of his own pocket), and refused huge offers to have Elvis appear overseas. For all of Colonel Tom Parker's bluff and colorful image, Andreas van Kuijk lived in a world of fear. Colonel Tom knew people who could fix things for Elvis. Van Kuijk didn't dare call them.

On Christmas Eve, Elvis sent a request to the draft board saying that he was ready to go in right away, but knowing that Paramount had already spent several hundred thousand dollars in pre-production expenses, asked to delay his induction for sixty days so he could make the movie. The board agreed to wait. A visitor, however, noticed that Elvis wasn't his normal cheerful self; he was visiting Graceland when the doorbell rang and Elvis signed for a package, returned to the room, and tossed it on the couch. Eventually, he was asked if he wasn't going to open it. He did. "Oh yeah," he said. "My gold record." He put on a good face for the public. "I'm kinda proud of it," he said about going into the Army. "It's a duty I've gotta fill, and I'm going to do it." But first there was a film to make, so Elvis and the Memphis Mafia packed up and went to California, where Elvis reported to the director, Michael Curtiz, the man who'd made *Casablanca* and *Mildred Pierce,* and started work on *King Creole.* Simultaneously, or, rather, around the scenes he was in, he was recording the soundtrack album under Leiber and Stoller's guidance, with some new songs from them. RCA was trying to load up the vaults with material they could release while he was in the Army, and Elvis had become somewhat superstitious about needing the two songwriters in the studio while he recorded, so with time being short, RCA scheduled a last session for February 1. Unfortunately, Jerry Leiber was recovering from a particularly nasty bout of pneumonia in New York, and his doctor refused to let him travel. Then the Colonel started threatening him, and asking him if he'd signed the publishing contracts he'd sent while Leiber was indisposed. Leiber replied that he'd looked at some, but not all, of them and Parker suggested he open the rest. One was a blank page with the Colonel's signature and a space for Leiber's. "Don't worry," he advised Leiber, "we'll fill it in later." It was too much. "We never worked with him again," Leiber said later. "That was it. We never talked to each other again." The men who'd written "Hound Dog" were out of the picture due to the Colonel's power play. It was only the first of many incidents that would pull Elvis away from his roots so that the Colonel could make a buck.

And there were bucks to be made, on Elvis, and on other rock & roll phenomena. Television dance shows, for instance: even the Memphis madman Dewey Phillips had one, at least until his on-screen sidekick, dressed in a gorilla suit, got a little too suggestive with a pinup of Jayne Mansfield on camera. Dick Clark's star was rising so fast that ABC-TV gave him a Saturday night show in prime time, one act after another lip-synching their hits in front of a seated theater audience. It didn't last very long, but the fact that a network would provide rock & roll such a visible slot was significant.

Another source of bucks was records, of course. New record labels were popping up all over the place, while others, unable to adapt to contemporary sounds, began to fade. In Los Angeles, Liberty Records was founded in 1955, and made a star out of Julie London, but it was Eddie Cochran who made them rock & roll fans in 1958, and just to make sure they had the R&B end covered, they signed Billy Ward and His Dominoes, current lead singer Eugene Mumford, formerly of the Larks. United Artists became the latest film studio to open a record label to distribute albums of their soundtracks, but they'd soon be looking at individual artists. ABC-Paramount came into the business, headquartered in New York, but also with an interest in soundtracks and individual artists. All of these were well funded through their other corporate connections. So was Roulette, opened by Morris Levy, owner of the legendary New York jazz club Birdland and friend of various well-connected people with money to launder.

Some of the pioneers weren't doing too well. Before joining the ministry, Little Richard had left a trove of recordings, so Specialty was able to make hits out of "Good Golly, Miss Molly," "Oooh! My Soul," and "Baby Face," as well as releasing an album, even though the star wasn't around to promote any of it with live appearances. They'd also signed Larry Williams, a flamboyant and unstable performer whose two 1957 hits "Short Fat Fannie" and "Bony Moronie" mined Little Richard influences, and then went on to record "Slow Down" and "Dizzy, Miss Lizzy" with Richard's recording band. His last recording for the label was the self-descriptive "Bad Boy," with "She Said 'Yeah!'" on the flip, this last produced by a new kid Art Rupe had found who had his ear on the Los Angeles scene, Sonny Bono. Bono also worked with a duo Rupe had found, Don (Terry) and Dewey (Harris), whose "Justine" was another Little Richard homage, also recorded with Richard's band. But with the exception of Richard's records, none of these were exactly smash hits, nobody was walking in the door, and Rupe had sent Sam Cooke and Bumps Blackwell packing, thereby seriously shooting himself in the foot.

Aladdin was doing much worse, probably because they concentrated on older-style urban blues and jazz; the Mesner brothers would eventually sell the inactive label's catalog to Imperial's Lew Chudd in

1961. Those other brothers, the Biharis, continued to put out singles on Modern, and release B. B. King records on RPM, but found it most profitable to re-package past triumphs as budget-style albums on the Crown label, notorious for covers featuring a painting of a star with the name in huge letters, and, once you got the thing home, finding out that the LOWELL FULSON album you'd just bought only had a couple of his tracks on each side, with the rest of the album filled by no-names from the Modern vaults, who were only identified on the record label itself. Well, what do you want for $1.98? And elsewhere on Central Avenue, John Dolphin, who'd been in business since the late 1940s, was talking to a disgruntled songwriter, one Percy Ivy, about their business relationship when Ivy pulled a gun and blew him away. The murder was witnessed by some white teenagers— Dave Shostack, Bruce Johnston, and Sandy Nelson—who were hoping for an audition. Shostack was hit by a ricochet and was bleeding from his leg, Nelson dropped his soda and ran to get the cops, and Johnston stayed behind, comforting the distraught Ivy—and offering to represent him as publisher for the songs he'd write in jail. Oddly, it didn't seem to discourage Nelson and Johnston from careers in the music business.

Atlantic was an exception to this decline. With the foresight to hire Leiber and Stoller for their teen touch with the Coasters while holding on to Ruth Brown and LaVern Baker and developing Clyde McPhatter into a nightclub act, their breadth of approach meant that they always had a record on the charts. They were still signing people and making them modern; Chuck Willis had had a long string of dull blues records on Okeh dating back to 1952, but when Atlantic grabbed him, he started making stroll records, catching the dance craze just as it was starting, and watching his popularity soar. As a gimmick, he wore a turban onstage, and there's no telling where he might have gone if he hadn't died while being operated on for a bleeding ulcer in Atlanta, aged thirty, on April 28. His posthumously released two-sided top-ten hit was "What Am I Living For?" and "Hang Up My Rock and Roll Shoes," hot on the heels of Atlantic's rewarding him with an album, *King of the Stroll*. (In 1963, they issued another album, which included these last songs, *I Remember Chuck Willis,* with a rare lapse in taste for an Atlantic album cover, a photo of his gravestone.)

Chess was certainly doing all right with Chuck Berry. With "Rock and Roll Music" still getting lots of play, he delivered the story of "Sweet Little Sixteen," about a teenage girl who can't get enough rock & roll—and rock & rollers. She's a nice girl, though, we're assured, which, given some of the stories beginning to make the rounds about Berry, was good news. And while she was ascending to #2 on the pop charts (Berry's best showing to date—and his best until 1972), he came out with another song for the ages. "Johnny B. Goode" certainly wasn't autobiographical, at least not in its precise details, but its story about a poor boy who rises to stardom thanks to his proficiency with a guitar certainly was, and Chuck showed off his playing ("Go! Go, Johnny, go!") brilliantly. Over the years, it became a song that transcended Chuck Berry, but not guitar players. Nor was Chuck Berry the only one making money for Chess in 1958. They'd introduced two new labels, Checker and Argo, with the idea that Checker would be more for rhythm and blues artists than the hard-core blues artists like Muddy Waters and Howlin' Wolf, and Argo would be for jazz. Argo signed a star out of the Pershing Hotel's lounge, a famous Chicago jazz club, pianist Ahmad Jamal, and then recorded him there for a hit live album. Jazz was still big on jukeboxes, especially in black neighborhoods, and by the end of the year, Jamal would have a hit single in "Secret Love." Chess also signed pianist Ramsey Lewis to Argo, but one of the biggest rock & roll records they had was also on Argo, and it was by a vocal group, the Monotones, high school students who, they claimed, were rehearsing their song "Book of Love" one day at school while other kids were outside playing basketball. The lead-up to the verse, "I wonder wonder who do-do do do do!" was suddenly punctuated by the thud of a basketball hitting the window in perfect time, providing the song with the hook that would take it to the top ten on both the pop and R&B charts. Meanwhile, Chess switched both Little Walter and Bo Diddley over to Checker, and Oakland blues singer Jimmy McCracklin's dance novelty "The Walk" (which was even easier to do than the stroll, since according to Mc-Cracklin all you had to do was close your eyes and walk) was also on Checker. There was probably a logic to it, but they were too busy selling records to explain.

Perhaps influenced by Chuck Berry's almost documentary approach to songwriting, rock & roll lyrics started getting into situations other than boy-girl dramas, although having a boy-girl situation to hang them on didn't hurt. America was undergoing an economic slowdown, which brought about one of the year's first big hits. The Silhouettes were a Philadelphia vocal quartet, and quite talented, so they had no problem getting the tiny Junior label to take a chance on them. Their song, "Get a Job," combined tough lyrics, skillful harmonies, and a bridge that featured them stomping their feet and clapping their hands, and immediately flew off the shelves. Dick Clark heard it and loved it, but he had a strict rule: *American Bandstand* went out nationwide, and he wasn't playing any record that didn't have national distribution. But New York's Herald-Ember Records had had hits before (the Five Satins' "In the Still of the Night," for one) and bought the record from Junior, and when Clark saw that it was now on Ember, he played it right away. Said Al Silver, who headed the label, "When I walked into the office the morning after he played it, there were telegrams with back orders for about five hundred thousand records underneath the door . . . Eventually, that record sold a couple million." What on earth was on that slab of plastic? Very simple: the travails of a (presumably black, male) teenager looking for a job. And there was something else: "When I get back to the house," went the bridge, "I hear my mother's mouth / Preachin' and a cryin' / Sayin' that I'm lyin' / About a job / That I never could find." Parents just didn't understand, did they? So Leiber and Stoller abandoned their feeding the Coasters exotica (they were just coming off a weak showing with "The Idol with the Golden Head") and wrote them the biggest hit they ever had, "Yakkety Yak." This featured yet another parent preying on yet another teenager, ordering chores, reminding about homework, and commanding him to "Tell your hoodlum friends outside / You ain't got time to take a ride / Yakkety yak /

(Don't talk back)." Ooh, that stung, and not even the gabbling saxophone, played by New York's new studio star Curtis Ousley (a.k.a. King Curtis) could take the edge off. It was hard out there for a teen, and not everyone could be Johnny B. Goode. (And, of course, there were vocal group records whose lyrics were perfectly impenetrable: "Shombalor," by Sheriff and the Ravels, a Brooklyn group discovered by a West Indian guy who wrote the song with Elmore Sheriff, the lead singer. It's virtually unknown, but you could make the argument that this rapid-fire tongue twister from which words like *Frankenstein* and *Nazi* emerge was a form of protest, too.)

Of course, no smash hit could be without an answer record in those days, and "Get a Job" spawned "Got a Job," full of perky can-do optimism and some fairly decent lyrics. It was by a group from Detroit that had been looking for a break, and got it when George Goldner's End Records picked it up. The Miracles was a group that was just one of the projects being developed by a young black entrepreneur in Detroit, Berry Gordy Jr. Gordy's family had a sort of corporation whereby family members could apply for a loan or other help and pay it back without having to resort to the banks, and they'd already financed Berry's failed jazz record shop. Gordy had been working with a former boxer—and, briefly, a former member of Billy Ward and the Dominoes—Jackie Wilson, a familiar face in Detroit's black club scene, who had a remarkable voice and stage presence, and a record deal with a Chicago label, Brunswick. (If you were a Detroiter and wanted to make a record, you more or less had to go to Chicago.) Gordy wrote songs with his friend Tyran Carlo, and managed to have four hits with Wilson in 1958: "I'm Wanderin'," "We Have Love," "To Be Loved," and, at the end of the year, "Lonely Teardrops," which was Wilson's breakout record, #1 R&B and top-ten pop. But the Miracles? Nothing. Oh, well, at least Brunswick would pay him. Maybe.

Slowly, a new crop of stars was appearing. Buddy Holly and the Crickets were red-hot; the end of 1957 had seen the release of "Peggy Sue," a Buddy Holly record using the name of Jerry Allison's girlfriend in the title and Buddy's trademarked hiccup in the vocal, followed by "Oh, Boy!" and "Maybe Baby" by the Crickets appearing in early 1958. In January 1958, the band toured in the summer sunshine of Australia with Jerry Lee Lewis and Paul Anka, then returned home to work the hits and jumped on another plane to play England in March, thereby igniting a love affair that has never ended; with the Colonel making Elvis unavailable overseas, Buddy was the kind of rock & roll star any British kid could emulate, and they did, although arcane import laws made it impossible to get American-made electric guitars, and the domestic ones were pretty weak. They also did a couple of appearances on *The Ed Sullivan Show*, and jumped into Norman Petty's studio to record whenever they had time.

The Crickets were evolving. Niki Sullivan was out, and they found guitarist Tommy Allsup, who'd been part of Johnnie Lee Wills's Western swing band and was a versatile player Norman Petty had found and offered session work to. After working with Buddy in the studio, he wound up going on tour with the Crickets, and his guitar solo on "Heartbeat," credited to Buddy and Bob Montgomery (although there's no record of them ever having performed it in the Buddy and Bob days), shows him off to good effect. But Buddy was very ambitious, and in August, the Crickets visited the offices of Peer-Southern Music to visit Murray Deutsch, and the minute Buddy's eyes beheld Deutsch's new receptionist, Maria Elena Santiago, he was in love. He took her out to dinner that night and asked her to marry him. On August 15, she flew to Lubbock and they got married, and Mr. and Mrs. Holley gave them their blessing, although they worried about the success of a mixed marriage; Maria Elena was Puerto Rican. Then things really started moving; Buddy and Maria Elena rented an apartment in Greenwich Village, and Buddy moved to New York. He severed his relationship with Petty, and also the Crickets, although he continued to use some of the members as sidemen for his solo performances. He was writing songs like crazy, including "Peggy Sue Got Married" (which she had) as a wedding gift to the new Mr. and Mrs. Jerry Allison, and he began recording with a string orchestra arranged by Dick Jacobs. When he wasn't doing that, he was in the apartment recording demos on an Ampex tape recorder he'd bought from Norman Petty, and on a couple of the so-called living-room tapes, you can hear Maria Elena in the kitchen frying something, and Buddy talking to her between songs.

Jerry Lee Lewis, for his part, was racking up hits, with "Breathless" coming first and then "High School Confidential," so titled because he played it at the start of the film of the same name, on an upright piano on a flatbed truck with his band in front of the high school where the film's action—a sordid tale of dope, sex, and Mamie van Doren—would unfold. In May, a British promoter set up a tour, and Jerry Lee took an entourage including his sister, Linda Gail, and his new wife, Myra Gale, and her parents. As with many American stars, a press conference was set up at the airport, and Myra wanted to share the spotlight with her husband. This was not a good idea. They'd gotten married in Mississippi in December, and both Sam and Jud Phillips had urged Jerry Lee to hush it up. For one thing, nobody was sure of the status of his previous two wives, one of whom he may not have finished divorcing. For another thing, Myra Gale was Jerry Lee's third cousin—her father was his bass player. At Heathrow, Jud Phillips, who was along as tour manager, suggested Jerry Lee leave her behind while he went out to talk to the press, but she wanted to stick to his side, and Jerry Lee told Jud, "Look, people want me and they're gonna get me, no matter what." Oscar Davis, Jerry Lee's new manager, begged him, but the star dug in his heels and went out into the press conference. Immediately, one of the reporters asked who the girl was. "This is my wife, Myra," he said, a bit defensively. The next question was how old she was. "Fifteen," said Jerry Lee. Then someone asked her if that wasn't a bit young, and she answered cheerily, "Oh, no, not at all. Age doesn't matter back home. You can marry at ten if you can find a husband." (This wasn't true; the current age of consent in Mississippi was seventeen, and she'd told the judge performing the wedding that she was twenty.) When news of the press conference hit the United States, a reporter at the Memphis paper did a little digging and discovered that she wasn't fifteen at all; she was thirteen, and the Phillipses' suspicion was well founded—Jerry Lee's latest divorce wouldn't be final for five more months. The first concert of the tour was a disaster; empty seats out-numbered full ones in a 25 percent–full house. The next night the hall had hecklers calling him a sissy and a cradle robber. The next night, there was no show; the promoter canceled the tour, and the Americans flew back home, but not before being mobbed by reporters and photographers at the airport, causing Jerry Lee to kick a photographer. It was the same in the United States: Jerry Lee insisted he hadn't been deported, which he hadn't been, and said he'd gotten homesick, which he might have been, but it wasn't the reason he was back. To the question of whether his bride was a bit young, Jerry Lee seethed, "You can put this down: she's a woman," and stomped off.

Sam Phillips must have been reeling. Although he paid for, and ghostwrote, a full-page ad in *Billboard* in which Jerry Lee defended himself, after a fashion, and although "High School Confidential" was still selling, Dick Clark had served notice to Oscar Davis that he wasn't going to book him again, "a very cowardly act . . . for which I've been very sorry ever since," Clark admitted in his autobiography. But Sam was having other woes: Carl Perkins and Johnny Cash had both signed with Columbia, he hadn't held on to Roy Orbison, whom the Everly Brothers had wooed away with a big publishing contract with Acuff-Rose, and his roster of stars was running low. That summer, he'd watch as Harold Jenkins, who'd recorded some stuff at Sun that didn't get released, took a page from Vernon Dalhart's book and put two Texas towns together for a stage name, and, as Conway Twitty, had a smash hit on MGM with "It's Only Make Believe." Jerry Lee was just about all Sam had until he could develop another star, so to his credit he stuck with him. At least for a little while.

Elvis was getting ready to go in the Army. On March 24, 1958, at 6:35 A.M., with his parents and some friends in tow, he reported to the induction center in Memphis. The Colonel worked the crowd, handing out balloons advertising *King Creole*, and eventually Elvis and his fellow inductees got on a bus for a hospital where they'd take blood tests and the other routine medical exams the Army needed. Finally, US53310761, as he was known after being sworn in, got back on the bus and headed to Fort Chaffee, Arkansas, to begin basic training. Every step of the way, he was followed by press, fans, and photographers, and there was more than a little schadenfreude expressed when the pictures of Elvis getting his military haircut hit the wires and started appearing in papers. Things got chaotic at that point, and Elvis forgot to pay the barber the sixty-five cents he owed him and had to go back and pay up. Next stop was to call his mother from a pay phone, but here the Colonel blocked reporters' access, figuring Elvis had a right to some privacy at that moment. The next day the Army announced that Private Presley had been assigned to the Second Armored Division, and would train at Fort Hood, just outside of Killeen, Texas. It was a famous outfit, once commanded by George Patton, and along with his regular training, Elvis would learn how to drive a tank, a long way from the "long, black sonovabitch" of a Lincoln he'd jokingly said good-bye to in Memphis.

Elvis arrived at Fort Hood on March 28, where the press had been waiting patiently for his bus. The base's information officer, Lieutenant Colonel Marjorie Schulten, had never seen anything like it, and told Colonel Parker, who'd arrived to manage things, that she was laying down the law: the press could have him for the first day, but after that, Presley was off limits. On May 31, he got his first furlough, and flew to Memphis to see his parents, hang with his friends, and go to Nashville for a recording session. When the time was up, he headed back to the base and found that Colonel Parker had found a paragraph in Army regulations that a soldier, once he'd completed basic training, could live off base if his dependents were nearby. Figuring that his parents *were* his dependents, he set about finding a house for them in the vicinity, and soon they moved in and were socializing with Eddie Fadal, a guy who'd briefly worked on tour with Elvis and lived in nearby Waco. Elvis stayed with the Fadals whenever he had time off, and they'd even gone so far as to add a wing to their house for him.

It was all very nice, but Elvis's mother, Gladys, was worried; after basic, the unit would deploy to Germany, and she wasn't sure she wanted to live in a foreign country. But that was a way off, and between the Presleys' house and the Fadals' there were plenty of visitors to entertain and cook for. As the summer wore on, though, Gladys started feeling poorly, her digestion acting up. For a while, she could eat nothing but watermelon and Pepsi, and her doctor told her he wasn't licensed to practice in Texas, so on August 8, the Presleys got on the train for Memphis. She was admitted to the hospital the next day, and nobody could figure out what was wrong. Elvis was beside himself with worry, even threatening to go AWOL if he couldn't get emergency leave. (The Army's position was that if he was granted leave, the press would say they were giving him exceptional treatment.) But things looked grim, and Gladys's doctor pleaded with the brass, and on August 12, Elvis flew back to Memphis and headed straight to the hospital. After a long visit, which her doctor said did her a lot of good, he left, but he was back the next day and spent the whole day and much of the night there. His father, Vernon, stayed on a cot in her room. At 3:30 the next morning, the phone rang at Graceland, and Elvis had an intuition what it was. After speaking with his father, he drove to the hospital: Gladys had woken up, struggled for breath, and died. Father and son broke down, wailing so loudly you could hear them down the hall, and finally a hearse came for the body. Graceland was in chaos, and Elvis was useless; except when he answered the door to let mourners in, he sat by the body, cuddling it, touching it, crying, or just sitting there in a daze. Finally, the funeral home took Gladys to get ready for the funeral. Elvis had arranged for her favorite gospel group, the Blackwood Brothers, to fly in and sing, and somehow everyone got through the funeral and the interment, and the well-wishers congregated at Graceland, waiting for Elvis to come out of his room. His friend Red West had applied for leave when he'd heard about Gladys, and it was denied, but then his father had died suddenly, so he, too, was back in Memphis and was shocked that Elvis showed up for his funeral—hadn't he had enough? But Elvis was supportive, and in the end, Red was happy to have him there. At the end of the week, Elvis returned to Killeen. Now there was nothing but to wait for the trip to Germany.

Elvis could not imagine a world without Gladys, but rock & roll was going to have to imagine a world without Elvis. There was Ricky Nelson, but he didn't have Elvis's edge. There were the Everly Brothers, who were good with the slow stuff—"All I Have to Do Is Dream" was a smash in the spring, and its B side was "Claudette," written by Roy Orbison (for their publishing company) in tribute to his new wife—but when they warned "Bird Dog" to "stay away from my quail," the threat didn't sound as real as when Elvis sang "Trouble" in *Jailhouse Rock*. In the Bronx, a vocal quartet fronted by a clean-looking lad named Dion DiMucci, Dion and the Belmonts, released a record, "I Wonder Why," that was a breakthrough for white vocal harmony groups, just as tough as a lot of the black groups, and he might be a contender. Although the next Elvis wasn't appearing, someone *did* find the next Little Richard.

Or, as it turned out in later years, the original Little Richard: Steven Quincy Reeder, a.k.a. S. Q. Reeder, a.k.a. Esquerita, was a piano-playing maniac that Paul Peek of Gene Vincent's Blue Caps had found playing in the same seedy bars the Blue Caps had hailed from. As Richard recounts in his autobiography, Esquerita taught him to play piano after picking him up at the bus station in Macon back in the early '50s, and he also helped Richard develop his hairstyle. At the time, he was touring with a female evangelist whose gimmick was selling "blessed bread," but he appears throughout the decade under a number of similar aliases, and during the disco era as Fabulash. Capitol didn't have a clue what to do with him, although they did record enough tracks for an album. Of course, Capitol didn't have a clue what to do with Gene Vincent, either; he was far more popular in Britain than in America. Eventually, Esquerita disappeared and popped up in New York in 1975 working as a parking attendant, but his records continued to confuse and entertain people, especially his operatic instrumental with wordless wailing "Esquerita and the Voola."

But wait: what if, as some people surmised, teenagers were fed up with all this hillbilly and ghetto music and what they *really* wanted was the next Sinatra? It was time for good music to make a comeback, and Chancellor Records in Philadelphia stepped up to the plate. Run by Bob Marcucci and Pete DeAngeles, it aimed for a stable of good-looking, traditionally oriented teens singing the kind of songs that teens' parents could reluctantly admire. "We now run a school where we indoctrinate artists into show business," Marcucci told *Billboard*. "We worked with Frankie Avalon for three months before making 'Dede Dinah.'" The record in question was a top-ten item at the start of 1958, and one might legitimately wonder what Avalon (originally Francesco Avallone) had sounded like before going to school, although it did take advantage of his Philly accent in rhyming "nothin' finah" with "Dinah." Avalon was good-looking in an anodyne, non-ethnic kind of way, and so was Fabian, whose last name was Forte, whom Avalon had introduced to Marcucci, and who required a lot more work in the vocal department. Needless to say, Dick Clark was all in favor of Chancellor, and featured their artists and records heavily on *American Bandstand*. Local boys and all, they could have been pulled off his dance floor.

Another contender was Canadian Paul Anka, whom ABC-Paramount snapped up and who began 1958 emoting "You Are My Destiny," a follow-up to the previous year's smash "Diana." Anka was a good investment; not only was he a talented pop singer, he was also a songwriter who produced material for other singers. He would chart sixty singles in a recording career that only ended in 1983.

The closest contender for the "next Sinatra" title was Bobby Darin, born Walden Robert Cassotto in the Bronx, who appeared on Atlantic in the summer of 1958 with "Splish Splash," a silly tune not unlike "Dede Dinah" that was twitchier than rocking, but his strategy seemed to be, like Frankie Avalon's, to grab the kids' attention with a novelty and then move into supper-club mode.

Both Darin ("Early in the Morning," "Now We're One") and Anka ("I Guess It Doesn't Matter Anymore") had their songs recorded by Buddy Holly without the Crickets. Nor were these purveyors of good music all male; Connie Francis (Concetta Rosa Maria Franconero) had been around for a couple of years, recording for MGM, before she broke through in February with "Who's Sorry Now," a weeper of a ballad that headed straight to the top ten and started a run of hits that lasted into the late '60s, recording in both English and Italian. Her other notable hit of 1958, though, was yet another wacky, twitchy number, "Stupid Cupid." There would be more of these people; their music fit into Top Forty programming brilliantly.

But a lot of the time the airwaves were filled with instrumentals or novelty records. Ross Bagdasarian was a songwriter who was tops in the apparently lucrative but little-known Armenian American pop market, and it was he who took the idea of "Flying Saucer"'s last words, "Good Bye Earth Pee Pul," clumsily spoken on tape and sped up, and turned it into a career. Using the name David Seville, he recorded one of the year's bestselling records, "Witch Doctor," whose nonsense chorus was rendered in a sped-up voice. That caused Sheb Wooley, a country singer with a side career in acting, to craft "The Purple People Eater," about the ultimate alien, who also spoke like that. Encouraged that the world needed more of this, Seville waited until Christmas, always a time for awful records, to unleash "The Chipmunk Song," featuring three voices singing in sped-up harmony, and starting a torrent of Chipmunk and Chipettes records that has yet to abate.

Seeking relief from squeaky artificial vocals, people turned to such instrumentals as Pérez Prado's cha-cha "Patricia," the "Tea for Two Cha-Cha" by the Tommy Dorsey Orchestra, bebop drummer Cozy Cole's monotonous drum solo "Topsy, Part Two," and a twangy guitar instrumental with an unusual echoey sound, Duane Eddy's "Rebel Rouser." This last was by a guitarist based in Phoenix who'd been collaborating with a young music-biz hustler there named Lee Hazlewood. It appeared on the B side of "Stalkin'," a slow instrumental that Hazlewood was certain was a hit, and the master tape had gone from Phoenix to Hollywood, where Hazlewood, in collaboration with another ambitious producer, Lester Sill, the guy who'd introduced Leiber and Stoller around Hollywood, added a saxophone to it. Sill had connections with Jamie Records, another up-and-coming Philadelphia label, and Dick Clark went on "Stalkin'" immediately, but it failed to sell. But when DJs turned the record over, they discovered a guitar instrumental that was considerably more sophisticated than Bill Justis's "Raunchy," and suddenly Eddy, Hazelwood, and Sill were going places.

Eddy had originally hoped to be a country star, although the path he wound up on was far more lucrative. But what *had* happened to country? The answer was that the guard was changing. For one thing, younger singers were blurring the line between old-style country and rock & roll; the Everly Brothers and Johnny Cash were harbingers of this, as was Johnny Horton, whose 1957 hit "I'm Coming Home" rocked like crazy, although the pop charts ignored it. Marty Robbins, too, was straddling the line, although more conservatively (he was over thirty), with titles like "A White Sport Coat (And a Pink Carnation)" and "Teen-Age Dream," the former of which was a pop hit. Over at RCA, Chet Atkins, a virtuoso guitarist who proved to be a canny producer, had begun taking hints from Harold Bradley's production techniques, and started de-emphasizing fiddles and steel guitars and adding strings, occasional brass, and backup singers to country records, with the result that Don Gibson, one of his early protégés, had a top-ten pop hit (and a #1 country hit) with "Oh, Lonesome Me." The Nashville Sound, as it was soon dubbed, was born in RCA Studio B and Bradley's Barn, and would become the new default for some country stars, including Ray Price, whose "Crazy Arms" Jerry Lee Lewis had covered, and who got a lot of mileage out of the so-called Texas shuffle his band, the Cherokee Cowboys, played like nobody else. (Price's road band around this time included guitarist Roger Miller and bassist Willie Nelson, both of whom he'd acquired in Fort Worth.) But it's evident what was happening by looking at the list of 1958's #1 country singles: they were by Marty Robbins, Jerry Lee Lewis, Johnny Cash, Don Gibson, the Everly Brothers, Faron Young (whose 1955 hit "Live Fast, Love Hard, Die Young" was attitudinally rock & roll, although he'd calmed down in later years), and Ray Price. And another performer who'd wanted to be a country star, Eddie Cochran, had a hit on the charts that summer, "Summertime Blues," a teen protest song about mixing life and work while out of school that was so hot that nobody realized he'd multitracked the whole thing, playing all the instruments himself.

On college campuses, students were abandoning rock & roll, the music of their childhood, for other things. Sophisticates went for jazz, which rarely made it onto the pop charts (except for Ahmad Jamal and Moe Koffman's catchy but insubstantial "Swinging Shepherd Blues") but sold substantial quantities of albums, particularly such contemporary stars as Miles Davis, Ahmad Jamal, and Chet Baker. Intellectuals went for folk music. This wasn't the first time this had happened; there had been a folk revival in the 1930s, when it was the soundtrack to the

American left during the Depression, most notably with the Almanac Singers, who lived in a sort of commune in New York, and whose numbers included a young Harvard graduate with a folklorist father, Pete Seeger, as well as future actor Lee Hays. Some of the survivors of that era (notably Seeger and Hays) banded together in 1948 as the Weavers, who had hits with Lead Belly's "Goodnight, Irene," and the Israeli folk song "Tzena Tzena," in which Pete Seeger's homely banjo did battle with Decca's house arranger Gordon Jenkins's massed strings. (Jenkins, remember, later worked with Buddy Holly.) The group's career was killed at its zenith by the McCarthy hearings in Washington (and, indeed, several of the members, including Seeger, had joined or supported communist-aligned groups in the '30s, not that such a thing was illegal), but Seeger continued to perform at schools, camps, and college campuses, his infectious personality and nonsectarian advocacy of peace and nuclear disarmament gaining him a growing number of fans, who also bought his banjo instruction books and his recordings for Folkways.

Folkways itself was a remarkable record label. Headed by Moses Asch, son of famed Yiddish author Sholem Asch, it, like its predecessor Asch Records, didn't shy away from politics—or anything else. Folkways had in its catalog Bela Bartok's recordings of Hungarian folk music, Alan Lomax's recordings of the British Isles, Italy, and the Deep South, Harlem stride pianist James P. Johnson playing his classical compositions, and Kansas City bandleader Mary Lou Evans's suite based on astrology, as well as recordings of the James Joyce Society's meetings with Joyce reading from his works. It also, in 1952, released six LPs that would change American music forever. Arranged in three boxes with two discs each, it was called *The Anthology of American Folk Music*, but it was in fact nothing of the sort. What it actually was was the record collection of 78s acquired by an eccentric painter, filmmaker, and amateur anthropologist named Harry Smith, who needed some quick money and offered Moe Asch the collection, further offering to arrange it for LP release by picking titles and writing about them, as well as designing the cover and the accompanying booklet. The price was right, so Asch went for it, and Smith got to work. The three volumes were Ballads (narrative songs), Social Music (dance and church music), and Songs (blues and other non-narrative songs, with a couple of Cajun recordings thrown in). The booklet was a collage of woodcuts and poorly reproduced pictures of some of the artists, each ballad summarized in headline style ("Frankie," by Mississippi John Hurt: ALBERT DIES PREFERRING ALICE FRY, BUT JUDGE FINDS FRANKIE CHARMING AT LATTER'S TRIAL), with notes ("Allen Britt shot Frankie Baker of 212 Targee Street St. Louis Missouri, October 15, 1899. The song was first sung by, and probably written by, 'Mammy Lou' a singer at Babe Conner's famous cabaret in that city.") and a discography and bibliography, which made it look like folklore scholarship, but in fact these were early commercial recordings (among the artists are the Carter Family and Blind Lemon Jefferson) and Smith noted in the foreword to the booklet that the records used were from 1927, when electric recording started, through 1932, when the Depression shut down folk music sales (or so Smith said). He also promised three more volumes, "devoted to examples of rhythm changes between 1890 and 1950," but the first three were enough for Asch, so he turned down volume 4, although Smith had it ready. The first three didn't sell, and they languished in the back room with copies of *Readings from the Ramayana and Bhagavad Gita in Sanskrit & English* and *Music of the Belgian Congo, Vol. 1 (East)*. Or, rather, they didn't sell well at first. But with such a definitive title, libraries and other institutions started ordering it, and people heard it, including some of the kids who'd been inspired by Pete Seeger. Some of them saved up for their own copies (Folkways Records, selling mostly to libraries, were expensive, several dollars more than normal LPs), and they became sources of songs for incipient folksingers to learn. They also inspired people to go out and find more of the kind of music that was on the six albums, going door-to-door in the South to buy old 78s, and, later, to find the artists who'd made them. (This wasn't as hard as it sounded; after all, in 1958, these recordings were barely thirty years old.)

But on most college campuses, folk music meant the occasional trio of guys playing banjo, guitar, and bass, a kind of stripped-down template of the Weavers' lineup that had been adopted by the Tarriers, the group that had had the original hit with "The Banana Boat Song (Day-O)" before Harry Belafonte. Scarcely interested in authenticity, groups like the Gateway Singers, the Easy Riders, Bud & Travis, and the Kingston Trio shared bills in clubs that also booked jazz, sharing sets with comedians. In 1958, Capitol Records took a chance with the Kingston Trio, named for the city in Jamaica, but more interested in Hawaiian music than calypso. Two of the group had grown up in Hawaii, and played Hawaiian music together at college, and on adding their third member started doing satirical songs and some light pop material, working with their new manager, Frank Werber, a Bay Area publicist, to develop an act that would be suitable for San Francisco clubs. Their break came over Memorial Day weekend 1957, when Phyllis Diller canceled her weeklong engagement at the Purple Onion, and Werber talked the club into booking his act. They went over well, and soon more bookings happened, and Werber, seeing the future, insisted that any record label that signed them would release LPs only. The first album did okay, but not spectacularly, until a disc jockey on a station in Salt Lake City played one track, "Tom Dooley," on the air and the phones went wild. Eventually, Capitol was forced to release it as a single, and it was a major hit in the summer of 1958, hitting #1. The album stayed on the charts for four years. Ironically, "Tom Dooley" was an authentic American folk song, collected by a folklorist, Frank Warner, in the 1950s from Frank Proffitt, a banjo maker and singer in Kentucky and released on Folkways, but the Kingston Trio mostly avoided that sort of material.

Pete Seeger's stepbrother, Mike, however, did not; the Seegers grew up in a house filled with folk music, thanks to their ethnomusicologist father, Charles (and their babysitter, left-handed guitarist Elizabeth "Libba" Cotton), and by the time he was twenty-five, Mike was not only a walking encyclopedia of old-time music, but also a multi-instrumentalist, capable of playing in a number of styles. In New York, he collected two like-minded friends, photographer John Cohen and mathematician Tom Paley, and they started playing clubs in Greenwich Village as the New Lost City Ramblers. They, too, made an album in 1958, self-titled, for Folkways, who else?

On September 22, at the military ship terminal of the Brooklyn Army Terminal, Elvis faced the media for the last time before sailing to

Germany. Representatives of his record company, his label, his family, the Colonel and his entourage, and about 125 reporters and photographers were there for a last press conference. Would he miss his singing career? (Yes.) What did he think about marriage? (It was a good idea to give a relationship time so you were clear about it; that was something he'd learned from his parents.) How would he characterize his ideal woman? ("Female, sir.") Finally, the Colonel arranged some photo opportunities and to the strains of "Tutti Frutti," arranged for military band, Private Presley marched with the rest of the soldiers up the gangplank of the ship, leaving everyone else in the United States to deal with Frankie Avalon and the Chipmunks as best they could. As for the Colonel, he took the tape of the press conference and had RCA edit it into the weirdest Elvis single ever, "Elvis Sails." It did not chart.

chapter eleven
1959: DEATH AND SOUL

Berry Gordy Jr. in front of Hitsville, U.S.A.
The action was in the basement studio.
(The Detroit News)

In January 1959, death entered the top ten. Actually, it had already been there with the condemned murderer Tom Dooley facing his last days on the charts, but another old murder came alive again in the hands of Lloyd Price, who'd moved over to ABC-Paramount from Specialty and was enjoying an enhanced production budget with female backup singers and an orchestra behind him. His first single for them was a reworking of a 1950 Imperial record by the mysterious New Orleans pianist Archibald, who got the song from who knows where and called it "Stack A-Lee." Price renamed it "Stagger Lee" and wrung as much drama as he could in three minutes out of the murder of Billy Lyons in St. Louis over a gambling dispute, beginning with a haiku-like verse sung almost unaccompanied ("The night was cold, and the moon was yellow, and the leaves came tumbling down") that wasn't in the original, and then picking up the tempo until by the end the backup singers were chanting, "Go Stagger Lee! Go Stagger Lee!"

Another bit of death making its way into the charts in January wasn't quite as overt. Doré Records was a label run by Lew Bedell, whose other label, Era, featured acts like Gogi Grant who played the boîtes of Hollywood. Bedell had married into royalty—Dede Barrymore, a non-acting member of the dynasty that went back to the early days of the film business—and had money of his own. When his next-door neighbor's son told him that there was a group at his school, Fairfax High, that didn't sound like any other, he offered to audition them, and very soon thereafter a spooky teenager named Phillip Spector showed up with a demo he and three other kids had cut at Gold Star Studios, "Don't You Worry My Little Pet." Bedell loved it, but reminded Spector that there also had to be a B side, so the kid went home and wrote another, "To Know Him Is to Love Him," and went back to Gold Star with it, minus one of the kids on the first song. Spector, Marshall Leib, and Annette Kleinbard sang with passion, if not complete accuracy, and Bedell put the record out, only to have Spector visit him every single day to see if there'd been any action. Months went by and finally Minneapolis reported some sales, and then Fargo, North Dakota, ordered fifteen thousand copies. The Teddy Bears, as they were known, were hot, and nobody knew the source of the lyric: the tombstone of Spector's father, which bore the inscription "To know him was to love him." The Teddy Bears managed to record enough material for an album, but Philip had already lost interest and was off on another tangent.

Some people might have wondered if all Los Angeles teenagers were shy and sang in muted voices like the Teddy Bears and another phenomenon who'd cropped up recently: Ritchie Valens's "Donna" was a smash, heard by more kids than had heard his debut, "Come On, Let's Go," or the B side, a traditional Mexican song, "La Bamba." Valens, whose real name was Richard Valenzuela, was a personable lad from East LA who'd been scooped up by would-be mogul Bob Keene, who saw great things in his future.

That future ended on February 3, 1959, along with that of two others. Valens had joined the Winter Dance Party, a revue that also included Dion and the Belmonts, Buddy Holly, the Big Bopper (a DJ from Beaumont, Texas, named J. P. "Jape" Richardson, who did humorous recitations like his current hit "Chantilly Lace," and wrote novelty songs for others), and Frankie Sardo. It was hardly an A-level tour, and although it was a good break for Ritchie and Dion and the others, Buddy—who was listed as Buddy Holly and the Crickets, although no Crickets were on board and he'd had to draft a country disc jockey he'd been producing, Waylon Jennings, to play bass—

needed money badly, possibly because Norman Petty was withholding royalties, so he signed on. Further evidence of how second-rate the tour was could be found in the buses they were traveling in, whose heaters continually broke down in the frigid midwestern winter, and the venues they played, like the Surf Ballroom in Clear Lake, Iowa, where they found themselves on February 2. When they got to the venue, Buddy called Maria Elena and told her that conditions on the tour were so bad that he expected someone to mutiny. Then he decided that he was going to take action; his clothes stank, and if he could get to Moorhead, the tour's next stop, early enough, he could do some laundry, a little advance publicity for the show, and get some rest in a heated hotel room. He chartered a plane with the help of the local promoter to fly himself, Jennings, and his guitarist, Tommy Allsup, to Fargo, North Dakota, leaving after the show at 12:30 A.M. He was already without his drummer, Charlie Bunch, who was in a hospital bed minus a bunch of toes, which he'd lost to frostbite when their bus had broken down.

During the time leading up to the concert in Clear Lake, word spread that Buddy had found a plane to take him to the next stop, and suddenly everyone wanted to fly. There were only three passenger seats, so when J. P. Richardson approached Waylon Jennings about taking his place, Jennings, who, not having been outside of west Texas much, was actually enjoying the tour, readily agreed in exchange for using Richardson's newly purchased sleeping bag on the bus. Tommy Allsup, though, was a harder sell when Ritchie Valens approached him about taking his seat, so they decided to flip a coin. Ritchie picked heads. It was heads. When the show was over, the three musicians headed out to the airstrip, where they met Roger Peterson, the twenty-one-year-old pilot, and Jerry Dwyer, owner of the charter service they'd booked with, who was helping prepare the aircraft for the trip. Peterson was a fully qualified pilot, and he'd been checking the weather, which was snowy and windy, but nothing he couldn't handle. What he didn't see, however, was two weather bulletins predicting low visibility due to developing snowstorms along the route. This would require flying with instruments—"by wire," as pilots say—but Peterson had taken lessons in that. Dwyer's service, however, wasn't licensed for this sort of work, nor was Peterson familiar with the particular instrument configuration of the plane, which read altitude in the opposite way from the ones he'd trained on. Slightly after 1:00 the plane took off, and Dwyer sat in the tower watching the taillight in the night sky. At one point, the plane seemed to descend, but Dwyer dismissed it as an optical illusion due to the angle of the plane and its distance from him. Oddly, though, Peterson hadn't filed a flight plan. Dwyer took to the radio, but there was no answer.

Meanwhile, in Lubbock, the actual Crickets were sitting at Jerry Allison's house having a discussion. Buddy had told them, "You ever want to get back with me, all you have to do is call," and they decided that Norman Petty had dealt them a bad hand and they hadn't gotten any work or made any records since Buddy and they had split. (It's also not impossible that the ever-ambitious Maria Elena had something to do with this, as she had with Buddy studying at the Actors Studio with Lee Strasberg.) They called New York to find out where Buddy was, and then called Clear Lake only to find out that he was on his way to the airfield. They called the next night's venue in Moorhead and left a message for him to call them.

Jerry Dwyer kept trying to contact the plane, and also radioed the Mason City and Fargo airports to see if they'd heard from it, with no luck. Finally, an alert for the missing plane went out, and as daylight returned, Dwyer lost his patience and climbed into another of his planes to follow the route he figured Peterson had taken. It didn't take him long to spot the wreckage eight and a half miles from takeoff and the bodies strewn around it; Richardson had been thrown forty feet by the impact, and Buddy and Ritchie were twenty feet from the wreckage. Peterson's body was still in the plane. The rest of the performers found out while checking into the hotel in Moorhead, Maria Elena found out from a business associate, Mrs. Holley from a gossipy neighbor. The rest of the country found out soon enough. In Moorhead, a contest was held to choose a local band to fill out the bill, which was won by the Shadows, fronted by Robert Velline, who called himself Bobby Vee. Frankie Avalon and Jimmy Clanton flew in to fill the other two slots on the tour. And the show went on.

Despite the words of a popular song written years later, this wasn't "the day the music died," but an unpleasant moment in an evolution that was already under way. The actual replacement of Buddy Holly, Ritchie Valens, and the Big Bopper by Bobby Vee, Frankie Avalon, and Jimmy Clanton was also symbolic. Had they lived, Richardson would no doubt have continued an already thriving career as a country songwriter, Valens might have had a further career, especially if he could have freed himself of Bob Keene, who was still an amateur player despite having had a few hits with Sam Cooke, and Holly might have balanced the string-laced Gordon Jenkins pop productions Decca was saddling him with and future recordings with the Crickets, had they been able to come to terms. What did happen was that the Crickets continued to record, Norman Petty overdubbed some existing Holly recordings he had in the can using the Fireballs, an instrumental group he was producing, and Jack Hansen did other overdubs on stuff that had been recorded in New York. Death, as always, was a brilliant career move, and Petty continued to help Decca issue Buddy Holly recordings through 1969.

But more and more, "good music"–leaning performers were taking over white rock & roll. Even black music was softening up, with the Platters' superb but square rendition of the old warhorse "Smoke Gets in Your Eyes" leading the charts in January and February, and Clyde McPhatter's "A Lover's Question" and LaVern Baker's "I Cried a Tear" close behind, polite but with teen appeal.

Some things remained the same while others were changing in the background. Elvis's entry into the Army was satirized by one "Bill Parsons"' record of "All-American Boy," the story of a kid who, with the assistance of a man with a cigar, makes it big with his voice and guitar, only to be drafted in the last verse. ("Parsons," it turned out, was the future country star Bobby Bare.) Vocal groups were still around, quietly breaking new ground; the Crests were a biracial quartet fronted by Johnny Maestro (Johnny Mastrangelo, no known relation to Carlo of the Belmonts), whose "Sixteen Candles" was the perfect mixture of Italian American nasality and vocal group soul, and the Flamingos, having left Chess (but not before playing Chess heir apparent Marshall Chess's Bar Mitzvah in Chicago—

they were Jewish, after all, and had met in a black synagogue) for George Goldner's latest New York–based label, End, released their first echo-drenched masterpiece in "Lovers Never Say Good-Bye" early in the year. Two other white groups made the pop charts; the Bell Notes' "I've Had It" was nasal and monotonous, but had something that sparked airplay, and, from Olympia, Washington, the Fleetwoods polished up the Teddy Bears' hushed, winsome sound with "Come Softly to Me," with its irresistible "dum dum, doobie dum dum" backing supporting Gretchen Christopher's barely audible lead vocal. It was hypnotic. And the Coasters continued to disrupt the social order with help from Leiber and Stoller by telling the story of "Charlie Brown," who wasn't the round-headed kid of the *Peanuts* comics, but a dangerous class clown who smokes in the locker room and calls the English teacher "daddy-o." The record made full use of the songwriters' knowledge of teenagers, King Curtis's sax, Bobby Nunn's basso profundo ("Who me?"), and even trendy sped-up vocals ("Yeah, you"). The rock & roll spirit, at any rate, continued to peek out despite everything.

But there was a generational change happening in blues. Muddy Waters and Howlin' Wolf had already charted their last singles, although they'd put out new ones for some time, and Little Walter would in October. A new generation of Chicago bluesmen was coming up on the West Side instead of the South Side. Fiery left-hander Otis Rush had had a hit with "All Your Love," and names like Magic Sam, Buddy Guy, and Junior Wells were drawing younger crowds to Chicago's clubs. A new generation of Memphis blues talent, too, was emerging, with Bobby "Blue" Bland blasting onto the scene in 1957 with "Further On Up the Road" and then putting out one great record after another and hitting the road, often with Junior Parker, who had signed with Don Robey's Duke label after Don Robey lured him away from Sun.

Ray Charles had sat 1958 out as a vocalist, for the most part, as Ahmet Ertegun's brother, Nesuhi, head of Atlantic's well-regarded jazz department, took him into the studio with selected players and recorded a couple of excellent instrumental albums with the Modern Jazz Quartet's vibraphonist Milt Jackson and Charles's own saxophonist David "Fathead" Newman. Ray then headed to the 1958 Newport Jazz Festival for a knockout set, recorded by Atlantic and released late in the year as *Ray Charles at Newport*, mostly instrumental until the end of the set when Raelette Margie Hendrix steps out during "(Night Time Is) The Right Time" to belt the word "Bay-bay" over and over, building incredible tension and helping cement this album's reputation as one of the greatest live sets ever recorded. Charles lost no time recording a single version of it, which climbed the pop and soul charts, signaling his return as a pop artist. And return he had; on February 18, 1959, he and his band went into Atlantic Recording Studios and made history again. Ray had a Wurlitzer electric piano he used on the road, and although jazz fans decried its dead, metallic sound, he was nonetheless able to use it to drive a revival service on a tune he'd made up on the road that was more or less a rhythm exercise with boilerplate lyrics ("See the girl with the red dress on" and the like) interspersed with call-and-response moans with the Raelettes. The thing, titled "What'd I Say," came in at over five minutes, but everybody who heard it knew it was a hit, and it had a convenient place to splice it in the middle, so Atlantic rushed it out as part one and part two on the 45. The only other song he recorded at that session was "Tell the Truth," by Lowman Pauling of the "5" Royales. With the help of Ray Charles and Sam Cooke and a few others, a new kind of black popular music was being born.

And with the help of the "5" Royales, too; although unless you were a fan, got lucky listening to a late-night radio broadcast, or managed to catch them live, you'd never know it. Was King trying to kill this act? Were they incompetent? Underfunded? Probably all three, it appears now. The Royales had recorded the original of "Tell the Truth" in April 1958, and it had been released as the B side to "Double or Nothing," a slow burner with solid vocal work. But the real insult came in September, when King relegated the group's top live showcase to the B side of their next single, "Don't Let It Be in Vain," another slow gospelly number. There's some debate about what the actual title of this number was, but they'd been doing it for some time, stretching it out to over twenty minutes at times and letting Pauling go nuts with his guitar, and after seeing it at a show in his hometown of Memphis, a teenage guitarist named Steve Cropper went home, took the belt off his jeans, and used it to extend his guitar strap in imitation of Lowman's low-slung Les Paul strap. The song came out under the incomprehensible title "The Slummer the Slum," and yet the group seems to be singing "the stompety-stomp," which makes sense with the preceding words ("I can do"). Nobody bought it, nobody played it. The "5" Royales continued to release superb records throughout 1959, but in 1960 their contract was over, and they and King parted company, no doubt with sighs of relief on both sides.

The gospelly lead singing that Ray Charles, Johnny and Eugene Tanner of the "5" Royales, and Sam Cooke (who was still finding his way in the pop world while putting out hits for Keen) had introduced was catching on, but it didn't have a name just yet. More new talents were doing it, though; in 1958 a group from Chicago, the Impressions, had a smash with "For Your Precious Love" with lead singer Jerry Butler pouring out his plea with emotion and precision, and in 1959, Mercury introduced Brook Benton, a silky-voiced veteran of the Camden Jubilee Singers who followed Sam Cooke's lead and went pop, scoring a #1 R&B hit and top-ten pop hit with "It's Just a Matter of Time." The word for this sort of music wouldn't fully emerge before the end of the year, when the Cannonball Adderley Quintet recorded a live album in a San Francisco jazz club that included a twelve-minute workout called "That There." Jazz was progressing nicely, and was popular, but some of its practitioners felt that it was becoming too abstract, including Adderley, a rotund, extroverted alto saxophonist. "That There" not only showed off Adderley's band, but it was also danceable, and, while adhering to blues changes, had a groove that helped propel sales of *The Cannonball Adderley Quintet in San Francisco* higher than any of his previous efforts. When the jazz press asked what he called this new approach, he told them it was soul. And, in fact, Atlantic had already used the word in the titles of the 1958 Ray Charles-Milt Jackson albums *Soul Brothers* and *Soul Meeting*. It was a term that was beginning to circulate in black communities.

Another milestone in the coming of soul was a strange revival of an old act. Early in 1959, George Treadwell, manager of the Drifters, had fired everyone in the group and hired a new batch of Drifters, a vocal group formerly known as the Five Crowns. The old group hadn't had a hit since Clyde McPhatter had left, but Treadwell figured the brand still had some miles left on it, so he informed Atlantic that the Drifters were ready to do a session. Atlantic put Leiber and Stoller on the case as producers, and Treadwell handed them a song that he had half credit on, "There Goes My Baby." The arrangement was based on a Brazilian rhythm that was popular at the time called the *baion,* so it looked ready to go until they got to the studio. It just failed to gel. A tympani was out of tune. Mike Stoller had a framework for an arrangement, and a guy named Stan Applebaum was filling it in. As Leiber remembered later, "Stanley wrote something that sounded like some Caucasian takeoff and we had this Latin thing going on this out-of-tune tympani and the Drifters were singing something in another key, but the total effect, there was something magnetic about it . . . We took the playbacks to Atlantic one afternoon to play them for Ahmet and Jerry . . . and we were saying 'Oh, there's nothing salvageable about this' and then we played this one side and Mike said 'There's something fascinating about it. You know, it's a fucking mess, but there's something very magnetic about it.'" Wexler proclaimed his disdain, but Ertegun thought it should be released. He was right; although it sounded like nothing anybody had ever done, the lead singer, Ben E. King, sold the song with his passionate delivery, and then, in the middle, there was a weird instrumental break featuring *strings*! Nobody had ever used strings on a rhythm and blues record before, so no wonder Leiber was so afraid; they'd spent a lot of money on this track, and it came out sounding sideways, due to the odd modal framework Applebaum had cast the string interlude in. "I'd be listening to the radio sometimes and hear it," he said, "and I was convinced it sounded like two stations playing one thing." But the radio *was* playing it, wasn't it?

In Detroit, the new sound was cropping up in the clubs, and Berry Gordy was tired of writing hits and misses for other people. He'd assembled a bunch of like-minded souls around him—mostly would-be performers, but also his sister Anna, his wife, Raynoma, and songwriters Bill "Smokey" Robinson of the Miracles and Roquel

"Billy" Davis. He still needed money, and after the flop of his 3-D Record Mart his family's Ber-Berry Co-op Savings Fund was reluctant to loan him any more money. He needed $800, he figured, and, after refining his plans and running the numbers, he finally presented them with a framework they'd accept. He began by setting up a music publishing company, Jobete Music, to administer the songs that he'd release on the label he envisioned heading eventually, and in December 1958, he went into United Sound, the best studio in Detroit, with a twenty-year-old singer named Marv Johnson, and a band consisting of Thomas "Beans" Bowles on flute and saxophone, Eddie Willis and Joe Messina on guitars, James Jamerson on bass, and Benny Benjamin on drums and cut "Come to Me" b/w "Whisper." He then pressed it up and released it on his new label, Tamla, as Tamla 101, in late January 1959. The record took off so fast locally that Gordy realized he couldn't yet keep up with the potential demand, so he leased it to United Artists, which got it to #5 on the R&B charts and #30 on the pop charts. (Johnson stayed on United Artists, and Gordy produced most of his records, including his bestselling one, "You Got What It Takes," in 1960.) Gordy took the money and put it back in the company, going back into the studio with a kid he'd used to demo songs he and Tyran Carlo had written for Jackie Wilson, Eddie Holland. Again, he had to lease Tamla 102 to United Artists, but it wasn't a hit. Gordy soldiered on; driving down West Grand Boulevard with his friend Mable John (older sister of Little Willie John, and a member of the Raelettes), he saw a house for sale. Since Gordy had no license, she was driving, and suddenly Gordy said, "Stop!"

"We stop and get out," she wrote later. "He walks up the stairs, peers in the window. 'That's it.' 'What's "it?"' I ask. 'Headquarters.' 'For what?' 'The operation. The music publishing company. The label. The studio. It's all going to happen here. Can you see it?'" Gordy seemed to be able to see things others couldn't, so she assured him that if he could see it, that was good enough. He bought it and put up a sign: "Hitsville U.S.A."

It only took him a few more months and a few more records to begin to make that sign make sense. The third Tamla release was by a guy from Mississippi named Barrett Strong, a friend of Jackie Wilson's who was singing in a gospel group with his three sisters when

Wilson came over one day and heard him playing the piano and singing and noted that a friend of his had just started a label and had written hits for him in the past. Soon afterward, he brought Gordy to meet
Strong, and in April, Strong had a single out on Tamla, "Let's Rock"
b/w "Do the Very Best You Can," recorded in somebody's basement. It
flopped, but Strong was impressed with Gordy's level of organization;
he'd even run an ad on a local radio station saying that his new company was looking for songwriters, musicians, and performers. The
same month "Let's Rock" came out, Tamla released "Solid Sender" by
Chico Leverett, another local singer, but restricted distribution to
Detroit. In June came "It," a novelty by "Ron & Bill," who were Miracles Ronnie White and Bill "Smokey" Robinson, which didn't do
much even when Gordy leased it to Chess's Argo subsidiary. Next up
was "Going to the Hop," by the Satintones, a vocal group that included
Chico Leverett. The flip side was "Motor City," and Leverett remembers Gordy offering $100 to anyone who could come up with a name
for a new label he envisioned. He suggested Motor City Records, but
Gordy held on to his money.

Gordy probably didn't like the name, but it's also possible he didn't
have the hundred bucks; he'd paid to press and distribute a lot of
records in a short time, and the only money anybody'd seen was for
"Come to Me," and that money went to United Artists, who under-
standably took a cut. Gordy was sitting at a piano at Hitsville one
day, and the receptionist, Janie Bradford, a high school student who
worked there after school, noted that "he had this riff going. We
stood there and kept writing and throwing out lyrics and improving
on the melody and the whole thing came together." "We" included
Barrett Strong, and a couple of white high school students who heard
the racket coming out of the house walked into the situation toting a
bass and a guitar. "Just walked up and asked if they could be on the
session," Strong remembered later. "Never saw them again in my
life." Nor have they ever been identified. They sat down with Benny
Benjamin on drums, Brian Holland on tambourine, and Strong on
piano in the brand-new Hitsville studio, and when they were done,
Tamla's first smash had been born. Write what you know, they say,
and Gordy and Bradford (he gave her co-writing credit) sure did;

"Money (That's What I Want)" was an instant smash in August, so much so that in order to make the jump to national success, Gordy had to license the record to his sister's Chess-distributed label, Anna, in early 1960. But it sold and sold and sold, and money: that's what they got.

Not everyone who was getting into the music business around this time knew as much about what they were doing as Berry Gordy did, of course. A lot of people were leaving the Sun Records ambit in Memphis, among them Jud Phillips, who started Judd Records; a former studio musician there, Eddie Bond, who started Stomper Time Records; Scotty Moore, out of a job even before Elvis went into the Army, who became a partner in Fernwood Records; Buddy Cunningham, who'd cut a couple of country records for Sam, who opened Cover Records; and Bill Justis and Jack Clement, both of whom Sam fired in March 1959, who started Play Me Records and Summer Records, respectively. Meanwhile, Sam broke ground on a new Phillips Recording Studio at 639 Madison. Another former Sun artist, Ray Harris, joined with a couple of instrumentalists who'd played on Sun records, Quinton Claunch and Bill Cantrell, to launch Hi Records, with investment money from record store owner Joe Cuoghi and a few silent partners, and started putting out instrumental records by another Elvis alumnus, Bill Black.

Then there was Jim Stewart. Stewart was a banker, an established figure in Memphis, but he also had an avocation that he just loved: he played country fiddle. Both he and his sister, Estelle Stewart Axton—who also worked in a bank—loved music, and she was a rock & roll fan who sought out the latest tunes. Her co-workers were amazed at her ability to pick the hits, and soon she was running down to the local wholesaler and buying records to re-sell to them at work for a profit. Jim entered the other end of the process. He had a barber, Marshall Ellis, who cut his hair regularly, and also wrote and recorded country songs, one of which had been picked up by country star Hank Locklin and, because Ellis had copyrighted it, made him a pile of cash. So Jim ran the numbers, started a publishing company, and went into partnership in a record company he called Satellite, after Sputnik, with some other people, including a disc jockey named

Fred Byler. They hung some drapes in a garage and cut Byler singing a couple of tunes, including one of Jim's. It flopped rather spectacularly, but Jim was hooked. Next, he recorded a local guy doing a rockabilly number, which, people who have heard it say, was really good, but although Ellis had schooled him in publishing, he knew nothing about distribution. Then Ellis moved and took his tape recorder with him, but Jim's new barber had a daughter who he thought had talent—plus, he had a storage building out in Brunswick, Tennessee, about twenty miles away, which he'd let Jim use to open a recording studio. Jim moved his operations to Brunswick, and Estelle, caught up in the fever of the new enterprise, convinced her husband to let her mortgage their house to get $2,500 to buy an Ampex 350 professional console tape recorder for Satellite to use. Then, out of nowhere, came the Veltones, five black guys singing harmony with an unissued single for Sun in their past and a pretty good song, "Fool in Love," ready to go. How they found their way to Brunswick is a good question, although it could have been that Estelle's son, Charles "Packy" Axton, had run into them while carousing in the black bars he liked to frequent, or else Lincoln Wayne "Chips" Moman, who had been on the road with Sun rockabilly Billy Lee Riley as a guitarist before signing on as an engineer at the fledgling label, and who had half credit on "Fool in Love," urged them to go to Brunswick. However they got there, the Veltones cut "Fool in Love," and Jim released it as Satellite 100 in September. Before too long, Mercury Records came calling and picked it up for distribution, and although it didn't light any fires, it made Satellite a few hundred bucks. Ellis was right!

And what *was* Sam Phillips doing, anyway? He'd put some of the Presley money into his radio station, KSHE, with the all-female announcers, put some more of it into a friend's scheme, a hotel franchise called Holiday Inn, and of course there was the plush new headquarters he was building. The studio there wouldn't be ready until October, but Sam had great hopes for two new artists he'd found. Carl Mann was a fresh-faced sixteen-year-old from Jackson, Mississippi, who'd had some experience on the road and decent guitar skills and a strong tenor voice to apply them to, and Sam saw his potential immediately. There'd be a gimmick, too, and one that'd be good for Phillips International: pop standards, but rocked up. His first release was a version of the silky Nat King Cole number "Mona Lisa," and although rocking it up was a gimmick, it was a gimmick that worked. In person, teens went for him. It looked like Sam had found something new. The other artist he was hoping would hit was another matter entirely. Charlie Rich was a bit of a greaser and a bit of a drunk, but his ability to sell a tune in the bars where he worked night after night, playing piano and singing standards and jazz tunes, was amazing. He wrote, too, in partnership with his wife, Margaret Ann, and had a pretty good parcel of original material. He, too, was signed to Phillips International, although Sam was waiting for the right moment—and the right song—to spring him on the public. But according to people who worked there, something had gone out of the Sun / Phillips International operation, something greater than the talents on both sides of the microphone that they'd lost. Sam still believed in Jerry Lee Lewis, but after Marion Keisker had left, he got way more interested in building and buying and selling radio stations than ever.

Summer had become a testing ground for trends; teenagers were out of school, many of them had jobs that they could work for longer hours than when they were in school, and, hence, had more disposable income, some of which they spent on records. But the kind of records they were buying was changing. Chuck Berry, for instance, was still making good records for the most part (we'll pass over his Italian-dialect flop "Anthony Boy") and while his first release for 1959, "Almost Grown," was a good teenage protest song and went to #3 on the R&B charts, it stalled at #32 on the pop charts, where its B side "Little Queenie" died at #80. His patriotic follow-up, "Back in the U.S.A.," which celebrated returning home after touring the world, got to #16 R&B and #37 pop. And a song that is regarded as a masterpiece, "Memphis, Tennessee," a superbly crafted tale of a man attempting to return a missed phone call that Berry only reveals in the last verse is not from a distant girlfriend, but from his six-year-old daughter, who is living with his estranged wife, a song that has been covered hundreds of times, never charted at all. Instead, the early summer saw Johnny Horton semi-mining the folk fad with a historical song written by Jimmy Driftwood, "The Battle of New Orleans," the exotica of Martin Denny's "Quiet Village" with its jungle sounds, Lloyd Price with another big production, "Personality," and a weird version of an early Leiber and Stoller hit for Little Willie Littlefield, "K. C. Loving," recast by an eccentric one-man band, Wilbert Harrison, as "Kansas City." Oh, and "good music" by Bobby Darin, Connie Francis, Fabian, Frankie Avalon, Carl Dobkins Jr., and the Browns.

Some of this was due to the spread of the Top Forty format among high-wattage stations with strong signals and conservative programmers, but some of it was due to the fact that a generational change was in the air; a disc jockey named Art Laboe broadcast his show live from Scrivner's Drive-In in Los Angeles over KPOP, and took live requests from the customers. He noticed that they often asked for older records rather than contemporary hits, and that certain older records, which had only been mild hits, were requested more than others. It didn't take Laboe long to figure out a way to make money out of this, and he drew up a list of the twelve most popular songs he'd been playing, then approached their record companies and offered to lease them for a given amount of time for use on an LP. This was a very attractive proposition; Dootsie Williams, for instance, had let his Dootone label languish and was existing on party records by the likes of Redd Foxx on his Laff label. He'd lost Dootone's main asset, the Penguins, to Mercury years back, but held on to the master (and the publishing rights) for "Earth Angel," their only hit, and one on Laboe's list. He took Laboe's modest lease payment, which, however much it was, was more than "Earth Angel" had earned in ages, and he'd make royalties if Laboe's project worked. Soon, Laboe had his dozen tracks and released his record, calling it *Oldies but Goodies*. It went to #2 on the album charts, and stayed on that chart for 183 weeks. For those of you who can't do the math in your heads, that's three and a half years, and it was later joined by seven annual siblings. It didn't hurt that Laboe gave his label an honest name, Original Sound, so that buyers knew they weren't getting copycat recordings, and in some cases, *Oldies but Goodies* would reignite interest in the oldie, causing it to chart again—as happened with "Earth Angel," actually, in 1959. Radio stations also realized this was enough of a trend to start featuring an "oldie of the week," or just adding occasional spins of an old hit to the playlist for a while. It was sure more humane than subjecting the DJ to another three minutes of Fabian.

A significant part of the audience for *Oldies but Goodies* was older consumers in their twenties or late teens, who were susceptible to nostalgia and more likely to have the cash for an LP purchase, but that was also the audience for the growing folk movement, and that movement prompted George Wein, who'd been putting on the Newport Jazz Festival since 1954, to try an experiment. He'd already stretched things by presenting Ray Charles in 1958, resulting in a great album, and that same year he'd also booked blues singer Big Maybelle and Chuck Berry, the latter of whom scandalized many jazz fans—including Wein, who'd never seen Berry's famous duck-walk. For 1959, Wein decided that a full-fledged folk festival might work, and got a friend and fellow nightclub impresario from Chicago, Albert Grossman, to help him pick a bill for the weekend. They picked fifteen acts for each night, headlined by Pete Seeger. The first night was largely commercial folksingers, albeit not pop-commercial, among them Odetta, John Jacob Niles, and the Clancy Brothers, and the second night was another fifteen-act show headlined by the Kingston Trio, with Earl Scruggs, the Stanley Brothers, Jean Ritchie, Bob Gibson, and the Reverend Gary Davis, a ragtime guitar-playing preacher from South Carolina living in Harlem, being big attractions. But if that Sunday is remembered for anything, it's for Gibson bringing onstage a beautiful eighteen-year-old girl who'd been making waves on the Boston folk scene to sing a duet with him. By the time they'd finished "Virgin Mary Had One Child," the name Joan Baez had gone out to a few thousand more people. The daughter of a nuclear scientist currently teaching in Boston, she'd already appeared on a compilation album for a Boston folksinger named Ted Alevizos, *Folksingers 'Round Harvard Square*, which also featured one Bill Wood, but the record was impossible to find—and, more crucial to the folk music media, impossible to find in New York. Shortly after Newport, she signed with Vanguard, a label that had released a little folk music (and a lot of classical music) and had also recorded that first Newport Folk Festival.

But the non-Madras-wearing crowd was busy being teenagers, and seeking out the best music they could so they could dance to it. Hank Ballard and the Midnighters, always dependable, found a dance craze that black teens had been doing for a while, and wrote a song around it, but the other side of the record sold better and got more airplay. The B side of "Teardrops on Your Letter" also sold some, but "The Twist," as it was called, would have to wait a while. Elsewhere on King, James Brown made a surprising return from a few years of fairly awful records, and, like "Please Please Please," this one was a plea to "Try Me."

Summer 1959 may have been a hot one, judging from the number of slow records that made the charts then. "Sleepwalk," a steel guitar instrumental by two Italian Canadian kids, Santo and Johnny, was one of the slowest records ever, and Sammy Turner's odd reading of "Lavender Blue" also wound up in the upper reaches of the chart, its producer an uncredited Phillip Spector, whose mother had noted his facility with language and sent him to New York to study to become an interpreter at the United Nations. He dutifully went to school, but also applied and was accepted to another "school," Leiber and Stoller's office, where they noted his talent and let him play around under their watchful eyes. Young Phillip no doubt perked up his ears at the summer's vocal group masterpiece. "I Only Have Eyes for You," like the Platters' version of "Smoke Gets in Your Eyes" earlier in the year, was a remake of a standard, done on a production shoestring for George Goldner's End Records, and was the record the Flamingos had been fated to make since they began. Awash in echo, it had an almost orchestral richness, largely using nothing but the group's voices. A soaring wordless falsetto line punctuated the song, as did the group chanting "do-bop sh-bop" under the verse, languidly sung by Nate Nelson. Goldner believed in this standards-done-vocal-group-style so much that he had the group record an entire album, *Flamingo Serenade*, that marks a separation line between the classic vocal group sound of the 1950s and the new sound that was about to emerge, a fitting milestone for the end of the decade.

It wasn't rock & roll's greatest summer by a long shot, but there were forces gathering that would have liked to see it be the last. In March, Chuck Berry had opened a nightclub in St. Louis, Club Bandstand. It made a point of stressing that it was open to all, and its manager, Francine Gilliam, was a statuesque blonde. The initial publicity from both black and white St. Louisans was strongly positive, and it looked like it would be a success. Meanwhile, its owner was on the road raising money to keep it alive, and in August, he played a gig at a high school fraternity dance in Meridian, Mississippi, which turned into trouble when a white girl kissed him a little too long in the autograph crush after the show. In the hubbub afterward, Berry was taken to jail, allegedly for his protection, and the $750 he'd been paid for the show was taken as a fine for his incitement to riot. Much worse was around the corner.

On December 1, Chuck and his band were spending the afternoon in Juarez, Mexico, before playing a show in El Paso that evening. They went into a bar called the Savoy and met a man remembered only as Venchi, who, hearing that they wanted to see the town, introduced them to a young woman, Janice Escalanti. Janice knew her way around, all right; she'd just gotten out of jail in El Paso for public drunkenness, her third arrest, the other two being for vagrancy and prostitution. At the moment, besides drinking, what she was doing was avoiding school; she was fourteen years old. But she hit it off with the group, and at the end of the afternoon, they returned to El Paso, where she confessed to Chuck that much as she'd like to see the show, she was broke. Well, fine—artists often sold pictures to be autographed after their shows, so he offered her the job and a cut of the profits. He then drove her to another bar, where they waited for a friend of hers to show up to let her into her apartment to change clothes. He asked her right off how old she was, and she told him she was twenty-one, of course, and he asked her what she did for a living. She admitted she'd been doing freelance prostitution but wanted to stop. Berry thought it over and told her he'd wanted to hire a hat-check girl at Club Bandstand; would she be interested? She'd be far from El Paso and the world she'd known. She could turn over a new leaf. She readily agreed and joined the band for the rest of the tour, finishing up in St. Louis, where Chuck introduced her to Francine Gilliam, who'd show her the ropes.

Right off, Francine asked her for her Social Security card and birth certificate, and Janice didn't have either, but she definitely didn't look her age, so Francine was fooled, too. Still, her work habits left a lot to be desired; she'd wander around the club talking to patrons, leaving the hat-check station empty. Francine put her on the door instead, and again, she'd just wander off and leave the cashbox un-attended. On December 17, Chuck had had enough, and went to the house where she was staying and told her she was fired, and that she was to pack her stuff and get ready to head back to El Paso. At the bus station, he gave her a one-way ticket and some money and left. In the time before the bus left, she got to talking to a guy who took her to a bar, and before long she was back at the Club Bandstand, where she hung out, talking to folks. Berry, seeing her there, blew up and had her taken to a hotel to sober up. The next day, he told her he'd give her the ticket and the money, but he'd have to watch her get on the bus. This apparently didn't sit well with her, so she sat tight, tried to call Berry on the phone, but couldn't get past Francine. She then started hooking again, trying to figure out what to do next. She didn't want to go back to El Paso and her old life, and she didn't want to go back to high school. For some reason she called the police in Yuma, Arizona, who were puzzled about the call, but urged her to stay where she was and wait for the St. Louis police. They showed up shortly afterward and arrested and questioned her, and then two de-tectives took her to Club Bandstand where, in the early minutes of December 22, they arrested Chuck Berry as he left the stage after his last set and arrested him for violation of the Mann Act: transporting a minor across state lines for the purposes of prostitution, a federal crime.

Oh, and speaking of federal crimes, there was a brand-new one about to be invented, if anyone could figure out how to word the law making it illegal: payola. In November, the chairman of the FCC had casually mentioned that radio stations taking payola might be in danger of losing their licenses. This was an interesting problem; as long as anyone could remember, promotion men visiting radio stations had done things to thank DJs—some of America's most underpaid entertainers, stars like Alan Freed and Bill Randle notwithstanding. These poor guys were happy to receive a pair of socks, one promotion man remembered, let alone a bottle of whiskey or maybe ten bucks. Of course, for someone like Freed, you could cut them in on the publishing for a hit song, as Chess had done with Chuck Berry's "Maybellene," but that was another thing entirely. One of the basic tenets of the increasing focus on payola in radio was that left on their own, teenagers would never buy the garbage the stations were playing and would go for "good music" instead. This shows how out of touch the lawmakers were; anyone who's been a parent knows that it's impossible to make teenagers do something they don't want to do. You could play a record for days on end, and if the kids didn't like it, they wouldn't buy it. But the crusade against communism was waning, and crusaders needed to find something else to do.

The question was, which among the manifold evils of the record companies should be tackled first? An editorial in the November 23 issue of *Billboard* suggested going after the time-honored "free goods" policy of providing a certain number of free records for every much larger quantity ordered by a store, as well as "the corruption of the programming of honest jockeys by crooked or poorly prepared popularity charts, disseminated by certain radio stations and trade papers, on which positions are bought by record companies in return for cash or advertising." The same issue had headlines like PAYOLA HULLABOO RAGES, over an article about lawmakers trying to figure out what to go after, and MORE READY TO MAKE LIKE CANARIES AS SCANDAL GROWS, in which a number of people were quoted, including a suburban Philadelphia distributor who'd gotten out of the business, who said that when it got to where he'd have to sell ten thousand records just to break even on the cost of "cash, checks, and household articles and baby items" he'd had to give DJs, he stopped handling pop music. He also said that stories of orgies with prostitutes for DJs were "probably" true. Meanwhile, the law was putting the squeeze on Tony Mammarella, the former producer of *American Bandstand,* and Dick Clark had been called to testify about some perceived business irregularities. In Cincinnati, Syd Nathan said he'd been blackmailed into providing payola, but knew very little about the details, except that he'd given the money for big East Coast markets to Henry Glover (a black A&R man) and had no idea "who got that loot." Dot Records, home of Pat Boone, was willing to open its books to scrutiny, and WNEW-TV, which was airing Alan Freed's show, said they were looking into allegations about "interlocking activities," but weren't going to pre-judge him. (ABC-TV, where Dick Clark's shows were, didn't pick up the phone when the reporter called.) Some record companies, reporting anonymously, the article said, were considering it a merry Christmas, indeed, since they'd stopped spending payola money for the time being. About the wildest things on the charts was "Reveille Rock," an instrumental by Johnny and the Hurricanes, and Sandy Nelson's "Teen Beat," another instrumental, albeit a drum solo by one of the kids who'd witnessed John Dolphin's murder. How bad was it? Also on the chart that week was "The Battle Hymn of the Republic" by the Mormon Tabernacle Choir, for whose success it is doubtful payola played a part. As if that weren't bad enough, Ross Bagdasarian announced that he'd set up thirty-two licensing agreements for Chipmunks-related merchandise. The pesky rodents were preparing for their second annual assault on the charts.

chapter twelve

1960: OLDIES, NEWIES, AND PAYOLA

Two faces of the new pop enjoy adult beverages:
Jackie Wilson and Bobby Darin.
(Donaldson Collection/photo by PoPsie Randolph/Michael
Ochs Archives/Getty Images)

In the last weeks of 1959, Atlantic released a single by Ray Charles. "I'm Movin' On" was a country tune, originally recorded by Hank Snow in 1950, but it wasn't surprising that Charles would know it; early in his career he'd found himself stranded in Seattle, where the only musical work he could get was as a pianist with a country band, and besides, in those days there was no black radio to speak of, and plenty of black Southerners gathered to listen to the *Grand Ole Opry* when its broadcasts came on. But, whether intentionally or not, the record had a message: in 1960, Ray Charles would be moving on, to a new contract that Atlantic couldn't—and wouldn't—attempt to match, from ABC-Paramount. He was guaranteed $50,000 a year, the ability to pick his own material (and his own publishing firm for original and contracted material), and a 75–25 split with Paramount on royalties; only a record company that had a huge network and a major film studio behind it could afford to take a mere 25 percent. Atlantic had been outbid on Elvis, and now they'd been outbid on a star they'd brought to prominence through hard work and support during the hard times. Business was business, though. It was just that Atlantic would have to find a new star of Ray Charles's magnitude—a tall order. For the moment, though, they still had great stuff by him in the can, and would leak it out bit by bit during the year.

Nor was Brother Ray the only star looking for greener pastures;

virtually unnoticed in *Billboard*'s back pages on December 14 was a short review of a record titled "The Mashed Potatoes" by Nat Kendrick and the Swans. Kendrick, it transpired, was James Brown's drummer, and James, touring incessantly while waiting for another hit, was becoming as well known for his instrumental numbers like "Night Train" as he was for his vocals. One night at the Palms of Hallandale, a major stop for the band in a Miami suburb, they watched as every single person on the dance floor did an odd dance, seemingly grinding out a cigarette on the floor with one foot while gyrating to the beat. During the break, a fan told them it was the mashed potato, the latest dance craze, and everyone in Florida was doing it. The band worked up an instrumental that you could do the mashed potato to, and James provided encouragement and verbal interjections and learned how to do the dance. As they headed back to Cincinnati to record, they saw other audiences doing it; it was a bona fide trend, and James and the Famous Flames were right on top of it. Syd Nathan, though, hated the number and refused to record it. Well, then, James had something up his sleeve: Henry Stone, a former big-band trumpeter turned Miami music-biz character who had almost signed James years ago and had (as was his wont) kept in touch, agreed to put it out on Dade, one of his many labels. Thus, "(Do the) Mashed Potato, Parts 1 and 2" came out under Kendrick's name and shot up to #2 on the R&B chart and even troubled the lower reaches of the pop chart. Nathan was nothing if not consistent; a month or so later, Brown released another single under his own name, and King put its weight behind "I Know It's True." It wasn't until public demand turned the record over that he had his next substantial hit, "I'll Go Crazy." Probably the only reason King got the right side of the follow-up, a searing version of the "5" Royales' "Think," was because they had a significant part of the publishing and the B side, "You've Got the Power," featured Brown's current female vocalist, Bea Ford, instead of him.

Sam Cooke, too, was getting itchy. His records for Keen were doing okay, and more than okay in black markets, but not nearly as well as he'd thought in the pop world. In some ways, he blamed Keen for not having the power to get his records out there, and he also blamed his management, the William Morris Agency. One thing the agency had done, though, was to put him in touch with RCA Records, and at the end of 1959, Sam was looking over a contract with them. They had a great idea for taking him pop: giving him Hugo & Luigi as producers. Hugo Peretti and Luigi Creatore were first cousins, and had a track record that included working for Mercury looking for R&B records for their white artists to cover, and they were co-running Roulette Records with Morris Levy when RCA offered them each a $100,000 salary and a lot of other perks. They engineered an amiable parting with Levy and went to work. Cooke was their first big client, and they were determined to cross him over. Their first effort with him, "Teenage Sonata," a Jeff Barry song, overproduced and laden with a big orchestra, stalled at #50 on the pop charts, and suffered even more when Keen released a song Sam had written with Lou Adler and Herb Alpert, "Wonderful World," a far superior number that almost made it into the top ten. Hugo and Luigi tried again, with another Sam Cooke original, "Chain Gang," where Sam sings lovingly to his girlfriend about how he spends all day breaking rocks, but yearns to be back with her. An odd choice, maybe, but it got to #2, and it looked like Sam, Hugo, and Luigi had hit on something.

Neither Ray Charles nor James Brown was bothering the pop charts, though. Instead, they looked like the triumph of the Nashville Sound, with Johnny Preston's "Running Bear" (written by the late J. P. Richardson), Marty Robbins's Western narrative (and longest song to make the top ten so far) "El Paso," Jim Reeves's "He'll Have to Go," Conway Twitty's "Lonely Blue Boy," and Johnny Horton's "Sink the Bismarck" all vying for the top slot, which was usually taken by Percy Faith's string instrumental "Theme from a Summer Place." Then there was Mark Dinning's "Teen Angel," a maudlin tale of a teen couple out on a date when their car gets stuck on a railroad track. They leave the car to its fate, but the girl goes back for the boy's ring just as the train hits the car. Since it sold like crazy, it was perceived as a trend, and soon there would be more death songs cropping up. But clearly Nashville was hitting the sweet spot between rock & roll and "good music," so in mid-February, another film studio took a huge chance. Warner Bros. had been mostly issuing soundtracks from their films, and had only nodded in the direction of the top ten by signing a fading Bill

Haley, who immediately recorded a version of the South African novelty tune "Skokiaan," originally done by the Bulawesi Sweet Boys in 1954. In mid-February, Warners made the announcement Nashville had been waiting for ever since it became obvious that the Everly Brothers weren't going to re-sign with Cadence Records once their contract was up: Warners signed them to an unprecedented deal, ten years at a guaranteed $75,000 per year. Their first record under the new deal, "Cathy's Clown," which they'd written, was just as good as the records that had established them, and sold better, too.

Not that some people were paying much attention to singles. Absent a craze like rock & roll selling millions of singles, the record industry's attention was all on albums. In 1957, a small New York label, Audio Fidelity, had released the first commercial stereophonic LP, although there were very few record players capable of handling it. This changed quickly; the high-fidelity craze had been building during the 1950s, with those who could afford it building or buying equipment capable of handling the higher frequency response of LPs, and buying classical, jazz, and soundtrack albums to play on their new systems. (This was also aided by the adoption of a single standard for playing back sound, the RIAA curve, a means of equalizing recorded material to de-emphasize lower frequencies and emphasize higher ones; ask your local hi-fi nut for details.) Stereo meant replacing the tone arm, amplifier, and preamplifier, and getting a matching speaker (or two new ones), which appealed to the largely affluent male gadget-freak hi-fi crowd. The thing was, as everyone noticed right off, stereo *was* better; the separation of the sounds resulted in more clarity and detail, and with the improvements in recording technology happening all the time, such labels as Mercury's Living Presence Sound issued records that audiophiles treasure to this day.

Once the appeal of Audio Fidelity's Formula One sound effects records and Enoch Light's gimmicky *Provocative Percussion* albums and their imitators died off, there were still lots of albums to choose from with actual music on them, and the original cast recording of *Sound of Music* lasted over five years atop the charts, in part due to its magnificent stereo recording. The songs on it were pervasive enough that John Coltrane, who'd signed to Atlantic in 1959, recorded it on

October 21, 1960, and it became a hit for him, or as much of a hit as a serious jazz player could have. And Atlantic, following a long-established tradition, listed the brands of microphones used to record it and the lathe used to master it in a little box of technical information on the back of his *My Favorite Things* album, just as classical labels did; for that matter, they did the same for Ray Charles's albums.

Manufacturers competed like crazy to come up with a home stereo system that didn't involve expensive, complicated components yet delivered superior sound, and in another corner of the industry, companies like Ampex and Magnecord were noting that records scratched and wore out, and that the *real* pure sound was direct to tape, so record companies started looking into pre-recorded tape as another way to release music. A whole subset of discount labels emerged, selling knockoffs of popular music and inexpensive (and not always awful) classical albums by Eastern European orchestras, leased on the cheap. An industry survey of the previous year noted that LPs (over six million) had overtaken singles (under five million) in sales for the first time, and some acts were releasing albums and then picking the single from the material there instead of the time-honored practice of building an album around an already-successful single. And adult customers, it was noted, preferred albums to singles.

What was making everyone nervous, of course, was the payola hearings, which were preparing in separate hearings of the FCC and Orrin Hatch's Senate oversight committee in Washington, but the first bomb the government dropped was, although not unexpected, not scheduled: Elvis Presley got out of the Army a little early, and suddenly things were different. Actually, it started getting interesting when Elvis began his trip from Germany back to the States. The Army put on one last press conference, a tightly scripted event at which Elvis was expected to speak. It didn't quite go that way. A captain in the Women's Air Corps who'd been assigned to Armed Forces Television to be part of the coverage of the event was waiting for things to happen, drinking coffee at the bar near a door. "Suddenly it flies open and in steps Elvis . . . I said, 'Hi, hon.'" Hardly officer-like behavior, but then, this was Marion Keisker, who'd pretty much discovered him. "Marion!" said Elvis. "In Germany! And an officer! What do I do? Kiss you or salute you?" She replied, "In that order," and hugged him. The public information officer was shocked and ordered her to leave. As Keisker remembered it later, "Finally, Elvis got free and he came over and he said, 'Captain, you don't understand. You wouldn't even be having this thing today if it wasn't for this lady.' The captain said, 'This WAC captain?' Elvis said, 'Well, it's a long story, sir, but she wasn't always a WAC captain."

After the press conference, he got on a plane and flew to McGuire Air Force Base, where he posed for pictures as he deplaned and then went to yet another press conference, this one featuring Nancy Sinatra, who gave Elvis a box of dress shirts as a present from her dad, whose Timex Spectacular TV special he'd tape in a month at the Fontaine-bleau Hotel in Miami. The next day, March 5, Sergeant Presley went to Fort Dix, adjacent to McGuire, and got his mustering-out check, $109.54, for travel, clothing, and food. Colonel Parker was there and huffed and puffed until Elvis handed him the check, then they stepped into a limo and blasted off down the New Jersey Turnpike, with a caravan of media following down snow-packed roads—there'd been a blizzard—after telling the media that there'd be another press conference in New York the next day. The Colonel had no such thing in mind; they hid out with some of Elvis's buddies in a Trenton hotel overnight, and the next day took a private railroad car to Washington, where they got on another private car attached to the back of the Tennessean, a regularly scheduled train, and headed to Memphis.

Life in the Army in Germany had been schizophrenic. The Colonel had gotten Vernon Presley and Elvis's grandmother a house in Bad Nauheim, where he was stationed, and he spent as much time as he could there. He had a live-in German girlfriend, a nineteen-year-old half American, Elisabeth Stefaniak, whom he'd hired as his secretary, but there were other girls, too. Out training near the Czech border, he'd been introduced to miraculous pills that kept you full of energy and awake during maneuvers, and when he came home, he bought several quart-sized jars of them, distributing them to his friends. (They'd been invented by the Germans during World War II to keep flyers alert on bombing raids, and were called amphetamine.)

The pills made Elvis weird; at one point Vernon and Elisabeth were in a serious car accident that destroyed Elvis's Mercedes, and the first thing Elvis thought to ask was whether Vernon was putting the moves on Elisabeth. Some of his Memphis friends decided to leave; he was getting a bit hard to handle. Meanwhile, RCA was trying to get the Colonel to let Elvis record something—*anything*—in Germany so they'd have some records to keep his name out there. The Colonel seemed to feel that the very scarcity of product was a good thing; there was the *Kid Creole* soundtrack, and then another greatest hits album called *50,000,000 Elvis Fans Can't Be Wrong*. That'd have to do while Elvis finished his service. A deal was signed for a film to come out immediately after Elvis left the Army, *GI Blues*, which was cleverly written around Elvis's scenes, so that all he'd have to do would be to plug them in, and location shooting began for that in Germany, although the film would be finished in Hollywood.

And then Elvis got his own fourteen-year-old. Priscilla Beaulieu had just moved with her family from Bergstrom Air Force Base on the outskirts of Austin, Texas, to Wiesbaden, and before they moved, she and a girlfriend looked it up on a map and discovered how close it was to Bad Nauheim, where Elvis was stationed. The girls giggled about it. But then, not long after the Beaulieus had moved and gotten settled in, Priscilla was hanging out with some friends at the Eagle Club, a facility for soldiers' families, when she noticed a guy staring at her, an older guy. He eventually came over and introduced himself as Currie Grant, the entertainment director of the Eagle Club, and asked if she were an Elvis Presley fan. She said she was, and he told her he and his wife visited Elvis often and asked if she'd like to come to dinner with them some evening. Captain Beaulieu was suspicious, but after meeting the Grants and inquiring about him with his commanding officer, he gave permission for a dinner, noting that she had to be back by 11:00, because the next day was a school day. Off they went, and when they arrived, Elvis said, "Well, what have we here?"

"Elvis," Currie said, "this is Priscilla Beaulieu, the one I've been telling you about."

"Hi," he said, extending his hand. "I'm Elvis Presley."

At first there was light conversation, during which she had to admit she was only in ninth grade. He took it in stride, and showed her the house, introduced her to his grandmother, and finally sat down at the piano for an impromptu series of songs. Eventually, Grant said it was time to go—that 11:00 curfew—and Elvis begged for more time, but Grant insisted, because he didn't want to get Captain Beaulieu angry. (Best-laid plans and all: dense fog on the Autobahn got them home at 2:00 A.M.) A couple of days later, Elvis asked her back, and Grant drove her to his house. After a while, Elvis told her he wanted to be alone with her—in his room. She didn't think that was such a good idea, but he said, "I'll treat you just like a sister," and, when she finally agreed, that's just what he did. They sat on his bed and talked and talked. Priscilla noted that there was a part of him that was like a little boy, insecure, frightened, and, most of all, afraid that the fans would desert him. But he kept his word and sent her home at the end of the evening. On the fourth date, he met Captain Beaulieu, who wanted to know right off what Elvis wanted from his daughter. "Well, sir, I happen to be very fond of her," he told him. "I guess you might say I need someone to talk to." Over the course of the conversation, the captain's misgivings vanished. From then on, Elvis and Priscilla saw each other every night.

Elvis's inner circle—including Elisabeth, with whom he continued to sleep—knew something radical had happened. There were still girls, but this one was special. Elvis plunged into new activities, beginning the study of karate, undergoing treatment with a South African dermatologist who offered to take care of Elvis's acne scars and turned out to be a publicity-seeking quack, but mostly getting ready for March 1, when he'd be going back home. Packing was a pain— among other things, Elvis had more than two thousand records— and of course there was the last-minute Army paperwork, as well as business details for his return, the Sinatra special (he was getting $125,000 to appear and sing two songs, the most any television guest had ever been paid), and a new publishing contract for the songs he'd eventually record. At last, the day came. Priscilla went out to the airfield to see him off but was prevented by the security contingent from seeing him or talking to him. Then the press conference, the reunion with Marion Keisker, and then . . . he was back.

After that, things moved fast. There was the film to finish, friends to catch up with, and records to be made. The March 28 issue of *Billboard* had a double-page ad from RCA welcoming Elvis back, and reporting that his new single had already sold 1,275,077 copies. Really? He hadn't even recorded it yet. He probably looked around at the competition, which included the Drifters' new string-backed ballad "This Magic Moment"; some good hard-core blues from Jimmy Reed, "Baby What You Want Me to Do"; B. B. King's latest, "Sweet Sixteen"; all that Nashville stuff; the Everlys' new record; a brilliant ballad from Jackie Wilson (an Elvis favorite), "Doggin' Around"; and, from Sam Phillips, Charlie Rich's first hit, "Lonely Weekends," described in the trade-magazine ads as "distinctively different," which it certainly was. Rockabilly? Pretty much a thing of the past, but that kid out in Los Angeles, Eddie Cochran, had not only recorded some good stuff, but had mastered multitracking so that on records like "Somethin' Else" and "Cut Across Shorty" he played most—or all—of the instruments himself. Carl Perkins's career had fizzled out, Jerry Lee Lewis's likewise, although both were popular touring acts, Perkins being part of Johnny Cash's show. Wanda Jackson, unsure about rockabilly, was still doing it (her most famous record, "Let's Have a Party," would come out in June) when she wasn't doing country. There were other rockabillies recording for tiny Southern labels, but they weren't being heard nationally—Top Forty radio had taken care of that. Elvis had his work cut out for him, and first he had to tape his homecoming special with the man who'd once characterized rock & roll as "sung, played, and written for the most part by cretinous goons . . . the martial music of every sideburned delinquent on the face of the earth." Hmmm, "sideburned delinquent." Wonder who that referred to? (Not Eddie Cochran, who'd died on April 17 when a car carrying him, Gene Vincent, and Cochran's girlfriend, songwriter Sharon Sheeley, crashed in Cheltenham, England, when the driver, speeding to take them to Heathrow Airport, misjudged a hill.)

One thing was for certain: Elvis was one "sideburned delinquent" who didn't need payola, not when he could sell a million and a quarter copies of an unrecorded record. But the rumble in Washington was getting louder because of the sensational subject matter picking up traction in the media, although surveys showed that most people considered payola a minor threat next to juvenile delinquency: in January, satirist and ad executive Stan Freberg issued a two-sided comedy routine, "The Old Payola Roll Blues," which obviously wasn't picked up by many radio stations. They were too busy quaking about the supposedly impending indictments. And then the inquiry had its first casualty: John Doerfer, one of the FCC commissioners, was shown to have accepted favors from a large broadcasting chain. Oops. Then they announced that they'd be formulating strict rules about radio stations accepting free records, which was ridiculous, some industry people felt: nobody was going to go out and buy a record they'd never heard of, and there were more coming out than anyone could listen to—or find in the stores. They also wore out and needed to be replaced. The FCC action was clearly intended to stop record companies providing many more copies than were needed so they could be resold, but few radio stations were doing that. And there was this: the FCC chairman, Frederick W. Ford, sent a memo to Congressman Tip O'Neill, who'd fulminated that the youth of America had to be protected from "a type of sensuous music unfit for impressionable minds," noting that the FCC had no information "which would enable it to determine with any degree of certainty" that a relationship existed between the popularity of rock & roll and payola.

Not that there hadn't been some dirt uncovered: on May 2, Dick Clark began his testimony in Philadelphia, a testimony one congressman characterized as "evasive at best." Clark controlled 162 copyrights, as well as recording, publishing, and pressing interests. He said that Jamie Records, a label he'd invested $150 in back in 1957 before it even got started, did pay payola, but he himself had never accepted any. Anyway, he'd sold his interest in 1959 for $31,575, because who knew how long this thing would last, and there was an opportunity to make a good return on that $150. The more they came after him, the cooler he acted. He knew nothing of his partner Tony Mammarella's payola activities, even though they'd worked inches apart at facing desks with only one telephone between them, while producing *American Bandstand*. Mammarella had quit the job rather than divest himself of the various connections he'd made. The congressmen asked Clark if he had been able to write his own anti-payola affidavit for ABC because he'd made the network $12 million, while another DJ (read: Alan Freed) had only brought in $250,000 and had had to sign a far harsher affidavit, which had caused ABC to fire him. He denied it, saying he'd sign any affidavit they put in front of him. In a second day of testimony, he explained to the congressmen that he'd taken opportunities to make money when they were offered to him, that he was just following the "rules of the game" by taking them. Sure, payola existed, but he didn't consider giving money, as opposed to accepting it, to be payola, and he hadn't accepted any. And he swore under oath that he had divested himself of all the interests he'd had before he signed the affidavit. Satisfied, Oren Harris, head of the congressional investigating committee, told him he was "an attractive and successful young man" who knew that what he'd done was wrong, but that he was "a product of that system, not responsible for it. You took advantage of a unique opportunity to control too many elements in the popular music field through exposure of records to a vast teen-age audience." And that was that.

In the room next door, Alan Freed, whose television show had also been on ABC, was sweating out a tough line of questioning, stating that he'd been told to "lean heavily" on ABC-Paramount records and play his live shows only in Paramount theaters. (Clark ridiculed this in his testimony.) He made the allegation about Clark writing his own affidavit and said that the network had a "dual policy" that allowed Clark to divest himself of his possibly tainted links. The next week Freed announced that he was going to work at KDAY in Los Angeles, a station that had made a big deal about not playing rock & roll, but where he would be playing only rhythm and blues. The week after that, indictments came down: Freed, Mel Leeds (a former DJ who'd become program director at KDAY), and Tommy "Dr. Jive" Smalls, Harold Jackson, and Jack Walker of WLIB, "The Voice of Harlem." Freed was indicted on twenty-six counts and was alleged to have accepted bribes of $30,650 from seven record companies in

1958–1959. And the hits kept on coming; producers Hugo & Luigi, country label Starday, and Specialty's Art Rupe were served, and complaints were lodged soon after against Sue, Fiesta, Scepter, Rank, Old Town, and Peacock—all, it should be noted, small, independent, largely black labels. Rupe, caught between an increase in the payola he alleged *American Bandstand* was asking for and the summons from Washington, called Sonny Bono into his office and said, "I know this is a big disappointment for you, and I'm really, really sorry, but I just can't do it anymore. I can't stand it; I'm getting out of this business. It's so crooked I can't stand it anymore." And with that, one of the great rhythm and blues and gospel labels ceased to exist as a living presence, although Rupe kept the company alive in suspended animation, to revive it decades later with a welcome flood of reissues. He was no fool; he then went into Los Angeles real estate and made far more than he ever would have done with a record label. As for Freed, he fought his payola case for years, exhausting his finances (no matter how they'd been obtained), wrecking his marriage, and drinking increasingly more. He died, a bitter and all-but-forgotten man, in 1965, aged forty-three. The death certificate said uremia because there is no recognized medical term for heartbreak.

The only thing yet to be worked out was Rule 317, where the FCC required that stations announce where they'd gotten any free records, presumably with a bit at the top of the hour: "In the next hour, we'll be playing records from ABC-Paramount, Atlantic, Top Rank, MGM . . ." This was clearly unworkable, so the stations petitioned for some kind of relief, and, well after the hearings had vanished into history, they got it. In December, *Billboard* ran a headline: DEEJAYS TAB PAYOLA PROBE AS BOOTLESS POLITICAL FOOTBALL: JOCKS FEEL FEDERAL INQUIRY HURT INDUSTRY, BUT CHANGED VERY LITTLE. Inside, the magazine ran a sanctimonious editorial disagreeing with the article that said, "The rug needed to be lifted," but in the end, the DJs were right.

The end of the hearings was also the beginning of summer, when teenagers were cut loose and able to have fun, and this summer, dire as it was in most respects, shows some interesting things happening. In the July 11 issue of *Billboard*, a record showed unusual action, breaking in high in the charts and moving upward with alarming speed. "Walk, Don't Run" was an instrumental by a bunch of guys from Washington State, the Ventures, all but the drummer playing solid-body electric guitars. The melody was simple enough, and the lead line used a feature of some guitars, a bar—which, when depressed, would lower the tone of all the strings simultaneously—the so-called whammy bar.

Guitar instrumentals were nothing new, although apparently they were a big thing in the Northwest, because the Ventures had been preceded by the Wailers, from Tacoma, who'd scored minor instrumental hits with "Tall Cool One" and "Mau-Mau" in 1959, and a drummer from Caldwell, Idaho, who was really named Paul Revere, whose first record, "Beatnik Stix," based on "Chopsticks," went nowhere but produced a minor hit at the end of the year with "Like, Long Hair," based on a piece by Rachmaninoff. There were a bunch of them all of a sudden; Duane Eddy had been cranking them out, and the Ventures were competing with his "Because They're Young." There was also the Fendermen, on Soma, a tiny independent label out of Minneapolis, whose "Mule Skinner Blues" was a wild rave-up of guitars and whooping, and later in the year the California band the Revels would release "Church Key." The important thing here was that the Ventures and the Fendermen and most of the rest were playing what should properly be called electronic guitars. With a solid body, they had no hollow interior to cause feedback or other distortion to the string's vibration, and thus they could be played louder. These instruments had been around for a while—Buddy Holly famously played a Fender Stratocaster, as did Carl Perkins—but they weren't very versatile in a jazz combo or backing band context. They were also cheap; if you didn't insist on a Fender, there were lots of other makes that could be had almost as inexpensively as a gut-string acoustic guitar, and sales were on the rise. Similarly, the solid-body bass that Fender had developed wasn't very popular with most musicians. True, an early model had made an appearance on "5" Royales records as far back as 1957, and jazz guitarist Wes Montgomery's band, the Mastertones, had one played by his brother Monk (Wes had a semi-hollow-body guitar), but it was scorned by most working bassists. The only customers for solid-body instruments besides teenagers seemed to be

West Coast country musicians, and they were still a local phenom-enon.

The payola hearings weren't the only court case in rock & roll, though. Chuck Berry's Mann Act bust that made the headlines hadn't been his first. That had occurred in 1958 with a young Frenchwoman, Joan Mathis, where Berry had essentially been busted for being a well-dressed black guy in a fancy car with a white woman. They'd decided against prosecution, but warned him not to let it happen again. Now that it had, he was charged with two more crimes, stemming from two trips with Mathis. Berry had been busted and convicted of a felony in 1944, when he and two of his teenage friends had gone on an armed robbery and car theft spree. Having that on his record sixteen years later meant that his three charges now saw him facing twenty years in prison and $17,000 in fines.

When the trial finally began on February 29, they faced Judge George H. Moore, whose record was somewhat mixed. He'd ruled for desegregating St. Louis's public housing in 1955, but had also re-fused, some years earlier, to speak at St. Louis University's law school because "they had that nigra out there," referring to the student who'd desegregated the school, Theodore McMillan. That was the Moore who was sitting at Chuck Berry's trial. As Janice Escalanti began to testify, Moore repeatedly asked her, when a new character in her story was introduced, "Is he a white man or a Negro?" Natu-rally, the jury hearing this was all white, and Moore must have real-ized he was playing to any racial prejudice among them. Berry's lawyer, Merle Silverstein, now had another job: not only did he have to get his client off three Mann Act charges, he had to get race off the jury's mind. But again and again, the judge pushed the racial issue; he had Escalanti describe the luxurious house she'd been put up in, and kept hammering her to tell the race of every person in her somewhat confused story. As for Berry, he was evasive and uncon-vincing, offering up numerous reasons for wanting to take Escalanti back to St. Louis with him, including that he wanted "so very much" to learn Spanish to keep up with the new trend of foreign-language songs. Despite the previous testimony by Escalanti and the bellhop at the hotel where they stayed, he claimed never to have had sex with her, even once. He argued about minor points: when, at one point, he was asked if a hotel registration card was in his handwriting, he pointed out that the writing in question was printing, not hand-writing. He disputed testimony about what Escalanti was wearing when the bellhop saw her on his bed. In short, he didn't make any friends in the courtroom, and Silverstein, who was pretty unhappy with his client's behavior, wound up attempting to have a mistrial declared. Unsurprisingly, the movement was denied. The jury was empanelled, and in two hours and thirty-five minutes, they found Charles Edward Berry guilty of violating the Mann Act. He was led to the municipal jail to await sentencing.

Moore showed no sympathy. "[Y]ou are not a very wholesome citizen," he told Berry, "and there is nothing about your situation to arouse much sympathy . . . You came into this courtroom with a flimsy story, and I can't believe that anybody that sat in this court-room and heard your testimony believed you when you talked about trying to reform her. You took her on this trip for the purpose of try-ing to reform her and get her out of a career in prostitution, and then used her for your own vile purposes." He then imposed the maxi-mum penalty: five years in prison and a $5,000 fine. He also refused bail. "I would not turn this man loose to go out and prey on a lot of ignorant Indian girls and colored girls, and white girls, if any. That man would be out committing offenses while his case is on appeal, if this court is any judge . . . I have never sentenced a more vicious character than that kind, I don't believe . . . society is well off with him incarcerated." Silverstein was aghast. "If I don't get this case re-heard," he said at the time, "I'm going to jump out the window." By filing to appeal Moore's sentence, he automatically overturned Moore's denial of bail. Chuck Berry, free for a while, zipped up to Chicago and over two days recorded nineteen sides. He returned on May 30, because one of the Mathis-related arrests, which also had a weapons charge—a loaded gun having been found in the car when the high-way patrol had stopped them—was going to be tried before a different judge. Mathis denied nothing, said she'd been in love with Berry, the jury found nothing immoral about the reasons for their crossing state lines, and the charges were dismissed.

Not that it was over, though; on October 30, the Eighth Circuit Court of Appeals noted that "what has given us concern . . . [is] the attitude, conduct and remarks of the trial judge," and added that "a trial judge who, in the presence of the jury, makes remarks reflecting upon a defendant's race or from which an implication can be drawn that racial considerations may have some bearing on the issue of guilt or innocence has rendered the trial unfair." However, they ruled that because of the evidence against him, he wasn't entitled to an acquittal, but a new trial.

With rock & roll being in such disrepute, between payola and Chuck Berry's woes, novelty records and "good music" by young artists on Philadelphia-based labels looked like they were going to be the soundtrack for a lot of teenagers. Someone named Bryan Hyland had released the tale of the "Itsy-Bitsy, Teenie-Weenie Yellow Polka Dot Bikini" and it got played over and over. Ray Peterson contributed the latest death song, "Tell Laura I Love Her," sung by a boy dying in a flaming race-car wreck. It was banned in England when it was released there in August. But not all the teen pop singers were awful; the Everly Brothers continued their string of hits, and the guy they'd enticed away from Sun with a deal with Acuff-Rose publishing put out his first song on the publishers' new label, Monument. "Only the Lonely" was identifiably by Roy Orbison, the same guy who'd sung "Ooby Dooby," but oh, the difference in the emotional content! Projecting the persona of the lonely, confused teenager who can only hope for redemption through a new love, Orbison scaled the heights of his vocal range in the bridge, backed with a socko orchestral punch, ending on a high note from which he gracefully fell to finish off the chorus. Teenagers across America (and, later, England) felt a jolt of recognition—*he understands!*—in the song, and Orbison and his producers knew they were onto something. Now, mused Monument's president, Fred Foster, if they could do something about his looks. Orbison was nearly blind, and his close-set eyes were jarring. The cover of his first album, *Lonely and Blue*, showed him alone in his car at a drive-in burger joint. It would be hard to put him on television looking like that. Then Foster had an inspiration: "Give him sunglasses." A star was born. (Or, somewhat more prosaically, one night Orbison had left his regular glasses on an airplane and only had his prescription sunglasses when he was ready to go onstage, and he wore them instead—and Foster insisted he continue to do so.)

Other stars were, too, as we can tell in retrospect. A half-page ad in *Billboard* featured one of them, although he wasn't a performer. "From out of the Midwest," the ad copy read, "comes a new label destined to take its place among the leaders in the industry. TAMLA, prexied by one of the young, driving geniuses of the music business today." Berry Gordy, Tamla's "prexy," smiled out of the photo, and the ad mentioned the latest release by the label's flagship group, the Miracles, "Way Over There." He'd released their previous single, "Bad Girl," on a label he'd named Motown, but once again had to give it up to a larger company, Chess, within weeks because it was selling so well and he still didn't have the resources to ride out a hit. He was ready this time, and "Way Over There" was a gospel-flavored work-out inspired by a date the Miracles had played with the Isley Brothers. But the young, driving genius made a mistake; unhappy with the unadorned backup, he took the tapes into United Sound and dubbed on strings, withdrew the original record, and put out the new version. They both had the same serial number, and everyone was confused. It broke the record's momentum and, no doubt, taught Gordy a lesson. (Also, when *Billboard* reported his next couple of releases, it listed them as being on "Talma." Another lesson: pay your advertising bills on time.)

It was the black charts where the action was, though; country was as sclerotic as pop. Hank Ballard and the Midnighters were still at it, and their "Finger Poppin' Time" was a lot of fun, and James Brown re-made the "5" Royales' "Think" and turned it into a hit. In mid-July, a record that out-shouted James Brown came out of nowhere—well, New York via Mississippi—to break into the R&B top ten; "A Fool in Love" was listed as being by Ike and Tina Turner, although Ike was mostly the facilitator to his latest wife, the former Anna Mae Bullock, from Nutbush, Mississippi, who had showed up in his life after he'd relocated to St. Louis. She became a huge fan of the music the Kings of Rhythm played in the clubs there and started singing with them, eventually singing backup (as "Little Ann") on one of their records. When Ike reconfigured his band and signed with black label owner Juggy Murray's Sue label, he abandoned blues for a new sound based around his new wife. On "A Fool for Love," she strutted and shouted and growled and produced unearthly sounds as the three female backup singers, the Ikettes, reminded her that she was a fool, she was only in love, to which she howled and shrieked, whether in agony or ecstasy was unclear. It eventually caught on with the pop charts, landing in the mid-twenties, and the concept of this record and Bryan Hyland's sharing space on America's airwaves is indicative enough of a revolution that was just beginning.

Of course, what's summer vacation without a new dance to do, and in Philadelphia, Ernest Jenkins, a teenager famous for his impressions of other performers, had one: "the Toot." Jenkins had changed his name to Chubby Checker, because his producer thought he looked like Fats Domino, and he'd already had a minor hit with "The Class," in which he imitated everyone from Fats to the Chipmunks, but he still wasn't making it. Heaven knows how one did the Toot, but Checker's producer had a brainstorm: that Hank Ballard B side from last year. Were black kids still doing the twist? They were? Let's re-record that! Of course, the request for copyright hit King, and someone took the hint and re-released Ballard's version; the race was on. In late July, a *Billboard* ad said that Checker's record was "already 200,000." King plugged on. The next week, Chubby broke into the pop charts at #49; Ballard was right on his tail at #53. The next week, Chubby was at #11, Hank at #95. Then Ballard rallied; he was at #61, although it looked like the race was going to Chubby, who was at #8. But there was more than a horse race going on here; the twist was actually happening. Chubby Checker knocked Elvis out of the top slot, and his fellow Philadelphian Fabian released something called "Kissin' and Twistin'." Santo and Johnny had another instrumental, "Twistin' Bells," Danny and the Juniors chimed in with "Twistin' U.S.A.," and someone named Bruce Coefield tried some fusion with the "Cha Cha Twist." It hadn't even started, though.

Whether it was because the twist was old hat to black teenagers or they were hearing more good stuff than other teens, it was clear from the music on black-oriented (and, by this time, even black-owned) labels that a major change was in the air. Some of it was the kind of slow-dance music that is so essential to summer dancers; in fact, one of the summer's greatest records was the Drifters' "Save the Last Dance for Me." Written by a long-standing songwriting partnership, Doc Pomus and Mort Shuman, its chorus was more poignant than the teens who loved it knew: "But don't forget who's taking you home and in whose arms you're going to be / Oh, darling, save the last dance for me." Pomus was actually the pseudonym of Jerome Felder, a white Jewish man from the Bronx who had had polio as a child and used crutches. Initially, inspired by Big Joe Turner, he was a blues singer who performed to appreciative audiences in Harlem, but standing and singing on crutches was exhausting, so he turned to writing lyrics for others. He still loved black music, though, and several times a week he'd hit the clubs in the company of his wife, who loved to dance. He'd let her, but there was no question that they went home together, and eventually this turned into a hit song.

Other midtempo hits included Shirley & Lee's "Let the Good Times Roll," Maurice Williams and the Zodiacs' "Stay," Jo Jones's "You Talk Too Much," Jerry Butler's "He Will Break Your Heart," and Hank Ballard and the Midniters' "Let's Go Let's Go Let's Go." (Ballard, despite losing the twist horse race to Chubby Checker, wound up doing very well this summer, with not only it and this record, but also "Finger Poppin' Time" on the charts at once.) But the ballad sweepstakes was conclusively won by Ray Charles's second single for ABC-Paramount, an ancient number by Hoagy Carmichael, "Georgia on My Mind," where, over a sparse arrangement, Charles's gospel-drenched voice does indeed convey how much he missed the state, and even convinced others that they missed it, too, even if they'd never been there.

In Detroit, Berry Gordy was finally gathering enough capital to start putting out records regularly. His first new signing was Mable John, Little Willie John's younger sister. She was the first act he signed to undergo a thorough training program, although she still had the job as his chauffeur; Gordy never learned to drive. Her first record for the label, "Who Wouldn't Love a Man Like That?" didn't go anywhere, but it was good and she was patient. Next up was Mary Wells, a teenage songwriter who asked Gordy to pass on a song she'd written, "Bye Bye Baby," to Jackie Wilson. Gordy told her he had his own company now and asked her and her mother to drop by the next day and show him what she had. He liked it enough to put her through twenty-two takes, winding up with what would eventually become a top-ten R&B hit and a moderate pop hit, his first break-through, although it was followed up shortly by the Miracles' first record for Gordy.

"Shop Around" was originally written for Barrett Strong, but Gordy wanted to keep it on his label (Anna was still taking Strong's records, although Gordy released them locally first), and issued it as the B side of "Who's Lovin' You." A few weeks after that record came out, Gordy called Smokey Robinson at 2:00 A.M. and told him to round up the group. Gordy couldn't sleep, because he'd had a great idea: record "Shop Around" at a faster tempo. An hour later, everyone had convened at the studio except the piano player, so Gordy sat down at the piano, and in short order a new version was completed. Every-one was amazed—it *was* better! So much so that it charged up the R&B chart and, not long after, the pop chart. In the end the statistics were plain: #1 R&B, #2 pop, over one million copies sold. Hitsville U.S.A. was on the map.

So, over in Chicago, Detroit's eternal musical rival, was another black-owned label. Vee-Jay had started earlier than Berry's enter-prises, and locally had Chess to compete with for acts. But Chess was acting conservatively; the label was sticking to its old-time blues stars, with only young Etta James taking up the standard of the new black music. Vee-Jay often found itself as a home for people Chess didn't want, and that's how they got their biggest blues star, Jimmy Reed, who kept them afloat for many years. Ewart Abner, who ran the day-to-day business of recording and signing, was given a subsid-iary label of his own, Abner, which had a hit in 1958 with a gospelish group, the Impressions, which featured a brilliant songwriter, Curtis Mayfield, and a soaring baritone lead singer, Jerry Butler. "For Your Precious Love" did well enough that Butler split with the group and signed a solo deal with Vee-Jay, which paid off in 1960 with the huge smash "He Will Break Your Heart." By 1960, the label was doing well enough that it was signing jazz artists (some of them from Detroit) and taking on gospel acts like Sam Cooke's old employers, the Soul Stirrers, who'd been dropped with Specialty's demise.

In Memphis, it was clear that the guard was changing, too. Sam Phillips seemed to have lost all interest in Sun, despite having bought the property at 639 Madison and, over the first half of the year, investing $750,000 in building what was to become Sam Phillips' Recording Service, an up-to-the-minute studio complex run day-to-day by Scotty Moore. But the gorgeous new facility that opened in September was just the main building of the company, which was building a satellite facility in Nashville in what had been Sonico Recordings, partially owned by a young producer, Billy Sherrill, who was retained as chief engineer when Sam took over. Sam also bought a record store, Select-O-Hits, which also served as a distributor for Sun, Phillips International, and other labels, and turned it over to his brother Tom and his wife to run. But except for pushing Charlie Rich, and occasional recording sessions that remained unreleased at the time on Jerry Lee Lewis, Sam was acting like a man with other things on his mind, which, with his all-female radio station chain, his buying and selling radio stations, a new girlfriend (although he stayed married to his wife and took a great interest in his two sons' growth), and his investment in his friend's hotel franchise, Holiday Inn, he was.

Jim Stewart and Estelle Axton had finally decided that Jim's recording studio way out in Brunswick was too far to go, and, looking around Memphis, found an old movie theater, the Capitol, for rent at the corner of College and McLemore, adjoining a middle-class black neighborhood. The rent was $100 a month, and Jim could move his recording equipment into the theater, which had great acoustics, while Estelle could set up a little record store, Satellite Records, in the lobby. It's not like there was much recording activity going on in Brunswick; the studio was currently used by a band of white high school kids called the Royal Spades. Originally it was a guitar group, with Steve Cropper on guitar, his friend Donald "Duck" Dunn on bass, Terry Jackson on drums, and Jerry Lee "Smoochy" Smith on keyboards, but they'd added on a horn section when Estelle's tenor sax–playing son, Packy, asked if he could join and then casually dropped the information that his mother had a recording studio. Soon, Wayne Jackson and Don Nix filled out the horn section, and Estelle was driving them out to the studio every weekend. But once they'd rented the Capitol, it became the focus of everything; when the boys weren't rehearsing, they were helping Jim and Estelle build out the interior, pulling out the old seats and putting down carpeting, hanging drapes, putting acoustic tile on the walls.

The neighborhood started taking notice of all the action taking place, and one day their postman, Robert Tally, who was also a songwriter and musician, told his friend Rufus Thomas that there was a new recording studio in town. Tally and a mortician friend of his with whom he wrote songs had done a couple of demo sessions there, despite the studio not being completely finished (Jim was cutting a few radio station jingles already), and had liked the results, as well as the modern equipment and the friendly white folks who ran the place. Rufus hadn't had much of a recording career since he'd cut "Bear Cat" for Sun, but he'd kept recording, doing a couple of sides for Lester Bihari's long-vanished Meteor label, and of course holding down his radio show on WDIA. So one day in August, Rufus and his daughter Carla, who was still in high school, got in the car and drove down to McLemore Avenue, and walked in the front door. By this time Estelle had the Satellite Records store up and running at the old candy counter, and she knew Rufus by reputation and because of his radio show. She called for Jim, who was surprised to see his visitors, because he'd met with Rufus promoting his Veltones record. Despite Rufus's misgivings about white folks, he and Jim settled a deal to cut a single using Rufus's piano-playing son and Robert Tally's band, recording a song Rufus had written as a duet, "Cause I Love You." It was soon decided to augment the band a little, so someone went to fetch a baritone sax player he knew, a high school kid named Booker T. Jones. Steve Cropper, who'd been manning the Satellite Records shop, came in to play guitar. Chips Moman ran the board, and then they dashed off a B side Rufus had been writing between takes. When the session was over, Booker T. had a chat with Moman and Cropper, letting them know he also played piano in case they needed him.

"Cause I Love You," Satellite 102, took off locally, selling four or five thousand copies in a hurry—of course, Rufus was playing it on the radio—and this caught the eye of a guy named Buster Williams, who ran a distributor that handled, among other labels, Atlantic. He was under strict orders to notice when a record was taking off in Memphis and the surrounding region, and he told the Atlantic rep next time he came in about the record. It didn't take long for Jim to get a call from Jerry Wexler, who introduced himself as the guy who'd produced Ray Charles. It just so happened that Jim had recently been knocked out by hearing Brother Ray, and was flattered by Wexler's interest in his tiny record company. A deal was hammered out whereby Atlantic would lease the record from Satellite, issue it nationally, pay a tiny royalty for it, and have first refusal on future Rufus and Carla records. Oh, and he cut a check for $5,000. As it turned out, "Cause I Love You" didn't do much nationally, but in November, Satellite issued a record by Carla on her own, "Gee Whiz." Atlantic picked it up and promoted the hell out of it—Wexler knew this was a hit, and it was: top-ten R&B and pop. Satellite had been launched.

And the most famous Memphian of them all? It didn't take long for Elvis to get back into the groove, finishing off *GI Blues* and recording its soundtrack. His first post-Army single, "Stuck On You," was a good enough effort, crafted by two professional songwriters, J. Leslie McFarland and Aaron Schroeder, but it was the second one that was a bit of a shocker; it was an Italian folk song that Caruso had recorded, and in its story lies a clue to what lay ahead. Elvis was calling the shots on his new sessions, carefully going through the material that the Colonel and his people were bringing to them. One song he wanted to do—apparently he'd wanted to do it for a long time—was "O Sole Mio," and this made some people nervous, not because it was a big departure, but because it was public domain, and there was no publishing money to be made from it. The English-language version Elvis had learned, "There's No Tomorrow," was published by people who wouldn't cut in the people at Hill and Range that the Colonel insisted had to be dealt a piece of any song Elvis recorded.

This situation had come together while Elvis was in the Army, and is very likely what would have shown up on that blank piece of paper Jerry Leiber had refused to sign had he signed and returned it. Some songwriters—Otis Blackwell, Doc Pomus, and Mort Shuman, among them—were okay with this, and in fact cutting the pie this way is a fairly standard music-biz practice. So when Freddy Bienstock, the Colonel's man inside Hill and Range, asked Elvis if he'd mind if they gave the tune new lyrics, he readily agreed. The tune, now known as "It's Now or Never," wound up credited to Wally Gold and (again) Aaron Schroeder. For the moment, there was no problem with quality, but in years to come, many talented songwriters would be cut out of the possibility of getting a song to Elvis by this rigidly enforced detail. "It's Now or Never," although some people (including Elvis) were apprehensive as to whether or not the teenage fans would go for it, proved to be a bigger hit than "Stuck On You," sailing easily to #1 and staying on the pop chart for twenty weeks.

Apparently, romantic ballads would sell if Elvis did them, and so he finished out the year with one of his most enduring songs ever, "Are You Lonesome To-Night?" It was the Colonel's wife's favorite song, first recorded in 1926, and had a sentimental recitation halfway through. Elvis made it his own.

As the year drew to a close, there was a palpable sense of an era passing, which was made explicit by a record store in New York's Times Square subway station. Irving "Slim" Rose had discovered that he could get up to five dollars apiece for old, out-of-print singles, and that all kinds of people were discovering his Times Square Records as the place to find obscure oldies. It had a lot of stuff on the Old Town label, which leased some old records (as well as being the home of proto-soul singer Billy Bland, whose "Let the Little Girl Dance" had been a big hit this year), including the Capris' "There's a Moon Out Tonight," which had failed to be a hit in 1959 and 1960 on two different labels. Old Town would take care of that in the early months of the coming year. Various deals were being announced for '61, the biggest by far was that of Frank Sinatra leaving Capitol (for whom he'd just recorded "Ol' McDonald," as it was titled; his friends told him he could record anything and it'd be a hit, so he did and it wasn't, but hey, he was out of the contract) for Warner Bros., who gave him not some high-dollar production deal, but his own label, Reprise, the first time any artist had been offered anything like that. The Chipmunks released a version of "Rudolph, the Red-Nosed Reindeer," and Atlantic released "Spanish Harlem," another beautiful record, this time by Ben E. King. It was written and produced by Jerry Leiber and Phil Spector, and Spector co-wrote the other side, "First Taste of Love," with Doc Pomus. The kid was getting around! And, as always, a silly story crept into the trade press as *Billboard* announced that the emir of Qatar, sitting on untold oil money, had bought jukeboxes for his harem, and then sent a couple of his eunuchs, with an interpreter, to Western Europe to learn how to maintain and repair them. Unfortunately, they couldn't learn, so he imported a couple of European mechanics, with their wives, and gave them a place to live and special dispensations from some of Qatar's laws. There was no indication of what the harem ladies were listening to, but it just could have been Elvis.

chapter thirteen

1961: LET'S TWIST AGAIN

The AFO Executives: *(left to right)* Melvin Lastie, John Boudreaux, Alvin "Red" Tyler, Peter "Chuck" Badie, and Harold Battiste.
(Courtesy of AFO Records)

As any pedant will tell you, the 1960s began at 12:01:00 on January 1, 1961, there being no year 0 in the Christian calendar. The media had already been frothing about the new decade for a year, and with the election of a new, young president, America seemed poised on the verge of a new era. The sixties, however, hadn't started yet, even if the 1960s had; to paraphrase the outgoing president, Dwight Eisenhower, things were more like they were then than they ever had been. Various pompadoured Italian American boys were recording "good" music with slightly rockish beats that their producers hoped the kids would like, while their female equivalents, Connie Francis and Annette Funicello, made their own anodyne records. In fact, Disney, from whose Mouseketeers stable on the wildly popular *Mickey Mouse Club* program Annette had sprung, spent the largest part of 1961 promoting her Hawaiian records, presumably in an attempt to get the kids interested in the music being played by the longtime hit radio show *Hawaii Calls*. Close, Disney, but no cigar.

There was a ton of music being released. As the after-Christmas returns piled up, distributors complained that there were too many LPs being issued, not that anyone was listening to their woes; any random issue of *Billboard* confirmed that there were major labels in those days who thought the public wanted records of strolling mandolins, sing-along records in Yiddish, Charlton Heston narrating the life of Christ, and comedy records. Tons of comedy records: this was the year that saw Nichols & May, Shelley Berman, Bob Newhart, Lenny Bruce, Mort Sahl, Belle Barth, Redd Foxx, and numerous others release albums. Comedy records were cheap to produce—one performer, one microphone, an unobtrusive recording setup in a club, hardly any editing and mixing, and it might be a hit. Bob Newhart's records were; *The Button-Down Mind of Bob Newhart* topped the LP charts and stayed on them for 108 weeks, and its successor, *The Button-Down Mind Strikes Back!*, did likewise and endured for seventy weeks, providing much-needed revenue for the fledgling Warner Bros. label. They both won NARAS awards, too, a new distinction bestowed by the National Association of Recording Arts & Sciences, an institution formed in the wake of the payola scandal to monitor major-label ethics and form an industry lobbying group. The award was shaped like an old-fashioned gramophone, and before long they'd become known as Grammys. That Newhart's first album won one of the first NARAS Record of the Year awards doesn't reflect too well on the state of popular music at that point, though.

There were, however, some interesting things happening, and they tended to be regional and flying under the wire. Top Forty had become pervasive in a lot of places, and it was playing a large role in determining the hits on the charts. But as many labels had proven before, you could make a decent living selling records locally. Take Jay Miller, for instance. Located in the rice-processing town of Crowley, Louisiana, he operated an electronics store, with a little recording setup he'd been running since 1948 to record local Cajun musicians. Paying them a pittance and not mentioning royalties, Miller could break even on a couple hundred copies of a record, and sold them in his store, as well as distributing them to stores and jukeboxes around local towns like Eunice and Mamou. Baton Rouge wasn't exactly in his backyard, but news travels quickly when there's money to be made, and in 1954, Otis Hicks, a Baton Rouge bluesman who performed as Lightnin' Slim, appeared and Miller recorded "Bad Luck Blues" for him. Miller saw the record begin to sell in quantities he couldn't keep up with and he knew that WLAC out of Nashville had paid programs sponsored by record stores, one of which had its own labels, Nashboro and Excello. Miller began licensing his blues stuff to Excello, and Lightnin' Slim became a local star. For one session in 1957, Slim showed up with his regular harmonica player, James Moore, and told Miller he was afraid that if he didn't let Moore cut a record, he'd leave him, and he needed him in his band. Slim had written a song, "I'm a King Bee," for Moore, so Miller devoted part of Slim's session to him. After a couple of takes Miller suggested that Moore sing through his nose; he liked the song, but thought Moore's voice was boring. Moore obeyed, and the results were astounding. "King Bee" only sold locally, but then, nobody expected more, and James Moore was christened Slim Harpo. He enjoyed popularity all over Louisiana and Texas, occasionally performing outside that circuit with or without Lightnin' Slim, and then, out of nowhere, in early 1961, one of his records, "Rainin' in My Heart," suddenly took off nationally, hitting #14 on the R&B chart and even #34 on the pop chart.

New Orleans, too, was ripe for an uprising, and it got it. Fats Domino had been churning out hit after hit—nothing exciting, nothing challenging, the only identifiable New Orleans elements being his Ninth Ward accent and his piano playing—which helped keep Cosimo Matassa's studio alive, but Joe Banashak, who owned A-1 Distributors, the city's largest record wholesaler, said, "I was fed up making hits for other people," and started Minit Records in 1958. Minit didn't make national news until 1961, when it had its biggest hit so far, "Mother-in-Law," by Ernie K-Doe. This being New Orleans, of course, it's a complicated story, and it centers on Allen Toussaint, one of the many hot piano players around town, who had had a shot at success in 1958 when RCA Records showed up auditioning people for a recording contract, and liked the instrumentals he was playing. Before he knew what had happened, the twenty-year-old had an album, *The Wild Sound of New Orleans*, credited to Al Tousan, out on the label, which had no idea what to do with it. It did, of course, raise his profile locally, and he became in demand as a session player and arranger. Banashak came calling with his new label, and Ernest Kador, a popular local club act whose first Minit single, "Hello My Lover," had flopped. Did Toussaint have any songs lying around for him? Why, yes, he did—a lot of them. So he assembled a bunch of musicians, among them Alvin "Red" Tyler on saxophone and Benny Spellman on bass voice, and made a catchy, funny record for the session, which, after Banashak had signed a distribution deal with United Artists, shot up the charts as "Mother-In-Law" by Ernie K-Doe.

Suddenly, there was a steady trickle of great music that didn't sound like anything else coming out of New Orleans. The opening shot had come in April 1960, when local bandleader Jessie Hill had released the nonsensical but catchy "Ooh Poo Pah Do," in two parts, on Minit, and a record by Joe Jones, "You Talk Too Much," that Roulette turned into a hit that September, but except for teenage keyboard prodigy James Booker's "Gonzo," not much had escaped local circles until K-Doe's hit, after which Clarence "Frogman" Henry, whose novelty hit "Ain't Got No Home" had gotten some play in 1958, resurfaced with an old standard funked up with a New Orleans beat, "(I Don't Know Why) But I Do" on Chess's Argo subsidiary, in February. Now, things were cooking.

Nor was Joe Banashak the only New Orleans musical figure tired of making hits for others. Harold Battiste, who'd arranged a number of hits (including "You Talk Too Much"), had been doing a lot of reading about black self-determination, much of it published by the Nation of Islam, a strange, pseudo-Muslim group headquartered in New York. Battiste's idea was simple: a musician-owned collective, sharing equally in profits and producing their own records, using black-owned distributors whenever possible. AFO was incorporated that spring, the initials standing for "all for one," which was the basic concept. The shareholders were Battiste, Alvin "Red" Tyler (sax), Allen Toussaint (piano), Peter "Chuck" Badie (bass), John Boudreaux (drums), Roy Montrell (guitar), and Melvin Lastie (cornet), who was their connection to the Musicians' Union so that they could release records and give the union its 2 percent, "which," Battiste commented later, "was all they wanted."

Now all they needed was money, and one day it just walked through the door. Juggy Murray was a black businessman from New York, just getting started with his new label Sue, which he intended to turn into the biggest black-owned label in the country. He already had Ike and Tina Turner, and he'd gone to Los Angeles looking for someone to be a talent scout for him, and looked up Sonny Bono, who told him to talk to Battiste in New Orleans. He did, and was very impressed with AFO's determination, talent, and idealism, so he laid down some investment money on the spot. Now it was time to make a record, and Melvin Lastie's uncle, Jessie Hill, showed up with two artists, a teenage girl, Barbara George, and a guitar player, Lawrence Nelson, who, for reasons having to do with black secret societies in the city, called himself Prince La La. La La had written two songs for the young woman, and outlined the first to the house band, who were calling themselves the AFO Executives—because they were. They settled into one of the slippery, herky-jerky rhythms that Battiste and Toussaint specialized in (although the pianist wasn't on the session and they used Marcel Richards instead), and Barbara George stepped up to the microphone and nailed the song, "I Know," in a couple of takes. Everyone knew they'd made a hit (Lastie blew a particularly inspired solo that sealed the deal), and now it was time to do the other song of La La's. Try as she could, Barbara couldn't do it. La La was tearing his hair out; it seemed so easy to him! Finally, he decided to do it himself, and AFO's second hit, "She Put the Hurt on Me," was in the can. Things were looking good.

The sound that was evolving in the New Orleans studios was just one of the new musics coming out of Louisiana, though. The other one had been coming together for a couple of years. Probably the first evidence of it heard nationwide was the release, on George Khoury's Lake Charles label Khoury 703, of Cookie and the Cupcakes' "Mathilda," in 1959. Huey "Cookie" Thierry was a Creole who led the house band at a popular Lake Charles club, and the song had an unusual but pleasing beat, anchored by a bass line that alternated quarter notes and triplets: *dum, duh-duh-duh dum*. Cookie's pleading delivery sold the song, and through some kind of bargaining, it went from Khoury's label to Judd (owned by Sam Phillips's brother), to Chess, where it stayed. George Khoury's next stop was Phil Phillips, whose "Sea of Love" was a #2 smash in 1959, picked up for Mercury by a Nashville hustler named Shelby Singleton, who came to western Louisiana to see what else was happening.

A barber and part-time radio personality from Winnie, Texas, Huey P. Meaux, was also scouting the area for talent, and leased his very first production, Jivin' Gene Bourgeois's "Breaking Up Is Hard to Do," to Mercury through Singleton and nearly went to jail for it; when he presented the check to his local bank, they called the local narcotics squad, because nobody who cut hair could have gotten that kind of money legitimately. But that "Mathilda" bass line did it again, and it, too, was a hit. Early in 1961, Meaux got a call from Floyd Soileau, a friend of his in the prairie Cajun town of Ville Platte; a singer named Joseph Barrios Jr., who performed as Joe Barry, had a strong local hit on Soileau's Jin label (he was already dominating the local Cajun and Creole market with his Swallow label), and it was threatening to get out of hand. "I'm a Fool to Care" was an old Les Paul and Mary Ford song, and Meaux, who listened closely to voices, thought Barry's voice bore an uncanny resemblance to Fats Domino's, albeit a Fats with an edge, and made a deal with Mercury for the record. Meaux was also keeping tabs on Jimmy Donley, who was writing songs that he sold to Fats Domino for a pittance, and who was, like Barry, white. Donley's problem was raging alcoholism, which is why he sold his songs for fifty bucks and some whiskey, but Meaux knew that if he could ever get him under control, he'd have something. Meanwhile, he found a left-handed guitar-playing woman who'd been playing in Houston clubs, Barbara Lynn. She wasn't "swamp pop," as some in the industry were calling this new music, but she had potential.

In fact, Barbara Lynn was at heart a blues player, and this was a very good time for blues, especially the new sounds that were mostly coming out of Chicago. Jimmy Reed continued to make hits for Vee-Jay—1961 was the year of both "Big Boss Man" and "Bright Lights, Big City"—and in late January, Junior Wells released his classic "Messin' with the Kid," yet another new voice from Chicago heard from, as was Freddie King, a Texan resident on the West Side whose instrumental "Hideaway" was picked up by would-be guitar virtuosos of all persuasions—including steel guitarists. In Houston, Don Robey's Duke label continued to showcase Memphis talent, releasing two classics early in the year with Bobby "Blue" Bland's "I Pity the Fool" and Junior Parker's "Driving Wheel." And the old-timers continued to produce worthy wax, even if it no longer made the charts; January saw Howlin' Wolf release "Back Door Man" b/w "Wang Dang Doodle," adding to his catalog of classics. Chess was paying a little attention to the new breed; they managed to get Otis Rush in for some sessions, one of which produced "All Your Love" and "So Many Roads, So Many Trains," but the real action was on tiny labels like Cobra, Crash, Chief, Bobbin, and Profile, most of which were lucky to be distributed in Chicago, let alone elsewhere. Fortunately, Chicago had a couple of radio stations that played blues, particularly on weekend nights.

On March 13, in St. Louis, Chuck Berry's legal woes continued. He was still represented by Merle Silverstein, and everyone concerned hoped that the Janice Escalanti matter would be settled at last. Just finding the witness was hard enough, and once found, they wound up putting her in a local convent, whose mother superior told them to hurry up and get the case over with; she wasn't a particularly welcome guest. Silverstein laid heavily on some of Escalanti's statements that someone would pay for what had happened, despite testimony that she hadn't done the jobs Berry claimed he'd brought her to St. Louis to do in his nightclub—hat-check and selling photos—while the prosecution more or less repeated their previous version of events that showed Berry as a sexual predator. That apparently worked on the jury, who once again found Chuck Berry guilty of violating the Mann Act, and Judge Roy Harper sentenced him to three years in prison and a $5,000 fine. He would appeal the sentence and lose. Chuck Berry was headed to jail. He recorded a few more sessions for Chess in 1961, which included two of his best (and least typical) songs, "I'm Talking About You" and "Come On," but they didn't even dent the charts.

It was like the old guard was being forced into change. Little Richard was still in the seminary, Jerry Lee Lewis was still in purgatory (although he'd have a mild hit in April with a version of Ray Charles's "What'd I Say"), Carl Perkins was an opening act for Johnny Cash and drinking a lot, and Elvis . . . well, Elvis was still making records, and they'd creep their way into the top ten for a few weeks before sinking back down. He was making soundtrack albums, too, for his two films this year, *Flaming Star* and *Blue Hawaii*, the latter of which not only had the semi-hit "Rock-A-Hula Baby," but also such attractions as his version of "Aloha Oe" and the "Hawaiian Wedding Song," along with "Ku-U-Ipo," "Slicin' Sand," and "Ito Eats"— and, to be fair, his best ballad effort in a while, "Can't Help Falling in Love."

Rock & roll was in short supply, with only Ricky Nelson (who was getting better: his two-sided smash "Travelin' Man" b/w "Hello, Mary Lou" brightened the airwaves in April and May) and the Everly Brothers sustaining careers from the old days. The new breed of teen crooners was downright spooky; Roy Orbison released "Running Scared," an operatic bolero with chilling, paranoiac lyrics in March, and Del Shannon (real name Charles Westover) had two hits in the first part of the year, "Runaway," which went to #1 in a hurry, and "Hats Off to Larry," both of which featured a weird keyboard instrument called the Musitron, an early synthesizer whose solos made the records stand out on the radio.

There were still lots of vocal groups around, although the ones who had hits tended to produce novelty records like Little Caesar and the Romans' "Those Oldies but Goodies," the Marcels' bizarre remake of the classic "Blue Moon," or the Edsels' "Rama Lama Ding Dong," which would spawn Barry Mann's answer record "Who Put the Bomp." The Vibrations, a Chicago group, contributed "Stranded in the Jungle," which followed up on their similarly African-themed "Watusi," which wasn't about tribesmen; it was a dance. There seemed to be a lot of dancing going on; Chubby Checker began the year by announcing that "It's Pony Time," and apparently it was, because that was yet another hit for him.

There seemed to be a lot of young girls making records, too: the Shirelles were four girls who went to school with Florence Greenberg's daughter at Passaic (New Jersey) High School, and Mrs. Greenberg owned a record label called Scepter that was in need of a hit. She'd wisely hired a veteran music-biz guy, Luther Dixon, to find her artists and material, and he liked the Shirelles right off the bat. First, he'd had them record the "5" Royales' "Dedicated to the One I Love" (they'd had a previous record, "I Met Him on a Sunday," on Tiara,

Greenberg's short-lived previous label, which she sold to Decca), but it didn't do too well, so he co-wrote "Tonight's the Night" with lead singer Shirley Owens, and it did a bit better. At the end of 1960, he'd found the right song, co-written by a husband-and-wife team of professionals, Carole King and Gerry Goffin, which he'd whittled down from a seven-and-a-half-minute demo done as a country song with a recitation: "Will You Love Me Tomorrow." It was a rather daring choice, since it all but makes explicit what every teenage girl knew was the subject: If you give in to your boyfriend's desire for sex, will he love or respect you anymore? It went to #1 instantly, carrying over to the new year, and the girls followed it up by re-releasing "Dedicated," which did very well, too, as did its follow-up, "Mama Said." All of this before summer came, too. Lest New York hog the spotlight too much, Vee-Jay released "Every Beat of My Heart" by the Pips, four guys who were related, fronted by the sister of one of them, Gladys Knight. If she sounded self-assured, it was because she was seventeen and had made her recording debut at five with the Wings Over Zion Choir. Despite there being two versions of the song (both by the Pips) on two different labels, it was a hit, too.

A *Billboard* headline in the March 20 issue summed the situation up nicely: R&B RESURGENCE AN OMEN: LONG VIGIL IS FORECAST FOR FAITHFUL HARBINGERS OF "GOOD MUSIC" RETURN. Translated, that meant that teens were now buying R&B records in such quantity that if you were waiting for them to come to their senses and buy "good music," you should be ready for a wait. Unheeding, the next week Cameo released *Bobby Rydell Salutes the Great Ones*, to wit Al Jolson, Bing Crosby, and Frank Sinatra. Al Jolson? Were they kidding? Rydell was nineteen years old! Were any nineteen-year-old Americans listening to Al Jolson? What the teenagers were buying was music that may not have been as wild as when Little Richard and company exploded onto the scene, but there was still the odd wild moment. The May 1 pop chart had "Runaway" at #1, "Mother-in-Law" at #2, Gene McDaniels's "100 Pounds of Clay" at #4, the Marcels' wacky "Blue Moon" at #5, and Frogman Henry's "But I Do" at #6. The very next week, the Duals' hot-rod themed "Stick Shift," the Regents' "Barbara Ann," and Ben E. King's magisterial "Stand by

Me" were all issued, in anticipation of a hot summer to come, and come it did, with the help of events in Memphis and New York.

In Memphis, it was Packy Axton's band who had figured out after long days and nights working on the studio Jim Stewart and Estelle Axton had leased that maybe the Royal Spades *wasn't* such a good name and changed it to the Mar-Keys. (Mrs. Axton had suggested Marquis, but they didn't like the *q*.) They threw together an instrumental based around a circular riff that keyboardist "Smoochy" Smith played on the organ, and after a couple of times around, the horns reinforced. Instead of a chorus, the music just stopped, and the band all went, "Aaaaaaaah! Last night!"

Actually, it wasn't the band that had been playing around town; bassist Duck Dunn had to drop out because his father had money troubles, so he and a friend opened a business giving helicopter rides. In his stead Lewis Steinberg was on bass, scion of a venerable black Memphis music family going back a couple of generations. Steinberg was older than the rest of them, but he was amazed to discover the scene around Satellite Records and its studio. Mrs. Axton spun records from her candy-counter record store while kids danced on the sidewalk outside, and she kept scrupulous notes on who bought what. It was she who'd told Packy to get his band working on something the kids who danced on the sidewalk could get into, and it was she who took a dub of the resulting tape to a local radio station, which couldn't stop playing it. The next day people dropped by her store and demanded a copy, even though they hadn't manufactured any, and she later claimed she sold two thousand copies of it over that counter, one by one, after Satellite pressed it up and issued it. "Last Night" was a huge nationwide hit, eligible for the title of that summer's smash, and with Atlantic's help it sold a couple of million copies. The Mar-Keys went on tour, first with Carla Thomas and Mrs. Axton chaperoning, but soon without them. Of course, it was the all-white version of the Mar-Keys; what went without any comment on McLemore Avenue didn't go in the clubs, black and white, that they'd been playing, so they rampaged around the South and had the summer vacation of their lives.

The thing that happened in New York was that a club opened. Big deal: clubs and bars opened and closed all the time in Manhattan, particularly close to Times Square, and particularly clubs owned by the Mob. In 1958, Johnny Biello was asked to take over a club at 128 West Forty-Fifth Street by his friend Sibbey Mamone, who found himself having to take a swift leave of absence for a while. Biello already ran another club, the Wagon Wheel, a couple of doors away, and to work out details of the deal (Biello paid $30,000 for 90 percent, the remaining money going to Mamone's wife to pay the bills in her husband's absence), he sat down there with some of his business associates and his son-in-law, Dick Cami. Biello wanted the new joint to make money—it's hard to launder money if you're not making some legitimately, after all—and it had a stage, so they had to book music. Cami noted that every other club in the neighborhood had some kind of jazz. He recommended rock & roll. This was not without self-interest; Cami had been trying to get his toe into the rock & roll business for some time and had financed a couple of flop records and knew a lot of musicians, so he had a pool to draw from. After the meeting, the businessmen wandered over to the new joint, which had been called the Gangplank. It needed a new name, of course, so after tossing a few around, one guy, Fat Jack Herman, who was forever popping candy, suggested the Peppermint Lounge, after the stuff he was currently chewing. Biello thought that was great—a red-and-white candy cane color scheme!—so that's what it became. Cami started booking bands in there, but it took forever to take off. Eventually, though, out-of-towners, the kids New Yorkers call B&Ts (bridge-and-tunnel people), discovered it and kept it busy enough.

Biello, looking to put his Mob career behind him, moved to Florida to open a carpet business. Cami took care of the Peppermint Lounge from a nice house on Long Island. In October 1960, he found a decent group to serve as a house band. Northern New Jersey and western Long Island were hotbeds of musical talent, and in Lodi, New Jersey, Joey Dee and the Starliters had just finished a two-month run as the house band in a club when booking agent Don Davis approached them about a gig at the Peppermint. It was just a three-day engagement, but they did so well that they were immediately hired to play six nights a week for $600 a week.

They were very talented; Joey had gone to school with the Shirelles and backed them up on a couple of sessions, and over time the band had attracted some of the best talent in New Jersey, including vocalist David Brigati, his drummer brother Eddie, organist Felix Cavaliere, and guitarist Gene Cornish, although the lineup changed over the years. One key to being a house band in a popular teen dance club was the ability to keep up with the hits, and to anticipate them if you could. That's why, when Chubby Checker (who clearly had a hipper A&R man than his labelmate Bobby Rydell) called out in June "Let's Twist Again," the Starliters took heed. By then, they had acquired some girls who danced on the stage, led by perky eighteen-year-old Veronica Bennett and her sister Estelle and cousin Nedra Talley. What they really wanted to do was sing—they'd made a record as the Darling Sisters already—but this was as good as anything for the moment, especially once they started getting paid for it.

Not all of America's youngsters were twisting, though. Some were turning to folk music, and not just the folk-influenced music being purveyed by the Kingston Trio (who were awarded an unprecedented four gold albums in January), the Limelighters, the Highwaymen (who had a hit that summer with "Michael (Row the Boat Ashore)") and the Chad Mitchell Trio, but something they perceived as more authentic. In Minnesota, Bobby Zimmerman had graduated from high school and headed toward the University of Minnesota in Minneapolis, where he fell right into the nascent folk scene in Dinkytown, the student ghetto. There, he met people like Jon Pancake and Paul Nelson, who had record collections full of the music he'd been attracted to, including a copy of Folkways' Harry Smith–edited *Anthology of American Folk Music* and another influential Folkways album, *The Country Blues,* which other students like John Koerner and Tony Glover were using as a source of songs to learn. Elektra Records, home to the folk popularizer Oscar Brand, had signed a young woman from Kentucky who played the dulcimer and sang the songs of the hills where she'd been raised, Jean Ritchie. These records had been out for a while, but Folkways kept coming up with more. Besides the contemporary revivalists the New Lost City Ramblers, they'd issued a tape that musicologist Ralph Rinzler had made in North Carolina featuring Folkways Anthology star Clarence Ashley and some of his friends, *Old-Time Music at Clarence Ashley's.* It was exciting to hear not only Ashley, in fine fettle (well, his recordings had only been made some thirty years previously), but a young, blind guitarist named Arthel "Doc" Watson, whose fluency and speed was incredible. Everybody was getting guitars and banjos or, at very least, a Hohner Marine Band harmonica, which was the instrument of choice for blues harmonica players.

After absorbing as much as he could, and discovering Woody Guthrie—who'd been around since the first folk revival of the 1930s, writing songs with political messages on the frameworks of traditional numbers and who was now confined to a hospital in New Jersey with a neurological disease, Huntington's chorea—Zimmerman knew what he had to do next and took off for New York, where he'd never been and knew nobody. He arrived in January 1961, an ideal moment. Israel G. Young had opened a storefront on Macdougal Street in Greenwich Village called the Folklore Center, where he sold sheet music, books, a few records, and the occasional instrument, and it was a magnet for the new folkies. Young also had a column in *Sing Out!,* a folk fan magazine that had been published since 1950 and gave notice of doings across the country, which attracted more people to his store. In December 1960, he'd promoted a concert by Elizabeth "Libba" Cotton, the left-handed guitarist who worked as housekeeper for the Seegers, and the New Lost City Ramblers. The concert drew well, and Young wanted to do more shows of young traditionalists and older artists, and thus, he, John Cohen of the Ramblers, Ralph Rinzler of the urban bluegrass band the Greenbriar Boys, Jean Ritchie (who lived in Brooklyn), and folk dancer Margaret Mayo formed the Friends of Old Time Music, which presented its first show on February 11, 1961, at P.S. 41 in Greenwich Village, with Roscoe Holcomb, a multi-instrumentalist singer from Kentucky, headlining over Ritchie, the Greenbriars, and the Ramblers. It was such a success that on March 25, they did another one at the same venue, with Clarence Ashley's group and Doc Watson and a singer from Virginia, Anne Bird. This show got written up by Robert Shelton of *The New York Times.*

Nor was this sort of action limited to New York. Boston had a thriving folk scene, thanks to its several colleges and universities, and thanks to young Joan Baez, who was already recording her second album for Vanguard. Entrepreneur Albert Grossman opened a club in Chicago, the Gate of Horn, in the basement of the Rice Hotel, to accommodate local and touring folksingers. In Berkeley, a young man who'd been on his way to becoming minor Polish royalty when the war had broken out, Chris Strachwitz, was taking things into his own hands. His family had been put up by relatives in Chicago upon getting to the States one step ahead of the Nazis, and Strachwitz discovered blues on the radio there, unsurprisingly enough. He found that he preferred the more basic performers, people like John Lee Hooker and Lightnin' Hopkins, who simply accompanied themselves on a guitar (and were still having hits and getting radio play), and, after he'd moved to California to go to college, decided to go find Lightnin' Hopkins in Houston, armed only with a tape recorder. Not much came of that initially, but Mac McCormack, a Texan folklorist who'd befriended him, told him of a tenant farmer in Navasota with a virtuosic guitar style and wide repertoire stretching back to the songster tradition before the blues, Mance Lipscomb, and Strachwitz went to see him, befriended him, and recorded him. He put the resulting album out himself, on a label called Arhoolie, after a name for the cries black field workers made to help them work, and in April Arhoolie 1001, *Mance Lipscomb*, was released. It was a sensation among people who heard it; like Roscoe Holcomb, Lipscomb had been passed by when record labels were recording the kind of music he made. How many more like them were out there? For that matter, if Clarence Ashley were still alive and making good music, how many more Folkways *Anthology* and *Country Blues* performers might also be out there to be found?

This was the milieu Bobby Zimmerman found himself in, and he quickly told people that his name was Bob Dylan, that he'd grown up touring with a circus, played in Little Richard's band (a lie, but it would be unhip to admit the truth, that he'd been in Bobby Vee's band very briefly and been fired), and that he was making regular visits to Woody Guthrie, at whose bedside he'd perform songs, much to the old man's apparent pleasure. By February, he'd started playing clubs in the Village and gotten to know some of the people on the scene: banjo/fiddle player Peter Stampfel, a gruff young man named Dave van Ronk, who'd started out playing with a Dixieland jazz band and soon moved on to blues, which he learned from a Harlem preacher, the Reverend Gary Davis, and Carolyn Hester, who'd started in Texas (where she'd had a song written for her by Buddy Holly) and moved to New York. The Twist mattered not to this crowd; they had far more important matters to pursue. Many were also involved in the nuclear disarmament issue and desegregation and voters' rights in the South, and they were cheered by folkies from the previous folk revival of the late '40s and early '50s like Pete Seeger, who traveled and performed anywhere they'd have him, from church halls to college cafeterias, reminding his audiences that songs could heal and there was a lot of healing that needed to be done.

You'd never know it from the records teen America was dancing to, though. *Billboard* was right on the money in July with an article headlined R&B DISK JOCKEYS IN HIT-MAKING ROLE; BREAK SINGLES & SPAWN FRESH ISSUES. The "fresh issues" were reprints of oldies that had been selling again, and there were a bunch of brand-new vocal group records that sounded a lot like the old days: Curtis Lee's "Pretty Little Angel Eyes," with its prominent bass singer; "My True Story," by the Jive Five with lead Eugene Pitt singing a song of teen love and loss; white Philly group the Dovells proclaiming hometown kids from Bristol "sharp as a pistol" when they did the "Bristol Stomp"; and Barry Mann's rather self-referential "Who Put the Bomp," in which he swore that the songwriter who put the bop in the bop-shoo-bop-shoo-bop had made his baby fall in love with him. Barry, of course, was an up-and-coming songwriter himself.

Solo artists, too, kept the summer warm, most notably Jerry Butler, who led off with "I'm A-Telling You" and then grabbed on to what was obviously the song of the year, from the film *Breakfast at Tiffany's*, "Moon River." Butler's version was hardly the only one, but his smooth baritone sold it in a way that demolished all rivals. Dion, now without the Belmonts, told the tale of "Runaround Sue" (shocker: "Sue goes out with other guys!"), and Elvis managed a two-sided hit with "Little Sister" b/w "His Latest Flame," which at least hit the top ten. In August, Atlantic thought they might have filled the void left by Ray Charles's departure with a chunky young man from Philadelphia who'd done a few recordings for other labels while leading a church congregation and running a mortuary to make money. Solomon Burke's debut for the label, "Just Out of Reach (Of My Two Empty Arms)," was a country song that had been recorded many times, but not like he did it, and it stormed the charts. Juggy Murray's Sue label had another hit with Ike and Tina Turner's "It's Gonna Work Out Fine," with Ike actually having a speaking role instead of just playing guitar.

In fact, Murray was at the center of one of the behind-the-scenes battles of the summer. Sue was just one black-owned label in New York. Another was Fire, owned by the colorful Bobby Robinson, who owned a record store very close to Harlem's famed Apollo Theater on 125th Street, Bobby's Records, founded in 1946. He'd played around with the record business as a label owner for years and claimed to have helped the Ertegun brothers set up Atlantic. What's certain is that he had a knack for selling music you'd think sophisticated New Yorkers wouldn't buy and then taking it national; in 1959, he'd taken Wilbert Harrison's ramshackle version of Leiber and Stoller's "Kansas City" to the top, and in 1960, he'd had a more modest hit with Elmore James's "The Sky Is Crying," following it up with yet another recording of his "Dust My Broom," total anachronisms in that era. He put out records by Lightnin' Hopkins, who would record for anyone who'd pay him, and had the distinction of releasing Lightnin's only known Christmas record, "Santa." In 1960, he went to New Orleans and came back with Bobby Marchan's "There Is Something on Your Mind," half a brooding meditation on a lover's betrayal and half a grisly first-person murder story. Marchan was best known as the lead singer of Huey "Piano" Smith's Clowns, but here he (actually, Marchan was transgender and also performed in drag as Bobbi) was on completely different ground. Radio sent part one of the song (the side without all the blood) to the top of the charts, and Robinson, after some success with the second Pips version of "Every Beat of My Heart," went back to New Orleans for more. He found a guy with an auto body shop, Lee Dorsey, singing in a bar and offered him a record deal. All they needed was a song, and as they sat on the porch at Dorsey's house drinking beer one afternoon, they heard some kids singing a jump-rope chant: "Sitting on the la-la, yeah yeah," and with a little work turned it into a song. The next day, they took it to Harold Battiste at AFO, and he promised an arrangement the next day and musicians ready to record it. He was as good as his word, and the AFO Executives were ready for them with a typically funky arrangement that they knocked off along with a B side. Robinson returned to Harlem a happy man. Meanwhile, AFO released their first record, Prince La La's "She Put the Hurt on Me," which didn't sell so well but served notice that there was a new sound in town. They followed it up with Barbara George's "I Know," which, with Juggy Murray's help, did very well indeed. And so, when Bobby Robinson reactivated his Fury label to launch Lee Dorsey's career with "La-La," Murray heard the track and knew only one combo in New Orleans could have recorded it. He bode his time, and after making his money off George's record, he called Harold Battiste, told him he'd signed her to Sue, and, alleging violation of his exclusive contract to use AFO's talent through recording Dorsey for Robinson, declined to distribute any more of their records. AFO would soldier on as a solid local label, but it took a while for them to realize that this was a mortal wound.

If this sounds like small potatoes, remember that the civil rights movement was just coming to national attention, and black record executives, no less than other black businessmen, were fighting for inclusion in the American dream. Berry Gordy certainly was; everyone was paying attention to the Shirelles, and everybody wanted a girl group. There were so many singers in Detroit who wanted a break that Gordy was sure to find something, and sure enough, he did. There were kids hanging around the studio all the time, and one group of girls, the Primettes, had made a record for a small local label called LuPine. Now they wanted to be on Tamla-Motown. Berry didn't encourage them at first—"Are you girls still hanging around?" was his routine greeting to them—but songwriter Brian Holland and Freddie Gorman, a postman who also hung around Hitsville writing songs, had something they thought the girls could do—"I Want a Guy"—so one day they grabbed him and made him listen. He got excited enough to perform some surgery on what Holland and Gorman had already done and decided to record it. One problem: the group's name had to go. Lists were drawn up, and eventually one of the girls, Florence Ballard, chose the name the Supremes from one of them. They recorded "I Want a Guy" and it sank without a trace. They tried again, with "Buttered Popcorn," about a gooey, salty, greasy treat that may indeed be the title subject, although hearing Ballard sing it one could be forgiven for thinking of other things. Gordy, who had co-writing credit on the song, hurriedly announced that the other side was the song being pushed, a lackluster Smokey Robinson number called "Who's Lovin' You," sung unconvincingly by another of the girls, Diane Ross.

Gordy must have been distracted around this time; his next move was to start another label, Miracle, as a sort of farm-team outfit, its first signing being the other, male, half of the Primettes, the former Primes, now known as the Temptations. He must not have heard the hoary old music-biz joke about calling a label Miracle because "if it's a hit, it's a Miracle." But he focused sharply when a high school guidance counselor from suburban Inkster drove some girls to Hitsville. They'd lost Inkster High School's talent contest, but the counselor thought they deserved to audition, anyway. They sounded good, but the label insisted on original songs, so they handed up a sketch one of their classmates had started, and Brian Holland and Robert Bateman got to work on it, finally calling in postman Freddie Gorman. The result, "Please Mr. Postman," upped the ante on girl groups and was Brian Holland's first production. Again, the group's name had to be changed from the Casinyets to the Marvelettes. The record took off almost immediately, becoming #1 on both the R&B and pop charts, a first for Hitsville.

The guy who would really put girl groups on the map, though, was having an uproarious year. At the end of January, Leiber and Stoller announced that they were setting up shop as an independent business, no longer under contract to Atlantic, and that they'd hire on to do production work, as well as starting two new publishing companies. They'd also be signing other production talent, and the first one signed was young Phil Spector, who'd been all but living in their offices, anyway. While his mentors were still with Atlantic, he'd contributed arrangements to some of Ben E. King's hits, most notably "Spanish Harlem," which he'd also co-written with Leiber, but he was still doing stuff on the side. He had an informal deal going with Dunes, a label owned by the Hill and Range publishing house that supervised Elvis's material, and for them he cut "Corinna Corinna," by Ray Peterson, which went top ten, and, with the company's trepidation about a young producer allayed, he went into the studio with Curtis Lee, a white vocalist from Yuma, Arizona, backed up by a black group, the Halos, and cut "Pretty Little Angel Eyes." Hill and Range then had him produce a number of records for their main label, Big Top, where he heard a songwriter named Bill Giant working with the Crystals, five high school girls he was developing. Spector took them into the studio, allegedly to run over some material, but Big Top felt they weren't ready yet.

Despite his fear of flying, Spector was spending a lot of time in California, where he was hanging out with Lester Sill and Lee Hazlewood, who'd brought Duane Eddy to fame. During one of those trips, he and Sill formed a label called Philles (Phil and Les) and without telling anyone signed the Crystals to it. When Big Top tried to sign them, he just had them call Sill, and when they got off the phone, Spector was fired. Not that he cared; Sill had signed a vocal trio, the Paris Sisters, and, unable to sell them to any label, he formed one of his own, Gregmark, and hired Spector to produce them. Apparently trying to invoke the hushed sound of the Teddy Bears, he developed a blurry, indistinct sound for them, and his first production on them, "Be My Boy," did modestly well, so they went back in the studio and came out with "I Love How You Love Me," which was blurrier still. Sill claims Spector did thirty or more mixes on the strings alone, but it went into the top ten, so it was worth it.

In New York, Musicor, a subsidiary label of United Artists, paired him up with Gene Pitney, a songwriter who'd written "Hello Mary Lou" for Ricky Nelson, and they had a minor hit with "I Wanna Love My Life Away," which gave them license to try again with

"Every Breath I Take," which again showed off Spector's increasingly odd use of the studio. Where it really showed up, though, was on a record released at the end of October, "There's No Other (Like My Baby)," by the Crystals, on Philles 100. A label and an era was being born.

Several eras, actually. The kids went back to school, the memory of the summer protracted by another echo-laden slow-dance hit by the Flamingos, "Lovers Never Say Good-Bye," but the twist kept right on happening. The B&Ts at the Peppermint Lounge had caught on to it, and on September 21, Cholly Knickerbocker, one of America's most-read gossip columnists, reported that Prince Obolensky had been seen doing the twist there (not true) and that "the Twist is the new teenage dance craze. But you don't have to be a teenager to do the Twist" (true). Fictitious appearances by Russian royalty were soon displaced by real appearances by American royalty: Truman Capote, Noël Coward, Marilyn Monroe, Judy Garland, and many others dropped in to see what the fuss was about. Phil Silvers was starring in a musical, *Do Re Me,* in one of the nearby theaters, and quickly added a twist number to the show.

Dick Cami was down in Florida relaxing with his father-in-law, Johnny Biello, when he got an incoherent phone call from New York about the club and . . . well, it was hard to tell. He needed to find out what was happening. He couldn't call the club—because of wiretaps there was no phone there—but there was a pay phone in the lobby of the Knickerbocker Hotel next door, near the back entrance to the club. Dick called and got one of the bouncers, known only as the Terrible Turk, who was guarding the back because so many people were unable to get in the front door that they tried to sneak in the back way. (The Turk was a very efficient way to discourage that.) Finally, Dick got Louie Lombardi, the manager, on the phone. "I'm telling you," Lombardi shouted into the phone, "this joint's exploding! You know who I was just looking at? Greta Garbo. That broad who just wants to be left alone. She's here tonight. You guys are the only ones who ain't here." He told Biello about the phone call, and they caught the first plane to New York. At the airport, they got into a cab and told the driver to head to the Peppermint Lounge, but he replied, "You kidding me? We can't get within fifteen blocks of that place!" They made it as far as they could go and did the rest on foot. As Dick noted when they got inside, if the place burned down right then, only half of New York society would be wiped out because the rest were standing in line, hoping to get in.

Why the society attention? There were other discothèques in Manhattan, but they were tame compared to the Peppermint, carefully curated to simulate a wild experience, while the Mob joint on Forty-Fifth Street *was* a wild experience. Ahmet Ertegun had one foot in the world of funky music and one in high society; in 1961 he'd married Mica Grecianu, a socialite from a Romanian diplomatic family. Their crowd depended on Ertegun to show them where it was at, and he wasn't above renting a bus to take a crowd to the Apollo Theater in Harlem for a show or to some dive nightclub like the Peppermint Lounge. Ertegun even tried to sign Joey Dee and the Starliters to Atlantic, but he was outvoted; Morris Levy of Roulette might not have gotten there first, but his vote canceled the others. Levy had strong ties to the Mob and had been acquiring record companies for years; Gee, End, and other rock & roll labels eventually came into his hands, he managed Alan Freed for a while, and Roulette was his crown jewel, having acquired Count Basie, among others. Levy's headquarters was called Birdland, and it was New York's top jazz club, the place you had to work if you wanted to be seen. Ahmet would have to be content with twisting the night away, and he was. Levy, meanwhile, called in Henry Glover, who'd worked at King when Hank Ballard had done the original "Twist," and had him write a song Joey Dee could release, and with a little work, Glover came up with "Peppermint Twist," and they recorded it—and a live album—while making a twistploitation film at the club. (Veronica Bennett and her friends weren't in it, owing to their mixed-race heritage, replaced by nice blond girls.) Chubby Checker's "Twist" came back into the charts and headed again to the top, the only record ever to have been #1 twice. It was reported that at parties at the White House, the Kennedys were doing the twist. Dwight and Mamie Eisenhower would never have behaved like that! Twist records started appearing by the dozen; Epic released *Twistin' in High Society* by famed elite bandleader Lester Lanin, and Atlantic, which had been shamelessly re-packaging Ray Charles's material, put out *Do the Twist with Ray Charles*. That was the cool thing about the twist: unlike the cha-cha or the stroll, it wasn't dependent on any musical signature. Hit a certain tempo, and you could twist to it. Anticipating the season to come, in late November, the Marcels released "Merry Twist-Mas." In a rare moment of clarity, the American public that had by now made TV stars of the Chipmunks, despite a long tradition of schlocky Christmas singles, did not make it a hit.

The end of the year saw a number of things happening that, in retrospect, would be important, although they were so scattered nobody knew just how important they were. The FCC, for one thing, was struggling to define standards for FM stereo radio. Ever since a ruling that any station with an AM and FM frequency had to present a certain percentage of separate programming on each band, a lot of stations had recognized that FM's superior sound quality was something they could market to hi-fi buffs, and it was an ideal medium for jazz and classical music. Now, a technology called multiplex allowed for two signals, right and left, to be broadcast simultaneously and decoded at the receiver, and it was important to make it uniform, for the sake of hardware manufacturers. They spent most of the year wrestling with this, but in the end, it was a major breakthrough. There were other ideas floating around, too; the compact 33 single, which would have better sound, could be recorded in stereo and allow for a couple of extra songs on the B side. Thanks to jukebox companies' unwillingness to replace every single jukebox in America, this idea died. So did a breakthrough by RCA, which invented a tape cartridge the size of a paperback book, but not as thick, which was as convenient as a record and delivered much better sound. This vanished within a couple of months, but the basic idea would return.

Musically, things were all over the place. In September, *Billboard* printed an article wondering why, if 38 percent of American radio stations played country music, country record sales were so pitiful, never taking into account that the largely rural audience had little time to play records, little money to spend on record players, and preferred to spend what little entertainment money they had on the country acts that frequently played the out-of-the-way towns near which they lived, and whom they could hear on the radio all the time. There was also the fact that country was, by and large, not crossing over to the pop market, with a couple of exceptions. Don Gibson's Nashville Sound singles found their way to pop radio, but the real triumph belonged to Patsy Cline, who'd been making mediocre country records until Harold Bradley of Decca found a formula for her that worked. She'd had a hit in 1958 with "Walkin' After Midnight," which was hardly country at all, but her career had languished until the spring of 1961, when two of Nashville's greatest songwriters, Hank Cochran and Harlan Howard, had given her a song that suited her emotional delivery, "I Fall to Pieces." She almost did, too, a few months into the song's run when she was in an automobile accident that killed a fellow passenger, but recovered to record "Crazy," a distinctive song with odd chord changes by an unusual songwriter, Willie Nelson, who'd been Ray Price's bassist for a while and, freshly out of the Army, had struggled as a songwriter and a DJ in Oregon (where he'd written a song about DJs, "Mr. Record Man," which was a minor country hit for him on Liberty), and now was employed by Tree Music in Nashville to write more strange songs. "Crazy" was a pop top-ten hit, and it was also a country smash, but Cline was clearly headed to pop stardom.

Another indication of the prevailing anarchy showed itself in September, when jazz pianist Dave Brubeck released an album, *Time Out*, that would have been a gimmick if it hadn't been so good. The idea was to record a number of compositions with unusual time signatures, instead of jazz's prevailing 4/4 and 2/4. This happened from time to time—Fats Waller's "Jitterbug Waltz" was a classic—but Brubeck was out of the West Coast "cool" school of white intellectual jazz (which also had plenty of black adherents). *Time Out* would have passed unnoticed except that hi-fi nuts picked it up, and Columbia, for some reason, released a single off it, a 5/4 tune called "Take Five." (Most jazz artists released singles for the black urban jukebox market, but they got next to no radio play, usually being edited for the jukebox version, whereas jazz radio would rather play the unedited track.) Despite the odd meter, it caught on with pop radio, Paul

Desmond's alto sax floating a catchy melody over the lumpy groove, and it climbed up to #25 on the pop charts.

Out in California, a scene was coming into being on the Balboa Peninsula, part of Newport Beach. People had been surfing here since the 1920s, when a man named George Freeth rode the waves to promote Los Angeles's streetcar to the beach, but it really took off after World War II, when a bunch of veterans who were having trouble fitting back into society used it as a sort of therapy, living in solitude near the water, taking odd jobs to support themselves, existing for the one-on-one communion—impossible to explain if you'd never done it—of man and ocean. These guys lived where the surf was good, which in California meant from Santa Cruz south and across the border into Baja. They had their own language and their own culture, and eventually they turned surfing into a sport with its own rules and learned to make boards lighter and more responsive to fluid dynamics and developed maneuvers like "hanging ten," walking up to the front of the board and dangling your toes over it. The big deal about surfing was that it looked like fun, and so some of these guys found themselves mentoring teenagers who wanted to learn.

Malibu Beach was a place where excellent waves met easy accessibility to well-off LA teenagers, so a thriving social scene developed there, where older surfers, teenagers, their girlfriends, and curiosity seekers all mingled. Into this world strode five-foot-tall Kathy Kohner, fifteen, daughter of a screenwriter and a girl who wanted to learn how to surf. Because of her height, she had a nickname: Gidget—girl plus midget. The guys gave her grief, but she was sincere, she'd sneak food from her house nearby to feed them, and as it turned out, she actually had some talent for surfing. She kept a diary of the whole thing, and, in 1957, her father, with her help, turned it into a paperback novel, called, of course, *Gidget*. It sold five hundred thousand copies. In 1959, it was made into a film using Kohner's buddies for the surfing scenes, and teenagers across the country were suddenly presented with a ready-made subculture made up of attractive young people (including other teenagers) wearing their own fashions (checked flannel shirts made by Pendleton were popular, bathing trunks were "baggies" for the boys and two pieces, if not outright bikinis, for the girls, and everyone wore sandals, particularly cheap Mexican-made huaraches), indulging in an activity that sure looked like fun if you could figure out how to do it—all in Technicolor. The big problem was that surfing was mostly limited to Southern California, and not everyone lived there. Still, it was the first new teenage culture since Elvis had appeared back in the distant past.

In 1959, an ice cream parlor in Balboa took a chance on an ambitious young guitarist, Dick Dale, who was looking for a place for a band he'd thrown together to play. Dale had been born Richard Mansour in Boston in 1937 and had moved with his family to LA in 1954. He exhibited plenty of musical talent from early childhood, playing traditional Lebanese music with his relatives. In California, he played trumpet in a country band, but he really wanted to play guitar, despite being left-handed, which required him to play the instrument upside down. With the support of his father, who formed Deltone Records to put out his son's work, he quit his job at Hughes Aircraft and went into music full-time. Only a few people showed up for the first Dick Dale and the Deltones gig at the ice cream joint, but as his reputation grew, so did his audience, to the point where he and his father had to negotiate a deal with the nearby Rendezvous Ballroom, a cavernous relic of the big band era that was standing empty. By early 1961, Dale's gigs were attracting four thousand people a night.

Dale's life fell into a nice routine. He'd get up in the morning, go surfing on his custom Hobie board, change, go to work in the music store he'd opened in Balboa, and spend the afternoon there. Then he'd hand the store over to an employee, go surfing again, and get ready for the evening's show at the Rendezvous. The music store not only helped bring in some cash, it was also a conduit to makers of instruments and equipment, and Dale was particular friends with Leo Fender, whose Fender Guitars was in nearby Santa Ana. Fender would present Dale with prototypes to test durability and viability, and Dale was responsible for testing the classic Fender Showman and Dual Showman amps, which, among other things, were louder than previous amps had been. In 1961, Fender gave him the first Fender Reverb Unit, and Dale's sound was fixed—as was the sound of surf music.

Dale swears it was his audience that was responsible for calling the loud, reverb-laden, guitar-dominated music the Deltones played "surf music." Surfers, who knew him from the beach and spread his reputation, were a large part of his audience, and the dance they did to the music was as primitive as their actions on the boards were sophisticated, hence its name: the surfer stomp. Dale's 1961 "Let's Go Trippin'" is frequently called the first surf record, and it's a stomper, but there's little else to distinguish it from numerous other instrumental records of the time, and its long sax solo is kind of an outlier in surf music. It didn't even feature Dale's famous reverb. The title, though, refers to surfing, "tripping" being a then-current term for riding the surf. It also managed to get to #60 on the national pop charts and spawn one surf-referencing instrumental after another, most of which remained local or regional hits: Dick Dale's "Miserlou" and "Surf Beat," "Pipeline" by the Chantays, "Wipe Out" by the Surfaris. The only way you could tell something was a "surf" instrumental was usually because of its title and/or some sound effects of waves or people having a good time; it was all about twangy guitars and that stomp beat. One thing surf music did, though, was very important: it established solid-body guitars and basses as the default instrumentation of the American rock band, something that, for all their importance, the Ventures couldn't do alone from Washington. In changing the way guitars sounded by utilizing direct electronics (and the tremolo lever, or whammy bar) instead of amplified acoustic sounds, it laid the foundations for the next era of rock & roll.

At the end of 1961, a lot of things were in motion, although the trends were too indistinct to discern, hard as people tried. Berry Gordy had set up nationwide distribution and embraced the twist: the Marvelettes' follow-up to "Please Mr. Postman" was "Twistin' Postman," and the Twistin' Kings (the Motown house band in an early incarnation) delivered "Twistin' Xmas" b/w "White House Twist." He also continued to work with the Temptations and a young man who'd done some session work at Chess, including singing backup vocals with Etta James on Chuck Berry's "Back in the U.S.A.,"

Marvin Gay, whose voice Gordy thought was ideal for supper-club music, although his single of "The Masquerade Is Over" stiffed. In Chicago, the Impressions, whom Jerry Butler had fairly crippled when he went solo, released a new record with their guitarist, Curtis Mayfield, singing lead, and his sinuous guitar winds all through "Gypsy Woman," the first of many hits for them. In Memphis, Jim Stewart and Estelle Axton had gotten a cease-and-desist notice from Satellite Records in California (which offered to sell them the name for $1,000), so they took the letters of their surnames and changed it to Stax. One of the kids who'd danced on the sidewalk came in one day with a song he'd written, and Stewart and Chips Moman heard a hit, a black record with a huge dose of country music in it, and that's how William Bell got to cut "You Don't Miss Your Water." Folkies gathered around the Christmas tree wondering if that flat, square gift was a copy of *Joan Baez II* (featuring two cuts with the Green-briar Boys, an album that *Billboard* had described as "stirring wax"), *Dave van Ronk Sings* (his debut for Folkways), the first album by a Denver folkie who was Baez's first real competition, Judy Collins's *Maid of Constant Sorrow*, or maybe even Pete Seeger's *How to Play the Five-String Banjo*, another Folkways release that paired an album demonstrating the techniques being taught with a book (also available as a standalone from Oak Publications, which also published *Sing Out!*), yet another milestone in the growing folk revival. It probably wasn't an album Columbia had quietly released in October, *King of the Delta Blues Singers*, by Robert Johnson, whose masters they'd discovered they owned, but that, too, would slowly grow in stature. And for good luck, Columbia had signed Pete Seeger to a non-exclusive contract, allowing him to record for Folkways while making more popular albums for them. If you wanted "good music," it was still there, but *Billboard* had instituted a new chart to stand alongside the country and R&B charts and was calling it "easy listening." Maybe that phrase was coined to warn teenagers off; they clearly wanted uneasy listening, and it was just around the corner.

chapter fourteen

1962: TEEN PAN ALLEY

Teen Pan Alley: Aldon Music songwriters, staff, and friends at an awards ceremony:
(top row, left to right) Jack Keller, Artie Levine, Lou Adler, Al Nevins,
Sheila Kirshner, Don Kirshner, Emil La Viola, Morris Levy, and
Howard Greenfield; *(bottom row, left to right)* Barry Mann, Cynthia Weil,
Gerry Goffin, Carole King, and Neil Sedaka.
(Photo by BMI/Michael Ochs Archives/Getty Images)

Up at Chess Studios, they were working on doing a lot of recording with Chuck Berry in the summer of 1961. He'd exhausted all his appeals and was going to prison. On February 19, 1962, he entered the federal prison in Terre Haute, Indiana, and was later transferred to Leavenworth Penitentiary in Kansas, and, toward the end of his sentence, to the Medical Center for Federal Prisoners in Springfield, Missouri, and he'd remain behind bars until his thirty-seventh birthday, on October 18, 1963. It wasn't the end of his career—he'd have the English to thank for that initially, and he'd have hits again starting in 1963—but it was a notable hiatus, and a warning, it would seem, to those who thought they could buck society. On the other hand, his time away coincided almost perfectly with the rise of the civil rights movement, and, ironically, if he'd been just a little less successful and a little less associated with pop music, some of the white civil rights supporters among the folkies might have taken up his cause. As it was, Chuck sat in his cells, reading books on accounting and business management. And there were other songwriters on the rise.

In a 1991 interview with Diana Reid Haig, Florence Greenberg remembered the events surrounding "Will You Love Me Tomorrow," which she claimed was partially written at the piano in her office. "Mr. Kirshner, who was a real big-shot publisher, came to me and said he had a song for the Shirelles . . . I think the world of Donnie

Kirshner, and he sure worked the record with us." He hadn't been a big shot long, and it's not like he had to take a cab to Scepter's offices, either; they were at 1650 Broadway, and Kirshner's office was at 1619 Broadway. Both addresses were hotbeds of activity; among the other tenants at 1650 was Atlantic (who also had their recording studio there), and as for 1619, it was the Brill Building. Built in 1931 and named for Morris Brill's clothing store on the street level, it soon became the central address of the music-publishing business, which had been scattered around midtown New York, particularly in the theater district near Times Square. The lobby card read like a Who's Who of publishing: Mills Music, Famous Music, Fred Fisher Music, and loads of unknowns, including, starting in 1958, Aldon Music.

Don Kirshner was a hustling young songwriter who'd sold his first song to crooner Frankie Laine while working as a teenage bell-hop at a resort, and in exchange Laine gave him enough knowledge to set himself up as a professional. It was Kirshner's opinion that a lot of the music being written for the teenage market was unsuccessful because the middle-aged men who were writing it were so far away from their own teenage experiences, whereas in 1958, he was only twenty-three years old. He met Al Nevins, who was in his forties, an ex-singer, and co-author of "Twilight Time," which had been a hit for the Platters that year. Having seen an old copyright of his given lucrative life by this new market, Nevins took Kirshner on as a part-ner, and they started looking for writers.

The first ones were Neil Sedaka and Howie Greenfield, whose "Stupid Cupid" was a big record for Connie Francis, a friend of Kirshner's, in 1958. Sedaka had been part of the Tokens, a vocal group that had had a hit with "The Lion Sleeps Tonight," borrowed from a Pete Seeger favorite, "Wimoweh" (which had actually been written by Solomon Linda, a black South African artist). Greenfield, three years older, had been a friend of Sedaka's since his early teen years. Then along came Barry Mann, of "Who Put the Bomp" fame, and his girlfriend and, soon, wife, Cynthia Weil. Carole King signed on in 1959, causing Greenfield and Sedaka to write Neil a top-ten hit, "Oh! Carol" (Sedaka had gone to the same high school as the former Carole Klein, and they'd gone out a couple of times), which of course prompted her answer record, "Oh! Neil." Whatever teenagers might have thought, it wasn't an Aldon office romance; Carole was married to another nineteen-year-old, Gerry Goffin, who was also her main writing partner, and, in fact, wrote "Oh! Neil." In 1962, Aldon added another songwriting couple, Jeff Barry and Ellie Greenwich, both of whom had been writing for others, including a stint with Leiber and Stoller for Greenwich. Nor did Aldon only work with couples; Paul Simon was a short, intense figure from Forest Hills, Queens, who'd had a hit in 1957 with a childhood friend, Art Garfunkel, as Tom and Jerry, and, later, Aldon added aspiring folksinger Neil Diamond, another Brooklyn kid, to its lineup on Ellie Greenwich's recommendation. If the Brill Building was already the headquarters of Tin Pan Alley (the name for New York's songwriting district, starting in the 1920s, because the open windows and multiple pianos colliding in different keys sounded like cookware being bashed together), it was, under the aegis of Aldon and the various Leiber and Stoller companies, morphing into Teen Pan Alley. Aldon writers weren't limited to their regular partners and sometimes helped each other finish or tweak a song. Then a demo was cut, with either the writer or studio musicians, to suggest the way the song might sound. Some of the demo recordings, particularly the ones featuring the vocal trio of Earl-Jean McCrea, Dorothy Jones, and Margaret Ross—the Cookies, as they were known—were good enough that they were released on Aldon's in-house label, Dimension.

One of Aldon's early customers was Phil Spector, who selected a Goffin-King song, "Every Breath I Take," for his second try at producing Gene Pitney, which, although not much of a hit, finally got him a record company job when Snuff Garrett, a twenty-four-year-old wunderkind in California who'd been elevated to head of A&R at Liberty Records, made Spector the East Coast head of A&R. Spector was busy building up his own label with Lester Sill, Philles, in California, though, and in the short time he had the Liberty job, he managed a whopping three singles for the label, none of which did a thing. Spector's office was well appointed, with an air hockey table that got lots of use, and he had a very respectable salary, especially considering he did nothing. Hired in March 1962, he made it all the way to July, at which point he was talking about taking a sabbatical in Spain. Instead, he left Liberty, taking his $30,000 advance with him, and used it to get serious about Philles.

Things were taking off. For the follow-up to the Crystals' "There's No Other Like My Baby" in February, he'd chosen a Barry Mann–Cynthia Weil number that was almost a protest song. "Uptown" had the singer's boyfriend waking up each day and heading downtown, where he's "a little man" and "just one of a million guys," but he heads back uptown after work, where the singer makes him know he's special. There were a lot of hidden codes in this song: minorities live in different areas in different cities, but in New York, "uptown" was clearly Harlem, and the singer was clearly black. The song only went to #13 on the pop charts, but it still sent a message about the way a record should sound and what kind of content resonated with kids. Then he almost blew it; who knows what Spector was thinking, but "Uptown"'s follow-up was "He Hit Me (It Felt Like a Kiss)," a Goffin-King song. Given his insistence on instrumental B sides, it was all or nothing for a Philles record, and this was a big stumble, right at the time he left the Liberty job. It didn't chart, it didn't sell, it didn't get airplay. Was he washed up at twenty-two?

Maybe he should have played it more conservatively and tried a twist novelty. After all, *Hey! Let's Twist*, the film shot at the Peppermint Lounge starring Joey Dee and the Starliters and Jo Ann Campbell, had opened the first week of January, and on the next week's album charts there were six twist albums, including three in the top ten. Despite the threat supposedly posed by the Popeye, a dance that started in New Orleans and, it was reported, was spreading as far as Baltimore, thanks to Eddie Bo's irresistible "Check Mr. Popeye," the twist was doing just fine. King Curtis had a hit with "Soul Twist," Chubby Checker got intimate with "Slow Twistin'," and Les Elgart released his *Twist Goes to College* album, Gary "U.S." Bonds released *Twist Up Calypso* containing his latest hit, "Dear Lady Twist," Sam Cooke released *Twistin' the Night Away* album and single, Bob Wills alumnus Tommy Allsup came out with *Twistin' the Country Classics*, and twist albums—or stuff that could be twisted to compiled by the record company—were released on Chuck Berry and Bo Diddley (who likely didn't know it was happening and hadn't recorded any explicitly twist-related material). Bobby Rydell and Chubby Checker also had "Teach Me to Twist," although Bobby was a little late in asking, and Ahmet Ertegun told *Billboard* that the public would keep on twisting, no matter what, and as a constant presence at the Peppermint Lounge, he ought to know.

But the twist was no longer teenage once it had been adopted by the Ahmet Erteguns of the world, and teenagers were on the rise again. In Southern California, in Hawthorne, a suburb south of Los Angeles, teenagers were taking matters into their own hands. "Surfin' is the only life, the only way for me," they sang, "they" being three brothers and two of their cousins. Actually, out of all of them, only Dennis Wilson surfed, while his brothers, Carl and Brian, were more into music, as were their cousins, Al Jardine and Mike Love. But the Wilson family was headed by father Murry, a failed musician with a lot of contacts in the Los Angeles music world, and when the kids wanted to make a record out of "Surfin'," he financed the pressing of the tape they'd made in their garage, with its engaging vocal interplay and stomp beat played (by Brian) on a garbage can. Released on the Candix label under the name the Beach Boys (they'd previously been the Pendletones, a reference to the plaid Pendleton flannel shirts that were part of the surfer uniform, and, before that, they'd been a vocal group, Carl and the Passions) the song only made it to #72 on the charts that spring, but that was pretty remarkable, considering what a shambles it was. (The B side was an instrumental, "Luau.") Murry cashed in some favors and got the boys heard by some of his friends at Capitol, and they offered a deal.

At least in California, surf records were coming out regularly now; Snuff Garrett already had the Ventures on Liberty, and added the Marketts, a bunch of studio musicians who recorded "Surfer Stomp" in late 1961 as well as signing Jan and Dean, an act that Doré, the label that had released Phil Spector's Teddy Bears, had been unable to break, while the Surfmen, formerly known as the Expressos, started recording instrumentals like "Paradise Cove" and "Malibu Run" for a small label, Titan, early in 1962. Del-Fi had signed the Sentinals [*sic*], and Bruce Johnston, another of the kids who'd witnessed John Dolphin's murder, released "Do the Surfer Stomp" in March. It was a little early to be thinking about the beach back east, but the sun always shone in California, right?

Anyway, teenage trends never really popped up before summer, and in March, Ray Charles dropped a bombshell on the American pop music world. *Modern Sounds in Country and Western Music* was proof that Charles was still entitled to the "genius" title that Atlantic had given him so many years ago. Charles understood the classic country repertoire, since he'd played it in Seattle early in his career, but he'd also internalized it so that now, when he sang it, it came out as pure Ray Charles. His first single from the album was proof: "I Can't Stop Loving You" was a 1958 hit for its composer, Don Gibson, and for Kitty Wells, both of whom communicated the regret the lyrics state over a medium shuffle rhythm. In Ray Charles's hands, though, the regret begins to come through in the agonized delivery of the second line—"It's useless, I've tried"—and the slow tempo makes it a far sadder song as he explores his pain. On the other side was "Born to Lose," a Ted Daffan oldie from the '40s, rendered in an even more funereal tempo, bringing out the blues in the song. Charles had jumped right into the middle of a genre most sophisticated pop listeners—the ones who were buying his jazz albums and who had celebrated his revision of Hoagy Carmichael's "Georgia on My Mind"—thought was corny and trite, a novelty at best, and whose songwriters, certain exceptions like Gibson, Cindy Walker, Willie Nelson, and Harlan Howard notwithstanding, were currently churning out less-than-memorable songs. (In fact, once "I Can't Stop Loving You" finally released its grip on the #1 position, his follow-up was a Cindy Walker song, "You Don't Know Me.") His discovery of the emotion one could get from this scorned material if one only took the time to see what was actually there was a rebuke to snobs everywhere, and, from the sales it generated, a very lucrative one.

In fact, a mini-movement of country soul was already happening in the South. As we've seen, William Bell's "You Don't Miss Your Water" was already out on Stax (although not selling), and in January, Dot released a single by Arthur Alexander, "You'd Better Move On," which was the result of a bunch of white guys in Florence,

Alabama (Sam Phillips's hometown), who'd been messing with some country and rockish stuff in the hopes of recording something, since two of them, Rick Hall and Billy Sherrill, had set up a studio above a drugstore in downtown Florence. Alexander was a bellhop at the local Holiday Inn and was co-writing songs with some of this crowd, and in 1960, he recorded a song, "Sally Sue Brown," on Jud Phillips's Judd label in Memphis. In the summer of 1961, backed by a band called Dan Penn and the Pallbearers, Alexander cut "You'd Better Move On," and Hall took it to Nashville to find someone to put it out. It was too black for country, and there was no black label worth approaching in Nashville (Excello was still only doing blues), but out of nowhere, a guy from Dot took a chance on it and turned it into a mild hit, which reached #24 on the pop charts. Hall made $10,000 out of the deal and used it to finish off a studio he was building in a former tobacco warehouse just out of town in nearby Muscle Shoals, calling it FAME, for Florence Alabama Musical Enterprises. Alexander would continue to record for Dot in Nashville (including a mild hit later in the year with "Anna,") while Hall looked for other talent to record the songs his musician friends, including Dan Penn, were writing. Nor was Alexander the only black singer straddling country and rhythm and blues; Solomon Burke had already had a hit with the old country song "Just Out of Reach," and his follow-up to that was "Cry to Me," which was written and produced by a Jewish guy from New York, Bert Berns, but very much in the ballpark (its B side was Ivory Joe Hunter's "I Almost Lost My Mind," a relic of an earlier age's country-blues fusion), and its follow-up was a rocked-up remake of a folk song, "Down in the Valley." All of them sold better with black record buyers, too.

Berns and Burke may have been hoping that the folk crowd would help them have a hit with "Down in the Valley," because folk was suddenly very hot. Joan Baez's two albums, without the benefit of a hit single or any radio play to speak of, hovered around the mid-twenties of *Billboard*'s LP chart for weeks on end, and Johnny Cash's management announced in mid-April that they were going to try to book him on college campuses as a folksinger (possibly because he wasn't doing very well on the country charts). Then Columbia

Records announced that their venerable A&R man, John Hammond, the man who'd discovered Count Basie and Billie Holiday, had signed Bob Dylan. Reviewing his first album, released in April, *Billboard* noted that "he plays, sings, and composes, and is one of the most interesting, and most disciplined youngsters to appear on the pop-folk scene in a long time . . . Dylan, when he finds his own style, could win a big following." Maybe so, but the album was a dud, except in some folkie circles, although others abhorred his voice and didn't see much to like about his guitar playing, either. No, the real hit came along almost simultaneously; Albert Grossman, whose Gate of Horn club was doing big business in Chicago, put together an act with two men and a woman—Peter, Paul & Mary—who had been doing solo gigs (Mary Travers and Peter Yarrow) and stand-up comedy (Paul Stookey) in New York. He rehearsed them for months before they made their debut at the Bitter End, a new folk club in the Village, and their album for Warner Bros. was an immediate hit in March— and stayed on the charts, including a seven-week stay at the top, for close to four years. Their first single, "Lemon Tree," was a notch above what the other commercial folk groups were recording, and it, too, was a mild hit, but the second one was exactly what they were aiming for: "If I Had a Hammer" had been in the Weavers' repertoire as "The Hammer Song" and had been written by Pete Seeger and Will Hays. There was a whole generation that hadn't heard it, though, and PP&M put it into the top ten. It was a nod to the folk elders, a pro-peace song at a time when that was a somewhat courageous statement, and a jolly sing-along, all in one—but it was polished enough for pop radio. And although teenage girls were already ironing their hair to straighten it into a Baez-like do and teenage boys and girls were picking up acoustic guitars, folk music remained an activity largely outside the charts, since it relied so heavily on personal participation and live shows, which were becoming more frequent as a touring circuit developed.

Black pop, especially stuff aimed at teenagers, was in an interesting place in spring of 1962. For one thing, the interest in oldies, and the injection of vocal group classics into the oldies played on the radio, meant that this style still had currency. Vee-Jay released "Duke of Earl," a very old-sounding record, in January, and while Gene Chandler's name was on the label, it was actually a recording his group, the Dukays, had recorded the year before. It went straight to the top. More modern sounding was the Falcons' "I Found a Love," which arrived a couple of weeks later on Detroit's LuPine label. The Falcons were a loose-knit group who'd had a hit a couple of years back with "You're So Fine," and singing lead on this throat-shredding, testifying song was Wilson Pickett, who'd done some time with Detroit-based gospel group the Violinaires. The backup group was the Ohio Untouchables, a Dayton-based band that worked constantly, backing up solo singers and playing clubs in the Midwest. In keeping with the gospel feel of the record, the Untouchables' guitarist, Robert Ward, who kept going in and out of the band as he returned to, then left, the church, is all over the record. The Falcons' next record would feature another vocalist, Mack Rice, though, because Pickett quit to try his luck with Detroit's Correc-Tone label, and then Double L, run by Lloyd Price.

Over at Motown, things were nuts; the Marvelettes followed up their "Postman" hits with "Playboy," which lead singer Gladys Horton co-wrote with some Motown staffers; Mary Wells had a hit with "The One Who Really Loves You"; and the latest Miracles record, "I'll Try Something New," was very much a classic vocal-group sound. The Miracles' Ronnie White was introduced to a young blind kid, Steveland Morris, eleven years old, who played harmonica like no one's business, and took him over to Hitsville to play for the folks. Berry Gordy allegedly heard him and said, "Boy! That kid's a wonder!" thereby giving him the name Stevie Wonder, and handed him over to Clarence Paul, the younger brother of the "5" Royales' Lowman Pauling, to develop some material. In no time, the kid had written "I Call It Pretty Music, but the Old Folks Call It the Blues." It wasn't a hit, but Paul didn't give up. Elsewhere the Shirelles pulled on some traditional heartstrings with "Soldier Boy," although there was no war going on (or so most people thought: the United States had "advisers" in Vietnam and were about to add some more), and for sheer wackiness, a group called the Rivingtons came out with "Papa Oom Mow Mow," which was mostly nonsense syllables, although very cleverly arranged. It was a huge hit with the surfers, oddly enough.

Over at Atlantic Records, things were mighty quiet on the pop front. Nesuhi Ertegun continued to produce great jazz records with Charles Mingus, Ornette Coleman, and John Coltrane, and Jerry Wexler struggled to break Solomon Burke and Ben E. King, while his older stars were either all but moribund, like the Coasters and the Drifters, or, like Ruth Brown, left for other labels in hopes of reviving their careers. It was Ahmet Ertegun who found the formula that would keep them afloat during 1962: foreign instrumentals. Mr. Acker Bilk (as he preferred to be known) went to the top of the charts with "Stranger on the Shore," which was the theme song of a British television show featuring his chalumeau clarinet stylings (the Drifters recorded a vocal version), while Danish pianist Bent Fabric not only hit the top ten but also picked up a Grammy for rock & roll Record of the Year (which it certainly wasn't) for "Alley Cat." Records like this were easy enough to pick up; a record company would hear from one of their foreign distributors or go to a European confab like the San Remo Song Festival in Italy and make a cheap one-off deal with an option for a record (usually an instrumental, but everyone still remembered Domenico Modugno's "Nel Blu Dipinto Di Blu (Volare)" #1 pop hit from 1958—and it didn't have a word of English!) and put it out. If it didn't hit, no option was exercised, and better luck next year. There seemed to be a lot of these storming the charts at this point, but only Kenny Ball's Jazzmen from England managed to challenge Atlantic with "Midnight in Moscow" on Dot. Of course, most European hits weren't salable in the States; *Billboard* reported in May that fourteen- and fifteen-year-olds in Belgium were buying a record by a nun who strummed an acoustic guitar while praising St. Dominic, the founder of her order, and French and Italian versions of rock & roll were . . . well, why bother?

Right on time as school let out, the summer records started. First out of the gate was "Twist and Shout," by the Isley Brothers, a Cincinnati group who had had a pop hit in 1959 with a little bit of church business called "Shout," and, with Bert Berns, reworked it, slowed it down, and put a Latin-ish beat behind it for their debut on Scepter. Was this the dance record of the summer? Miami was reporting a new dance called the bug, Dee Dee Sharp was reporting that it was still "Mashed Potatoes Time," and her fellow Philadelphians the Orlons were doing the "Wah Watusi," so the jury was still out. Someone named Little Eva popped up on Aldon's new Dimension label with "The Loco-Motion," where everyone got in a line and made like a train. It was a Goffin-King song, and the story was that Eva (Eva Narcissus Boyd to her mom) was the Goffins' babysitter and they caught her doing the dance in their living room one day. Actually, she was a friend of the Cookies' from North Carolina who finally gave in to her friends' demands to move north, and the gig at the Goffins' was as much a favor to the Cookies as anything; she spent as much time helping the Cookies cut demos as she did looking after Louise and Sherry Goffin. She also had an abusive boyfriend, who was the inspiration for "He Hit Me (It Felt Like a Kiss)." "The Loco-Motion" was Dimension's first record, and it went to #1, although whether the abuser was the guy she married to celebrate that fact is unknown. But probably the biggest dance record of the summer came from Motown's Contours, who dropped into Hitsville one night on their way back from a gig to find Berry Gordy pounding out a new tune he'd written. "You guys seen the Temptations?" he asked them, figuring he'd finally found a tune to break the group at last. They hadn't (the Temptations were at a church watching the Dixie Hummingbirds on a gospel program), so Gordy taught the Contours the song instead, and "Do You Love Me" became their first, and biggest, hit. The singer asks his girl if she loves him now that he can dance, and then the group goes through a list of different dances that they undoubtedly demonstrated onstage. It's a total dance workout, and has the maddening addition of a fake fade toward the end, with the shouted "Do You Love Me" waking the record back up—and driving disc jockeys insane.

Out in California, school was out, giving the Beach Boys the opportunity to see what they could do with their new Capitol Records contract. Carl and Dennis Wilson were in high school, Al Jardine and Brian Wilson were going to junior college, and Brian was writing songs like crazy. By the time they went into the studio, though, Jardine had decided to go back to dental school, so he dropped out and a friend of Carl's, David Marks, became a non-singing, guitar-playing member of the group. Nick Venet, the man who'd signed them to Capitol, insisted that they cut a song that appeared on the demo tape they'd put together for the label, "Surfin' Safari," a Brian Wilson–Mike Love number, but he wanted something non-surf for the B side, so Brian and Gary Usher, a songwriter who was also from the neighborhood and had been in a few bands, collaborated on the first of many tunes they'd write together and came up with "409," an ode to an engine Usher wished was under the hood of his 348 Chevy. The car sounds were Usher's 348, recorded as he drove past the Wilson house and captured on their tape recorder. As it turned out, the insurance was hardly necessary; "Surfin' Safari" was the hit, going as far as #14 and lingering on the charts and the radio the entire summer, while "409" spent a week in the mid-70s and then vanished. But it did give Usher ideas, and he would be behind further car-oriented records by fake bands of studio musicians a year or so down the line. The fact of the hit made Capitol—virtually without pop acts at this point (having lost Frank Sinatra and Dean Martin to Frank's Reprise label and then gotten sued over reissuing Sinatra's Capitol stuff)—demand an album, and one was hastily thrown together, including a re-recorded "Surfin'," a cover of the Gamblers' influential 1959 instrumental "Moon Dawg," and another of Eddie Cochran's "Summertime Blues," a song all the garage bands had to know at that point. There weren't any other surf songs besides the hits; Capitol thought this would exhaust the surf craze, and didn't figure they'd have to deal with the Beach Boys—or Murry Wilson—much longer. The *Surfin' Safari* album cover showed the band in a colorful surfer vehicle, an old pickup truck painted yellow with palm thatching for a roof, parked right at the ocean's edge with David Marks, seated on the hood, pointing, presumably at a wave. All are attired in white Levis, blue Pendletons, and no shoes. Surf's up!

The surf craze—which had yet to peak—was nationwide, although actual surfing was limited to California and a couple of places in Texas. It was not only about music but about accessories; even if you didn't have a can of Sex Wax for your board (or a board), you could sport a T-shirt advertising it, or one with the enigmatic word "Hobie" (a brand of surfboard) on it. There was money to be made, and in July, the Small Business Administration published a pamphlet (a "small marketer aid") on how to reach the fifteen million teenagers out there. Noting that fifteen- to nineteen-year-olds had ten to fifteen dollars a week to spend, it counseled that 1) you must treat them like adults; 2) cater to them; don't ignore them or shoo them off if they show up in your store; 3) they want fast service; and 4) they like personal recognition. Catch them early and you have a customer for life: 25 percent of high school graduates go to work, 40 percent go to college, and 25 percent get married (presumably girls who drop out of the workforce picture to have families). These ideas may seem obvious to today's retailers, but teenagers were still perceived by many as children.

Summer records were all over the place. Besides the usual up-tempo dance records like the Contours', there were a lot of slow-dance records (no how-to lyrics necessary): breakup songs like "Breaking Up Is Hard to Do" by Neil Sedaka, "Make It Easy on Yourself" by Jerry Butler, and "You'll Lose a Good Thing" by Barbara Lynn all showed possible ends to summer romances, and Carole King, speaking for the already jilted, opined that "It Might as Well Rain Until September." There were also more optimistic ballads: the Jive Five's "What Time Is It," where the singer counts down the minutes until he sees his girlfriend, and Sam Cooke's silky "Bring It On Home to Me."

An indication of how confused things were included the fact that the Jamies, a vocal trio who made most of their money singing jingles, saw their 1958 "Summertime Summertime" become a hit all over again although they didn't know at first that it had been re-released. The Valentinos, another brother act like the Isleys, came out with "Lookin' for a Love," their first secular record after going secular under the guidance of Sam Cooke and J. W. Alexander on Cooke's SAR label; previously, they'd been the gospel-singing Womack Brothers.

The only sure trend visible was Motown; Hitsville was on fire, with the August 11 chart showing "You Beat Me to the Punch" (Mary Wells) at #73, "Beechwood 4-5789" (the Marvelettes) at #79,

"Your Heart Belongs to Me" (the Supremes) at #96, and "Do You Love Me" (the Contours) at #100. That week also saw the label release "Stubborn Kind of Fellow" by Marvin Gaye, the *e* now affixed to his last name and the supper-club sound on abeyance. All of these except the Supremes' record would go on to glory, but it was beginning to look like the Supremes weren't going to be a very good investment.

That week also saw an instrumental, "Green Onions," by Booker T. and the M.G.'s, on Stax, break in at #90. Booker T. was Booker T. Jones, the young prodigy who'd been hanging around the Stax studios, and the Memphis Group—that's what M.G. stood for—was Al Jackson Jr., son of a prominent local bandleader, on drums, the similarly pedigreed Lewis Steinberg on bass, and Steve Cropper on guitar. Cropper had survived touring with the Mar-Keys and had watched Packy Axton dissolve further into alcoholism along the way. Stax had released several follow-ups to "Last Night"—"Morning After," "About Noon," "Foxy," "Pop-Eye Stroll," and "Whot's Happinin'!"—and none of them had done anything at all. Neither had any of the other records Stax had released since, including an instrumental, "Burnt Biscuits," by the Triumphs (actually Chips Moman), until this low-key, minimalist record based around a riff played on the Hammond organ's lower register by Booker T. somehow caught the nation's ears. By then, some changes were going on at Stax. In an argument over "Burnt Biscuits," Moman, who felt it had sold better than he was being told, managed to make Jim Stewart mad enough to fire him, and he left in a huff for Nashville. As for Stewart's sister, she had a nervous collapse, and the doctor had told her something would have to go, and what went was her job at the bank. As "Green Onions" grew into a hit, the M.G.'s were faced with a bizarre reality; they couldn't play, legally, in Memphis, even when the reluctant Lewis Steinberg was replaced with Cropper's friend Duck Dunn. They played shows up north, and in the Stax studios, race just plain wasn't an issue. It may have been a coincidence, but Jim Stewart put up a sign at the old theater that, in contrast with Berry Gordy's Hitsville U.S.A. sign, read Soulsville U.S.A.

Soul, that indefinable, know-it-when-you-hear-it quality that Ray Charles, Sam Cooke, and the "5" Royales' Tanner brothers had pioneered, must have been a popular sound in the clubs, because young artists who would gain fame later were putting out their first, unsuccessful records. A duet from Florida, Sam and Dave, had stuff out on regional labels, and got one, "I Need Love," picked up by Roulette. A refugee from her mother's gospel group, Fontella Bass, was being recorded by Bobbin and playing clubs in St. Louis, while Little Milton, who'd recorded for Sun pre-Elvis, was still trying for a break on Chess, as was Etta James, another veteran, whose "Stop the Wedding" might have been a bigger hit if she'd been a little more reliable about showing up at gigs. And down in Nashville, Joseph Arrington Jr., who performed as Joe Tex, recorded Dan Penn's "Meet Me in Church." Most of these singers were playing with the latest trend in gospel, which was dramatic solo singing, sometimes supported by a group. The pioneer was Clara Ward, who began playing nightclubs with the Clara Ward Singers, who spun off another notable star of the era, Marion Williams, whose Stars of Faith were an off-Broadway sensation when they appeared in Langston Hughes's 1961 show *Black Nativity*. The great heiress to Ward's and Williams's style was the daughter of one of Detroit's most famous black ministers, the Reverend C. L. Franklin, whose LPs of sermons were the backbone of Chess's gospel series. Aretha Franklin made her first recording for Chess live in church at fourteen, where an amazed listener can be heard saying, "Listen at her! *Listen* at her!" as her voice rises to the heavens, and at eighteen, she got her father's blessing to pursue the same road as their friend Sam Cooke had. Shortly afterward, John Hammond signed her to Columbia, which should have been a ticket to fame. Unfortunately, Columbia's longtime head of A&R, Mitch Miller, was notorious for his disdain of rock & roll and famous for his endless series of *Sing Along with Mitch* albums. Black music barely existed at the label, and Franklin was shunted off to the jazz division where she was backed by the Ray Bryant Trio and other light jazz combos. Her singles adorned upscale black jukeboxes along with the many other jazz 45s coming out at this point, but didn't sell too much, and she played the supper-club and jazz-club circuits, never really attracting much of a following. Among those listening at her and no doubt grinding his teeth in frustration by how badly she was being served by her record company was Jerry Wexler at Atlantic, but she was locked tight into her contract, and Columbia kept renewing it.

Still, there was no stopping the future, which arrived in a number of ways. On August 12, at Stax, it came in a car driven by a big, lanky kid who was chauffeuring Johnny Jenkins, a guitarist with a wild live act who wanted to cut a record on Stax and had been recommended by Joe Galkin, a regional promo guy for Atlantic out of Atlanta. Jenkins went into the studio with the M.G.'s, and they played around for some time, and didn't find much to agree on; Jenkins's live act obviously didn't translate to the studio, and he didn't seem to have much good material. As the day wore on, Al Jackson Jr. came up to Steve Cropper and asked him if he could get the chauffeur off his back by letting him record a song; the guy'd been making a pest of himself. When it was obvious the session was a fiasco, Galkin told Jim Stewart, who was sitting behind the control board, that this big kid was also good—he did relief spots in Jenkins's show—and maybe they should take a chance on him. He sweetened the deal by offering half the publishing in exchange for half the sales royalties, and Jim caved in. Cropper had to go outside to catch Steinberg before he left for his evening gig, and after dragging him back in as the kid was setting up, Booker T. played some chords, and the kid began to sing. "I'd never been with anybody that had that much desire to express emotion," he said later. Said Estelle, "He had that different sound, but we didn't know he was going to bust it wide open." The song, which the kid had written, was "These Arms of Mine." The kid was named Otis Redding. Four days later, Jim signed him. They put the record out in October, and it crept up to #20 on the R&B charts.

Make no mistake, though, "good music" was still with us, although Frank Sinatra wasn't charting many single hits, and not even Tony Bennett's Grammy-winning Record of the Year, "I Left My Heart in San Francisco," troubled the top twenty for long. Another hot prospect, Bobby Darin, left Atlantic after four years and signed with Capitol. The record business as a whole was making out on albums, with 1962 seeing the release of several original cast albums—*Oliver!, No Strings,*

I Can Get It For You Wholesale (featuring Columbia's latest hot signing, Barbra Streisand), *Stop the World—I Want to Get Off*—sharing space with already established hits like *Camelot, West Side Story, Fiorello,* and *The Sound of Music,* which seemed nailed to the charts. And of course there were the Elvis soundtracks (this year's was *Girls! Girls! Girls!*). Plus, there were signs of a new generation of "good music" stars: Bobby Rydell's latest, a tribute to the big bands, wasn't exactly shifting units, but in California, a couple of Phil Spector's buddies, Herb Alpert and Jerry Moss, started a new label, A&M, to put out Alpert's trumpet instrumentals with a group of studio musicians he called the Tijuana Brass, and a very sophisticated new sound from Brazil, a rhythm called bossa nova, appeared in the stores, first on a Stan Getz album with guitarist Charlie Byrd called *Jazz Samba,* then with various artists trying on "One-Note Samba" from the album. "Is the Bossa Nova the New Twist?" *Billboard* asked breathlessly in October. No, but the title of the second Joey Dee and the Starliters film had been changed from something with "twist" in the title to *Two Tickets to Paris.* As the Contours knew, there were a lot of dances out there now.

There were a lot more people buying popular music, too, with two generations now having been shaped by rock & roll. It wasn't just Original Sound's *Oldies but Goodies* records anymore; lots of labels were re-packaging their old records into albums with nostalgic packaging and either selling them as hits packages or under the name of a locally famous disc jockey, whose face appeared on the cover. Chess, for instance, scored Murray "the K" Kaufman, the fabled WINS jock from New York, whose live shows had taken over from Alan Freed's as the showcase to be on, and whose riffs and catchwords were on teenagers' lips, as epitomized by his album's title: *Murray the K's Gassers for Submarine Race Watchers.* What was a "gasser"? Murray's listeners knew, like they knew that parking on the Palisades over the Hudson was the best way to watch those nonexistent submarine races with your girl. If you were doing singles, you hoped for transgenerational appeal—Ray Charles's "I Can't Stop Loving You" was at 1.5 million and still going in August—or something the kids would jump on. That's where Phil Spector was putting his bets; after the success of the Crystals' "Uptown," he liberated a demo of a Gene

Pitney song Liberty was going to get Vikki Carr to record, told Lester Sill to book Gold Star, his preferred Los Angeles studio, and grab the Blossoms, another girl group that did demos for publishers, and went in and cut "He's a Rebel," and put the Crystals' name on the record. Liberty went ahead with the Vikki Carr version, but the punchy song about a guy who didn't do what everybody else did—and got the girl's love, anyway—was totally irresistible to teenagers, who were by nature rebellious, and, thanks to the new spirit in America that President Kennedy had unleashed, getting more so. Not content with putting out a Crystals record without the Crystals on it, Spector then issued an open letter to the record business as a whole: "I am pleased to advise that I have acquired complete and absolute control of Philles Records, Inc. I have purchased all other interests in this company. Lester Sill and Harry Finfer are no longer associated with Philles Records." So Philles without Les. And like magic, "He's a Rebel" went to #1.

Spector knew his teenagers, though, and certain songs spoke to them alone. For teenage boys, surfing or silliness was the key. Bobby "Boris" Pickett and the Crypt-Kickers (a bunch of Hollywood studio musicians, including Gary Paxton of "Alley Oop" fame and a pianist, Leon Russell, who would be on Phil Spector's Gold Star A-team) topped the charts with "Monster Mash" ("It was a graveyard smash!"), a new dance done by horror-film characters, described in Pickett's sleepy baritone recitation. And for all teens, Ruby and the Romantics assured them that "Our Day Will Come," whose full-page ad in *Billboard* showed clasped hands, one white, one black. Kennedy had promised a "New Frontier," which might very well be on its way, and the late-1962 records had their share of optimism. The Drifters (remember them? They hadn't had a hit since "Save the Last Dance for Me" in 1960) went to the Goffin-King well and returned with their biggest record in ages, "Up on the Roof," which showed one thing that uptowners were doing: escaping to a place with a good view and nobody to hassle them, an oasis as near as the stairway, as new a frontier as you were likely to reach in a tenement.

Once the Cuban Missile Crisis was over in October, the nation gave a mighty exhalation of breath and went into a kind of mass silliness. Allan Sherman, a schlubby, middle-aged Jewish comedian, released an album of comic songs and humorous routines called *My Son, the Folksinger,* on Capitol and stood by as it blasted off. Capitol even got a hit single, "Hello Muddah, Hello Fadduh," out of it. Then the November 24 issue of *Billboard* noted another comedy album, *The First Family,* by someone named Vaughn Meader, on Cadence, of all labels, former home of the Everly Brothers. A satire on the Kennedy family—Meader's JFK was almost perfect because he was from Maine, so the accent came naturally—was just what everyone seemed to have been waiting for: it shot to the #1 LP position in two weeks, having sold 2.75 million records in that time, the fastest-selling album ever. In the great record-biz tradition, there were imitators out as fast as they could be recorded—*The Other Family* (Khrushchevs) on Laurie, *At Home with That Other Family* (Khrushchevs again, starring George Segal, Gwen Davis, Joan Rivers, and Buck Henry) on Roulette, *My Son, the President* on Clan, another *My Son, the President* on Strand, *The President Strikes Back* on Kapp, and *The Poor Family* on Mercury all showed up in one week—but nobody could touch Meader. Kennedy may or may not have given copies to friends for Christmas, depending on who you believe.

So at the end of 1962, there were some different songs in the air. Folk music, both authentic (the urban bluegrass band that had backed Joan Baez, the Greenbriar Boys, released their first album, which would prove very influential, and Baez herself went into the top ten with *Joan Baez in Concert*), commercial (the Chad Mitchell Trio hoped to have a hit with Woody Guthrie's "This Land Is Your Land," and the Rooftop Singers did have a hit with "Walk Right In," a Gus Cannon jug band song from the '30s, and, being on Vanguard and under the scrutiny of the folk crowd, gave him writing credit and presumably paid him), and a curious mixture of both (Lester Flatt and Earl Scruggs, one of the top bluegrass acts in the business, recorded "The Ballad of Jed Clampett," the theme song for what turned out to be a highly successful television sitcom, *The Beverly Hillbillies*) was now part of the landscape, and a label called Dauntless released an album, *Sit-In Songs,* which alerted folkies to the use of music in the nascent civil-rights movement. Among those songs was a hymn that had been repurposed by Southern folkie Guy Carawan and tweaked by Pete Seeger, "We Shall Overcome."

Blues was still going, and still selling, although the "Muddy Waters Twist" was a little late getting there. Chess was leaning more toward soul, although this was the year that Bo Diddley unexpectedly returned with "You Can't Judge a Book (By Looking at the Cover)." It was Duke-Peacock who were releasing the cutting-edge blues: Junior Parker's amazing *Driving Wheel* album, or *Here's the Man!* by Bobby Bland, which helped push his remake of T-Bone Walker's "Stormy Monday" and his own "That's the Way Love Is" and "Call Me." Country was at last showing signs of life as younger performers got a chance; Patsy Cline had a very good year, with four crossover hits, albeit mild ones, and Loretta Lynn, a friend of hers, newly arrived in Nashville, announced herself with the assertive "Success" and drove it into the country top ten. George Jones recorded a bunch of classic country, including "She Thinks I Still Care" and "Just Someone I Used to Know." Nashville's pop singers, one of whom was Cline, had a good year, with Roy Orbison releasing one of his spookiest songs yet, "Leah," while the Everly Brothers paid a call at Aldon and came away with a Howard Greenfield / Carole King song, "Crying in the Rain," that went into the top ten.

Soul was still establishing itself. Don Gardner and Dee Dee Ford went to church on "I Need Your Lovin'," which was a hit on Bobby Robinson's Fire label, and Ray Charles came out with a second volume of *New Sounds in Country and Western Music*. And, although Berry Gordy seemed to think soul alienated white teens, the next two Miracles singles, "Way Over There," and especially its follow-up, "You've Really Got a Hold on Me," had a lot of churchy singing in them. Ike and Tina Turner were on their way to success when Ike decided to sue Juggy Murray for what he estimated was $330,000 in unpaid royalties, stopping their career cold. Spector obviously disagreed with Gordy; his new vocal discovery, the woman who sang on the Crystals' record he'd just hit with, sang lead on his next release, "Zip-A-Dee-Do-Dah," which came out as by Bob B. Soxx and the Blue Jeans, although what you heard was Darlene Love. He also featured her on a single by the Crystals that came out at the end of the year: "He's Sure the Boy I Love."

And there were other, stranger, sounds out there. Bob Crewe, who'd been trying to make it as a teen idol for years, discovered a white vocal group from New Jersey, the Varietones, who'd made a couple of singles for RCA but were getting nowhere. Entranced by the lead singer, Frankie Valli, who had a piercing falsetto that stayed in tune with the other singers, he decided they could be a success if he co-wrote their songs with Bob Gaudio, the group's main songwriter, and got them a deal with Vee-Jay, of all the labels, in Chicago. They christened themselves the Four Seasons, after a bowling alley, and their first record, "Sherry," went to #1, as did "Big Girls Don't Cry." The Seasons were a polarizing group; you could either take the New York accents and the nasal singing or you couldn't. And speaking of weird sounds, what was this bizarre instrumental with all the odd sounds in it? "Telstar," named after the communications satellite, was apparently by the Tornadoes, and it was from . . . England?

chapter fifteen

SECOND INTERLUDE
IN ANOTHER LAND

A skifflesploitation flick, *The Silver Disc*, retitled for American release
and made to look like a rock & roll movie. It wasn't.
(The Michael Barson Collection)

The way American rock & roll finally got to British teenagers was thanks to Mantovani. This will seem odd to people who know the music of Annunzio Mantovani, who used his last name as a kind of trademark for album after album where he conducted string orchestras playing pop songs in semi-classical arrangements (specializing in his "cascading strings" gimmick), as well as light classics like Strauss waltzes. Mantovani was living in England, and his records, which were very well recorded, were huge hits during the early years of high fidelity, since you could pop them on and have twenty or so minutes of background music in your home. On Decca in England, he had his albums released by an American subsidiary, London (British Decca had lost the rights to the Decca name in America), where they did very well indeed. With this money flowing in, Decca decided that the trick might work in reverse and formed the London American label in England and appointed a woman named Mimi Trepel in New York to acquire American records to lease for Britain. She began studying the charts and welcoming offers from record companies, mostly independents because the majors already had overseas branches. It turned out that she had a great nose for a popular record; among the records London American released in 1956, its first year, were "Rip It Up" by Little Richard, "See You Later, Alligator" by Bobby Charles, "One Night" by Smiley Lewis,

"Honey Don't" by Carl Perkins, and less-well-known efforts by Chuck Berry ("Down Bound Train"), the Drifters ("Soldier of Fortune"), the Clovers ("From the Bottom of My Heart"), Big Joe Turner ("The Chicken and the Hawk"), and Willie Dixon and the All-Stars ("Walking the Blues"). There were also American pop records, including a version of "The Ballad of Davy Crockett" that wasn't the American hit version, and records by Kay Starr, Jim Reeves, the Fontane Sisters, and Cathy Carr. The next year saw "Great Balls of Fire" by Jerry Lee Lewis, "Keep a-Knockin'" by Little Richard, "I Walk the Line" by Johnny Cash, and "You Can't Catch Me" by Chuck Berry, among many others. They were careful to include songs featured in films like *The Girl Can't Help It* and *Rock Rock Rock!*, and soon British teenagers were alert to the blue-and-silver label with the three-pointed spindle adapter pressed into the record, and were bringing some of them home. Not all the American hits became British hits, of course, and there was only one radio station, which gave very little needle time to popular music. And sales didn't count as much as airplay did, although just like anywhere else, airplay helped sales.

Of course, there was a bit more rock & roll becoming available; RCA had Elvis, Decca already had rights to Buddy Holly and Bill Haley, and somebody was putting out Frankie Lymon's records, because he did several tours and recorded a live album at the London Palladium. But Atlantic, Chess, Sun, Mercury, and Liberty had no such representation, and gladly licensed the records Ms. Trepel wanted. And these records were giving British kids ideas. Just how to implement them in a time when Tommy Steele was the epitome of British rock & roll (and he was saying he didn't need a "rock and roll crutch" for his intended career as an all-round entertainer) was something of a problem, but skiffle was both helping and hurting there. The fact of a do-it-yourself music, provided you could come up with a couple of guitars or a banjo, was irresistible, and despite not having much of a presence on the radio, skiffle spread like crazy during 1957 in England. Although London, and specifically Soho's Denmark Street, was the nexus of it, its essential amateurism was contagious, and it quickly spread outside of London.

In 1957, just as he was announcing his retirement from skiffle,

John Hasted, a scientist, antiwar activist, and folk song fan who'd championed the earliest skiffle groups, said in a magazine column, "When skiffle dies down, it will split in two directions: rock 'n' roll and folk music." Early evidence of this was already cropping up in London; Alexis Korner and Cyril Davies were an established country blues duet, Ramblin' Jack Elliott had reappeared and summoned a banjo-playing friend from the United States, Derroll Adams, to come over and spread folk music with him, and a certain kind of teenager was showing up at the 2 I's coffee bar in Soho, banging away on guitars, and attempting to duplicate the records on the joint's mostly rock-and-roll jukebox.

And they kept getting discovered there. Terry Williams came in from the suburbs with a friend to see what was happening, took a look around, and returned with his guitar, asking for an audition. He passed, a manager type showed up, and suddenly he was Britain's newest rock sensation, Terry Dene. Alex Wharton and Michael "Mickie" Hayes worked the upstairs and downstairs bars at the 2 I's and became very much a part of the place, Hayes standing out because of his outrageous jive vocabulary (or what he thought was jive, anyway), calling everything "the most." He soon became known as Mickie Most. Eventually he and Wharton sat in with the house band, Les Hobeaux, as the Most Brothers, and got themselves a manager. Late in 1957, BBC Television's *The 6.5 Special* did a live show from the 2 I's, featuring a lot of its current talent, and the entire country was suddenly made aware that London was rocking—and skiffling. 1958 saw more stars; Colin Hicks, Tommy Steele's little brother, was signed to a management deal, and so was Reg Smith, who changed his name to Reg Patterson after he moved to London, but after signing with Larry Parnes, the hottest agent in town, he became Marty Wilde. Terence Nelhams confessed to a member of the Vipers that he was about to chuck it in; he'd been playing spots at the 2 I's for three months and hadn't been signed yet! He changed his stage name to Terry Denver, but that didn't help, but he and his group, the Worried Men, worked their way up to house band for a summer so the Vipers could go on tour, and soon television producer Jack Good came and saw them. They recorded backing up a couple of singers (with Mickie Most adding some guitar), and finally Terry walked to go solo under Good's guidance and changed his name again, this time to Adam Faith. Then there was Larry Page, who had the distinction of cutting a British version of the Crickets' "That'll Be the Day." Of course, when British youth heard the original version, they left Page in the dust, but his career had begun, a tour beckoned, and he needed a band. So, of course, he went to the 2 I's, and there was Ian McLean, a guitarist looking for a gig. Page told him to show up at a rehearsal hall to try out for the Page Boys, which included bassist Jet Harris and drummer Ray Taylor.

Rock & roll was slowly leaking into Britain, but for the most part it was deep underground; the British musical establishment insisted that the American records be strictly controlled for content and rationed because of their country of origin. The Director General of the BBC wanted "the creation of a market and a taste for songs and music which are British not only in the sense of being written by British composers, but British in sound and idiom and capable of performance in a British way." The Controller of Sound Entertainment added, "We should look at existing programmes with an eye to the ultimate possibility of removing the American element and replacing it with something un-American, if we can find it, which will do the same job." And they quoted the BBC's first Director General, Lord Reith, who had said, "It is not autocracy, but wisdom, that suggests a policy of broadcasting on the basis of giving people what they should like and will come to like." Add to this strict controls on lyrics, not only for matters of sex, but also religion (no mention whatever, in any context, of "the Lord," "God," or even bending one's knees in supplication) and commercialism (forget any Chuck Berry song about cars, which invariably named the make and model, let alone references to soft drinks or items of dress). Yet in the middle of all of this, little Larry London, a child singer from East London, managed to have a hit in England *and* America with an old Negro spiritual, "He's Got the Whole World in His Hands," which cleverly never specified who "He" might be. But thank him or whoever for the Grand Duchy of Luxembourg, from which Radio Luxembourg, a powerful AM station with English language programming—a powerful *commercial*

AM station at that—blasted anything they wanted over a directional signal aimed at the United Kingdom and Ireland. They handily shut out the BBC with their own chart-countdown show, with records the BBC didn't or wouldn't play: ten times the listenership, so horrifying that the BBC offered Tommy Steele the job of hosting their count-down show, even when his manager, Larry Parnes, held them up at the last minute for a per-show fee that was many times what the rank-and-file DJs there earned. He didn't last long.

Down at the 2 I's, there was a new group coming up, the Rail-roaders, a duet of Bruce Welch and Brian Rankin, the latter one of the most talented guitarists the scene had tossed up in a long while, both of whom were from Newcastle. Rankin called himself Hank Rankin for the sake of the group, and the two of them studied Everly Brothers records like they were scripture—which, to a rock & roll–inclined British kid, they were. The Railroaders played with whatever rhythm section they could find, although Jet Harris was a favorite bassist, and the more they played, the better they got. When Les Hobeaux, the Most Brothers, Wee Willie Harris, and a few other proto-rockers came off a thirty-date tour of England, they went down to the club to see what was shaking, and as Alex Wharton, the Most Brother who wasn't Mickie, reported, "They were amaz-ing, everything we weren't." Now Hank Rankin was calling himself Hank Marvin, after the part-Cherokee American country star Mar-vin Rainwater. Hank's virtuosity stood out; he was a serious scholar of American country-style records and knew who the players were, and he would play records over and over until he figured out how to play like them. He and Brian also worked out duo arrangements, so that one would back the other and then they'd switch. Skifflers just tended to whack away at chords. Inevitably, Hank was lured away from the 2 I's by an older group, in this case the Vipers, who were going for a more modern sound, and he went with them for a week's engagement in Birmingham, where they tried to augment their nor-mal skiffle fare with the likes of "Johnny B. Goode," to the utter in-difference of their audience. At the end of the week, Marvin quit and went back to working with Bruce at the 2 I's, while the remaining Vipers slunk back to London and dissolved.

Then, in March 1958, Buddy Holly and the Crickets came for a twenty-one-date tour. This was the real thing, close up. They were loud. They were cheerful. And they rocked. Nobody had seen a Fender Stratocaster before—so *that's* why American records sounded like that!—and everyone wished Britain could produce a star like Buddy. Perhaps you had to actually be American—something in the water. And then *pow*! An American rock & roller, clad in black leather, turned up at the 2 I's! Vince Taylor, he said his name was, and much of the rest of him was shrouded in a self-created mystery. It was said that in California, where he'd come from, he was a star; that he'd gone to Hollywood High School; that he had a pilot's license. The part about Hollywood High School was true, but he'd been born Maurice Brian Holden, in Middlesex, and had moved to America with his family when he was very young. Eventually his family moved to California, where his oldest sister married Joe Barbera, of the Hanna-Barbera animation studio, and Holden began playing clubs at the beach. Somehow he managed to hear a Tommy Steele record and told himself that if that's what passed for rock & roll in England, he'd show 'em. So he, his sister, a guitarist friend named Bob Frieberg, and a manager, Joe Singer, arrived in London in the summer of 1958, and Brian became Vince Taylor. He assembled a band from the talent at the 2 I's, and once he started playing, everyone agreed: he had the looks, he had the moves, he had the taste in songs to cover. Oh, and he couldn't sing. Still, he didn't seem like a degenerate, like Jerry Lee Lewis, who'd just come and gone from England.

Backstage at Jerry Lee's first British gig, a bunch of fans had waylaid him long enough to have their pictures taken with him. One of them had noticeably darker skin than the others; Harry Webb's grandmother was Spanish, and he'd grown up in India, son of a diplomat who'd been forced out during the post-independence riots with the rest of his family. Young Harry joined a skiffle group, and they played the 2 I's, but truthfully, his heart wasn't in it. He finally quit and formed a trio called the Drifters and worked up some Elvis numbers. On the Drifters' second gig, one of the other guys from the backstage photo appeared and asked if they'd like a lead guitarist, so Ian Samwell was suddenly a Drifter. A gig in the north beckoned, and the promoter thought that a two-part name would work better than just the Drifters, and he also thought that Harry Webb wasn't very inspiring, so Harry was re-christened Cliff Richard, and off they went. When they came back, they booted their other guitarist and signed with George Ganjou, a former vaudevillian who listened carefully to a couple of songs and then asked them if they'd rather be on Decca or Columbia. The group chose Columbia, and at the end of July they went into the studio to cut the song the record company had chosen, "Schoolboy Crush," which Columbia was so certain was a hit that they let the band knock off one of their own tunes, "Move It," for the B side. Then they pressed it up, and Aberbach Music, who published "Schoolboy Crush," sent their record plugger around to try to generate sales. One of his stops was Jack Good's office, and Good was about to ask the guy to leave, having listened to "Schoolboy Crush" and having hated it, and then, for some reason, he turned the record over. He got very excited, broke out in a sweat, and asked where he could see the Drifters. He had to get them on *Oh Boy!*, his television show on the new ITV network, before anyone else knew about them. He played "Move It" for Marty Wilde, who said, "Yes, it's marvelous, but, of course, you could never get a sound like that on this side of the Atlantic."

"He's from Hertfordshire, his name's Cliff Richard, and I've just booked him for *Oh Boy!*," was Good's reply.

By the end of 1958, Cliff had a top-ten single with "Move It" and was about to head out on a package tour with the latest edition of the Drifters: Ian Samwell, now on bass; Terry Smart on drums; Bruce Welch on rhythm guitar; and Hank Marvin on lead. Two more tweaks lay ahead. Samwell was asked if he'd mind stepping down and letting Jet Harris play bass. Samwell knew that Harris was a much better bassist than he was, so he acquiesced. And early in 1959, Cliff's new manager fired Terry Smart and installed Tony Meehan. Britain had its first serious rock & roll band.

The summer of 1958 saw skiffle totally evaporate in London, symbolized by the Vipers' breakup. Everybody wanted to be a rock & roll singer instead, inspired by the young men managed by Larry Parnes who kept popping up on the scene: Vince Eager, Marty Wilde, Tony

Sheridan, and Tommy Steele. Some might not have wanted to put up with some of Parnes's antics—both Wilde and Sheridan have told of having to rebuff his sexual advances on several occasions—but they all admired his power to create stars. But the word that skiffle was out didn't penetrate very far outside London, so the square teens in the provinces were still keen on it. On July 6, 1957, a skiffle group was playing at a church fete in Woolton, a neighborhood of Liverpool. The Quarry Men were mostly students at Quarry Bank High School, and in the audience was a kid who wanted nothing more than to be a musician. Paul McCartney was already playing the trumpet, but a neighbor kid, George Harrison, sometimes joined him on a guitar his father had given him. They both sought out those blue-and-silver London American records, as well as anything else that sounded good, hanging out at NEMS (Northern England Music Services), Liverpool's big furniture and radio store, which had the best-stocked record department in town, and which, like many record stores in those days, had listening booths where you could check out a prospective purchase. On this particular day, Paul's friend Ivan Vaughan had told him that an old friend of his had this band, the Quarry Men, that would be at the Woolton church fete, so the two of them biked across town to see it. When they got there, Paul could see what the excitement was about; the kid who was obviously the leader exuded attitude, although he wasn't such a great guitar player. The band struck up the Dell Vikings' hit "Come Go with Me," and it slowly dawned on Paul that this guy was making the lyrics up as he went along—clever lyrics, at that. After the band quit, Ivan took Paul over to meet the leader, John Lennon, his childhood friend. They were wary toward each other, but Paul was fascinated, so he and Ivan stayed for the Quarry Men's second set and then went with them to another gig they had at the church's assembly hall, opening for a small dance band. While they were hanging around waiting for the hall to get set up, Paul asked if he could borrow John's guitar and noticed it was tuned like a banjo. He asked if he could re-tune it, and after he did, he launched into Eddie Cochran's "Twenty Flight Rock," a song from the soundtrack of *The Girl Can't Help It*. John was very impressed; the song has a lot of fast-paced lyrics, and Paul was nailing them. Seeing that everyone was enjoying his playing, he slipped into "Be-Bop-A-Lula," and a couple of other tunes, after which he took off the guitar, sat down at the piano, and played "Long Tall Sally." The guys hung out until about ten o'clock and then went to a pub to see if they could pass for old enough for a drink (McCartney was fifteen, Lennon almost seventeen). Eventually they went their separate ways, and John, walking home with a friend, asked him if he should ask Paul to join the Quarry Men. He was so much better than the other guys that there might be hard feelings. But John Lennon wasn't one to let hard feelings get in the way of his ambition.

Not long afterward Paul went down to a local music store and traded in the trumpet his father had bought him for a guitar. Jim McCartney, who played music professionally, wasn't offended; he saw that that's what the boy wanted. As soon as school was out, the Quarry Men discovered that they were eligible for a skiffle competition at the Cavern, a coffee bar in a space that had been a vegetable warehouse for the Liverpool docks—a dank, often odorous place that was a big hit with the kids. The Quarry Men didn't win that night, and Paul McCartney was off at Boy Scout camp with his brother, Mike, for another Quarry Men gig there in August. With the fall came school again, with Lennon enrolled in art college and McCartney still in high school and still hanging out with George Harrison. McCartney was still a Quarry Man, although gigs were few, and he was hanging out more and more with John, much to Jim McCartney's displeasure. "He'll get you into trouble, son," he warned Paul. Not only that, he'd get young George Harrison in trouble, too; Paul invited him to a Quarry Men gig early in 1958, and another of the bands on the bill was the Eddie Clayton Skiffle Group, whose drummer was a young man named Richy Starkey. Starkey was the hot young drummer on the scene, which was what he was doing with the hot local skiffle band, who were getting lots of gigs, far out of the league of the Quarry Men. Lennon was getting to know Harrison, and although he was embarrassed to be playing with a young kid like McCartney, there was no doubt that Harrison, an even better player (and the only one of the three of them with an actual professional-level guitar), was a catch, even though he was even younger than

McCartney. At some point in early 1958, he joined the band. Not that there was a lot of work: they managed to get booked into the Cavern again but were banned for playing rock & roll on what had been billed as a skiffle show. John and Paul settled for playing guitars with George over at his house, which Mrs. Harrison encouraged. And John and Paul were writing songs, singly and together. Somewhere along the line, they pooled some money and cut a record: an acetate demo of Buddy Holly's "That'll Be the Day" on one side and a Paul McCartney composition, "In Spite of All the Danger," on the other.

Lennon was going into his last year in art college and had no plans for the future, although he'd been living with his mother's sister, Mimi, because his mother, Julia, couldn't handle him (his father had vanished years ago), and her rather bohemian lifestyle wasn't conducive to raising a teenager. Mimi was strict, but fair, a single woman with a good job and a nice house, and taking care of John meant that her sister was a frequent visitor. Mimi usually walked her partway to the bus stop at the end of one of her visits, but on July 15, Nigel Walley, a friend of John's, showed up looking for him, and Julia asked him to walk with her instead. Walley had no sooner parted with her to head back to his house when he heard a screech of brakes and a thump: Julia had been hit by a car and died on the spot. His mother's sudden and random death pulled John into a deep depression, which manifested itself in some of his less likeable personality traits surfacing: he picked on people, was sarcastic and cruel toward people who were different and passed it off as humor. In a student pub, though, he met a new friend, Stuart Sutcliffe, an art school student a year younger than he was and opposite him in every way—he was serious about painting and art and had enormous talent and was very easy to get along with—and yet they still became friends. Stu was someone John could talk art with, and he was in awe of his new friend's work. And it was a good thing John had art to occupy him, because the group, who were now calling themselves Johnny and the Moondogs, weren't getting a lot of work. They did audition for a TV program called *Star Search,* and passed the audition and played the first half of the show in Manchester, but they never found out if they won the prize (the chance to maybe appear on a television show) or not; the last train to Liverpool left before the show ended. There went one possibility. Then Larry Parnes came to town and signed Ronnie Wycherly, who immediately became Billy Fury. Then "Move It" by Cliff Richard and the Drifters exploded onto the radio, and the Moondogs—who were already trying to change their name again—knew they were on the right track.

Cliff Richard and the Drifters finished off 1959 in grand style; he was all over television and radio and had a film in the works, *Serious Charge,* for which they'd recorded four songs. They knew they should get Decca to release one of them to promote the film, but they'd lately come under the influence of Ricky Nelson's records, which Decca was releasing, and knew the best song from the film was "Living Doll," and they'd botched it on the soundtrack. They convinced Decca to let them re-record it, and they slowed it down a bit and let Hank play a languorous James Burton–inspired solo, and it was a hit. Because they were suddenly rich, Hank Marvin actually went about importing a flamingo-pink Fender Stratocaster into Britain. American guitars were not allowed to be sold in Britain (although German makes like Framus were), and going to the expense of messing around with customs and dealing personally with Fender was the only way to get one. The only guitar in Britain that even came close belonged to Jim Sullivan of Marty Wilde's band, who owned a 1955 Gibson Les Paul Goldtop that Marty had bought from Sister Rosetta Tharpe, a guitar-playing evangelist from the 1940s who had toured Europe on a folk-blues tour, and given to Sullivan for his contribution to Wilde's success. But Cliff outdid Marty on one matter. "Living Doll" was shaping up to be a hit in the United States, and he and the Drifters—oops, the *Shadows*—since "There Goes My Baby" by an American group called the Drifters, who'd been around a lot longer and were insistent on no competition for the name, had just become a hit—were off on an American tour, which ended when the record only went to #30. The Shadows, however, had taken the opportunity to hit New York's Forty-Eighth Street and its legendary music stores and got themselves some instruments. Somewhere in there, Cliff also made his best film, *Expresso Bongo,* which was the cinematic version of a hit play that had been packing them in since 1958 in London's West End. It's the story of a young man, Bongo Herbert, and his rise in showbiz through the sleazy scene in Soho, aided by his shady manager, and caused immense controversy when it was released. Cliff apologized to his fans and promised a more wholesome film next time, a promise he's still honoring.

None of which had much to do with what was happening in Liverpool, where Japage 3, the supremely awful name Lennon, McCartney, and Harrison were currently using (*John And Paul And GE*orge) were still juggling school (and art college), had so few gigs that George took a position with the Les Stewart Quartet, another band that wasn't working much, although they sure did rehearse a lot. They were going to be the house band in a new space a woman named Mona Best was going to open, but meanwhile, George was also doing construction work, as was John Lennon, while Paul had a job in a department store with a record department. One weekend George and Paul went off hitchhiking and for some reason were very late in getting back to Liverpool, which wouldn't have made any difference except that George had stood up Les Stewart for a gig (as had another band member, leaving him to perform as the Les Stewart Duo), and, infuriated, Stewart broke up the band and told Mrs. Best that she'd have to find another group for her club—two weeks before it was due to open. George had an idea and told her that he knew a couple of guys he'd been playing with who might want to do it, and, after a four-month layoff, Japage 3 had a steady gig. Not only that, they pitched in on getting the club ready. Paul painted the ceiling, and at the end of August, the Casbah opened in the basement of the Best home. Entertainment was by . . . well, they'd added a guy named Ken Brown, so the old name didn't make sense. Meanwhile, Paul was back in school, as was John, who seemed to be knuckling down to study under the influence of his friend Stu Sutcliffe and his new girlfriend, Cynthia Powell. George took a job in the maintenance department of a big store downtown, learning a trade while being paid for it. He celebrated by buying a new guitar, a Czech Delizia Futurama, which at least looked snazzy.

The Casbah featured two group nights a week and the Quarrymen—

yes, they were back to that name, but one word now—played Saturdays and a succession of other bands Sundays. At the end of November 1959, Jett Storm and the Hurricanes got a gig there and featured their new drummer, easily the best in town. Richy Starkey had been given the nickname "Rings" because he was wearing three rings on his hands, one his grandfather's wedding ring, which he intended to give to his girlfriend one of these days. The entire group had a fascination with cowboys, and guitarist Johnny Byrne became Johnny Guitar shortly after the leader became Rory Storm, after Western actor Rory Calhoun. Rings Starkey didn't fit that pattern, so after tossing around a couple of other possibilities, Richy became known as Ringo Starr.

The Hurricanes were a notch or two above the Japage/Quarrymen, and not only because they had a drummer and bassist, which Lennon and his group didn't. Nor were they going to depend on places like the Casbah for exposure; the Cavern had just been sold after it became evident that jazz and occasional skiffle—which had even died away in far-off Liverpool by this time—wasn't paying the bills. Just the place for the local gigs, although they were also getting bookings all over the country: New Year's Eve was spent in Fife, way up in Scotland. The Quarrymen didn't have a gig that night.

But one of them had something amazing happen right after 1960 had started. Stu Sutcliffe had a painting in an annual competition exhibition at the local Walker Gallery, and the sponsor of the exhibition, John Moores, a local industrialist, liked it enough to buy it for £90. Stu had no sooner deposited the check than John was on him to join his group. He could choose either drums or bass—they needed both—and he wouldn't even have to dent his prize money too badly. John was relentless, and Stu was tempted. Well, not drums—they required more effort than he was willing to put in—but the bass? It wasn't a pressing problem, though; the Quarrymen had somehow lost their regular Saturday-night slot at the Casbah and argued with Mrs. Best, while at the same time letting Ken Brown go.

Across town, Allan Williams, who was as close as Liverpool had to a beatnik at that point, was running a room called the Jacaranda along with his wife, Beryl, and a mysterious black West Indian who was known to one and all as Lord Woodbine, after the cigarettes he smoked, which often contained tobacco. Woodbine also fronted a steel band and ran a couple of illegal clubs around town. At the end of January, Williams and Woodbine saw a flyer for a cheap long weekend in Amsterdam, which certainly appealed to them, so they signed on. But they also had another plan: instead of returning with the rest of the package tour, they were going to head to Germany. One night a German guy had come into the Jacaranda and convinced a few of the steel band guys to go home with him, and they'd sent the club a postcard saying what fun they were having in Hamburg. Hamburg? A club scene to investigate? The intrepid Liverpudlians decided to check it out. If it was Liverpool musical talent the Germans wanted, they didn't have to sneak into clubs and steal musicians: Williams could make them a deal for talent he already managed, like Cass and the Cassanovas. He carefully assembled a tape of some of his clients playing live and packed it in his luggage. When the duo arrived in Hamburg, they were amazed: not only was there a thriving red-light district near their hotel, but the Reeperbahn, the main street, had side streets like Grosse Freiheit that had any kind of bar or club that you could imagine. It made London's Soho look like a tawdry few blocks in a repressed city. Williams walked around and located a club, the Kaiserkeller, that had a live band that was playing rock & roll, so he went in, ordered a beer, and was suitably appalled by the band, who were doing phonetic approximations of records they'd heard and not exactly moving the audience, which only danced to the jukebox during the interval. Okay, Williams knew he could beat that, so he asked the waiter if he could talk to the boss and was soon face-to-face with Bruno Koschmider, a hulking man with a clubfoot and not a word of English—the waiter had to be found to translate. Williams told Koschmider that he was a noted British agent and had bands that could wipe the floor with the one currently playing, and that he could have one of them for £100 a week plus £10 commission for him. Look, he said, pulling out the tape, check these groups out. Koschmider cued up the tape and pressed the button and . . . well, whatever was on the tape wasn't what Williams had put there. Before he could stammer out an apology, the noise of a fight came from the club, and Koschmider reached into his desk, came out with a truncheon, and waded into the melee. When all was calm, he came back into the office, cleaned off the truncheon, and put it back in his desk. Williams, knowing he'd blown it but good, slunk into the night.

Williams was hardly finished, though. Jack Good had been presenting Gene Vincent, long washed up at home, on his latest TV show, *Boy Meets Girls,* and now he'd convinced Eddie Cochran to come over by telling Eddie, who was scared to fly after Buddy Holly's death, that all the transportation on the British tour he and Larry Parnes were building up around Gene Vincent would be by road and rail. When the tour reached Liverpool, John and Stu went, as did George, on his own. So did Allan Williams, who on the spur of the moment and thinking, *This is the future,* called Parnes up the next morning to see if there were still dates open on the tour for which he could supply opening bands. Parnes said there were, because Vincent and Cochran were coming back after a break at home in mid-April, and he could have them on May 3. Williams sent him £475 to nail down the date and started thinking of Liverpool acts to pad the bottom of the bill.

The Quarrymen were looking for work, and both Paul and Stu sent off letters hoping to get something at one of Britain's many summer camps, where families would go for a week or two and there was a lot of musical entertainment for dances. Of course, it was much too late to get hired, but they didn't know this (although Rory Storm and the Hurricanes did: they'd been hired by Butlin's, the top name in the business, for the 1960 season). A draft of a letter Stu wrote has surfaced, and it captures a moment. "I would like to draw your attention," it reads, "~~to a band~~ to ~~the Quar~~ 'Beatals.'" It was John, of course, who'd come up with the name; he was inspired by the Crickets, of course, but he also liked that it didn't fit the Somebody and the Somethings template all the other groups seemed to have. (He spelled the name right, too: Beatles.) Nobody knows who Stu's note was aimed to, but one thing's for certain: they weren't getting work, and the few gigs they played during the first half of 1960 were at the Liverpool College of Art, which actually owned an amplifier they could use. They still didn't have a drummer, either. And on April 16, what could have been their introduction to the wider world evaporated when, trying to reach Heathrow for the long-needed break before resuming their tour, Gene Vincent, Eddie Cochran, and Eddie's girlfriend, songwriter Sharon Sheeley, were involved in a high-speed collision with a lamppost in Chippenham. Gene and Sharon were badly injured, but Eddie had massive head injuries and died a couple of hours later in the hospital. (And, as with bookings at Butlin's, the pros were ahead of the Beatles: Rory Storm and the Hurricanes had already been added to the resumption of the tour along with Cass and the Cassanovas.) Still, the show must go on, and go on it did at Liverpool Stadium on May 3 with Gene Vincent the sole American headliner, and Stu and George the only Beatles in attendance, in the audience, of course. After the show, everyone repaired to the Jacaranda, where Parnes and Williams huddled over how they could further work together. Parnes had two acts that would be working the north of England, Duffy Power and Johnny Gentle, and he needed reliable backing acts for them. Williams had brought together a dozen of them for the stadium show, so he was obviously the man to talk to. A couple of days later, Parnes's office called back with another request: he needed a backing group for Billy Fury, too. Williams agreed to have musicians ready that Tuesday the tenth.

Not long after the stadium show, John Lennon was in the Jacaranda and walked up to Williams and said, "Allan, why don't you do something for us?" He then had to explain that "us" was the band he and Stuart had together, so Williams added them to the audition schedule and, hearing that they didn't have a drummer, he offered to get them one, and Cass found twenty-nine-year-old Tommy Moore, who worked in a warehouse. The day of the audition, though, he was having trouble getting out of work, and as the Beatles pleaded to play later and later, eventually they had to do something, so one of the other groups' drummers stood in, and Moore arrived in time to play the last couple of numbers. Ringo Starr and Johnny Guitar showed up to check out the action but were totally unimpressed. So, apparently, was Parnes. But then an emergency came up: Johnny Gentle's appearance in Scotland had changed from a one-nighter to a nine-day tour, and he needed a group. The Cassanovas had been ready to help, but they had a regular Saturday-night gig at the New Brighton Pier, and couldn't very well blow that, and on one of the other dates they had a gig opening for Rory Storm and the Hurricanes at the Cavern's first Rock Night. Williams quickly called Stu and asked if his group could do it; there was a fat £75 fee for the week but they had to have a drummer. Tommy Moore, fortunately, liked the money, so he took the job. The other Beatles were going to miss out on one of the last weeks of the school year—in Paul's, Stu's, and John's case— or a week of work in George's, and devised various schemes to cover for that.

It was quite a week. Most of the band took fake names—Paul Ramon, Stuart de Stael, Carl Harrison—and yet they and Johnny Gentle got the girls screaming although they were barely rehearsed. Seven gigs in eight days, one moment when Johnny Gentle and Lennon were hanging out and John showed him how to write a song— one he subsequently recorded without crediting him—and innocent encounters with fans, one of whom mended a shirt of Lennon's that some fans had ripped. Ten days later, they were back in Liverpool, having seen for themselves what life as the backing band of a third-level Parnes star was like. The only one of the group who'd had trouble on his return was George, who'd been fired from his job. Tommy Moore kept on with them for a little while, but eventually his girlfriend told him that a steady wage was something she wanted her man to have, so one day he just didn't show up for a gig, and nothing Allan Williams or the others could say could change his mind. Various drummers sat in, and one, Norman Chapman, might have worked out but for being drafted. But the basic fact was that Allan Williams had gotten them professional work and taken a percentage for himself: he was now the Beatles' manager. That's why, on August 8, when he got a call from Koschmider saying he was opening another club, the Indra, and needed a band in just over a week, he offered the Beatles. One thing he didn't tell him: they needed a drummer. That was when someone reminded them of Mrs. Best's son Pete. He'd played with a band and then given up, his drums stored upstairs from the club she ran. It was too good to be true, and he'd just been mooching around the house, so that when Williams and the Beatles showed up, he was easily dragooned into joining the expedition. On August 15, they squeezed into a van, and George and Paul revived a joke the band had had going for a while: "Where are we going, Johnny?" they'd chant, and Lennon would reply, "To the toppermost of the poppermost!"

Well, not quite. They—Williams, his wife, her brother Barry Chang, Lord Woodbine, and the five Beatles—stopped in London to pick up another passenger, thought to be a bilingual waiter named Steiner to whom Koschmider had offered a job. London to Harwich, ferry to Hook of Holland, and then off they went. In Koschmider's office, they were informed of their duties: Tuesday to Friday, four and a half hours, 8:00 P.M.–2:00 A.M.; Saturday, six hours, 7:00 P.M.–3:00 A.M.; Sunday, six hours, 5:00 P.M.–1:30 A.M. Half-hour breaks were scattered in there, and it was assumed they had enough material to fill all that time. Sign here, please, and here. Oh, and here: the notice for the police that they were here. Notably absent were work permits, although the boys knew nothing of that. Williams also signed a paper making him Koschmider's exclusive source for British bands—there was already one, Derry and the Seniors, who were none too happy to see another Liverpool band arrive, at the Kaiserkeller. And for a place to crash, there were some small rooms in back of a cinema, the Bambi, across the street from the Indra. The Beatles took the stage of the Indra on the twentieth anniversary of the German bombing of Liverpool, August 17, 1960.

They were all teenagers and, thus, indestructible, and nobody in their audience knew much about rock & roll, anyway; they were mostly in the bar to get drunk. But the Beatles were getting better at performing; at one point, one of Derry and the Seniors looked in to scoff at them and admitted that they'd gotten really good in a very short time. There was a problem, though: an old lady who lived above the Indra, who protested the noise the group was making. This finally reached the courts, and Koschmider was served with an order to cut out the music at the Indra, so he told the boys (and Williams) that he was extending their contract and sending Derry and the Seniors home at the end of theirs, and that from October 4 they'd be alternating sets at the Kaiserkeller with Rory and the Hurricanes.

And so it happened, the two bands egging each other on in fierce competition, the audience getting the benefit. Then, one night in late October, an art student had an argument with his girlfriend and went on a long, moody walk by the Hamburg harbor. On his way back home, he cut down Grosser Freiheit and, as he walked by the Kaiserkeller, he heard some live rock & roll, the first he'd ever heard. He found the courage to go in—this was no student hangout—and was amazed by Rory and the Hurricanes' Butlin's-perfected stage act, with antics and choreography. It was the end of their set, though, so he sat awhile, and then this other group came on, and Klaus Voormann's world changed forever. Totally disoriented by what he'd seen, he left after their set and went back to his girlfriend's house, woke her up, and said, "You've got to see this." And the next night, Klaus, Astrid Kirchherr, and their friend Jürgen Vollmer went down to the Kaiserkeller to see what Klaus was raving about. Terrified of the audience, they sat in a corner and applauded each number, and during the break approached the band shyly—none of them spoke particularly good English, Astrid none at all—and tried talking to the boys. They were shunted off on Stu, who chatted amiably with them and, somewhat surprised, agreed to sit for a photo session the striking blond girl wanted to conduct. Of course he did; it had been love at first sight, something Klaus wound up accepting after it became obvious that it was fate.

As was what happened next: Koschmider gave the Beatles thirty days' notice to leave, after saying he'd gotten a notice from the police that they'd discovered that Herr Harrison was only seventeen and ineligible to hold a work permit. Of course, they didn't have work permits because he'd never gotten them for them, so a notice from the police was unlikely, and Koschmider was probably acting in reaction to a blowup he'd had with Williams, who'd booked Liverpudlians Gerry and the Pacemakers into his hated rival Peter Eckhorn's Top Ten Club. This was in violation of their agreement, and soon enough Williams served notice that it was null and void. Meanwhile, the boys had been down to the Top Ten to see former Larry Parnes client Tony Sheridan, who'd pretty much moved to Hamburg and was drawing fans, and signed a piece of paper with Eckhorn that they'd play the club in April 1961. Now that Koschmider had fired them, they tacked some condoms to the wall of their miserable room at the Bambi and lit them on fire. No damage was done, but the police arrested Paul, Pete, and John, and Stu, accompanied by Astrid (to whom he'd just become engaged), turned himself in. No charges were pressed, and Paul and Pete were deported in handcuffs at the airport and banned from Germany unless they filed an appeal within thirty days. George was already on his way out at the Hook of Holland. John hung out for a few more days with Stu, who was the only one who was staying on legally. What a mess. They could hardly wait to do it again.

chapter sixteen

THIRD INTERLUDE:
ENGLAND AND GERMANY

Sound check: The Beatles' last gig at the Cavern.
(Photo by Michael Ward/Getty Images)

The Liverpool the Beatles returned to, even though it had only been a couple of months, was subtly different from the city they'd left. They barely had time to investigate it, though, because they had to figure some way to keep alive until they could get back to Hamburg. Paul McCartney took a job winding coils for an electrical firm right away, at his father's insistence, but the others tried to delay finding work as long as they could. There was a problem: Allan Williams had opened a Liverpool outpost of the Top Ten Club, and soon after it had opened it burned to the ground, and part of the aftermath was Williams checking into the hospital with ulcers. The band didn't have a management contract with him, and he'd definitely screwed things up with Koschmider, so they were hustling their own gigs. Bob Wooler, the DJ at the Cavern, was sort of looking after them in the meanwhile, and when Stu arrived from Hamburg in mid-January, they were back to a five-piece. Stu was going back to art school in Liverpool and had applied for a teaching position, but Astrid was coming for a visit soon; otherwise his plans were vague. John was hanging around Nems, the furniture store–turned–record shop owned by the local Epstein family, whose son Brian had, after failing to make an acting career in London, taken the store and modernized it, emphasizing televisions, radios, record players, and records. He aimed to make Nems the best record store in

Liverpool, and claimed he could get anything in print. One thing he got was the latest London American 45s, and Lennon was often in the listening booth, finding material for the band, and he unsurprisingly zeroed in on the Aldon writers, and on records produced by Scepter's A&R man, Luther Dixon.

It was important to come up with new songs, because now they had competition: Rory and the Hurricanes had returned from Hamburg, King-Size Taylor and the Dominoes had gotten a lot better, as had the Big 3 (Cass and the Cassanovas minus Cass), and, of course, there were Gerry and the Pacemakers, who also returned from Hamburg in February. All of them were stunned by the Beatles, who'd been whipped into shape by the Hamburg experience and were actually working seven days a week. A lot of the gigs were in tough clubs in the north end of town, and one night some yobbos had cornered Stu in the venue's toilet and beat the crap out of him. The rest of the band came to his rescue, and in the melee, John broke a finger.

Meanwhile, though, they really wanted to get back to Germany, so Paul drafted a letter in which he apologized for the incident at the Bambi, expressed his opinion that deportation was out of proportion to the offense, and turned it over to Allan Williams's secretary, who wrote out two copies, one for Paul and one for Pete, had them sign it, and mailed it off to the head of the Ausländerpolizei. Bob Wooler lobbied the Cavern's new owner, Ray McFall, to let them play the club, but the only slot open was the lunchtime show, kind of hard to make for anyone with a day job like Paul. Hot dogs and soup were available, but no alcohol, and their smell now competed with all the Cavern's other smells, as the band tried hard to win over a new crowd of office workers, secretaries, and other working types. This left evenings open, and Mrs. Best was hustling gigs for those nights. By March, the Cavern offered them an evening, and things were starting to move in Germany, too. Williams had a tentative agreement with Eckhorn for a Top Ten residency once the legal issues were worked out. Sometime around April, Stu and Astrid moved back to Hamburg. Stu and his mother had been fighting incessantly about the couple cohabiting (although they were living with Williams), and Stu hadn't gotten the position at the art college he'd applied for. Fine;

he'd go back and paint, and Beatle, too, if they ever returned. Which, around the end of March, they did. The German police had put Paul and Pete on a sort of probation, good for a year, and charges would be dropped if they didn't get in more trouble. George was now legal, and the Top Ten was a nicer place—marginally—than the Kaiserkeller. Some of the time was spent backing up Tony Sheridan, and in order to keep up the long hours, he introduced them to Preludin, a diet drug (but not an amphetamine) that kept you going. The Top Ten's toilet attendant had a little jar and sold them to the musicians; John in particular loved them.

There were still problems for the band, though. For one thing, Williams was taking a managerial cut of their salary, and Eckhorn was also deducting income tax and Germany's church tax (government-required tithing) from their pay, which was illegal since they weren't German citizens. This had them upset; they had been the ones who secured the invitation from Eckhorn to play the Top Ten, yet they were paying Williams as if he'd done it. They also resented the German tax thing, although Eckhorn quickly folded on that. But there was a deeper problem that they were going to have to deal with. As Tony Sheridan saw it, "Pete was a crap drummer . . . He was just not competent, and there were discrepancies between his feet and his hands." In Liverpool, they kind of needed him, and they definitely needed his house to store equipment in, and Mrs. Best to hustle for them, but he wasn't cutting it in Hamburg. Whatever, they were stuck with him for a while, because they soon extended their contract until the beginning of July.

One Beatle who wouldn't be long for the group, though, was Stu, who began excusing himself from gigs, forcing Paul to get up off the piano and play bass, which he really didn't want to do. But Stu had applied to a Hamburg art school, his plans to marry Astrid were moving forward, and in the end, he felt more like a painter than a Beatle.

In the middle of this, on June 22, they had a recording session. Polydor Records, a major German firm, had decided to take a chance on Tony Sheridan, and Bert Kaempfert, a staff producer, had them show up at 8:00 A.M. (which, after all, was just after work) to cut a few numbers. Tony was hot on "My Bonnie Lies Over the Ocean," which they sometimes played, and the band was allowed a couple of numbers without him, "Ain't She Sweet," a number that dated to the '20s, and an instrumental called "Beatle Bop." These tunes, they were told, would be released in America as singles. But the session's clear focus was on Tony Sheridan. The sound isn't all that good, because Pete had had his bass drum and tom taken away by an engineer who thought he was better off the fewer drums he had to manipulate, and not all the Beatles played on all the tunes (Stu was there, but only as an observer), and, in fact, when the record came out, Polydor—invoking a clause in the contract they signed—identified the band as the Beat Brothers.

On July 1, the Beatles played their last show at the Top Ten on this visit. Stu officially left the group, and Klaus Voormann asked if he could join on bass—he'd been given Stu's—but John told him that Paul already had the job. They told Peter Eckhorn they'd be back, while hoping all the way back to Liverpool they wouldn't.

The Beatles returned home on July 3, and not long afterward, Liverpool had its own music magazine. *Mersey Beat* was the brainchild of Bill Harry, one of their friends, which started to chronicle the sudden eruption of musical talent in the city. The first issue had a piece of writing by John Lennon about "The Dubious Origin of Beatles," and if that went over, he'd left a bunch of stories and poems with Harry to plug holes in future issues. Harry needed investment, and he approached Brian Epstein, who turned him down, and the Cavern's owner, Ray McFall, became the primary investor. Epstein did, however, make sure copies were delivered to Nems for the teenagers who came in to buy records, including the Beatles.

Mona Best was getting them work at a far higher price than ever—£15 was where negotiations started—and, even better, she'd found them a van. Somewhere around the time they'd left for Hamburg the second time, Pete's best friend, a guy named Neil Aspinall who spent a lot of time on the scene, entered into a relationship with Mona, who was twice his age, and after quitting his accounting course, which he hated, he'd bought a van. He'd previously driven the band to gigs, and now he was their roadie. And they were getting gigs. Suddenly the lunchtime session at the Cavern was packed, and they shocked the local music scene with that £15 fee the Cavern paid them for their first evening show. But they were also attracting crowds like never before, and the walls of the Cavern ran with condensation from the bodies packed inside. The second issue of *Mersey Beat* came out with the headline BEATLE'S SIGN RECORDING CONTRACT! above Astrid's picture of them (Paul unfortunately identified as Paul Mac-Arthy), and news about the Polydor session and Stu staying behind. Nems took seven dozen copies, and Brian asked Harry if he'd be interested in having him write a record review column, a suggestion Harry was happy to agree to.

Allan Williams came back into the picture at the end of July, hiring lawyers to try to get £104 from the band, and so Paul went to a lawyer's office and counter-filed with a document that began "I am a member of the Jazz Group known as the Beatles." Williams's claims had very little legal weight—he still didn't have a contract with the group, nor would they have given him one—and he folded a few weeks later. But the incident pointed out something essential: they did need a manager now that Neil had given them the means to traverse the country. Bob Wooler, Bill Harry, Ray McFall, and others considered it, but all discarded the idea. Mona Best was doing what she could—they were now making £25 a week, far more than most of their peers—but she didn't want to do it, either. At the beginning of August, some local girls organized the Beatles Fan Club, and at the end of the month, Bob Wooler wrote the first straight article about the band for *Mersey Beat* (John's "Dubious Origin" had contained such possibly inaccurate details as a man on a flaming pie appearing in the sky and giving them their name). Things were in suspended animation, and at the end of September, John and Paul announced they were going on holiday and decamped for Paris. Their intent was to visit with Jürgen Vollmer and to soak up some of the local music scene, but the most momentous thing that happened was that, after looking at the locals, they induced Vollmer to cut their hair into a kind of bowl-like, comb-down style similar to what young Frenchmen were wearing. The Beatle haircut was born.

In late October, Stu mailed them copies of their record. Well, actually, Tony Sheridan's record: "My Bonnie" b/w "The Saints," by Tony Sheridan and the Beat Brothers. Not exactly what they were expecting, but it was a record, and it was them. This led to a story every Beatles fan knows, although the details are usually wrong. On October 28, a kid named Raymond Jones walked into Nems and asked its manager, Brian Epstein, if he had the record, adding that the backing group was the Beatles, a local band. Reports that Brian had never heard of them are unlikely, what with those seven dozen *Mersey Beat*s trumpeting THE BEATLE'S and their recording contract, even if there had been a couple of issues of the paper since then. Still, he was having trouble finding the record, and he called Bill Harry, who arranged for him to attend a lunchtime show at the Cavern on November 9. It wasn't the kind of place Epstein usually went, and he stuck out with his fine clothing (he was planning to head to his tailor's after the show), but he was very, very impressed. He thought the band looked great, and although they needed to work on their stagecraft some, there was an energy there that couldn't be denied. Of his first impression, he later said, "I knew they would be bigger than Elvis. I knew they would be the biggest in the world." He was so knocked out that he almost forgot why he was there, and after the show, backstage, he asked George about the record (he now had three special orders for it), and George asked Bob Wooler to play it. He copied down the details, excused himself, and went on to his fitting.

He knew right off that he wanted to manage them, but he also knew that he'd have to be very careful how he approached them about it. He attended a number of evening shows, and as many Cavern lunchtimes as he could squeeze in, and he set up a meeting to talk about management on November 29, after telling his family that he was thinking of doing it. He'd ordered a couple of boxes of "My Bonnie" and put a BEATLES RECORD AVAILABLE HERE sign in the window, watched them evaporate, and ordered more. The Beatles finally showed up for the meeting hours late, accompanied by Bob Wooler, and Brian asked them about their history, how the record had come about, and so on. He agreed, in the end, to act as manager for a while to see if it would work and said he'd be headed down to

London with a few copies of the record to see if he could get some action from the record companies whose product he sold in enough quantity that they all knew his name. He also checked with Allan Williams, who cautioned him to get something in writing or they'd screw Brian like they had him.

In London, his best connections were with EMI, where Ron White, the general marketing manager, remembered him from when he'd been a salesman and called at Nems. He promised to show it to the company's A&R men, and also took a copy of the band's contract with Kaempfert and Polydor to show to a German-speaking colleague. Next stop was Decca, where they were polite—how could they not be, when he was moving so much of their product?—and took a copy. Then he went to another department, where he met with Tony Barrow, a Liverpool lad who'd moved to London to take a job with Decca writing liner notes, and who, under the pseudonym Disker, wrote a record review column for the *Liverpool Echo*. He didn't much like the record but promised he'd mention it to his superiors. Having done what he could, Epstein got on the sleeper train for Liverpool. On Sunday, December 3, the Beatles, as they'd been told to do, knocked on the door at Nems, which was closed for business, but Brian was there working on Christmas sales. Well, three of them did: Paul was missing, and when they called his parents, it turned out he'd just gotten out of bed and was taking a bath, which didn't impress Epstein at all. "Well, he may be late," said George, "but he's very clean." He finally showed up, and Brian filled them in on the London trip, adding that nothing could happen until it became clear what the German contract said. Brian also set up a meeting with Pete, who'd been handling the bookings at this point, to learn what he knew. He was shocked that they were only getting £15 a night, too; he knew enough about show business to know they were worth more. The pubs were now open, so they moved the discussion to the Grapes, the pub next door to the Cavern, where the band unwound after gigs, and in the ensuing conversation, John and Paul mentioned that they'd written a bunch of songs, although they weren't currently performing any of them onstage. Brian knew that this could be as lucrative a source of revenue as live performance and records, and he filed the info away for further contemplation. At the end of the session in the pub, the band had heard enough, and John said, "Right, then, Brian. Manage us."

He got right to work. The fan club hadn't really done anything, and Paul had Roberta "Bobby" Brown, a friend of his current girlfriend's, take it over. Brian, however, told her to stop, which led to a meeting between them, out of which Brian realized she was really on the ball, and he acquiesced. Then he had a visit from Graham Pauncefort, who worked for Deutsche Grammophon (Great Britain), and wanted to talk Christmas sales, as well as the plans the parent company, Polydor, had for expanding into pop music in Britain. As a result, DG announced that they'd release "My Bonnie" on January 5, 1962. He also took the time to meet the Beatles' parents (or, in John's case, Aunt Mimi), all of whom were very impressed—Mona Best in particular: she was pregnant with Neil's baby and was going to have to cut back on Beatle activity.

Brian sent a letter to EMI following up on his visit, and got a translation of the Kaempfert contract back, which said that if the band's management served notice they wouldn't renew it, it would expire at the end of June 1962. Meanwhile, the sneaky Beatles had an obligation to fulfill: a local music-biz figure named Sam Leach had gotten them a gig in Aldershot, a suburb southwest of London proper, over two hundred miles from Liverpool. Leach had advertised three bands and put an ad in the local paper, which failed to run it. The other two groups were figments of Leach's imagination, and in the end, the Beatles played to about a dozen and a half people, and the gig was immortalized by Liverpool photographer and Beatle buddy Dick Matthews, the last Beatles show that virtually nobody attended. Leach had promised them £20 but could only come up with £12 from his own pockets, so the group refused to talk with him for the entire journey home, and Leach's dreams of wealth through undercutting Brian Epstein and managing the Beatles evaporated.

So, shortly, did the Beatles' chances with EMI, or so it seemed. They sent a stiffly worded letter stating that they had "sufficient groups of this type at the present time under contract and . . . it would not be advisable for us to sign any further contracts of this nature at present."

But Brian wasn't too concerned yet; Decca had just hired a new man, Mike Smith, and he was eager to sign his first blockbuster, so he came up to Liverpool to see the band at the Cavern on December 13. This caused an enormous hubbub: a London A&R man had come to Liverpool! Brian hustled to get a proper, legal set of management papers together. The band closed the year out with a big blowout at the Cavern, a Christmas party with Gerry and the Pacemakers and King-Size Taylor and the Dominoes. But the show was almost a disaster—Pete called in sick. At the last minute, they found a replacement, Billy Fury and the Hurricanes' drummer, Ringo Starr. Everyone remembered the show as a lot of fun; Ringo fit right in. Too bad that he was going to emigrate to America, or so he said. In the end, he found the emigration papers too much and left the country, anyway: to Hamburg to play with Tony Sheridan. This followed a post-Christmas visit by Peter Eckhorn to Liverpool with Sheridan. There was the matter of assembling a band for Sheridan, but he also wanted to find out what was going on with the Beatles, who'd realized that much as they hated Hamburg when they were there, they missed it when they weren't. Eckhorn found out, all right; the new manager was plenty tough with him, and in the end, Brian had gotten a better price for the boys, who'd start at the Top Ten on March 1 if all else panned out.

Next on the band's agenda was a "recording test," a session that would be recorded, for Decca in London, on January 1. It wasn't an audition; Mike Smith had seen them in the Cavern and noted their competence, but now it was necessary to see if they could hold up in the studio. They knocked off fifteen songs, from Chuck Berry ("Memphis") to show tunes ("Til There Was You") to corny old favorites ("Besame Mucho") and even three Lennon-McCartney tunes (including "Love of the Love"). John Lennon later characterized the resulting tape as "terrible." Smith thanked them and noted that because of various goings-on at Decca, it would be at least three weeks until there was any decision at all. They all trekked back to Liverpool and saw the latest issue of *Mersey Beat*, with its headline BEATLES TOP POLL! They'd beaten all the competition, and the paper had spelled their name right! (Not Paul's, though; he was now McArtrey.) The next day, Polygram released "My Bonnie" in Britain, and despite good reviews in both the trade and fan press, it sank without a trace. Brian ordered a bunch of copies for the shop, but pretty much everyone in Liverpool who'd wanted one had bought a German pressing when they'd first come in, and they sat in the back, unsold. Well, that was the retail business for you. Brian still had the management contract his lawyers had prepared, and on January 24, they signed it (or some of them did: Brian never affixed his signature to it for some reason), appointing him manager until February 1967. He would take 15 percent. The next order of business was to apply to the BBC for an audition for a performance on the radio, which was sent off to the regional office in Manchester and accepted practically by return mail: they were on for February 8. Things were chugging right along when Brian received a summons to London for lunch with Decca.

It wasn't what he thought or hoped for, though; according to his autobiography, Dick Rowe, the head of A&R, told him, "Not to mince words, Mr. Epstein, we don't like your boys' sound. Groups of guitarists are on their way out." Another executive told him, "The boys won't go, Mr. Epstein. We know these things. You have a good record business in Liverpool. Stick to that." Rowe later disputed the quote attributed to him, not least because the only "guitar group" in England was the Shadows, who were doing quite well, thanks. What actually seems to have been the case was that Decca was trying to decide between the Beatles and another group, Brian Poole and the Tremilos, and Rowe was pressuring Mike Smith toward the latter, because the idea was not only to record the group's own records, but to keep them on hand as a house band for when a singer needed rock backup. Brian was mortified and slunk back home. At least the BBC was interested, and they headed off to Manchester, where they went through their paces and were accepted for a broadcast (the auditioner noting that they at least had "a tendency to play music" despite being "rocky"), and they were given a date of March 7 to record a program to be broadcast nationally the next day.

Brian wasn't going to give up on the recording contract, though, so he took a copy of the Decca audition with him and returned to London. He took the occasion to visit an acquaintance, Robert Boast, manager of the HMV record store on Oxford Street, and, sitting in his office, he complained that he knew the band would be big if only someone would listen to them. Boast couldn't—his job was selling the records, not making them—but HMV had a small studio in the basement where they cut discs, and Boast suggested that he could make demo discs out of the tape because not everyone had a tape deck in their office. So they went into the basement, and as Jim Foy, the disc cutter, ran off some discs, he told Brian he liked what he was hearing, and Brian told him that three of the tunes were by the band. That was something few groups could claim, and Foy asked Brian if he'd published them, and Brian said no. Foy offered to call the general manager of EMI's publishing wing, Sid Colman. In no time, Brian and Colman were talking. Colman wanted to publish the Lennon-McCartney numbers. Brian wanted a recording contract and told him EMI could publish them if they had a contract. Exactly what happened next is unknown, but on February 13, Brian had an appointment with an A&R man, George Martin, at EMI. (It's unlikely that Colman set this up, because he didn't like Martin at all.) Martin didn't much like what he heard but took a disc from Brian and thanked him. Meanwhile, across the street, Sid Colman had been listening to some of the discs and asked one of his song pluggers, Kim Bennett, what he thought about this Lennon-McCartney song, "Like Dreamers Do." Bennett liked it, but not the group's name, and agreed to go to EMI and tell them that the publishers were willing to finance a recording session so they'd have publishing on the song. EMI told them to stick to publishing and let them make the records.

The beginning of March saw two more milestones for the band: the BBC broadcast and a present from Brian, who took them to his tailor to be fitted for matching suits to wear onstage and for the broadcast, even though it was radio. It was about image; all four had adopted Jürgen Vollmer's shaggy haircut, they'd found some Cuban-heeled boots that they all liked, and these suits—pale blue mohair, with narrow lapels and tight pants—were certainly not like anything any other provincial beat group was wearing. Still, Brian wouldn't let them wear the suits at the Cavern, and certainly not on their upcoming trip to Hamburg. There'd been some changes there, and Brian had had a visit from Horst Fasching, a criminal who'd been caught but never convicted, as hard a man as Hamburg had produced, who informed him that the Top Ten gigs weren't going to happen, but, instead, the Beatles would play a new club that was still being renovated, owned by his confederate Manfred Weissleder. To seal the deal, he pressed a DM 1000 note into Brian's hands. And since the probationary period for John, Paul, and Pete was about to expire, Brian would have to go through more German bureaucracy to get them visas. Waiting for the new club to be finished—it now had a name, the Star-Club—they still didn't have a date, although they heard that Tony Sheridan would be opening it. He'd be doing it without Ringo, though; Ringo's grandmother had taken ill and died, and he was in Liverpool sorting that out. Plus, the Hurricanes had had a good offer that would carry them until Butlin's opened in June, playing American Army bases in France. Before he went off to join them, he played a couple of more gigs substituting when Pete Best was sick or couldn't make the show for some reason. He loved the whole experience—these lads were on a much higher level than anyone else he'd ever played with—and just before he got ready to leave for France, they asked him to join. Ringo appreciated the invitation, but he had obligations to fulfill.

So did the Beatles. April 10 saw all but George (who'd been sidelined by a case of German measles) fly to Hamburg, where Manfred Weissleder treated them to steaks and showed them the club. It was pretty impressive: an old cinema, with a huge stage, excellent sound system, a balcony, and, most importantly, guest quarters for the bands, and a brand-new bathroom with tub and shower. Boy, Stu should see this! Of course, he had it better staying with Astrid and her mother. Or rather, he had had; on the very day the Beatles arrived in Hamburg, one of the many headaches he'd been having got much worse around noon, and he went into convulsions. Astrid's mother called an ambulance and then Astrid, and at 4:30, in the ambulance with Astrid holding him, Stu Sutcliffe died. The band found out the next day, when Weissleder loaned them his car to pick up Brian and George at the airport. They got there and found Klaus and Astrid, who broke the news. Millie Sutcliffe, Stu's mother, was on the plane with Brian and George, coming to pick up her son's body. The funeral was set for

Liverpool on April 19, and Klaus and Astrid flew over for it. It was a small affair; the Beatles were working, although they were represented by Cynthia, John's girlfriend, and George's mother. Astrid stayed with Millie until Millie accused her of murdering Stuart, whereupon she went to stay at Allan and Beryl Williams's place. John plunged into a deep depression, but there was work to do, so they got down to it. Brian typed up an account of opening night to mail to the fan club, and it was also reprinted in *Mersey Beat*, and in it he didn't mention Stuart, but did mention that the boys would play again at the Cavern on June 9.

In London, there'd been a scandal at EMI. Not the kind of thing that would interest the general public, but one that called out for action within the company. George Martin had left his wife and moved in with his longtime secretary, Judy Lockhart Smith, with whom he'd been having an affair for several years. It was also time to see if EMI would renew his contract as A&R man and producer for Parlophone, which was likely because he'd been doing remarkable things, particularly with comedy records, but also film soundtracks and miscellaneous pop records. Martin had requested royalties on the records he'd been producing, but EMI turned him down flat. Angry about the scandal, they renewed his contract but added a stipulation: that band Sid Colman and Kim Bennett had been on about? The one Martin hadn't liked? He was going to produce their record. In fact, the company was preparing a contract. On May 9, Brian went down to London to talk to George Martin. They sat down and went over the offer, which was the same boilerplate EMI gave all their new acts: six sides over the first year, EMI paying for studio time, no advance, contract was for four years with an option to renew coming up annually, worldwide rights. First recording session would be on June 6, and they shook hands. Excited, Brian went to the nearest post office and sent telegrams, one to Bill Harry to break the news in *Mersey Beat*, and one to the Beatles: CONGRATULATIONS BOYS EMI REQUEST RECORDING SESSION PLEASE REHEARSE NEW MATERIAL. To which the boys cabled back: WHEN ARE WE GOING TO BE MILLIONAIRES (John), PLEASE WIRE TEN THOUSAND POUND ADVANCE ROYALTIES (Paul), and PLEASE ORDER FOUR NEW GUITARS (George). Such comedians! Maybe Cliff

Richard had seen £10,000 in royalties, but a beat group from the north of England? In their giddiness over the news, Paul and John may have read it wrong, because they took "rehearse new material" to mean "write new material," so that's what they sat down and did.

The rest of their stay in Hamburg went by in a blur of Preludin and beer, but on May 24, they went back into the studio under Bert Kaempfert's direction to cut some backing tracks for Tony Sheridan, two traditional American songs (which shows how little Kaempfert understood what they were doing), "Swanee River" and "Sweet Georgia Brown." That was it for Polydor and Germany; the next day, Brian signed the contract with EMI. Brian signed on behalf of his clients, the Beatles (Parlophone had spelled it "Beattles"), and it was countersigned and witnessed by Bob Wooler. Wooler negotiated the Beatles' return to the Cavern, where they would appear exclusively for the two weeks following their return, and also have use of it for two afternoons to rehearse for the recording date. Then he did the Beatles another favor: he let Rory and the Hurricanes know that Allan Williams had just booked Jerry Lee Lewis for a night in Liverpool, and they cut short their French adventures—which were due to end soon, anyway, as the summer season at Butlin's loomed—to come back and catch the show, which was a triumph. It was a season for American rock & rollers, apparently, thanks to promoter Don Arden; he sent Gene Vincent to Hamburg, where he overlapped at the Star-Club with the Beatles for several hair-raising days. Vincent was out of control, drinking scotch from the bottle and waving around a gun he'd somehow acquired, at one point kidnapping George on a mission to his hotel to shoot his wife, and handing George the gun. Fortunately, the situation dissolved before it could get serious.

On June 2, they landed back in Britain at Manchester Airport to be greeted by Neil with manila envelopes from Brian containing copies of *Mersey Beat* with the article about their signing and several typed pages showing their schedule for the next weeks. They unpacked, they rehearsed, and Pete went home immediately to check on his mother, who was now seven months pregnant and had just lost her mother, Pete's beloved grandmother. And then, a few days later, they piled into the van (Brian took the train) and headed off to London. They had a day off once they arrived and wandered around a city they knew mostly from hearsay: "It was like fellows down from the north for a coach trip," as Paul put it. And then on June 6, they went into the studio and cut "Besame Mucho," "Love Me Do," "PS I Love You," and "Ask Me Why," of which two were understood to be for the single, one of which had to be a Lennon-McCartney song that Sid Colman would publish. What was odd about the session, and telling of what was to come, was that the band insisted that they had new material that was better than "Like Dreamers Do," the song that had gotten them signed, and Martin had let them record it, not a thing any other producer would have allowed. The session took twenty minutes, and afterward they all crowded into the control room to hear the playback. Martin sternly ran down some technical details about the microphones and filled them in about their future with Parlophone. They listened silently, taking it in. Finally, Martin said, "Look, I've laid into you for quite a time, you haven't responded. Is there anything you don't like?"

There was more silence, and finally George Harrison gave Martin a hard stare and said, "Yeah. I don't like your tie." There was a bit of tension, and suddenly everyone started laughing, and the laughter continued for some minutes. Finally, the band left, and Martin reflected that they had charisma, and it was contagious. Too bad about the drummer, though; he was absolute crap and would have to go. In the end, Martin decided the session hadn't produced anything they could issue. Time to try again.

It's odd to consider now, but on their night off in London, the Beatles didn't go see a band in a club because there weren't any. London was the center of England's government, cultural industry, record and music publishing business, and media, and there was no pop music scene to speak of. Promising lads would be swept up and recorded, but there were no long nights of bands sweating it out in front of crowds the way there was in Liverpool, no chance for a young band to figure out what they were doing and get better. But although the Beatles didn't see it on this first trip down, something was stirring; despite roadblocks thrown up by the Musicians' Union, some American music was filtering into the clubs. Chris Barber was behind some of it; in late 1957, he'd sponsored Sister Rosetta Tharpe, a hot-guitar-playing evangelist who didn't mind performing with jazz bands or in nightclubs, and then Sonny Terry and Brownie McGhee, a harmonica-and-guitar duo who'd been discovered by New York's folk scene some years back, came in the spring of 1958. The crowds loved them. Later that year, Barber managed a coup: his old idol Muddy Waters, along with Otis Spann on piano. Knowing he could sell out the Roundhouse club for this kind of music anytime he wanted to, he organized a secret gig there, which drew a full house—ninety people—who sat in stunned, respectful silence. Then there was a short British tour, with the last gig in London. Although some jazz fans disliked Muddy's singing, the younger ones, like a gangly teenager named John Baldry, were astonished by having the good luck to actually see something like this. Muddy went home and talked up the Round-house, and Memphis Slim's ears perked up. He'd just moved to Chicago, but when Barber asked him to come over, he agreed immediately. Before the end of the next year, he'd made plans to move to Europe; these people actually *listened*, and they really didn't care if you were black. Of course, Alexis Korner and Cyril Davies couldn't believe their good fortune as they continued to play with Barber and watch these Americans perform. Later they and Long John Baldry would join together in something called Blues Incorporated, an all-electric blues band that debuted on March 17, 1962, in a basement club in Ealing, where one tiny ad in *Jazz News* drew over one hundred people to the gig. People were said to have come from as far away as Cheltenham, which seemed ridiculous but wasn't; a serious young man from there with a thick head of blond hair asked to sit in and play guitar on the second night the club was open (Saturdays only), and introduced himself as Elmo Jones. Korner knew him from when the Barber band had had Sonny Boy Williamson over and done a short tour: Jones had waylaid him after the gig in Cheltenham and wanted to talk blues, which surprised Korner. The drummer, a trainee advertising guy with a fondness for jazz named Charlie Watts, was a bit boggled; he'd never heard a harmonica played like Cyril Davies did. Within a month, people were hitchhiking from Scotland to be at the Ealing Club on a Saturday night.

Or they came from closer in: at the railroad station in suburban Dartford, Keith Richards was headed in for a day at the art school in Sidcup and spotted a kid his age with a bunch of albums, including Chuck Berry's *One Dozen Berrys,* under his arm. He approached the kid, Mike Jagger, who was headed into the city to attend the London School of Economics, and for the next twenty minutes they talked about music until Keith had to get off the train. By that time, the two had agreed to meet at Jagger's house to explore his record collection, which, since Jagger was pretty well off, he'd gotten through mail order from the United States. It turned out they had a friend in common, Dick Taylor, who, like Keith, tried to play the music on those records on his guitar. By the fall of 1961, they'd put together a band of sorts, called Little Boy Blue and the Blue Boys. At some point, they even cut a tape in someone's living room, featuring a lot of Chuck Berry songs, an Elvis song, and "La Bamba." Nor were they the only blues group in the suburbs: Paul Pond, who lived in Oxford, fronted a band called Thunder Odin's Big Secret.

Cheltenham blues fan Elmo Jones (real name Brian, by the way) sought Pond out, and soon they were playing together. They, too, made a tape, and they thought it sounded great. Brian invited Paul to join the (nonexistent) band he led. Pond replied that he had a band, and he was its leader, but they remained friends. Still, Brian wanted a band of his own, so early in 1962, he moved to London and got serious. The May 2 issue of *Jazz News* had a classified from him: "Rhythm and Blues: Guitarist and Vocalist forming R&B band, require Harmonica and/or Tenor Sax, Piano, Bass, and Drums. Must be keen to rehearse. Plenty of interesting work available." He immediately heard from Ian Stewart, a pianist with a good command of blues piano. Rehearsals started at the White Bear pub in Leicester Square, from which they were tossed because Brian kept stealing cigarettes. Alexis Korner sent a guitarist, Geoff Bradford, to rehearse, but he was a stiff-necked blues purist, and then in June, Jagger appeared, and the next week he brought along Dick Taylor and Keith Richards. At this point, Bradford stopped coming to rehearsals when he was asked to play Chuck Berry and Bo Diddley. This was getting interesting.

Up north, the Beatles played their big welcome-home show at the Cavern on June 9 and on June 11 went back to Manchester to tape another BBC appearance, which was broadcast on the fifteenth. At about the same time, George Martin wrote Brian a letter saying that Pete had to go. He knew the other Beatles agreed, but he had his signed agreement and didn't know how to terminate one of its signatories. While they mulled this over, Mona Best announced she was closing her club, the Casbah; the Beatles played one last time, and it shut. Brian went to Manchester to talk to Granada Television, a private network that now existed alongside the BBC and was proud of its regional operation, to see about getting them on TV, which resulted in a producer coming over to see the boys at the Cavern. Brian also bought a decent van for the band to use, although they were already worried about whether or not Neil would stay on when they canned Pete. Epstein was a busy man; Manfred Weissleder had been in touch about having the band come back for two weeks in November, sharing the billing with none other than Little Richard, who was still nominally preaching the gospel back in the United States but picking up some money to live on with gigs like this overseas. He also wanted them for the last two weeks of the year, including New Year's Eve. And Brian signed his second act to a management contract: the Big Three, supposedly on the recommendation of John Lennon. He sent them to Hamburg to relieve Gerry and the Pacemakers, and then signed *them* to a management deal. He was becoming a mogul. And he was also trying to find the Beatles a drummer, offering the gig to Bobby Graham of Joe Brown and the Bruvvers (he declined) and Johnny "Hutch" Hutchinson of the Big Three (likewise). The Beatles themselves wanted Ringo, but he was off at the Butlin's camp in Skegness, which had made the news that summer when its pet elephant had drowned in the swimming pool. John and Paul actually drove all the way there to talk to Ringo, apparently, but nothing changed. King-Size Taylor and the Dominoes approached him about swapping drummers with Rory Storm when they got back from Hamburg at the beginning of September, and he said yes. Next, Granada came calling: they'd be at the Cavern on August 22 to film the Beatles. Now they *had* to get Ringo.

It seemed that the media was waking up to electric music. In

London, Alexis Korner's Blues Incorporated was playing the Ealing Club and the Marquee, a prestigious jazz club on Oxford Street, each week, and BBC Radio contacted him about appearing on their *Jazz Club* show on July 12. That was a Marquee night, so Alexis worked it out that Brian Jones and his band should take the gig for that night, with Long John Baldry's Kansas City Blue Boys opening for them. They needed a name, quick, and got one from Muddy Waters's "Mannish Boy," where he yells out, "Ooh, I'm a rollin' stone!" Both *Disc* magazine, which reported the substitution, and the Marquee's ad spelled the name Rolling Stones, and although Brian would attempt to keep the Rollin' part of it, he lost the battle. He couldn't have been happy with the Marquee ad, which called them Mick Jagger and the Rolling Stones (but he was going up against the same British tradition that had George Martin trying to decide whether he was going to rename this new band he was producing John Lennon and the Beatles or Paul McCartney and the Beatles). The band on this night was Jagger, Richards, Jones, Dick Taylor, Ian Stewart, and, on drums, Mick Avory. Nobody seems to have written the night up (and why would they have?), but it did leave the band feeling charged up. Before long, Mick, Brian, and Keith were sharing a flat at 102 Edith Road in Chelsea, then a rather down-market part of the city, with one James Phelge, whom they called "Nanker" for no discernible reason. They'd rehearse at the Weatherby Arms, the corner pub. Good thing they had a place to live, because they weren't getting gigs; the Mann-Hugg Blues band (with Paul Pond, who performed as Paul Jones) and an organization called Blues By Six were. They implored Charlie Watts to join them—most of the time they rehearsed without a drummer—but he was wary; the band had a bad reputation, largely because of Brian's unpredictable behavior, and the jazz community was in an uproar over the way they looked—dirty, disheveled.

Things in Liverpool were chaotic. Mona Best gave birth to Vincent Rogue Best on July 21, and John Lennon's girlfriend, Cynthia Powell, discovered that she was pregnant. Dreading it, she sat down with John and gave him the news, and, after a long silence, he said, "There's only one thing for it, Cyn, we'll have to get married." A date was set. Cynthia's mother, who hated John about as much as anyone could hate someone, was due to sail to Canada on August 22, the day of the Granada filming at the Cavern. Brian made an appointment at the registrar's office for the twenty-third—but he didn't have a drummer. John Lennon was about to have a child—although everyone, including Cynthia, knew that it would be forbidden to mention that or their marriage in connection with the group. What had to happen was to legally release Pete from the partnership agreement he'd signed and for Brian to find him gainful employment as per the agreement. But Brian had an idea: one of the many groups that had erupted in Liverpool was the Mersey Beats, a bunch of teenagers who weren't bad and whose drummer was leaving. When he met with Pete to give him the news, he could offer him immediate employment as their drummer and leader. He picked up the phone and called Butlin's on Tuesday, August 14, and asked that Ringo be paged. When he got on the line, Brian asked him if he'd join the Beatles, and he said yes. Would he come back to Liverpool tonight to start rehearsing? No, he had to give notice, but he'd be there on Saturday. The meeting with Pete was now set for Thursday, and it wasn't an easy one. Brian laid the Beatles' case out: the band didn't think he was good enough, and EMI didn't want him on the next session. Pete didn't get it, and on his way out he passed the Mersey Beats in the hallway. They hadn't even come up in the conversation. Brian went into his office and told them he couldn't see them just now. Finally, he wrote up a memo to his lawyer asking for a revision in the contract with the Beatles in which Richard Starkey's name was substituted for Pete Best's. Pete couldn't stand the idea of seeing the Beatles again and wanted to go on a bender with Neil, but Neil pointed out that Pete was the one who was fired, not him, and the band had a gig that evening, so he couldn't get too wrecked. The Beatles' relief at seeing Neil was palpable, as was their relief on Saturday when Ringo showed up at the Cavern for an afternoon rehearsal. The gig that night was at Hulme Hall in Port Sunlight during the annual horticultural society show. After a bit of a set-to with Neil about setting up the drums (Pete had always set up his own and Neil didn't know how to), the band took the stage with Ringo for the first time, and suddenly they sounded much, much better—other musicians on the bill and Bobby Brown, the fan club secretary, all noticed it. And on Wednesday, Granada filmed it for TV.

The next day, John and Cynthia got married, and as a wedding present—the only one they got—Brian gave them use of his private apartment, where they could settle into married life (and good thing, too; they hadn't thought this far ahead). It was a tiny ceremony. Paul and George attended, along with Cynthia's brother and his wife. John's aunt Mimi refused to come because she thought John was too young to get married. There were a lot of adjustments over the next few weeks: the Lennons to married life, and the Beatles to their new drummer. Cynthia stopped coming to gigs immediately; the secrecy of their marriage mustn't get out, although there were a couple of close calls. A fan, one of the original fan club girls, had spent the summer in Norway and brought John a wooden statue of a troll sitting on the toilet with his pants down—she certainly knew his sense of humor well—and the other Beatles said things like, "Will you put it with all the toasters?" and, more nakedly, "Is this another wedding present?" but John just grinned and asked her, "What's this, Norwegian wood?" EMI wanted them again in September and had sent a song for them to learn, "How Do You Do It," which the band detested as a piece of lightweight pop crap, the kind of thing they felt the songs they were now writing should replace in their repertoire. But there were record company politics at work, and they'd already blown their first session with a bad drummer, so down they went to London, and at an evening session on September 4, they laid down "How Do You Do It" and "Love Me Do." They also played some other stuff for George Martin, including "Please Please Me," which he felt might sound like something if they sped it up considerably. Then John confronted him, saying, "We can do better than this," and Paul backed him up, saying he'd rather have no contract at all than to put out "How Do You Do It" under the Beatles' name. Then they went back to Liverpool. In London, various people listened to the two new songs, and for a number of reasons—not least because Ardmore & Beechwood, the publishers Kim Bennett worked for, didn't own "How Do You Do It"—the hated song was dropped.

Thus, the Beatles were recalled to London on September 11 and walked into the studio to find the drums set up and a session musician, Andy White, at the kit. That afternoon, they put down "PS I Love You," "Please Please Me," and "Love Me Do." Ringo wasn't mollified much when he was asked to play maracas on "PS I Love You," but at least he was now on the session. This afternoon, though, was a landmark in the band's career: their contract with EMI had been fulfilled, and they signed papers assigning publishing of "Love Me Do" and "PS I Love You" to Ardmore & Beechwood, the firm that had seen to it they'd record in the first place. Now what? Now it was time to attend to the record release in early October.

First, they needed a press kit, and although EMI was preparing one, Brian felt the Beatles should have their own, so he got Tony Caldwell, a.k.a. "Disker," to write one. Brian added a questionnaire for each Beatle about his aims and ambitions (which came down to "money") and compiled a few of John's writings, including the story about the flaming pie. After all, they needed to stand out from the mob. Then there was a bit of a problem: Granada announced they were shelving the Cavern footage. It wasn't the Beatles' fault (although the film, in black and white, is pretty awful, and the sound distorted), but, rather, the fact that Granada had chosen to contrast them with the Brighouse and Rastrick Band, thirty members strong, all due a payout at Musicians' Union scale—which would completely destroy the show's budget if Granada went through with it. Then came a setback Brian could do something with: Pete Best had decided to sue for "unwarranted and unjustified dismissal." But that was no problem; the Beatles of which Pete had been a member had broken up, if only for a second, and a new Beatles partnership had been formed with Ringo. In fact, that partnership was about to sign new management papers with Nems Enterprises Ltd., firming up the nature of their relationship to Brian and in particular the percentages due him. Since he was acting as their booking agent, the rather high maximum percentage of 25 percent on earnings over £800 was actually a bargain because they weren't paying two parties, a manager *and* an agent. And it would appear that Pete was out of the way temporarily; he'd joined Lee Curtis and the All Stars (who, to his annoyance, put ads in the press saying, "We've got the Best! Yes—great ex-Beatle drummer"), which helped raise the struggling group's profile.

And then, it all came together. On October 5, Parlophone R 4949, a 45 RPM single of "Love Me Do" b/w "PS I Love You" came out, although nobody was pleased that the writing credits read "Lennon/McCartney" instead of "McCartney/Lennon," as Brian had, on the band's instructions, ordered. The BBC wouldn't touch it, but Radio Luxembourg would, and late that night—the Beatles had had a gig—George burst into his parents' bedroom with his radio blaring "Love Me Do" and yelling, "We're on! We're on!" In the next few days, people throughout the north of England ran to their local record stores—Nems was swamped—and bought copies. A record distributor pulled up at the shop just as Brian was arriving and informed him that the record was selling by the boxful. "Oh, really?" Epstein said, since this was the first news of any sort he'd heard. "That's *wonderful!*"

"He was *so* excited," John Mair, the distributor, remembered later. "Suddenly he was not the cool, imperious, arrogant Brian I knew, he was like a schoolboy." Of course, it was only regional, not national, and Epstein was accused of buying boxes of records to hype his own act, but they really were selling.

That same night, in the back room of a pub at the Woodstock Hotel in North Cheam, Surrey, south-southwest of central London, the Rolling Stones were slogging out a gig in front of two people (although four more were listening outside so they wouldn't have to pay to get in). It was their first time away from Ealing, where they were beginning to draw crowds, and they still had no drummer. Dick Taylor was getting tired of these guys and decided to concentrate on his art school exams, and by the end of October, he'd left the band amicably. (He'd been bitten by the bug, though, and in the months to come would assemble another, very Stones-like band, the Pretty Things: as photos show, the name was at least slightly ironic.) A few days later, the Beatles were in London promoting themselves, knocking on the doors of the press (who were mildly amused that a bunch of hayseeds from the north thought their record was worth any notice) and getting ready to tape one of EMI's Radio Luxembourg shows, *The Friday Spectacular.* This rather odd event took place at EMI House on Oxford Street before a live audience, but the performers lip-synched their songs even though it was a radio show and then met the fans and autographed records. After that, they went back to touring the press and getting shut out.

They weren't getting shut out only in London, either; in the United States, Capitol was now owned by EMI, and Dave Dexter Jr., their international director of A&R, had first refusal on all EMI-produced records from other countries, and refuse them he did. He was famous for hating British acts, unless they were novelties, having turned down the Shadows with and without Cliff Richard, Adam Faith, Helen Shapiro, and Matt Monroe, all British chart toppers. "Love Me Do" didn't even get to play all the way through before he rejected it. Anyway, Capitol was having enough trouble trying to break the Beach Boys. Parlophone would have to try elsewhere, so they sent the record to Transglobal Enterprises Inc., a company EMI secretly owned that licensed records Capitol turned down. Right off the bat, Liberty Records was interested . . . and then they weren't. Transglobal put it on the back burner.

They'd just have to conquer Britain first, and in mid-October, Don Arden's Little Richard tour (with Sam Cooke) came to the Tower Ballroom in New Brighton, with the Beatles the next-to-last act before the star. His first couple of nights, Richard had done a lot of gospel and a quick medley of his pop hits, but by the time he hit the north, he'd put the set list in order. And he was also paying attention to the opening acts, telling a journalist from *Mersey Beat,* "Man, those Beatles are fabulous! If I hadn't seen them I'd never have dreamed they were white. They have a real authentic Negro sound." The paper's photographer got a shot of Richard and the Beatles together backstage. And coming up, they'd be working with him at the Star-Club at the beginning of November. Which was a bit unfortunate: it would be right around when the record would be in its most crucial phase. The Beatles tried to get out of the gig, Richard or no Richard, and failed. Of course, nobody was playing the record, either, although Kim Bennett was trying hard; he got it on a lunchtime program for housewives, *Lunch Box,* and got a BBC producer to give them a shot at a live radio performance after they got back from Hamburg. He *almost* got it on *Saturday Club,* an important broadcast aimed at teens, but they'd gotten so many requests for the record from Liverpool that they figured it was an organized campaign: nothing could be that popular. Finally, toward the end of the month, even though it had no airplay, "Love Me Do" crept into the *New Musical Express* charts at #27. This was news; NME was fairly hostile to rock & roll, seeing itself primarily as a sophisticated jazz paper, but its charts were taken seriously. So seriously, in fact, that George Martin called Brian to arrange for another session at the end of November.

But it was off to Hamburg nonetheless. Things were much better this time, from the pay to rooms in an actual hotel for the duration of their stay. Also, they got to watch Little Richard do his thing, which involved, among other things, ending his set with a striptease on top of the piano, almost certainly not a part of his gospel act back in the States. Richard had his own organist along, sixteen-year-old Billy Preston (Weissleder's pull with the authorities must have been strong, because George had been deported for being seventeen), and was backed by the English band Sounds Incorporated, and the Beatles and Preston began a lifelong friendship there at the Star-Club. Brian flew over for the last couple of days, but when Weissleder wanted to book some dates for 1963, he told him he couldn't do it just yet. And they had two more weeks to do, including that New Year's show, starting on December 17. As the time in Hamburg ticked away, all they knew was that on November 16 they'd be back in Britain, flying into London to do the press—Kim Bennett had gotten them on some more BBC radio shows, and the record was still selling—and to talk to George Martin, who'd requested a sit-down with them that afternoon.

The news was good: Martin had been thinking, and he decided there was really something there with this group, and he wanted another single as soon as possible. He also—and this was unprecedented for such an untried group from the sticks—wanted an album. A live album, recorded at the Cavern, the bulk of it to be original material. George Martin was known for his unconventional ideas and success with offbeat releases—one thing John Lennon revered him for was his production of the wonderfully surrealistic *Goon Show* LPs—and this, apparently, was the latest one. He didn't have a title for it, and Paul suggested *Off the Beatle Track*, and grabbed a pad and mocked up an album cover for it. Martin was impressed by that. Righto: first things first, and on November 26, the band went back into the studio to record "Please Please Me" and "Ask Me Why." Meanwhile, "Love Me Do" continued slowly, slowly ascending the charts. All very well and good, but George Martin, after the last note of "Please Please Me" faded away, pressed the talkback button and told the band, "Gentlemen, you've just made your first number one record." The band cracked up. They broke for tea and then went back in and recorded the other side. All they had to do was wait until January 11, 1963, five long weeks away, for the record to be released.

Brian now had a bit of work to do. George Martin wasn't happy with what Ardmore & Beechwood had done with "Love Me Do," and he told Brian that he was going to recommend his talking to Dick James, an old-time music publisher, unaffiliated with any American companies (and, thus, free to negotiate with any of them), and when Brian got an appointment with him, it turned out that James's fifteen-year-old son was a fan, as was his receptionist, Lee Perry. When James heard the acetate of "Please Please Me," "I just hit the ceiling." He knew he'd just heard a #1 record, and Brian told him they had lots more original material as yet unrecorded. And as they hammered out the details of the contract between them, Brian insisted on an unusual clause: nobody could record Lennon-McCartney songs unless everyone signed off on it. Thus, James's main job was to promote the copyrights *through the records*, not via amassing a lot of cover versions. The Beatles came first. And as this deal was wrapping up, the Beatles showed up at the BBC Paris Street studio and taped a show called *The Talent Spot*. When they came offstage, their friend Alan Smith from Liverpool showed them something he'd just bought: a copy of *NME* with the year-end poll. The Beatles had come in fifth for British Vocal Group and eighth for British Small Group. Not bad, a year after they'd won that *Mersey Beat* poll! (They'd won that one again this year, of course.) And as December wore on, all the Beatles had to do was play one gig at the Cavern and a taping for Granada TV's *People and Places* show. This time, it ran.

Next up was Hamburg, playing on a bill headlined by Johnny and the Hurricanes from the States—has-beens at home, but very much in demand in Hamburg—and with the Beatles getting yet more pay, better housing, and shorter sets, but Germany in December is nobody's idea of paradise, and the red-light district of Hamburg even more so. In London, Dick James offered Brian a great deal: he'd split publishing revenues with a company Brian would form fifty-fifty, so confident was he of what would come. Oddly, the single was still on the charts, never going north of #17, but there nonetheless. It seemed to be still selling. The Beatles knew nothing of this; they had their eyes fixed on that New Year's show and the plane tickets for January 5, flying into Scotland.

And elsewhere in London, the Rolling Stones were coming along, albeit slowly. Bill Perks was looking for work, more work than his regular band, the Cliftons, could get him. He saw an ad Brian Jones had placed in *Jazz News* and went to audition for this band that was already working regularly—or so the ad said—and needed someone on bass. "Regularly" meant every week in Ealing, but a gig's a gig, and the guys seemed to like Perks, as well as the fact that he had an amplifier and was very generous about handing out cigarettes. The band quizzed him on his knowledge of American black music and found he knew rock & roll but not rhythm and blues, but they put him through his paces, in the middle of which, an exasperated Perks said, "You can't play fucking 12-bar blues *all night*!" Ah, but they thought they could. No matter, Perks was asked to return. He went through another rehearsal, which went much better, and the band made him an offer. The Cliftons were clearly not going anywhere, but the Stones might. They'd already made a demo record, which they'd sent to a couple of record companies, and Decca had returned it with the note "You won't get anywhere with that singer." But Perks felt that, somehow, "the Stones were a better bet." So on December 14, he played his first gig with them, at the Ricky Tick Club at the Star and Garter

Hotel in Windsor. "The crowd was a mix of students and a smattering of American servicemen who knew Chicago R&B," he reported. "They were impressed." Perks spent Christmas with his wife and infant son, and the Stones enjoyed a cheap lunch together. Then it was back for the last gig of the year, at Ealing. Surely next year would be better.

chapter seventeen

1963: THE END OF
THE WORLD

The Beach Boys in a woody on an actual beach: *(left to right)*
Carl Wilson, Mike Love, Dennis Wilson, Brian Wilson, and David Marks.
(Photo by Michael Ochs Archives/Stringer)

The new year started off with a bang for some people. Ricky—sorry, he was now Rick—Nelson signed a million-dollar contract with Decca, and at the end of January, BMI's songwriting awards saw a huge sweep by Aldon artists, with Jobete, Motown's publishing company, coming in second. In fact, Jobete looked like they'd be doing pretty well in '63: they'd sneaked out Marvin Gaye's "Hitch Hike" single at the end of 1962, capitalizing on yet another dance craze, and in mid-January three girls who'd been doing backup vocals on a lot of Motown sessions (and working as secretaries and in other jobs around Hitsville) finally got the chance to step in front of the microphones as a kind of test run for a songwriting/producing team. Brian and Eddie Holland and Lamont Dozier wanted to streamline the recording process by having one team in charge from writing the song to supervising the session. They grabbed a song Lamont Dozier had started writing a couple of years back for Loretta Lynn, one of the more dynamic young country singers coming up whose "Success" had been a summertime country hit in 1962, and finished it. Dozier thought "Come and Get These Memories" was a good country title, but when the team got through with it, it was something else indeed. Rosalind Ashford, Annette Beard, and Martha Reeves became Martha and the Vandellas, and when they played the song back, Berry Gordy said, "That's the Motown Sound!

That's the sound I've been looking for." Dozier agreed. "I've always thought that the Motown Sound started with 'Come and Get These Memories' because that one song had a mixture of all those musical elements—gospel music, pop, country and western, and jazz." The Holland-Dozier-Holland partnership was off to a good start, and because the Supremes were going nowhere fast, Motown finally had a hit girl group. And another interesting songwriting team, Burt Bacharach and Hal David in New York, had written a harmonically fascinating song for former gospel singer Dionne Warwick, "Don't Make Me Over," another match of performer and songwriter/producers that had a lot of promise.

Phil Spector, too, was doing quite well. January saw another Bob B. Soxx single, "Why Do Lovers Break Each Other's Hearts," and another hit by the Crystals, "He's Sure the Boy I Love," followed quickly by a Bob B. Soxx and the Blue Jeans album, *Zip-A-Dee-Doo-Dah*, and the Crystals' *He's a Rebel* album, with a cute cartoon hoodlum on a motorcycle on the cover. And of course there was surf music, with Dick Dale's "Misirlou," leading to Capitol, which saw a future in surf music all of a sudden, signing Dale and buying out his Deltone label, which they would distribute, as well as his new album *Surf Beat*. Dion, newly signed to Columbia, put out "Ruby Baby," the Four Seasons continued their hit run with "Walk Like a Man," Roy Orbison continued to be spooky with "In Dreams," and the Orlons, in Philadelphia, asked the musical question "Where do all the hippies meet?" The answer, of course, was "South Street," and "hippies" must have been local slang for young hip kids, because those other people were still a couple of years in the future.

The folkies continued to get stronger, with talk in the television industry of a hootenanny-type weekly show, and the Chad Mitchell Trio releasing a version of "Blowin' in the Wind" that went nowhere, while its author, Bob Dylan, recorded a single of "Mixed-Up Confusion" b/w "Corinna" that featured a raucous rock & roll band—a single that was quickly withdrawn and would remain unheard for some years to come. Now, what you want from a folk act is Peter, Paul & Mary's latest single, "Puff the Magic Dragon," whose "hidden message" (Puff? Little Jackie Paper?) was later discovered by pot smokers, but denied, probably with some justification, by its co-writer Lawrence Lipton (with Peter Yarrow).

On March 5, a plane crash near Nashville in bad weather killed Cowboy Copas, Hawkshaw Hawkins, and the bright hope of Nashville's pop crossover, Patsy Cline, as they returned from a benefit concert for the family of Cactus Dick Call, an important DJ. And on the way to the services, Jack Anglin, of the duo Johnny and Jack, was involved in a fatal one-car accident. Copas and Hawkins were pure 1950s Nashville, as was Anglin, whose partner, Johnny Wright, was married to Kitty Wells. Country music was losing its fascination with rockabilly and trying to cross over in a more traditionally pop way after seeing how Roy Orbison and Patsy Cline (and Brenda Lee, another Nashville-based singer who wasn't strictly country, but straddled the line) were doing, but finding that a good traditional sound mixed with up-to-date lyrics could do well. Loretta Lynn, a friend of Cline's, had blown into town from Oregon, where she'd been living, and signed up with Harold Bradley at Decca, and the songs she was recording were challenging the status quo. "Success," she claimed, was breaking up her marriage, and "The Other Woman," her follow-up hit in June, put a different spin on cheating songs. Texas songwriter Willie Nelson had a contract with Liberty, and he, too, was doing interesting work, like "Half a Man," which, like most of his Liberty material, only had minor sales but made people in Nashville pay attention. After all, he'd written one of Patsy Cline's big hits, "Crazy." And country fans were beginning to pay attention to the stuff that was coming out of Bakersfield if they could get it. Buck Owens had been having hits since 1959 in a fairly traditional style that didn't sound too far from Nashville, but under the influence of the music coming out of the clubs (most notably the Blackboard) in Bakersfield he began crafting a harder honky-tonk style that emphasized the Fender electric guitars he and Don Rich, of his band the Buckaroos, played. Rose Maddox, who'd barnstormed the west for years with her family act, the Maddox Brothers and Rose, also fit naturally into this style, as did Buck's wife, Bonnie. Fuzzy Owen and Lewis Talley were musicians who made enough money in the bars to invest in some recording equipment, and the Tally label started recording some of the talent, including a young ex-con, Merle Haggard, who had some powerful songs in his repertoire like "Skidrow," which he recorded for Tally in early 1963. Capitol immediately came calling, but he turned them down, saying Lewis Talley had believed in him too long for him to turn his back on him. But that was okay; Capitol was about to release Buck Owens's "Act Naturally," his first #1 country record.

Avoiding crossover was actually a pretty smart move. There was more than enough pop music to fill the airwaves, and Ray Charles was still doing his "modern sounds" with country material, the latest of which was "Take These Chains from My Heart," from the ever-dependable pen of Hank Williams. Girl groups were everywhere; besides Spector's Crystals and Scepter's Shirelles, the Cookies were requesting you "Don't Say Nothin' Bad About My Baby," and the Chiffons were noting that "He's So Fine." There were dance crazes aplenty, too. Rufus Thomas did "The Dog," which did well until Jocko Henderson's TV show broadcast dancers actually *doing* the dance, which involved some snooping down low that was plenty scandalous (and ended Jocko's syndication), Chubby Checker suggested, "Let's Limbo Again," which nobody seems to have taken him up on, and Freddie King probably thought he'd covered all the bases with "Bossa Nova Watusi Twist," which must have carried a medical warning from the American Chiropractic Association.

The March 16 issue of *Billboard* carried a small story on page 37 that announced that "Vee-Jay Records, through its tie with EMI, has the U.S. rights to the two leading records in last week's British charts—Frank Ifield's 'The Wayward Wind' (Columbia) and the Beatles' 'Please Please Me' (Parlophone)." That's not quite what happened, of course; Capitol had turned the records down, and Vee-Jay had done business with Transglobal. But again, Ifield was at #1 in Britain, and the Beatles weren't far behind at #5. By the time Vee-Jay got its ad in the trades it was #2, and in its haste to get "Please Please Me" out, they misspelled the band's name as the "Beattles" in the trade ads and on the record. The laugh was on Capitol, though— Ifield's record sold! Certainly nobody was expecting much from the Beatles—a rock & roll band from a provincial city in England?—and

Ifield had already hit for Vee-Jay the year before with "I Remember You," a nice middle-of-the-road song. But Brian Epstein was hard at work; he'd added Gerry and the Pacemakers and Helen Shapiro to his stable of stars and was fast becoming the impresario of the north. Laurie Records, the company that had given Dion and the Belmonts to the world, released "How Do You Do It" in Gerry and the Pacemakers' version in early May to no great effect, despite its rampaging up the U.K. charts and doing battle with the Beatles. Hey, it was another world, one that provided novelty records like Lonnie Donegan's "Does Your Chewing-Gum Lose Its Flavour (On the Bedpost Overnight?)"

In America, black music was changing rapidly (a fact that didn't get past these English folks, who still crowded the record stores looking for black American music), and alongside the teen girl group songs, a steady stream of more sophisticated material was coming from both veterans (the Drifters' magnificent "On Broadway," a Leiber/Stoller/ Mann/Weil top tenner produced by Leiber and Stoller, who'd also been producing Jay and the Americans, who weren't from Philadelphia, but might as well have been with their "good music" sound, to pay the rent) and newcomers (Irma Thomas's sophisticated non-hit "Two Winters Gone," Barbara Lewis's "Hello Stranger," Doris Troy's "Just One Look," and two versions of "If You Need Me," by Wilson Pickett and Solomon Burke, both of which charted, but with King Solomon rising higher). James Brown had his biggest hit in a while with "Prisoner of Love," slow enough to almost stop time, with a small string section (a first for Brown), and he was getting disgusted. He knew that the best way to show what he was doing would be to record him live, but Syd Nathan at King was predictably saying he couldn't afford to. Fine—Brown took $5,700 he'd been saving for a forthcoming tour and paid to record his show at the Apollo Theater in Harlem on October 24, 1962. He spent some time working on the tape and then helped King's chief recording engineer, Chuck Seitz, boil it down for an album. Seitz injected some screaming and crowd noise from a white sock hop, and they both made sure that moments that were mostly visual were edited so that it kept going and there was no dead space. Nathan still didn't like it, but Brown had some acetates made up and made some strategic gifts to DJs. Jerry Blavat, the influential Philadelphia jock, visited James backstage at a show in early 1963 and he handed him one, and Blavat took it home, played it, and then played it on the air the next day. A second copy went to Allyn Lee in Montgomery, Alabama, who did the same thing, and his phones went wild. Crucial to the success of the album was the fact that, except for cutting the show into two pieces so it fit on two sides of the LP, there were no individual tracks—you *had* to play it all. Nathan began to get phone calls; disc jockeys wondered why they hadn't been sent a copy—it wasn't out? Release it! And so, in May, he did. "Prisoner of Love" whetted the appetite; *Live at the Apollo* was a feast. It was also a way for young white kids to experience James Brown without going to a scary show in an unfamiliar part of town (although they began doing so right about this time), and it went on to the album charts and stayed there for sixty-six weeks. James Brown had arrived. It had only taken him seven years.

Perhaps sensing this energy, a bunch of investors decided that this sort of gospel frenzy was the next big thing, and in mid-May opened a nightclub, Sweet Chariot, in Times Square. Robe-clad waitresses—excuse me, "angels"—served drinks, and a search was on for rather secular gospel groups. Clara Ward was fairly broad-minded about these things and did a short stay there, and the house group made an album, but the idea was doomed from the start. Why not book gospel-oriented singers, ones who were doing this so-called soul music? Probably they wanted to keep too many black folks from turning it into an all-black scene. At any rate, the club failed in a couple of months, and the angels flew on to other venues.

In May, the RIAA announced the Grammys, a good snapshot of where the music industry was at the time: Record of the Year went to Tony Bennett for "I Left My Heart in San Francisco," Best Vocal Group and Best Folk Record was Peter, Paul & Mary for "If I Had a Hammer," Best Rock and Roll Record was Bent Fabric's "Alley Cat," believe it or not, Best Rhythm and Blues Record went to Ray Charles for "I Can't Stop Loving You," a country song, and the Album of the Year was of course *The First Family*, a second volume of which was just hitting the stores. In other words, the music industry was just a bit, but not totally, out of touch, as it was to remain. At least it wasn't as out of touch as whoever presented that year's British National Record Awards, presented a week earlier, whose trophy for Best Light Vocal Record went to the George Mitchell Minstrels, a blackface duo. That's right: blackface in 1963. But Britain had only lately acquired a black population as it welcomed West Indians from its colonies in the late '40s to come work in low-level positions, mostly in transportation as conductors and the like on buses, the Underground, and British Rail. Thus, the Rolling (or was it Rollin'?) Stones' appropriation of American black music wasn't hailed as a racial thing at all, at least in Britain. The band was struggling and inching its way upward. In January, Charlie Watts reluctantly joined, and Bill Perks adopted a new surname for the stage. From now on he would be Bill Wyman. Brian Jones, in his role as bandleader, wrote letters to the press about rhythm and blues, and Ian Stuart, the only guy in the band with a phone, albeit at his workplace, took the bookings, such as they were. They had their regular gig in Ealing and went for a second one on Tuesdays, but early in the year they lost their regular stints at the Flamingo and the Marquee. Taking any one-offs they could get, they were performing at the Red Lion in Sutton in February when an affable bearded gent Brian had met and invited to see them introduced himself as Giorgio Gomelsky, and he told the boys he was running an R&B club on Sunday nights at the Station Hotel in Richmond, where Dave Hunt's band was the regular. (One bit of interest about Hunt was that his guitarist was a youngster named Ray Davies.) Gomelsky was knocked out by the Stones and told them, "The first time Dave goofs, you're in." And thus it happened; Brian and the guys went down one Sunday, and Hunt was late showing up. Gomelsky admitted this wasn't the first time, and Brian was furious, offering the Stones for free, something he was wont to do in fits of missionary passion and which promoters often took him up on. Gomelsky, though, was a man of the world, and he called Stu at work that week and offered the Stones the coming Sunday, guaranteeing them £1 apiece and, perhaps, a residency. Then Ken Colyer, who was running R&B afternoons at his club in Soho, offered them a steady Sunday gig, so Sundays saw the Stones rushing from Soho to Richmond. Wednesdays at the Red Lion, too, were doing well, and suddenly girls were asking for their autographs. In April, Gomelsky gave his Sunday night club a name: the Crawdaddy. There, a second generation of R&B musicians would see them: members of the Roosters, for instance, whose members included Eric Clapton and Tom McGuinness, who'd soon be joining the Manfred Mann group. "They drew a cross-section," he remembered later. "Mods, guys in smart Italian suits, bohemians, art students, mixed couples, everyone. The venue was a dingy, hot, sweaty function room—all tobacco-stained everywhere."

On April 14, Gomelsky went to Twickenham to watch the Beatles film the *Thank Your Lucky Stars* television show and approached them about letting him put them into a film. He also invited them down to the Crawdaddy club, and that night Bill Wyman was plunking along during their first set when he saw something that almost caused him to fumble his rock-hard pulse: the four Beatles, in identical leather jackets, staring up at him. They stayed for the entire evening, and, in fact, after the show, went back to the flat on Edith Grove and stayed up almost to sunrise talking music and listening to the Stones' record collection. They left after issuing an invitation to their Thursday night show at the Royal Albert Hall. Of course, there was no such thing as a guest list, so the Stones came in the back door, carrying the Beatles' instruments. Said Jagger of this show, "I'd never seen hysteria on that level before. We were so turned on by those riots." They wanted a riot of their own.

As spring turned into summer, in America, thoughts turned to surfing. Now that Capitol had Dick Dale as well as the Beach Boys, they began a promotion; apologizing for the sound, they mounted a flexible single of Dale's latest, "Misirlou," in ads in the trade magazines, which was unprecedented, and it was announced that *Beach Party*, a film starring Frankie Avalon and former Mouseketeer Annette, with Bob Cummings and Dick Dale, had started shooting. Jan and Dean, now on Liberty, released an album called *Jan and Dean Take Linda Surfin'*, in hopes that their single "Linda" would do better than it did, and it had the Beach Boys (whose "Surfin' U.S.A." had just stormed the charts, borrowing Chuck Berry's melody for "Sweet Little Sixteen," and paying for it) providing instrumental help on the backing tracks. Their next single, "Surf City," co-written with Brian Wilson, followed along shortly. The Chantays based an album on their "Pipeline" single, and June saw the release of the Surfaris' "Wipe Out," which immediately found its way into the repertoires of thousands of wannabe surf bands.

And Murry Wilson explained surf music to *Billboard* in a special section they printed devoted to the new genre: "The basis of surf music is a rock & roll bass beat figuration, coupled with a raunch-style, weird-sounding lead guitar, an electric guitar plus wailing saxes. Surfing music has to sound untrained with a certain rough flavor to appeal to the teenagers. As in the cases of true country and western, when the music gets too good, and too polished, it isn't considered the real thing." Thanks, Dad! Why, even Bo Diddley and Freddie King released surfing albums, although in both cases it was a question of their record companies' jumping on the bandwagon and throwing together old instrumental recordings rather than any actual change in their music.

For those who took their guitars acoustic, folk music was picking up steam, too. In early March, ABC-TV announced that it would air a weekly *Hootenanny* program, emceed by Jack Linkletter. It ran into trouble immediately when it was revealed that the most beloved of all the current folksingers, Pete Seeger, had been asked—and refused—to sign a loyalty oath before he could perform on it. Banjoist Billy Faier led a fan boycott, which Seeger himself downplayed, even babysitting his stepbrother Mike's kids so that his group, the New Lost City Ramblers, could do a taping. In April, Bob Dylan (who hadn't even been asked to appear on *Hootenanny*) played the Town Hall in New York, and Columbia announced his second album, *The Freewheelin' Bob Dylan*, would appear in May, but his appearance on Ed Sullivan's phenomenally popular Sunday night television show was canceled after he wasn't allowed to perform "Talkin' John Birch Society Blues," a track satirizing a radical right-wing political organization that was subsequently removed from future pressings of *Freewheelin'*. George Wein announced the year's Newport Folk Festival lineup, and the first Monterey Folk Festival was announced, with the New Lost City Ramblers, the Greenbriar Boys, Bob Dylan, Peter,

Paul & Mary, Roscoe Holcomb, Mance Lipscomb, and Clarence Ashley. And it was announced that a proposed bossa nova film was being shelved, the production money going to a hootenanny film, staring the Gateway Singers, the Brothers Four, Judy Henske, Cathy Taylor, Sheb Wooley, Johnny Cash, Buck Owens, and George Hamilton, a lineup not exactly calculated to set *Sing Out!* talking, but not too different from *Hootenanny's* idea of folk music, either.

Traditional pop music was doing okay, too. In March, Screen Gems Music, a huge music publisher, bought Aldon Music outright for $2.5 million, wisely leaving everything intact, including Dimension Records and that amazing lineup of songwriters. A new duo, the Righteous Brothers, appeared with a catchy record, "Little Latin Lupe Lu," which their tiny record label wasn't able to push as hard as it deserved, but Phil Spector was listening. He had his hands full at the moment, though, with Bob B. Soxx and the Crystals, whose "Da Doo Ron Ron" was as catchy as it was silly. Seventeen-year-old Lesley Gore, from New Jersey, zeroed in on teenage girls' secrets—as she would make a career of doing—with "It's My Party (And I'll Cry If I Want To)." Nor was Rick Nelson the only old-timer doing well; Imperial Records sold Fats Domino's contract to ABC-Paramount, which promised him $50,000 a year and sent him straight to Nashville to cut his next record. A newly re-secularized Little Richard, who hadn't done too well with gospel music on Mercury, switched over to Atlantic, where he promptly disappeared after one single. Jerry Lee Lewis announced he was thinking of switching record labels, and did, to Mercury, which put him on their Smash subsidiary. On the other hand, Chuck Berry (whose never-ending court case had made him radioactive) released an excellent record that was ignored, "Talkin' About You," and for the first time, an Elvis Presley single, "One Broken Heart for Sale," never went near the top ten. He was probably too busy making his next movie to notice.

Motown was having the time of its life. The year 1963 established the label commercially and in which many of its stable of stars recorded their first iconic hits. With the debut of Martha and the Vandellas kicking the year off, the Miracles were on the charts with "You've Really Got a Hold on Me," and Marvin Gaye showed up in the spring with "Pride and Joy." The Motortown Revue was knocking them dead whenever it toured, so much so that when it hit the Regal Theater in Chicago, so many people wanted tickets that the theater's management put the show on four times a day instead of three. Stevie Wonder had recorded an instrumental called "Fingertips" on his album *The Jazz Soul of Little Stevie,* and, shorn of the studio musicians, he performed it as the finale of his segment of the Revue, causing pandemonium in the audience; he was a tough act to follow. Hearing that the number was going over so well, Berry Gordy dispatched a mobile recording unit to a Revue show in March; maybe this was the hit Gordy knew Stevie had in him. The resultant recording was so long it had to be split in two parts, one on each side of the record, and it was the second part that drew the attention: Stevie exhorting the audience, playing with them, tossing off a fragment of "Mary Had a Little Lamb" on his harmonica, and slowly leaving the stage, although teasing that he might be back. The show was already running overtime, the Marvelettes were next, Stevie's bass player had already unplugged, and the Marvelettes' bassist, Joe Swift, was getting ready when sure enough, on walked Stevie, playing up a storm. The band started riffing, Swift can be heard asking, "What key? What key?" (and you can barely hear the piano player say, "In C," and play a couple of arpeggios to orient him), and the whole thing rises to yet another climax. Suitably promoted, the single of "Fingertips, Part 2" went to the top of the pop and R&B charts, the first Motown release to do that since the Marvelettes eighteen months previously. No need to stop now; the Supremes tried a Smokey Robinson tune, "A Breath Taking Guy," but for some reason it stalled at #75 pop and disappeared. Would they ever have a hit? In mid-June, however, Martha and the Vandellas, with help from Holland-Dozier-Holland, blew the door open, making the coming summer even hotter with "Heat Wave," a top-ten smash.

Yes, it was summer, all right. The first slow-dance hit, the Tymes' "So in Love," came out in June, and Capitol Records added cars to surf with an album called *Shut Down,* with contributions from the Beach Boys, including their new hit single "Little Deuce Coupe," although it wound up getting overtaken by its other side, another slow-dance sensation, "Surfer Girl." Jack Nitzsche, a mysterious guy who'd been doing some arranging for Phil Spector, released a lovely instrumental led by a six-string bass, "The Lonely Surfer," but who knows what Al Casey was thinking with "Surfin' Hootenanny." This was the full flowering of surf music, with such mostly local hits as "Surf Bunny" by Gene Gray and the Stingrays, the Astronauts' "Baja," "Soul Surfer" by Johnny Fortune, and "Shoot the Curl" by the Honeys, a female vocal trio, Ginger Blake and the Rovell sisters, Diane and Marilyn, who were actual surf bunnies signed to Capitol and backed by an all-star band, including Al Jardine, Billy Strange, Carl Wilson, Leon Russell, and David Gates, and produced by Beach Boys producer Nik Venet and Brian Wilson, who soon married Marilyn.

There were some amazing records coming out, with a new sound, brighter, more aggressive, all across the board. In pop, you had the Crystals' "Then He Kissed Me," Trini Lopez rocking up Pete Seeger's "If I Had a Hammer" and reviving "La Bamba," Dion singing about "Donna the Prima Donna," and R&B not only had the James Brown *Live at the Apollo* album selling almost like a single throughout the summer, but brother-sister team Charlie and Inez Foxx's odd but catchy "Mockingbird," Chris Kenner's "Land of 1000 Dances" coming out of New Orleans, Garnet Mimms and the Enchanters' "Cry Baby," Major Lance celebrating "The Monkey Time," Arthur Alexander noticing "Pretty Girls Everywhere," and the Jaynettes' haunting, mysterious "Sally Go Round the Roses." Even country music seemed to be waking up and getting tough again; at the end of July, the top three country records were Buck Owens's "Act Naturally"; Johnny Cash's "Ring of Fire," written for him by his new sweetheart, June Carter, of the by-now-second-generation Carter Family; and Dave Dudley's "Six Days on the Road," a song depicting the life of a truck driver, thereby kicking off a new genre of country songs. Who knew truck drivers bought so many records? And mixed in with all of this was a fresh-faced lad from Cincinnati, Lonnie Mack, with two instrumentals played on his odd Gibson Flying V guitar, Chuck Berry's "Memphis" and his own "Wham!" getting airplay. Folk music didn't really show up on the pop charts (although Joan Baez's latest tour had grossed $100,000), but Peter, Paul & Mary did, grabbing the lead track off Bob Dylan's *Freewheelin'* album and having the hit

Chad Mitchell didn't get with "Blowin' in the Wind," and following it up with another from the same album, "Don't Think Twice, It's All Right." And folksinger Oscar Brand decided to go on the *Hootenanny* TV show "with misgivings," stating that "I have never seen any evidence that Pete Seeger has tried to overthrow the government with his banjo." In Cincinnati, WCPO announced it was going "100% hootenanny" in its programming.

All of this hot hootenanny action may seem silly in retrospect, but it's emblematic of a change that had overtaken America's teenage record buyers—and teenage America at large. Coarsely stated, there was a divide between the people singing "Blowin' in the Wind" and the ones singing "My Boyfriend's Back." "Blowin' in the Wind" is a notoriously noncommittal song; it asks a bunch of questions about important issues and unjust conditions, and then declares that the answer is out there somewhere, in the wind. But it asks those questions, no matter how vaguely they're stated. This was something new. Furthermore, the folk thing was about participation, be it a Carnegie Hall audience singing along with Pete Seeger or a bunch of kids with guitars in a basement trading favorite songs. Didn't like Peter, Paul & Mary's arrangement of "Blowin' in the Wind"? Come up with your own. Or, for that matter, write your own song. And people were buying guitars (or banjos—Pete Seeger's instruction book had never been selling better) and gathering to play them. This had been going on in New York's Washington Square Park (where a ban on folksingers led to a riot) for long enough that a news item claimed that a "folk statue" was being planned there. (Nothing came of it.) But teenagers seeking social engagement and doing it in public was a new thing, utterly so. It was, depending on which side of the fence you were on, either scary or a cause for optimism.

And Americans were asking some of the same veiled question Bob Dylan was. On August 28, a quarter million people gathered the Lincoln Memorial to hear a young Baptist preacher who'd be making headlines, Dr. Martin Luther King Jr., deliver a speech h delivered before, but never to so many people. Enshrined in his as the "I Have a Dream" speech, it, like the rest of the program, been recorded, and the record business leaped into action, resu

in King having to sue the Mr. Maestro, 20th Century-Fox, and Motown labels over releasing albums of the speech—and retracting the suit against Motown, with which, it turned out, he actually had a deal to record his stuff. Motown's barely active Divinity gospel label also prepared a single of "We Shall Overcome" (credited to George Fowler and Clarence Paul) by Liz Lands and the Voices of Salvation, but, distracted by the lawsuit, shelved it for five years until after Dr. King's assassination.

Nor is this to disparage the other kids, happily surfing and working on their cars and worrying about their girlfriends and boyfriends and buying records they had no interest in making themselves. After all, they were still minors, many people considered Dr. King and his followers to be inspired by communism, including many of their parents, and as has always been the case, there was always a large part of the teenage cohort that was terrified of being considered weirdos. But surfing (even if you didn't do it) and cars (even if you didn't have one) and thinking about boys and girls (again, even if you didn't have one—maybe especially if you didn't) were teenage preoccupations that were gaining their own vocabulary (especially surfing and cars: what on earth was a "deuce coupe" or a "gremmie" or a "woody"?) that, as it always had, encouraged solidarity of the group. When, next January, Bob Dylan released "The Times They Are A-Changin'" as the title track of his latest album and sang, "Your sons and your daughters are beyond your command," he wasn't just talking about the folkies; a larger, more diverse and inclusive teenage nation was forming.

In May, a music industry group announced that there were 230 singles and 100 albums released *each week*. Naturally, not all of them, especially the albums, were aimed at teenagers, and in fact, not all teenagers were making rock & roll. This was the year that Barbra Streisand, a teenage fixture on Broadway, made her first album, which caused a sensation (although she was twenty at the time of its release, no longer a teenager). Nor were all the albums in predictable categories; Phillips Records released a version of the Catholic Mass, brilliantly recorded in Brussels, performed by Congolese singers and percussionists, *Missa Luba*. Hi-fi enthusiasts scooped it up; it was a much better demonstration of what your equipment could do than

those silly Provocative Percussion discs. Encouraged, the company then released the album by the Dominican nun that had been selling like crazy in Europe, calling it (and her) *The Singing Nun*. But a glance at any week's listings of single releases in *Billboard* will just confirm that overall, the record business was as clueless as ever, throwing records at the wall and hoping one of them would stick, and this applied not only to the independent labels but to the majors as well.

This was very different from what was happening in England, although there were some deep commonalities. England had come out of the war with strict food rationing still in effect, but this was ended at last in 1955. Teenagers like John Lennon and Paul McCartney, living in middle-class households, witnessed this as a sudden improvement in their lives, and the psychological effect was that a generation suddenly saw a future without the scarcity they'd been raised in, which resulted in a similar teenage nation forming there. These were the kids at the Cavern's lunchtime sessions and the Sunday R&B club nights at the Crawdaddy club. They were hoping that the new economic recovery would allow them to participate more openly in British society, while chafing under the restrictions British tradition and the older generation imposed on them. As we see in the stories of the youths who joined bands, getting an education or signing on to an apprenticeship or training program in a trade was essential. Since nobody in the upper classes went into bands (Mick Jagger, son of a physical education instructor and a student at the London School of Economics, was as close as they came), the stories of those who did find them learning trades (George Harrison and, intermittently, Paul McCartney) or using an art school degree to find work in an ad agency (Charlie Watts, Bill Wyman). There was no going it alone unless you were very eccentric. Brian Jones stands out in this regard in his monomaniacal devotion to blues and R&B, a middle-class kid with no intention of becoming an apprentice or pursuing academic matters. This is why the events in England, although they were ignored in America at first, were just as important as what was going on in the States, as well as why they were ignored: the adults, youthful though they were, some of them, had enough on their hands trying to figure out how to sell these arcane hootenanny and surf cultures outside their home turf. Clearly, if Joan Baez could gross a hundred grand on tour, the little girls in Iowa City and Phoenix were getting it, but how on earth to sell Bob Dylan, her closest analog? How do you sell surfing to kids in landlocked Dayton?

So the Brits went their merry way. George Martin had wanted an album from the Beatles, and in February he'd gotten one, recorded in one session of nine hours and forty-five minutes. They'd only come up with nine tracks, and he'd wanted ten, so at the last minute, John Lennon, his voice shredded from the day's work, did a one-take recording of "Twist and Shout." The album, *Please Please Me*, was rush-released, topping the U.K. album charts on April 11, just as their new single, "From Me to You" (title inspired by *NME*'s letters column, "From You to Us"), hit the top of the singles chart, the first of an unprecedented eleven consecutive #1s from eleven different releases. The group toured constantly and signed a deal with the BBC for a series of regular radio shows called *Pop Go the Beatles*, and in August they appeared for the last time at the Cavern; they'd just gotten too big. (Not for Vee-Jay Records, who released "From Me to You" Stateside to the predictable indifference, although at the time the company was going through some huge changes, as longtime president Ewart Abner stepped down and the company was wrestling with the demands the unanticipated popularity of the Four Seasons made on them.)

For the Rolling Stones, the world changed when a brash nineteen-year-old hustler named Andrew Loog Oldham, who'd been working in the fashion industry for Mary Quant and in pop PR with an older man, Eric Easton, dropped in with Easton in tow at the Crawdaddy club on April 28 to see what all the noise was about. "I was probably forty-eight hours ahead of the rest of the business" getting to the Rolling Stones, he later remarked. "The combination of music and sex was something I had never encountered in any other group." He moved fast; on May 1, he and Easton signed the band to a management deal with the Impact Sound company, which they'd just formed for the purpose. Among the demands Oldham and Easton made at first was the restoration of the *g* to Rolling Stones and the demotion of Ian Stewart, who looked too ordinary for the group, and anyway, their reasoning went, five boys was the maximum that any teenage girl could be expected to keep up with. (Stewart took it well, continuing to play keyboards with the group onstage until his death in 1985.) Having signed them, Oldham covered the next vital step and took them to buy identical clothing—skinny black jeans and black turtleneck sweaters—and get them booked for a charity show sponsored by the *News of the World* newspaper. Now to get them a record deal. Fortunately for him, Dick Rowe, of Decca, was up in Liverpool helping to judge a talent contest with George Harrison. "You know," Rowe said to George, "I really got my backside kicked for turning you lot down."

"Well," said George, "why don't you sign the Rolling Stones?"

Rowe said he'd never heard of them, and George told him to go see them in Richmond. He did, on May 5, and took his wife. It was so dingy in the room that he could hardly see anything, but his wife told him the lead singer looked pretty good. Two days later, Oldham, Easton, and Rowe met to begin talks on a record contract (Impact would lease tapes to Decca), and Andrew and the band had already decided on a debut record, an obscure recent Chuck Berry title, "Come On." They recorded it on May 10, and Decca released it on June 7. The band hated it, and in fact it wasn't an auspicious debut. It went to #20 on the *NME* charts and then vanished. Then another problem arose: the brewery to which the Station Hotel was tied (pubs and hotels signed contracts with breweries, which then supplied beers they made and distributed) became concerned about what they saw as the goings-on at the venue, and there had been numerous complaints to the fire marshal about overcrowding, so Gomelski's Crawdaddy club there was shut down. Brian Jones immediately contacted a man named Ronan O'Rahilly, a promoter with his own club in Soho who was also managing Alexis Korner and Cyril Davies, and the Stones' residency moved to Thursday nights there. The more central location, plus the buzz building around the band, brought in larger audiences; around five hundred showed up on the first night.

The Stones needed a follow-up record to their non-hit, and they needed it fast; their popularity as a live act was growing, and their managers were working on getting them onto a major tour. On August 11, they played a jazz festival in Richmond, and the promoter reported a fifty-fifty split between the thousands of jazz fans and the thousands of Stones fans who had just shown up for their favorite band and left afterward. Their next single would come from a seemingly unlikely source. Lennon and McCartney had uncorked an unstoppable flow of songwriting, and Brian Epstein's clients were getting first pick of the numbers the group wasn't recording: Billy J. Kramer and the Dakotas got "Do You Want to Know a Secret?," "Bad to Me," and "I'll Keep You Satisfied," and Cilla Black got "Love of the Loved" and only Gerry and the Pacemakers had "How Do You Do It"'s Mitch Murray producing songs for them. (Late in the year, they recorded a Broadway show tune, "You'll Never Walk Alone," which was turned into an anthem for Liverpool's football team, thereby eventually making the Pacemakers the second-richest Liverpool band.)

On September 10 during a lull in a seventy-eight-shows-in-seventy-six-days tour, Oldham walked into a Stones rehearsal in London with John Lennon, Paul McCartney, and a song. "I said to Mick, 'Well, Ringo's got this track on our album, but it won't be a single and it might suit you guys,'" Lennon said later. "I knew Mick was into maraccas from when I saw them down at the Crawdaddy." And so "I Wanna Be Your Man" became the next Stones single. American showbiz was waking up to some of this excitement. Ed Sullivan went to England in July and signed Cliff Richard and the Shadows, Frank Ifield, the Dallas Boys, Mayo Henderson, and Kenny Ball for appearances on his show come fall. Somehow he missed the foofaraw over the Beatles' "Twist and Shout" EP selling 150,000 copies despite two other versions on the market. The group did even better than that in late September, when their next single, "She Loves You," was released and sold five hundred thousand copies in its first eight days out. In America, Capitol passed again, but the chaos at Vee-Jay, which had just replaced its two top executives, coupled with the complete indifference to their first two singles the label had picked up, caused them to pass, too, and it was released on a shady Philadelphia label, Swan, again without any significant action.

And why would America need the Beatles, after all? There were plenty of good records coming out domestically in the fall of 1963. Rufus Thomas came up with "Walkin' the Dog," which would keep

Stax solvent for a while longer, Paul Revere and the Raiders, formerly an instrumental act, released "Louie Louie," an old Richard Berry track, only to be challenged by another band from the Northwest, the Kingsmen, a week later, with their version on Scepter. The folk thing kept on rolling. *Billboard* ran an article on October 19 headlined FOLK TREND SHOWS NO SIGN OF LET-UP, and its album chart for November 2 showed Peter, Paul & Mary at #1, #2, and #6. Elektra had signed Koerner, Ray, and Glover, an acoustic blues act who'd come out of the same Minneapolis scene as Bob Dylan, as well as New York's Even Dozen Jug Band, featuring guitar virtuoso Danny Kalb and a fetching female vocalist, Maria d'Amato, while a ham-handed ricky-tick jazz band called the Village Stompers tried to ride the fad with their single "Washington Square."

Pop music continued its mixture of silliness and seriousness as Don Robey announced he'd eat his hat, as promised, since Billy Bland's "Sometimes You Gotta Cry a Little" hadn't made top twenty on all the charts, and was photographed doing so while promising to do the same thing for his shoes if Bland's next record, "The Feeling Is Love," and Al "TNT" Briggs's "Drip Drip" didn't succeed similarly. The pop gospel fad may have fizzled, but the church was still in the air, as Marvin Gaye released a title based on a common gospel trope, "Can I Get a Witness?" and the Impressions, who hadn't had a hit in two years, came up with a #1 record in "It's All Right." Phil Spector took a slightly different approach to religion when he released an album that eventually became a classic: *A Christmas Gift for You from Phil Spector*, which featured the Ronettes, the Crystals, Bob B. Soxx and the Blue Jeans, and Darlene Love singing a mixture of pop Christmas classics ("Frosty the Snowman," "Rudolph the Red-Nosed Reindeer") and originals (Darlene Love singing a Phil Spector / Ellie Greenwich / Jeff Barry song, "Christmas (Baby Please Come Home).") Weirdly, though, the fastest-moving single in the country was "Dominique" by the Singing Nun, which had reached #9 on the pop charts in only three weeks; her album was #8.

Then something awful happened. On November 22, President Kennedy, riding in a motorcade in Dallas, was shot dead. The last presidential assassination had been William McKinley in 1901, long enough for the public to have forgotten such things, and before the birth of modern communications, particularly television, which broadcast film from Kennedy's visit as well as the murder, live on air, of the alleged assassin, Lee Harvey Oswald, as he was being trans- ferred to another jail from his holding cell, by Jack Ruby, a Dallas nightclub owner with Mob ties whose connections also supported some of the Dallas teen-club scene. The national trauma was on a level the United States hadn't felt since Pearl Harbor had been at- tacked. In pop music, the people hardest hit were the folkies, many of them deeply politically engaged thanks to the young president's support for civil rights and nuclear disarmament, the two causes young people were particularly attracted to, but there were other re- actions. Brian Wilson withdrew for a couple of days and emerged with his first contemplative masterpiece, "The Warmth of the Sun," and in San Antonio, where Kennedy had stopped the day before Dallas to generally adoring (and largely Hispanic) crowds, the radio stations played "Why, Why, Why," a song by local hero Doug Sahm, an Anglo kid who played with West Side soul bands, over and over. The Singing Nun's sales skyrocketed. Archie Bleyer got ready to take back lots and lots and lots of *First Family* albums.

The show, as they say, had to go on, and go on it did. It probably wouldn't be much of a Christmas season for the record business, but there were those Singing Nun records, and hey, look on the bright side: there'd be JFK memorial product to flog, and sure enough, two weeks later there were three albums out there, pasted together from Kennedy's speeches and news broadcasts. One Millicent Martin wrote and performed a song, "In the Summer of His Years," on the BBC, and versions (including one by Mahalia Jackson) appeared Stateside almost immediately, only to face a near-universal ban by radio, a ban not faced by a gospel release, "That Awful Day in Dal- las," by Thurman Ruth and the Harmoneers, which didn't sell, any- way. Motown released a Christmas album by the Miracles—good thing Christmas albums were perennials—and the Beach Boys re- worked "Little Deuce Coupe" into "Little St. Nick."

Almost unnoticed in all of this were two carloads of men leaving New Orleans and driving to Los Angeles. In December 1963, the

AFO executives, confronted by a New Orleans union that would not desegregate and join the "colored" union into the main one, gave up in disgust. There were opportunities out there for musicians, and so Harold Battiste, with his composing and arranging skills, Alvin "Red" Tyler, with his prowess on the saxophone, and especially Earl Palmer, the man who'd invented rock & roll drumming behind Little Richard back at what now seemed like the dawn of time, headed west. In a few short weeks, they'd be reconvened in Gold Star Studios in Hollywood, most of them impatient for Battiste to finish the song their client—Art Rupe's young talent scout, Sonny Bono—wanted to record with his teenage girlfriend, Sherilynn Sarkosian, something about the beat going on. As it would.

England wasn't as traumatized by Kennedy's death, but their music business was becoming traumatized by the Beatles. Along with the singles, there was their first album, *Please Please Me*, which had sold 250,000 copies for a gold record, and a similar number of advance orders were on hand for the next one, already announced, *With the Beatles*. Brian Epstein had approached Ed Sullivan and gotten contracts for TV appearances for the Beatles and Gerry and the Pacemakers for early 1964. The December 14 issue of *Billboard* reported that Capitol had suddenly had the blinders removed from its eyes and was going to start negotiating exclusive rights to the band, shutting down Vee-Jay and Swan's contracts with Transglobal-licensed product. The group's latest single would be released in mid-January 1964, but they probably moved things up once 950,000 advance orders flooded in to their distributors. Sure enough, the year's last issue of *Billboard* had a full-page ad showing four haircuts and the words "The Beatles are coming!" And that single was officially released on December 26, 1963. Reviewing it in 1964's first issue, *Billboard* said of "I Want to Hold Your Hand," "This is the hot British group that has hit gold overseas. Side is driving rocker with surf on the Thames sound and strong vocal work from the group. Flip is 'I Saw Her Standing There.'"

Whenever an event like the Kennedy assassination occurs, talk of a conspiracy surfaces, and it certainly did this time. But when analyzing a conspiracy, the best question to ask is "Cui bono?"—who benefits? The four lads from Liverpool were thousands of miles away, and Britain couldn't have foreseen the immense financial benefits of their, and others', success, so they're off the hook. And if 1963 needed a theme song, it would have been Skeeter Davis's latest, "The End of the World," a country hit that was a smash crossover at the beginning of the year, even showing up on the R&B charts. In it, she marvels that stars still shine, birds still sing, and life goes on, even though her boyfriend has dumped her. Marveling at it all, she cries, "Don't they know it's the end of the world?" It never really is, except for teenagers in love, of course, but the American record business was facing something it had never seen before: an invasion from overseas. The Beatles' success would kill Vee-Jay Records and relegate the Philadelphia boy crooners to even further irrelevance. It would also spur electric guitar sales even faster than the Ventures' ascendance and surf music ever did, and, perversely, set up a false dichotomy between the ultra-successful Beatles and the not-so-successful Rolling Stones, which, in turn, would focus some folkies' attention to the rich, as-yet-unexplored heritage of Chicago and Southern electric blues. It would also eventually change youth culture in unimaginable ways all over the world, but for now, let's put on Phil Spector's Christmas album and listen to the present receding into the past. Something amazing was on its way, and the ever-increasing number of teenagers would bring it on.

BIBLIOGRAPHY

Books

Bernard, Shane K. *Swamp Pop: Cajun and Creole Rhythm and Blues.* Jackson: University of Mississippi Press, 1996.

Broven, John. *Record Makers and Breakers: Voices of the Independent Rock 'n' Roll Pioneers.* Urbana: University of Illinois Press, 2010.

———. *Walking to New Orleans, the Story of New Orleans Rhythm & Blues.* Bexhill on Sea, Sussex, UK: Blues Unlimited, 1974.

Bryant, Clora, Buddy Collette, William Green, Steven Isoardi, Jack Kelson, Horace Tapscott, Gerald Wilson, and Marl Young. *Central Avenue Sounds: Jazz in Los Angeles.* Berkeley, CA: University of California Press, 1999.

Fancourt, Les. *Chess Blues: A Discography of the Blues Artists on the Chess Labels 1947–1975,* 3rd ed. Faversham, Kent, UK: printed by author, 1989.

———. *Chess R&B: A Discography of the R&B Artists on the Chess Labels, 1947–1975,* 2nd ed. Faversham, Kent, UK: printed by author, 1991.

Frame, Pete. *The Restless Generation: How Rock Music Changed the Face of 1950s Britain.* London: Rogan House, 2007.

Goldrosen, John. *The Buddy Holly Story.* New York: Quick Fox, 1979.

Gordon, Robert. *Can't Be Satisfied: The Life and Times of Muddy Waters.* Boston: Little, Brown, 2002.

———. *Respect Yourself: Stax Records and the Soul Explosion.* New York: Bloomsbury, 2014.

Guralnick, Peter. *Last Train to Memphis: The Rise of Elvis Presley.* Boston: Little, Brown, 1994.

———. *Careless Love: The Unmaking of Elvis Presley.* Boston: Little, Brown, 1999.

———. *Dream Boogie: The Triumph of Sam Cooke.* Boston: Little, Brown, 2005.

———. *Sam Phillips: The Man Who Invented Rock 'n' Roll.* Boston: Little, Brown, 2015.

Johnson, John Jr., Joel Selvin, and Dick Cami. *Peppermint Twist* New York: St. Martin's Press, 2012.

Lauterbach, Preston. *The Chitlin' Circuit and the Road to Rock 'n' Roll.* New York: Norton, 2011.

Lewisohn, Mark. *The Beatles: All These Years, vol. 1, Tune In.* New York: Crown Archetype, 2013.

Palmer, Robert. *Deep Blues.* New York: Viking, 1981.

Pavlow, Big Al. *The R&B Book: A Disc-History of Rhythm & Blues.* Providence, RI: Music House, 1983.

Pegg, Bruce. *Brown Eyed Handsome Man: The Life and Hard Times of Chuck Berry.* New York: Routledge, 2002.

Perkins, Carl, and David McGee. *Go, Cat, Go: The Life and Times of Carl Perkins, the King of Rockabilly.* New York: Hyperion, 1996.

Rees, Dafydd, Barry Lazell, and Roger Osborne. *The Complete NME Singles Charts.* London: Boxtree, 1995.

Rees, Dafydd, and Luke Crampton. *The Guinness Book of Rock Stars.* London: Guinness, 1991.

Rohde, H. Kandy. *The Gold of Rock & Roll 1955–1967.* New York: Arbor House, 1970.

Santelli, Robert. *The Big Book of Blues.* New York: Penguin, 1993.

Smith, R. J. *The Great Black Way: L.A. in the 1940s and the Lost African American Renaissance.* New York: Public Affairs, 2006.

———. *The One: The Life and Music of James Brown.* New York: Gotham, 2012.

Wald, Elijah. *Dylan Goes Electric!: Newport, Seeger, Dylan, and the Night that Split the Sixties.* New York: Dey Street, 2015.

Ward, Ed, Ken Tucker, and Geoffrey Stokes. *Rock of Ages: The Rolling Stone History of Rock & Roll.* New York: Summit, 1986.

Whitall, Susan, and Kevin John. *Fever: Little Willie John's Fast Life, Mysterious Death, and the Birth of Soul.* London: Titan, 2011.

Whitburn, Joel. *Hot R&B Songs, 1942–2010.* 6th ed. Menomonee Falls, WI: Record Research, 2010.

———. *Hot Country Songs, 1944–2012,* 8th ed. Menomonee Falls, WI: Record Research, 2012.

———. *Top Pop Albums*, 7th ed. Menomonee Falls, WI: Record Research, 2010.

———. *Top Pop Singles, 1955–2010*, 14th ed. Menomonee Falls, WI: Record Research, 2012.

White, Charles. *The Life and Times of Little Richard, the Quasar of Rock*. New York: Harmony, 1984.

Wyman, Bill. *Rolling with the Stones*. London: DK Publishing, 2002.

Yagoda, Ben. *The B-Side: The Death of Tin Pan Alley and the Rebirth of the Great American Song*. New York: Riverhead, 2015.

Liner Notes

Blackwood, Scott. *The Rise and Fall of Paramount Records, Vol. 1*. Austin, TX: Revenant, 2013.

———. *The Rise and Fall of Paramount Records, Vol. 2*. Austin, TX: Revenant, 2014.

Blair, John. *Dick Dale and His Del-Tones, King of the Surf Guitar*. Burbank, CA: Rhino, 1989.

———. *The Surf Box*. Burbank, CA: Rhino, 1996.

Bowman, Rob. *The Complete Stax Singles, 1959–1968*. Los Angeles: Atlantic, 1991.

Cohen, John, and Peter K. Siegel. *Friends of Old Time Music, the Folk Arrival, 1961–1965*. Washington, D.C.: Smithsonian Folkways, 2006.

Dahl, Bill. *Buddy Holly: Not Fade Away: The Complete Studio Recordings and More*. Universal City, CA: Hip-O Select, 2009.

Dahl, Bill, Keith Hughes, Craig Werner, and Mable John. *The Complete Motown Singles, Vol. 1, 59–61*. Universal City, CA: Hip-O Select, 2004.

Dahl, Bill, Keith Hughes, Gerald Early, and Claudette Robinson. *The Complete Motown Singles, Vol. 2, 1962*. Universal City, CA: Hip-O Select, 2005.

Dahl, Bill, Keith Hughes, Craig Werner, and Martha Reeves. *The Complete Motown Singles, Vol. 3, 1963*. Universal City, CA: Hip-O Select, 2005.

Davis, Hank, Colin Escott, and Martin Hawkins. *The Sun Blues Box*. Holste-Oldendorf, Germany: Bear Family, 2013.

———. *The Sun Rock Box*. Holste-Oldendorf, Germany: Bear Family, 2013.

Escott, Colin. *Johnny Burnette: The Complete Coral Rock 'n' Roll Recordings*. Universal City, CA: Hip-O Select, 2004.

———. *Patsy Cline: Sweet Dreams: The Complete Decca Studio Masters, 1960–1963*. Universal City, CA: Hip-O Select, 2009.

Escott, Colin, Martin Hawkins, and Hank Davis. *The Sun Country Box*. Hambergen, Germany: Bear Family, 2012.

Finnis, Rob. *The Doré Story: Postcards from Los Angeles, 1958–1964*. London: Ace, 2011.

——. *Phil Spector: The Early Productions*. London: Ace, 2010.

Finnis, Rob, and Rick Coleman. *Little Richard: The Specialty Sessions*. Los Angeles: Specialty, 1989.

Haig, Diana Reid. *The Scepter Records Story*. Macon, GA: Capricorn, 1992.

Hannusch, Jeff, and Adam Block. *They Call Me The Fat Man: Antoine "Fats" Domino, the Legendary Imperial Recordings*. Los Angeles: EMI, 1991.

Hawkins, Martin. *Buzzin' the Blues: The Complete Slim Harpo*. Hambergen, Germany: Bear Family, 2015.

Hinckley, David. *Phil Spector: Back to Mono, 1958–1969*. Los Angeles: Phil Spector Records, 1991.

Hyde, Bob, Wayne Stierle, and Donn Fileti. *The Doo Wop Box*. Burbank, CA: Rhino, 1993.

Isoardi, Steven. *Central Avenue Sounds: Jazz in Los Angeles, 1921–1956*. Burbank, CA: Rhino, 1999.

Palao, Alec. *Love That Louie: The Louie Louie Files*. London: Ace, 2002.

Patrick, Mick. *The Leiber & Stoller Story, Vol. 2: On the Horizon, 1956–1962*. London: Ace, 2006.

Ribas, Michael. *Vee-Jay: The Definitive Collection*. Los Angeles: Shout! Factory / Vee-Jay, 2007.

Ritz, David. *Ray Charles: Pure Genius: The Complete Atlantic Recordings, 1952–1959*. Burbank, CA: Rhino, 2005.

Rothwell, Fred. *Chuck Berry: Johnny B. Goode: His Complete '50s Recordings*. Universal City, CA: Hip-O Select, 2007.

Varela, Chuy. *Pachuco Boogie*. El Cerrito, CA: Arhoolie, 2001.

Vera, Billy. *The Specialty Story*. Los Angeles: Specialty, 1994.

Vera, Billy, and Bob Hyde. *The Doo Wop Box II*. Burbank, CA: Rhino, 1996.

Young, Iain, John Firminger, and Peter Kirkpatrick. *James Burton: The Early Years, 1956–1969*. London: Ace, 2011.

Periodicals

Billboard, Cincinnati, Ohio, 1944–1963 inclusive, 1960–1963 accessed at http://www.billboard.com/magazine-archive.

Films

King Creole. Directed by Michael Curtiz. Hollywood: Paramount Pictures, 1958.

The Girl Can't Help It. Directed by Frank Tashlin. Los Angeles: 20th Century-Fox, 1956.

Rock, Baby, Rock It. Directed by Murray Douglas Sporup. United Pictures, 1957.

LINER NOTES

In 1969, I actually had the temerity to teach a rock & roll history class at my famously tolerant college, and one day I intoned the common-knowledge "fact" that Elvis Presley was the first white country-based performer to combine black and white popular styles. One of the students raised his hand. "What about Bob Wills?" he asked. This guy's name was Charlie Burton, and auditing the class was the music department's assistant, Ray Seifert. I asked Charlie who Bob Wills was, and he said, "Oh, man, you've never heard Bob Wills? Come to my dorm room after class."

Seifert then asked, "What have you got by him?"

We adjourned to Charlie's room afterward, and I got educated, not only about Bob Wills, but George Jones, Charlie Rich, and several other of Charlie's favorites. Charlie went on to lead a very successful rockabilly-revival band, and Ray started using his middle name professionally and, as Ray Benson, leads a Western swing band, Asleep at the Wheel, to this day.

I moved out to San Francisco not long afterward to work at *Rolling Stone,* and my education went into overdrive. One of my first teachers was John Goddard, proprietor and overlord of Village Music, in Mill Valley, California, whose comprehensive knowledge of American musical history was, conveniently, for sale at $3.88 per album, three for $10, in most cases. "Have you ever heard this?" and

"I've got something you'll be interested in" were magic phrases, supplemented on occasion by a phone tree that sprang into life when a veteran country performer, a great blues artist, or a multi-artist gospel program came into the vicinity. Besides John, Michael Goodwin and John Morthland were usually along for the ride. Working at *Rolling Stone*, I got guidance from Peter Guralnick, Jerry Hopkins, Grelun Landon, Langdon Winner, John Burks, Lenny Kaye, Greil Marcus, Rich Kienzle, and Michael Ochs, to name just a few. Afterward, Asleep at the Wheel moved to town and joined Commander Cody and His Lost Planet Airmen in creating a vibrant East Bay roots scene. Members of this crowd, particularly George "Commander Cody" Frayne, Bill Kirchen, Reuben "Lucky Oceans" Gosfield, LeRoy Preston, Jim "Floyd Domino" Haber, Chris O'Connell, Tony Garnier, and Kevin "Blackie" Farrell introduced me to jump blues and considerably deepened my knowledge of Western swing and hard-core country. Also in the Bay Area, the staff at Down Home Music, Flower Films, and Arhoolie Records—most notably Chris Strachwitz, Les Blank, Maureen Gosling, and Johnny Harper—were founts of learning. Occasionally running into Doug Sahm and Michael Bloomfield didn't hurt, either.

I moved to Texas the first time in 1979 to work on the *Austin American-Statesman*, the city's daily paper, and made sure I covered a good balance of old and new, leading, for instance, to meeting the last surviving Texas Playboys at a multiday recording session, and seeing shows by scores of blues, country, gospel, rhythm and blues, Cajun, and rock & roll legends, often interviewing them for the paper beforehand. Texas is fairly unique because it provides a place for these people to play, and support for them came from fans like Joe Nick Patoski, Leon Eagleson, Mike Buck, Clifford Antone, Margaret Moser, Keith Ferguson, Mark Rubin, John T. Davis (who introduced me to Lubbock and shared a graveside encounter with Buddy Holly's brother Lawrence with me one windy afternoon there), Clyde Woodward, Lucinda Williams, and Steve Dean. The paper enabled me to start taking vacations in England, where I stayed with Pete Frame in his thatch-roofed house and picked his commodious brain, as well as being guided by Ben Mandelson, Roger Armstrong, and

Ted Carroll (who worked together at Ace Records), Andrew Lauder, Simon Frith, Charles Shaar Murray, and Alexis and Bobbi Korner. I also freelanced while at the paper, most notably for the *Village Voice*, under the tutelage of Robert Christgau.

After I left the paper, the CD reissues began in earnest, and it was a golden age of having access to stuff you'd have to haunt dusty record stores for. By this time, I was a contributor to *Fresh Air* with Terry Gross on NPR, doing rock & roll history in six- to eight-minute segments, and thanks are due there to Naomi Person, Danny Miller, Amy Salit, Phyllis Myers, and, of course, Terry Gross for the opportunity over the decades to dole the story out, nugget by nugget. In Berlin, I became the educator, with my *Blue Monday* show on Jazz Radio, which was not only fun, but a lifesaver financially. Much thanks to Wilhelmina Steyling for her brave, doomed project. Also thanks to my friends there, Kevin Cote, Andrew Roth, Susan Hannaford, Andrew Horn, Natalie Gravenor, Michael S. Moore, Susanna Forrest, John Borland, Aimee Male, Michael and Karen Nickel Anhalt, Volker Quante, Ina Rüberg, Johannes Waechter, Dave Rimmer, Nikki Zeuner, Uwe Efferts, Dr. J. J. Gordon, Ingo Stoik, "Steven Seven Augustine," Kean Wong, and, in New York, another great editor, Raymond Sokolov, who put me on the culture beat of the *Wall Street Journal Europe*. In France, many thanks to Prof. Claude Chastagnier, Peter Hornsby, Chuck and Judi Fowler, Lillis Urban, Etienne Podevin, Erwin and JoAnn Beck, Gerry Patterson, and Kirsty Snaith.

Returning to Austin to write this book wouldn't have been possible without Roland Swenson, and Jeff Kramer taking a chance on me as a tenant—albeit one with no credit history (illegal in Europe)—meant I've had a nice roof over my head. Thanks also to Bob Simmons, Rob Hamlet, "Minerva Koenig," Jon and Marsha Lebkowsky, Andrew Halbreich, Margaret Moser, Jason Saldaña, Kelly Saragusa McEntee, the good folks at Waterloo Records, David Alvarez at KUT, Shane Matt, DDS, and Kris Cummings.

Cyberspace is everywhere, and helped immensely, not only with research, but with friends in places I'm not sure of. Terry Byrnes has been a brilliant correspondent for over forty years, and e-mail has just made it easier, and he and Patricia Woodburn have made my visits to

Montreal over the years great fun. My friends on the Well have been supportive and informative for fifteen years, and I treasure that place. Facebook, too, has been immensely helpful. Neil Porter has brought some great stuff to my attention; a bunch of music lovers have posted more music and articles than I can keep up with. Then there was the day, early on, when Bill Beuttler, who'd worked at a magazine I'd contributed to, heard that I needed an agent and suggested I contact David Dunton at the Harvey Klinger Agency. Don't even get me started on the parade of crooks, imbeciles, and incompetents whom I've dealt with (or tried to) over the decades: this one stuck. He's done his best to sell my stuff, and with this book succeeded magnificently, and I value his expertise. Thanks also to Well friend David Gans, who asked Bob Miller why he'd turned this book down and suggested splitting it in half, and thanks to Bob Miller, Jasmine Faustino, and the whole crew at Flatiron for giving me a second chance with it.

Nor is it over after the last word's been typed. There aren't many photos here, but chasing them down involved a lot of people's help, including Michael Barson, Dr. Ira Padnos, Hudson Marquez, Dennis Wilen, Leo Sayer, Patty Brady, Harlis Battiste, Ace Records (UK), Susan Archie, and everyone who tried to help me find an Elvis picture that seems to have vanished in cyberspace.

There are, without a doubt, many others whose names need to be here, and I could sit here all day and try to come up with more—and succeed. If you're not in this list, I'll do better next time, promise.

—Ed Ward, Austin, Texas, November 2016

INDEX